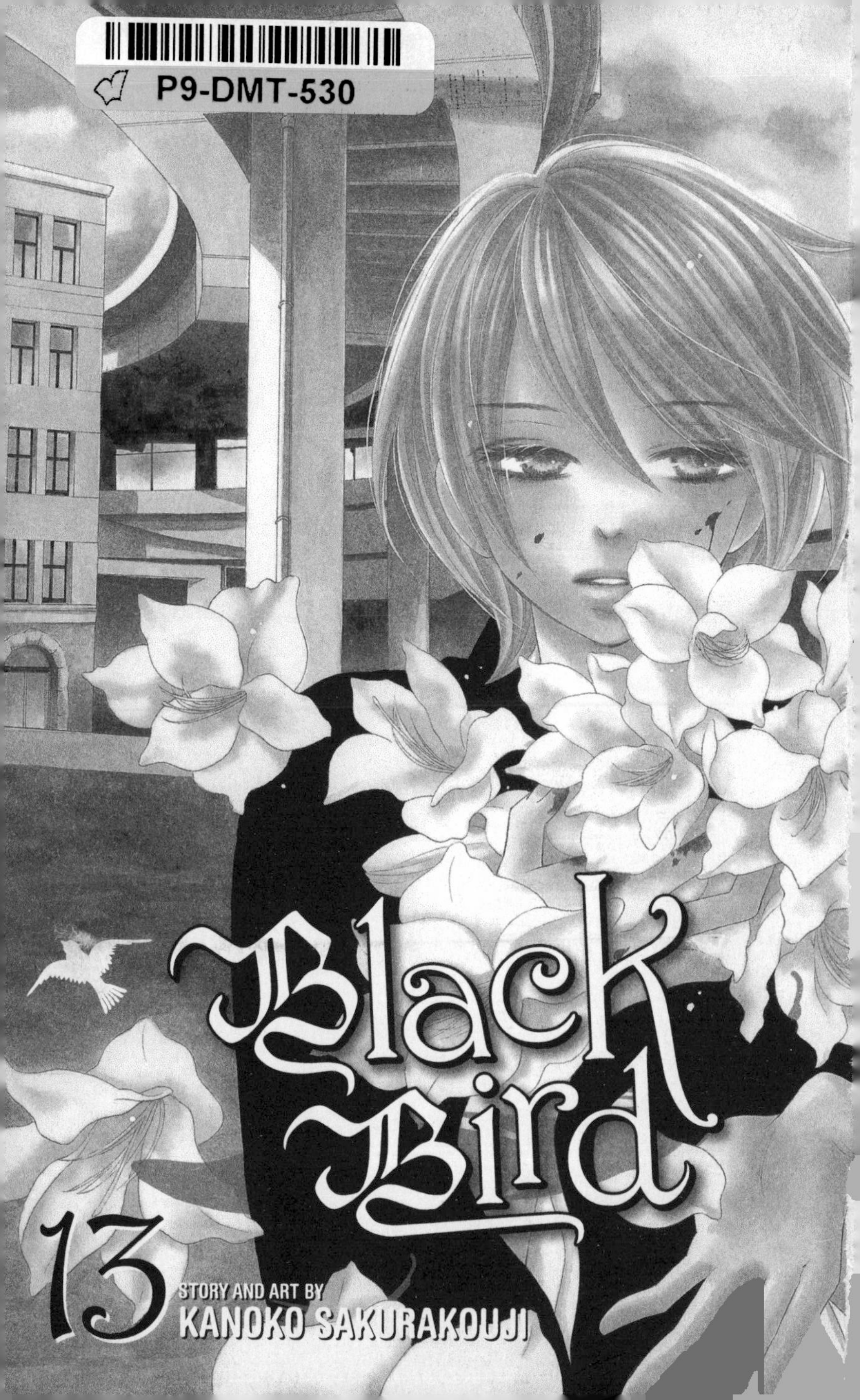
Black Bird
13
STORY AND ART BY
KANOKO SAKURAKOUJI

Black Bird

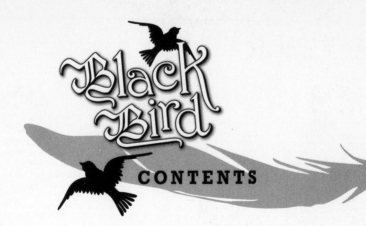

CONTENTS

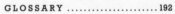

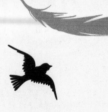

CHARACTERS

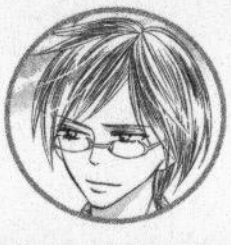

TADANOBU KUZUNOHA
Kyo's close friend since childhood. Current leader of the Kitsune clan.

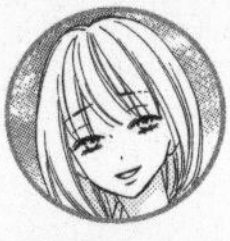

KAEDE
Her father Roh supported Sho's ambitions to seize the clan leadership. She is Sho's attendant.

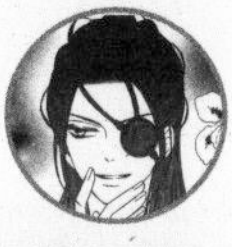

SHO USUI
Kyo's older brother and ar ex-member of the Eight Daitengu. He is also know as Sojo. His attempted cou failed and he is currently plotting near the tengu village.

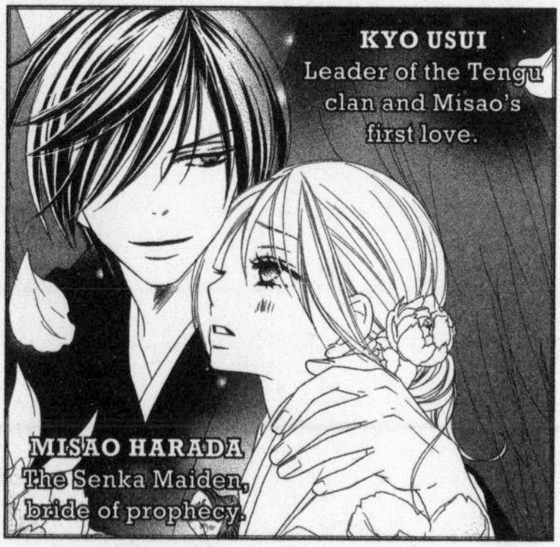
KYO USUI
Leader of the Tengu clan and Misao's first love.
MISAO HARADA
The Senka Maiden, bride of prophecy.

THE EIGHT DAITENGU
Kyo's bodyguards. Their names designate their official posts.

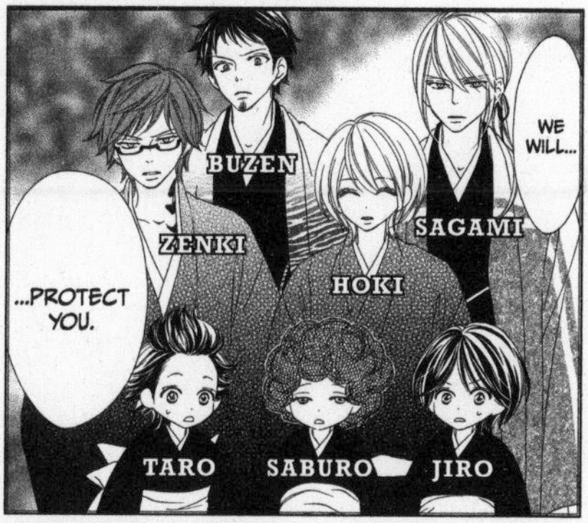
WE WILL...
SAGAMI
BUZEN
HOKI
ZENKI
...PROTECT YOU.
JIRO
SABURO
TARO

STORY THUS FAR
Misao can see spirits and demons, and her childhood sweetheart Kyo has been protecting her since she was little.

"Someday, I'll come for you, I promise." Kyo reappears the day before Misao's 16th birthday to tell her, "Your 16th birthday marks 'open season' on you." She is the Senka Maiden, and if a demon drinks her blood, he is granted a long life. If he eats her flesh, he gains eternal youth. And if he makes her his bride, his clan will prosper...And Kyo is a *tengu*, a crow demon, with his sights firmly set on her.

Kyo avoided sleeping with Misao because he knew that sex with a demon is somehow dangerous for the Senka Maiden, but when poison nearly killed him, he finally gave in and took Misao.

Now that Kyo's powers have no equal, his older brother Sho, presumed dead, reappears. Sho plans to use the might he obtained through his resurrection, Misao's blood, and his domination of other demon clans to throw the tengu village into confusion to create a world of anarchy.

Sho captures Zenki, one of Kyo's Eight Daitengu, and removes the seals that contain his volcanic powers. Kyo manages to halt Zenki's rampage, but is badly wounded in the process. Meanwhile, Hoki has convinced Sho that he has left Kyo's service and wants to join Sho's side!

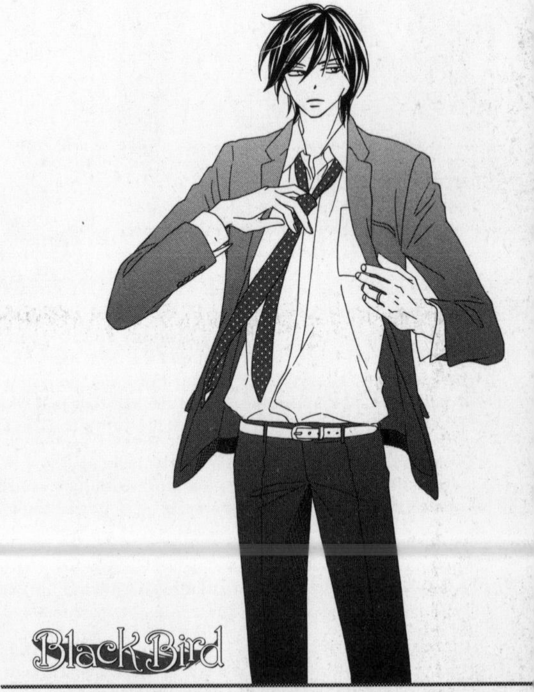
Black Bird

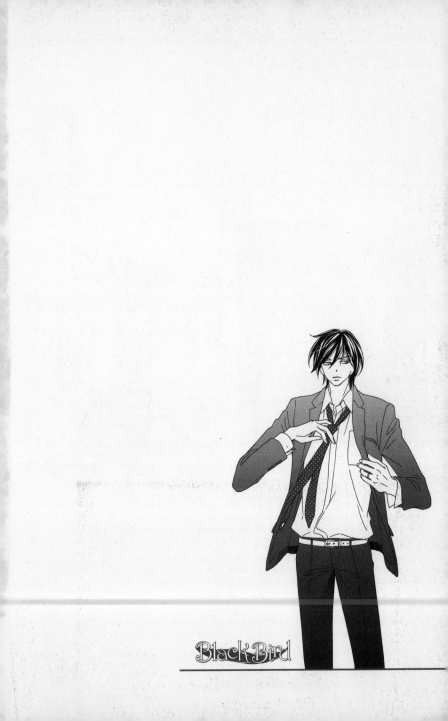

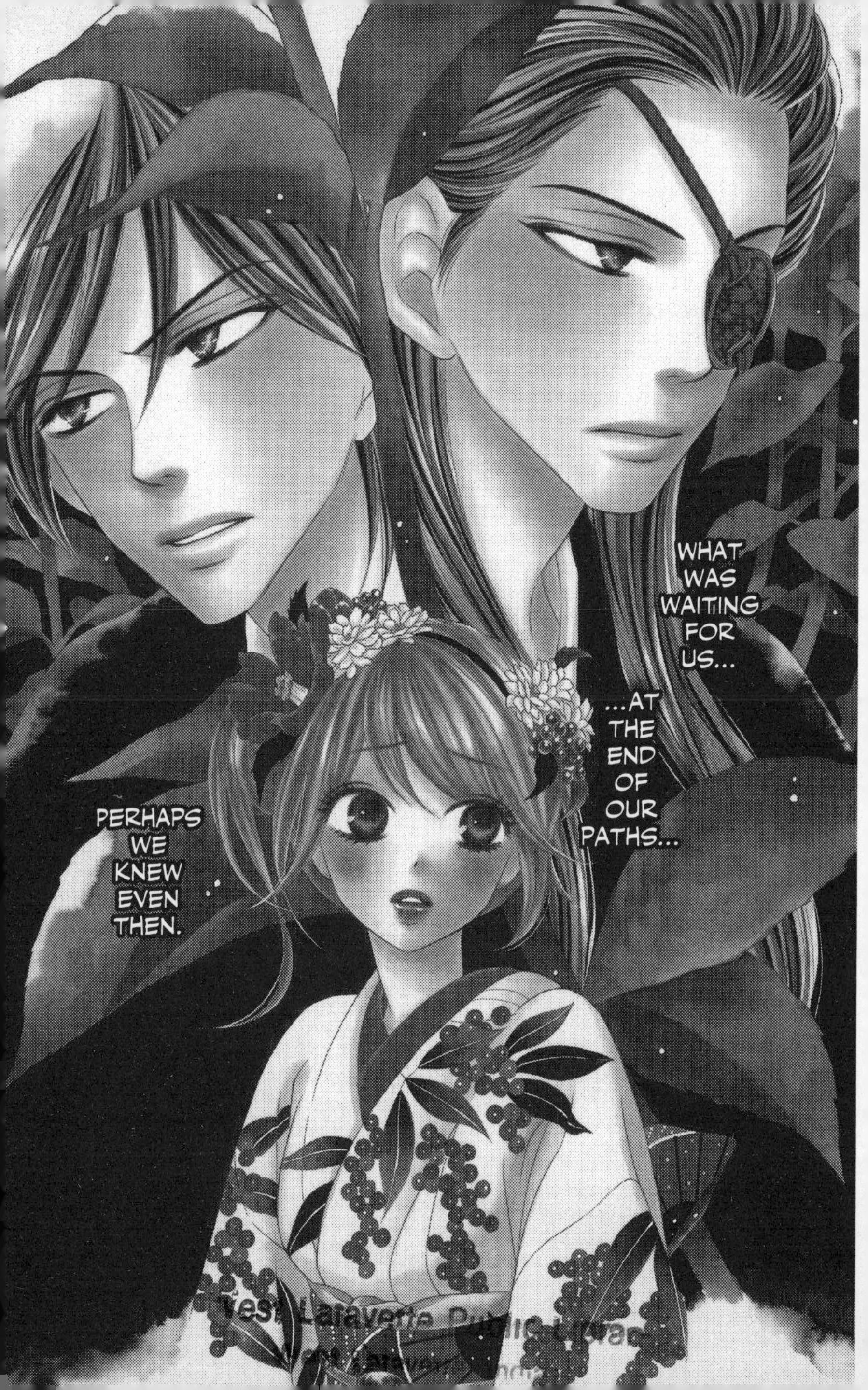
WHAT WAS WAITING FOR US...
...AT THE END OF OUR PATHS...
PERHAPS WE KNEW EVEN THEN.

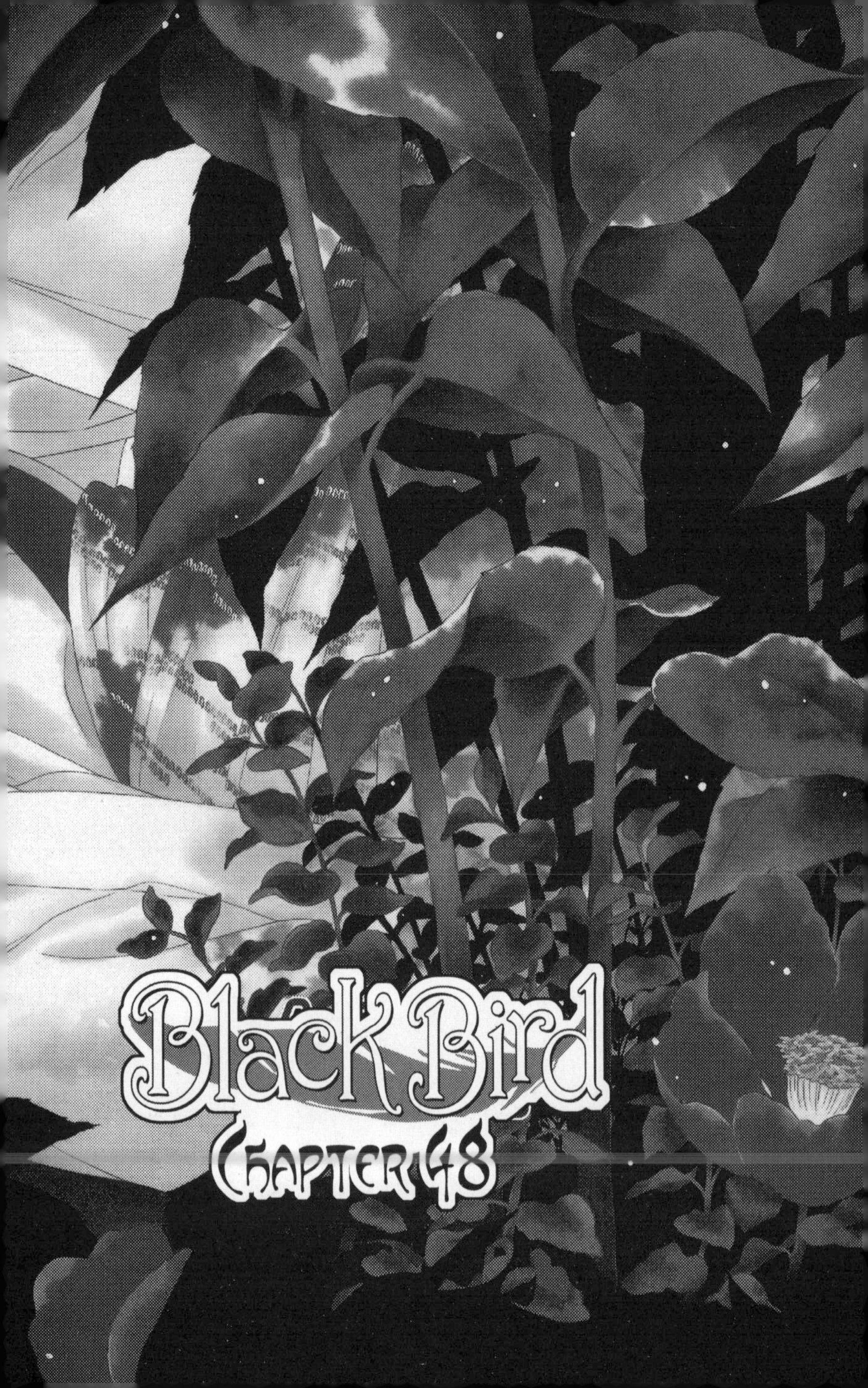
Black Bird
Chapter 48

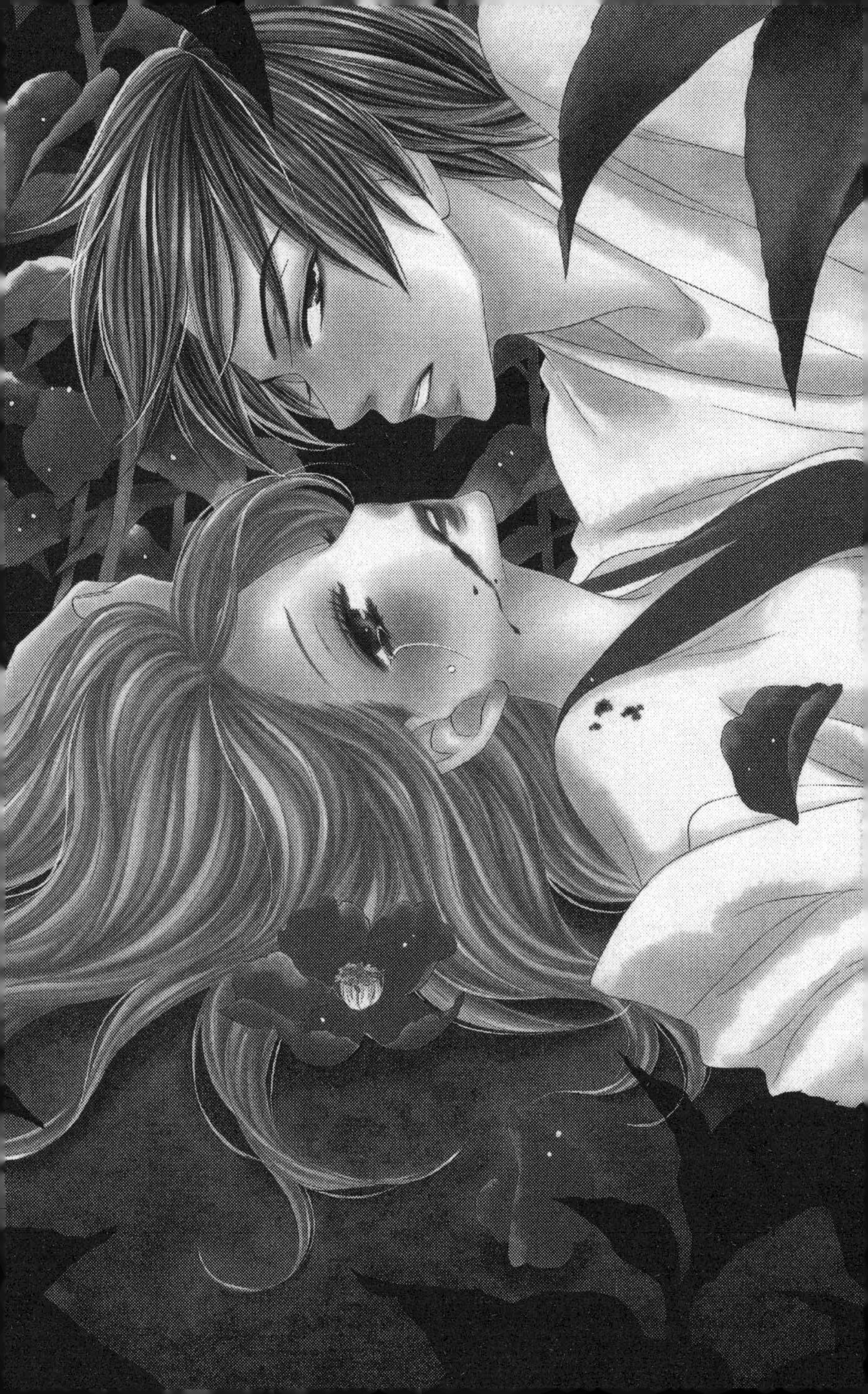

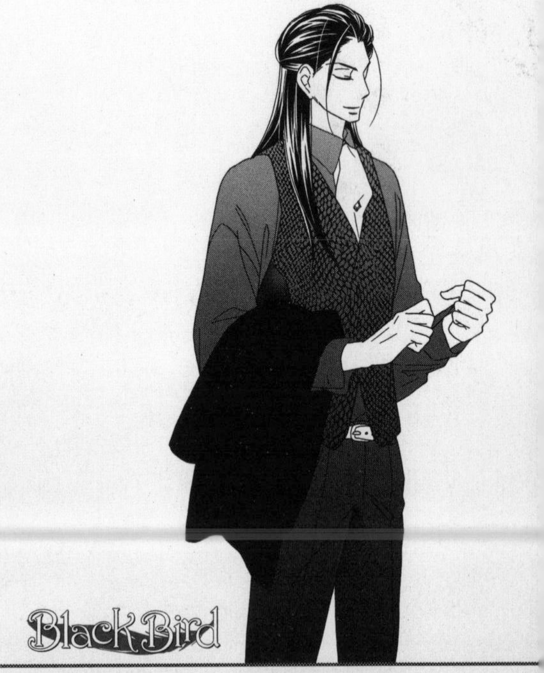
Black Bird

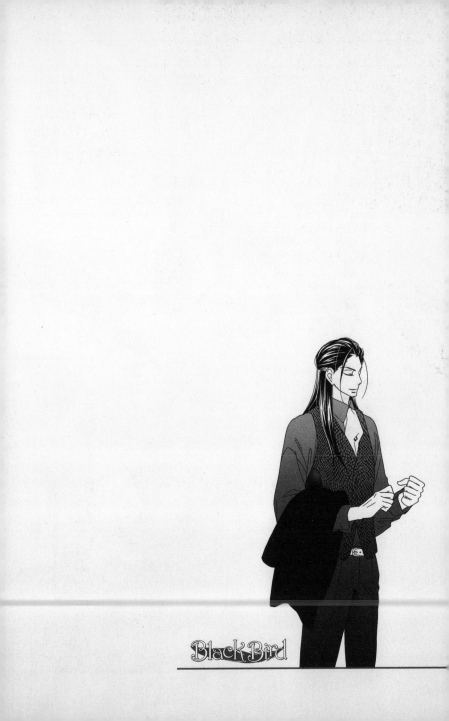

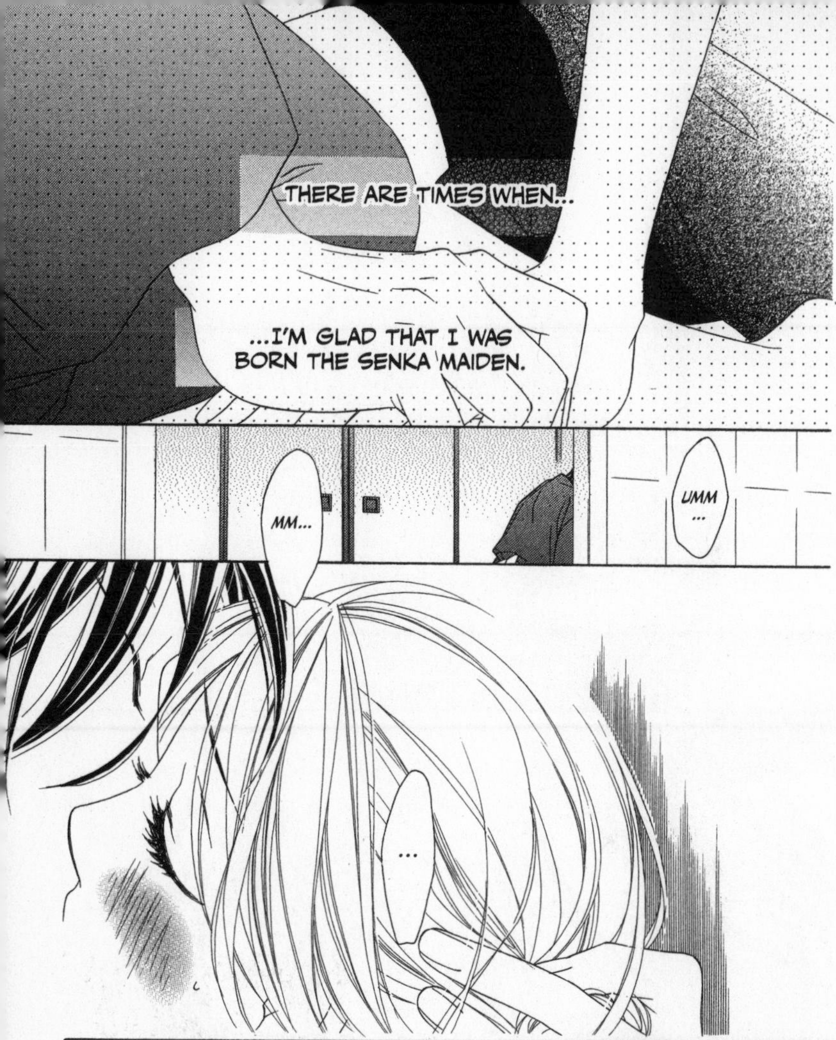
THERE ARE TIMES WHEN...
...I'M GLAD THAT I WAS BORN THE SENKA MAIDEN.
UMM...
MM...
...

Hello, everyone.
This is Sakurakouji. Here is the thirteenth volume of *Black Bird*.
I'm pleased to see you all again.

We moved studios between Chapter 48 and 49 of this volume. This means I've worked on this manga series in three different places.

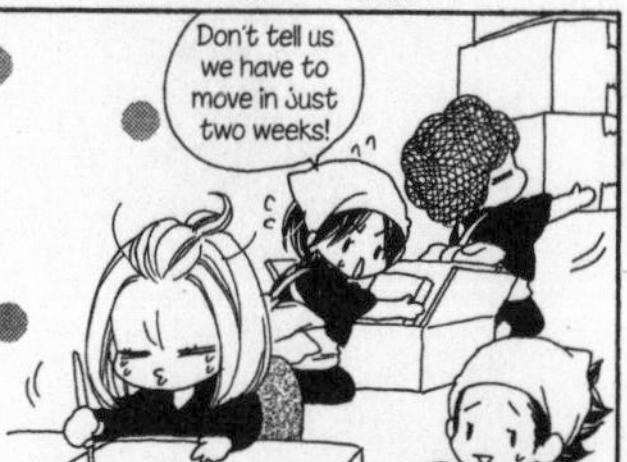
Don't tell us we have to move in just two weeks!
It would have been easier if I'd had the triplets...

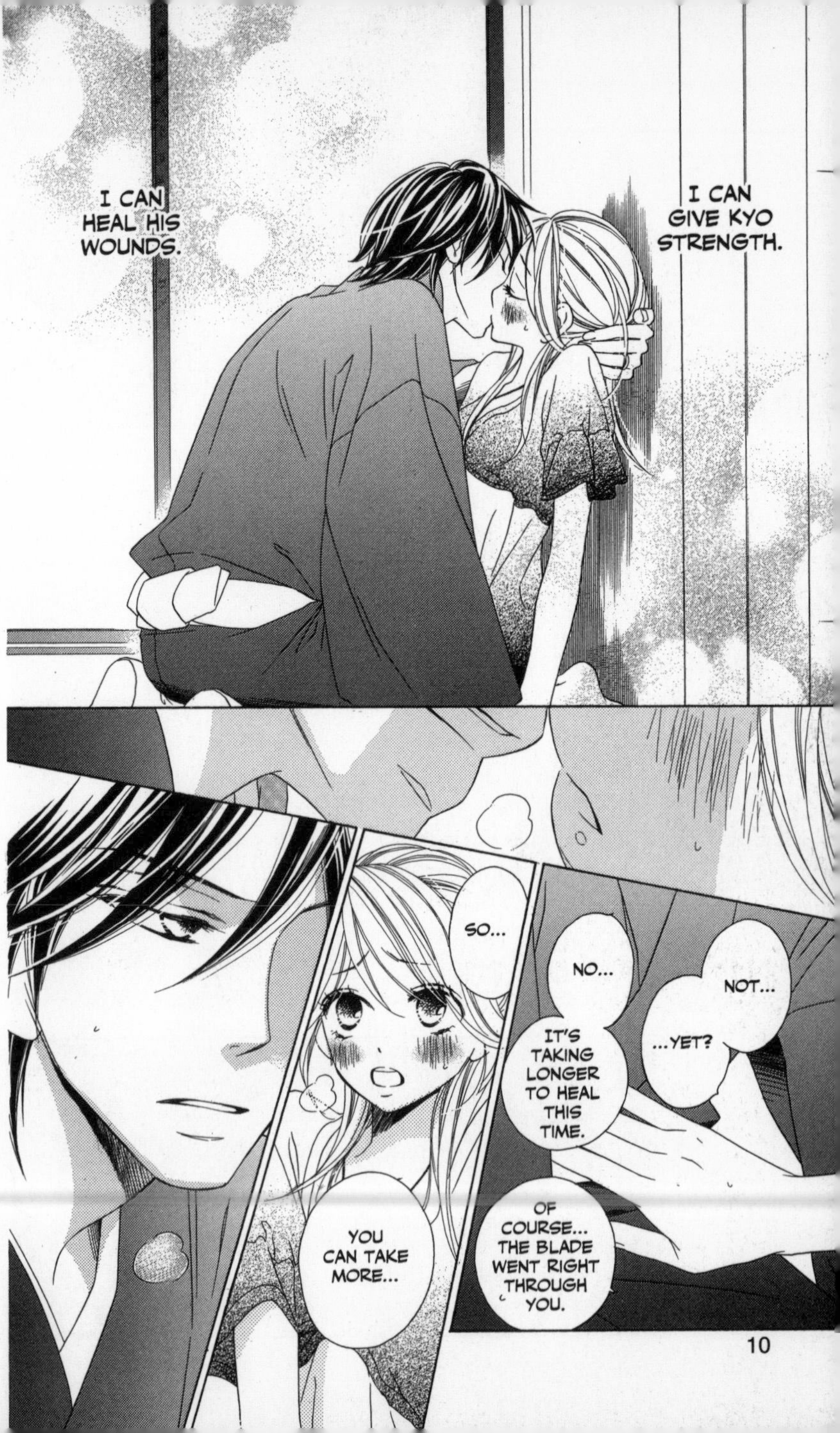
I CAN GIVE KYO STRENGTH.
I CAN HEAL HIS WOUNDS.
SO...
NOT...
...YET?
NO...
IT'S TAKING LONGER TO HEAL THIS TIME.
OF COURSE... THE BLADE WENT RIGHT THROUGH YOU.
YOU CAN TAKE MORE...

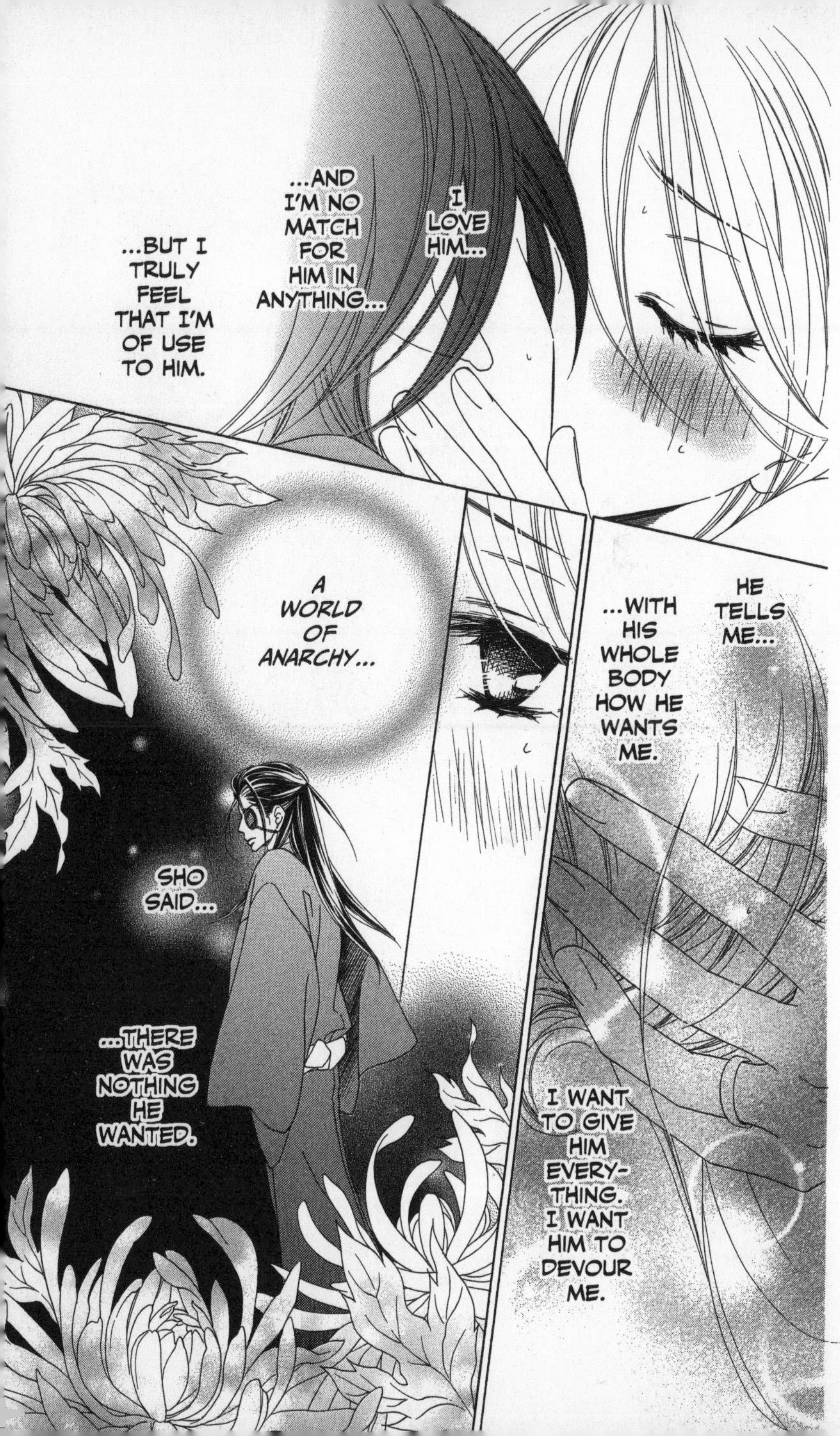
I LOVE HIM...
...AND I'M NO MATCH FOR HIM IN ANYTHING...
...BUT I TRULY FEEL THAT I'M OF USE TO HIM.
HE TELLS ME...
...WITH HIS WHOLE BODY HOW HE WANTS ME.
I WANT TO GIVE HIM EVERY-THING. I WANT HIM TO DEVOUR ME.
A WORLD OF ANARCHY...
SHO SAID...
...THERE WAS NOTHING HE WANTED.

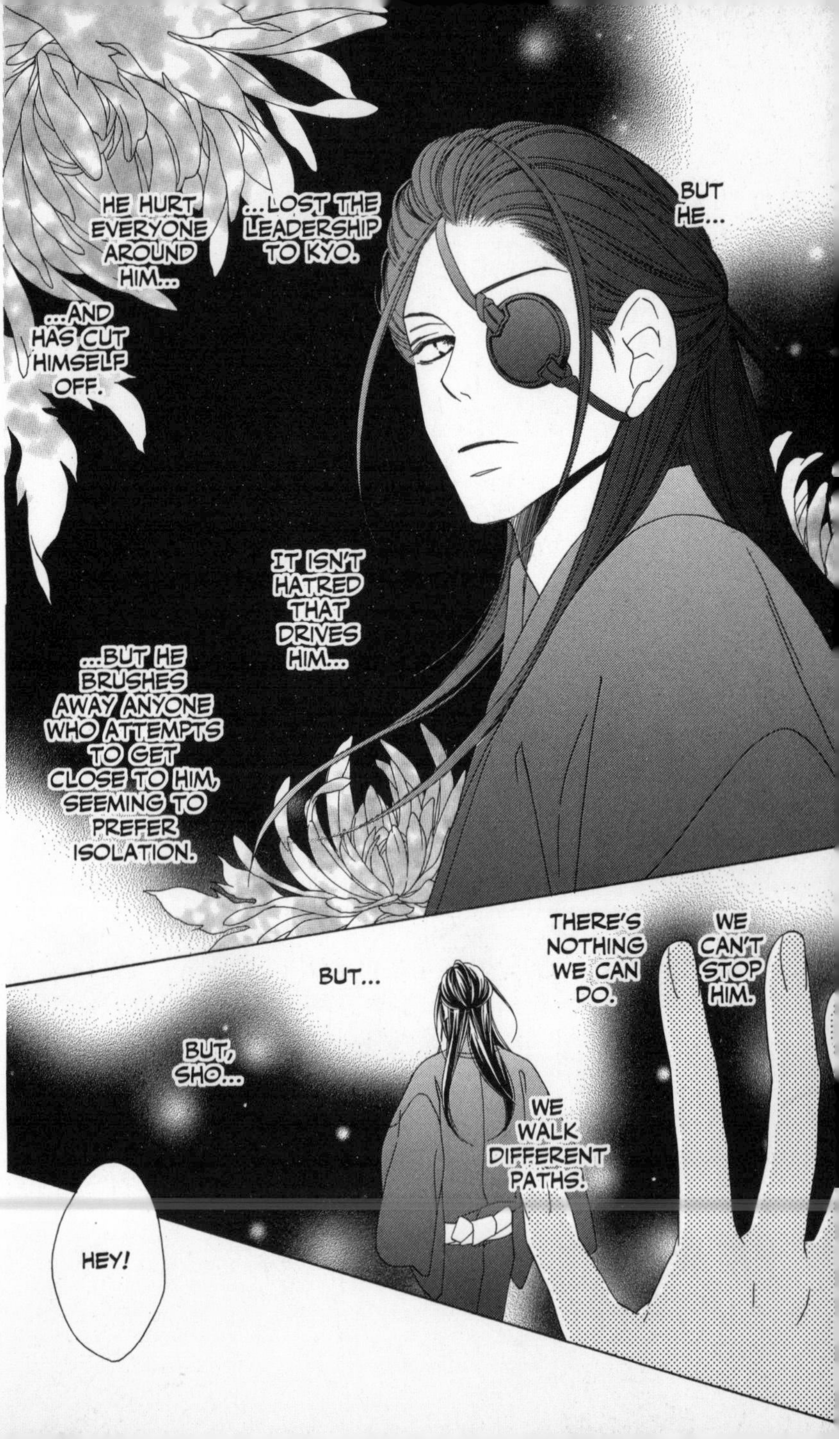
BUT HE...
...LOST THE LEADERSHIP TO KYO.
HE HURT EVERYONE AROUND HIM...
...AND HAS CUT HIMSELF OFF.
IT ISN'T HATRED THAT DRIVES HIM...
...BUT HE BRUSHES AWAY ANYONE WHO ATTEMPTS TO GET CLOSE TO HIM, SEEMING TO PREFER ISOLATION.
WE CAN'T STOP HIM.
THERE'S NOTHING WE CAN DO.
BUT...
WE WALK DIFFERENT PATHS.
BUT, SHO...
HEY!

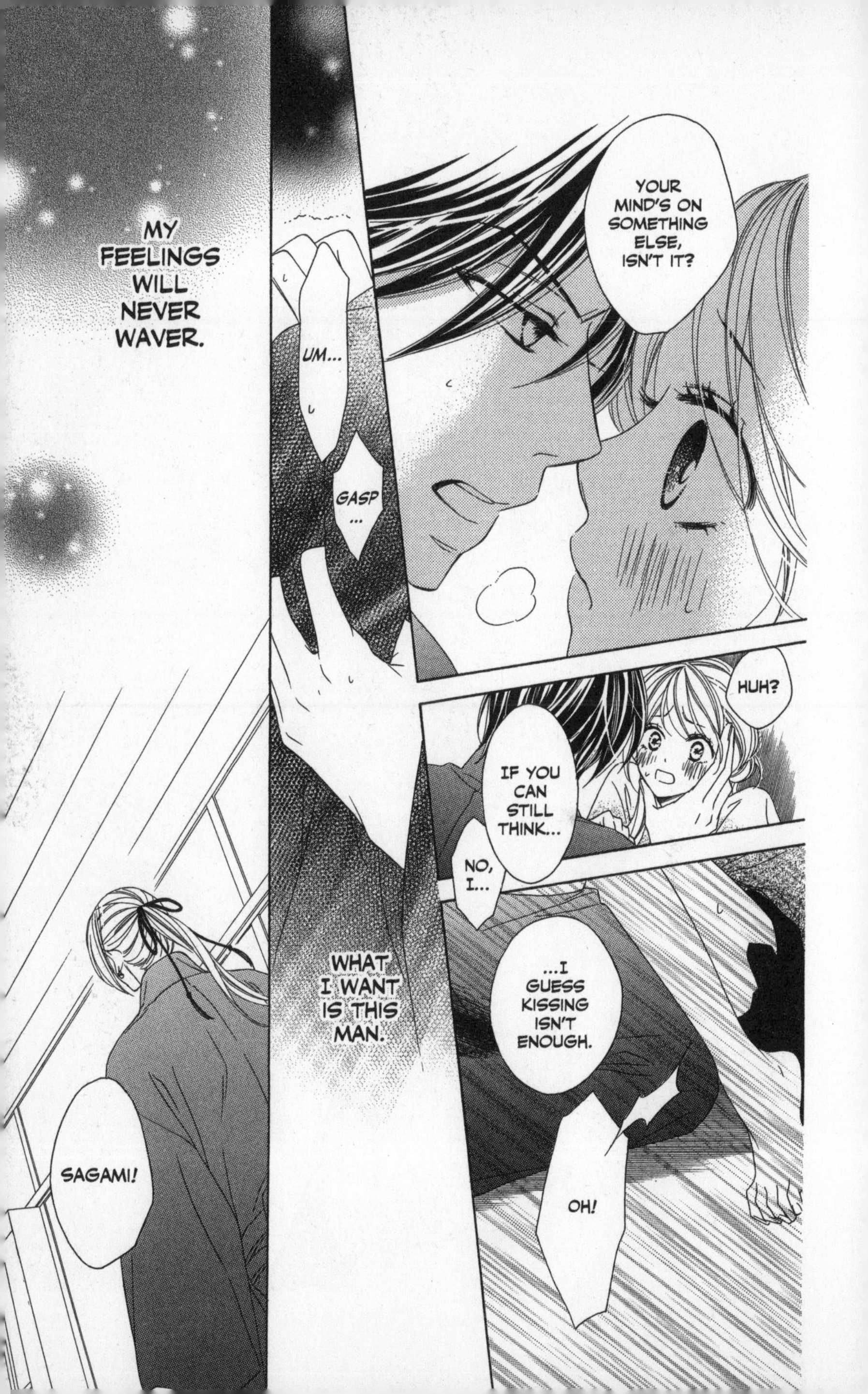
YOUR MIND'S ON SOMETHING ELSE, ISN'T IT?
UM...
GASP...
HUH?
IF YOU CAN STILL THINK...
NO, I...
...I GUESS KISSING ISN'T ENOUGH.
OH!
WHAT I WANT IS THIS MAN.
MY FEELINGS WILL NEVER WAVER.
SAGAMI!

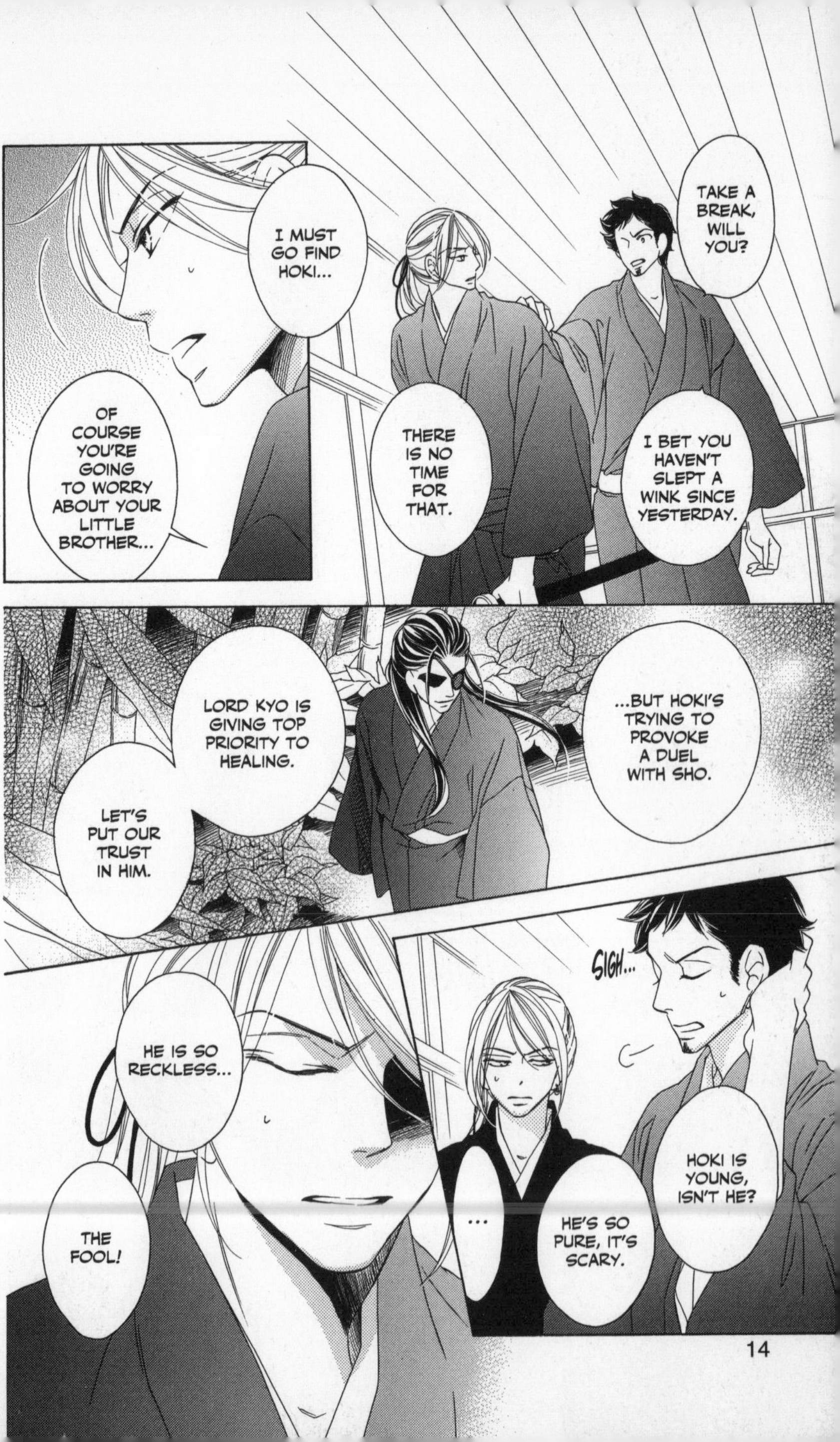

TAKE A BREAK, WILL YOU?
I MUST GO FIND HOKI...
I BET YOU HAVEN'T SLEPT A WINK SINCE YESTERDAY.
THERE IS NO TIME FOR THAT.
OF COURSE YOU'RE GOING TO WORRY ABOUT YOUR LITTLE BROTHER...
...BUT HOKI'S TRYING TO PROVOKE A DUEL WITH SHO.
LORD KYO IS GIVING TOP PRIORITY TO HEALING.
LET'S PUT OUR TRUST IN HIM.
SIGH...
HOKI IS YOUNG, ISN'T HE?
HE'S SO PURE, IT'S SCARY.
...
HE IS SO RECKLESS...
THE FOOL!

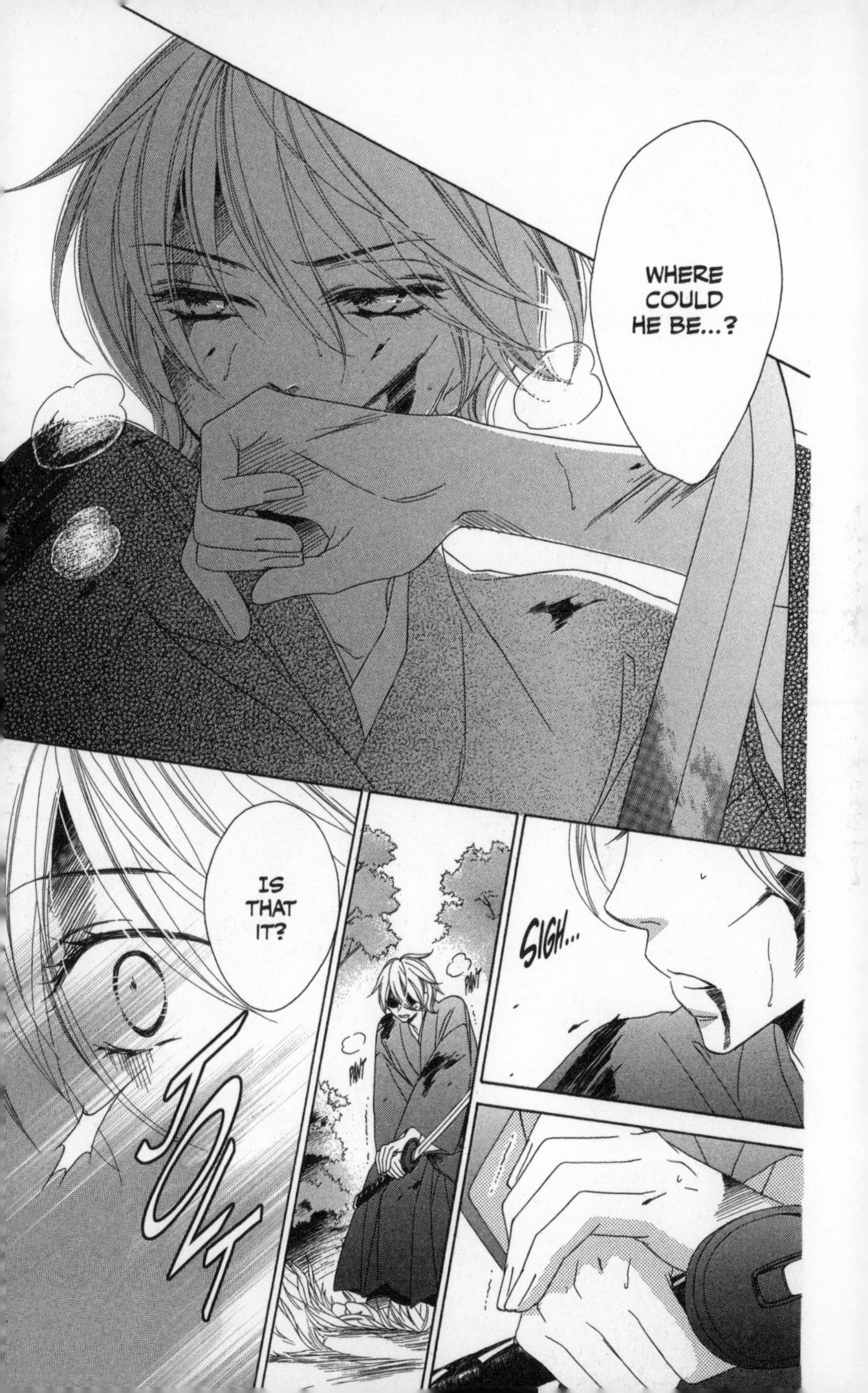
WHERE COULD HE BE...?
SIGH...
PANT
PANT
IS THAT IT?
JOLT

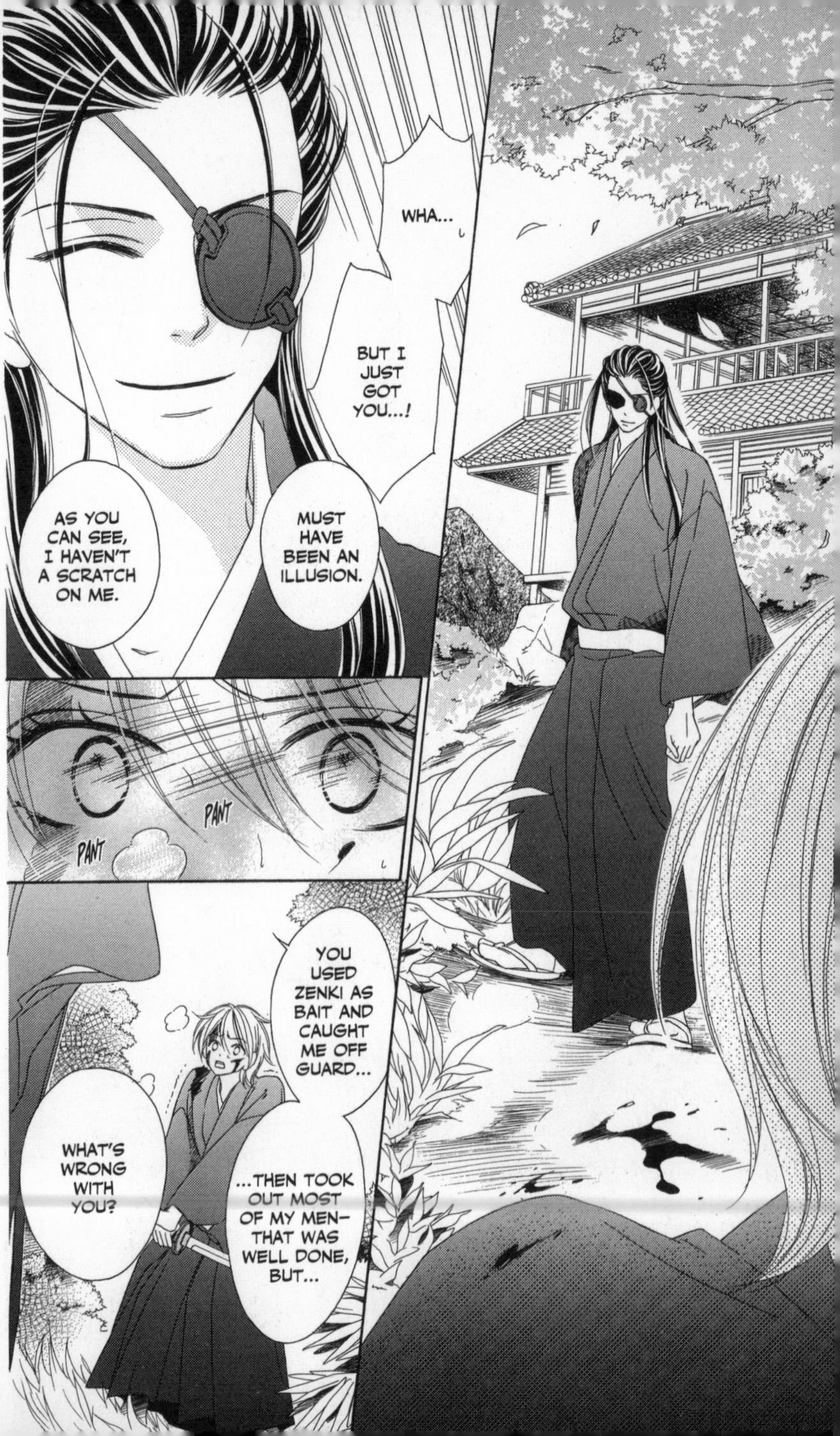
WHA...
BUT I JUST GOT YOU...!
MUST HAVE BEEN AN ILLUSION.
AS YOU CAN SEE, I HAVEN'T A SCRATCH ON ME.
PANT
PANT
YOU USED ZENKI AS BAIT AND CAUGHT ME OFF GUARD...
...THEN TOOK OUT MOST OF MY MEN—THAT WAS WELL DONE, BUT...
WHAT'S WRONG WITH YOU?

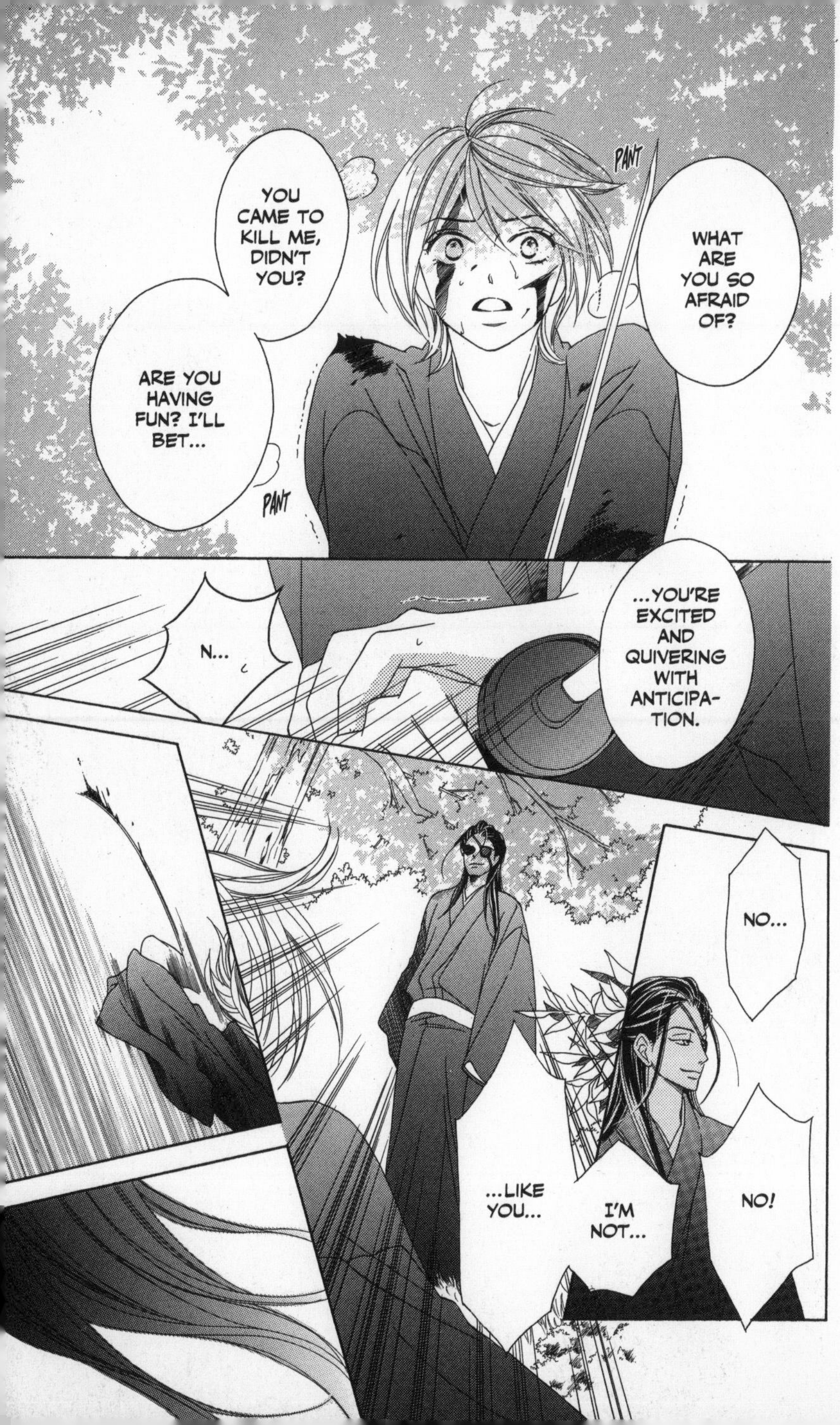
PANT
WHAT ARE YOU SO AFRAID OF?
YOU CAME TO KILL ME, DIDN'T YOU?
ARE YOU HAVING FUN? I'LL BET...
PANT
...YOU'RE EXCITED AND QUIVERING WITH ANTICIPA-TION.
N...
NO...
NO!
I'M NOT...
...LIKE YOU...

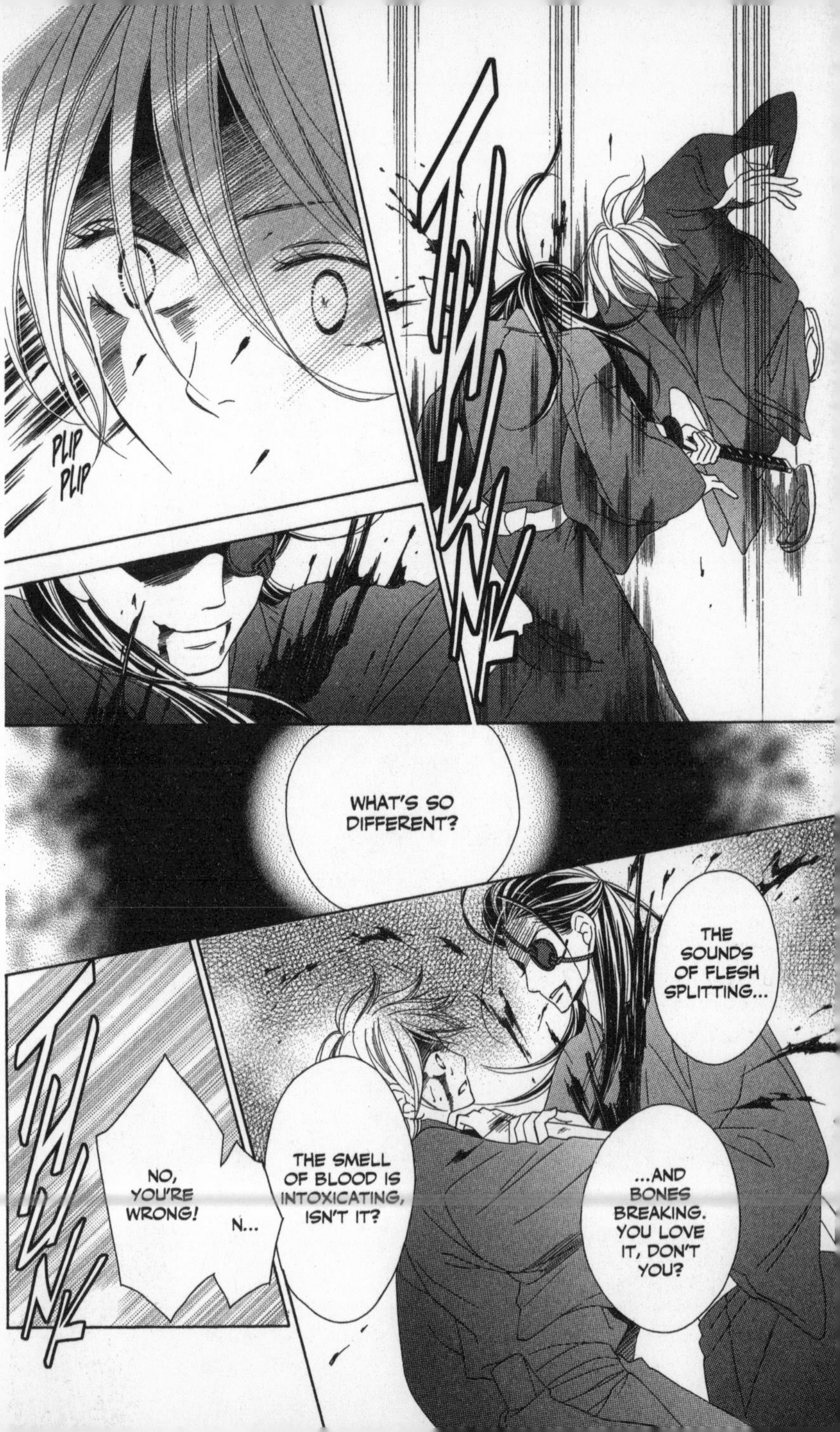
THUNK
PLIP PLIP
WHAT'S SO DIFFERENT?
THE SOUNDS OF FLESH SPLITTING...
...AND BONES BREAKING. YOU LOVE IT, DON'T YOU?
THE SMELL OF BLOOD IS INTOXICATING, ISN'T IT?
N...
THUNK
NO, YOU'RE WRONG!

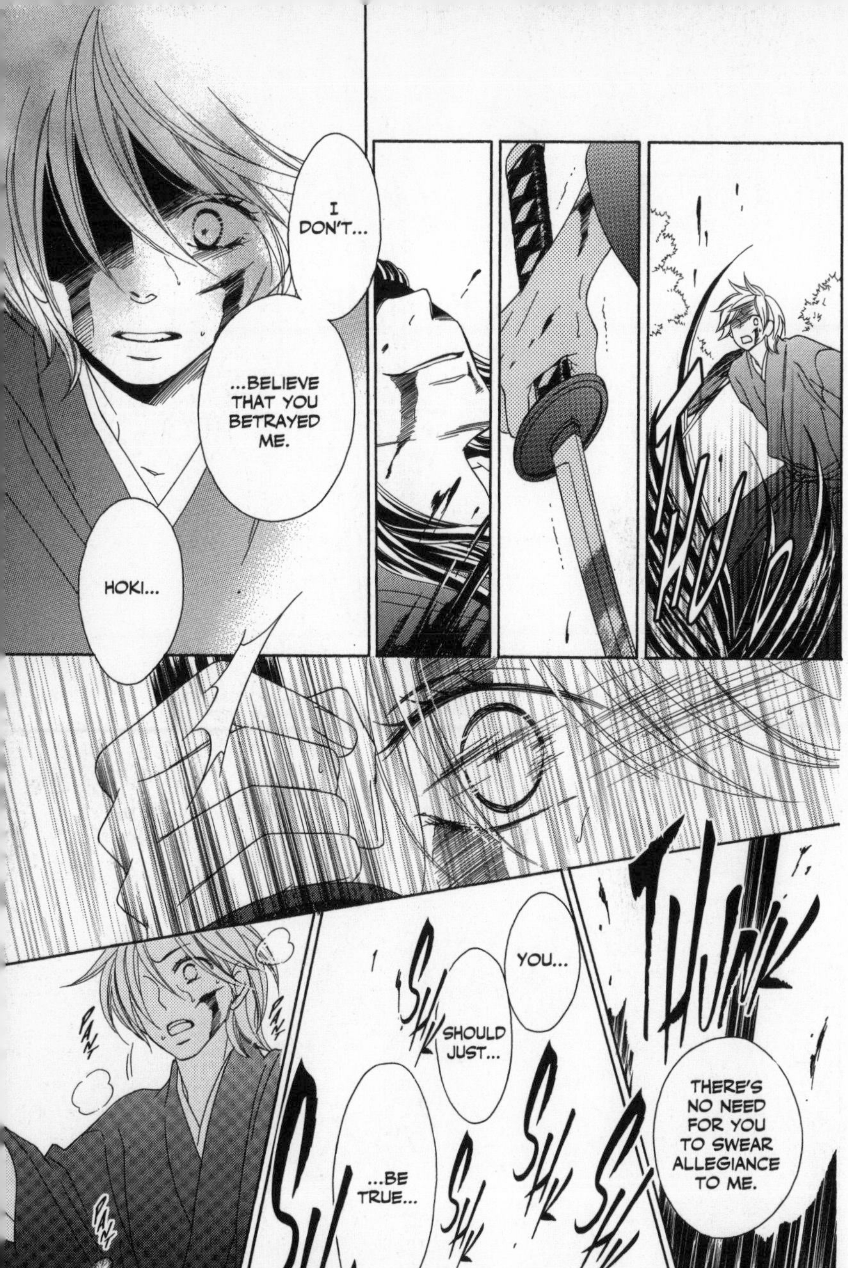
I DON'T...
...BELIEVE THAT YOU BETRAYED ME.
HOKI...
THUNK
THERE'S NO NEED FOR YOU TO SWEAR ALLEGIANCE TO ME.
SHK
SHK
YOU...
SHOULD JUST...
...BE TRUE...
SHK
SHK
SHK
PANT
PANT

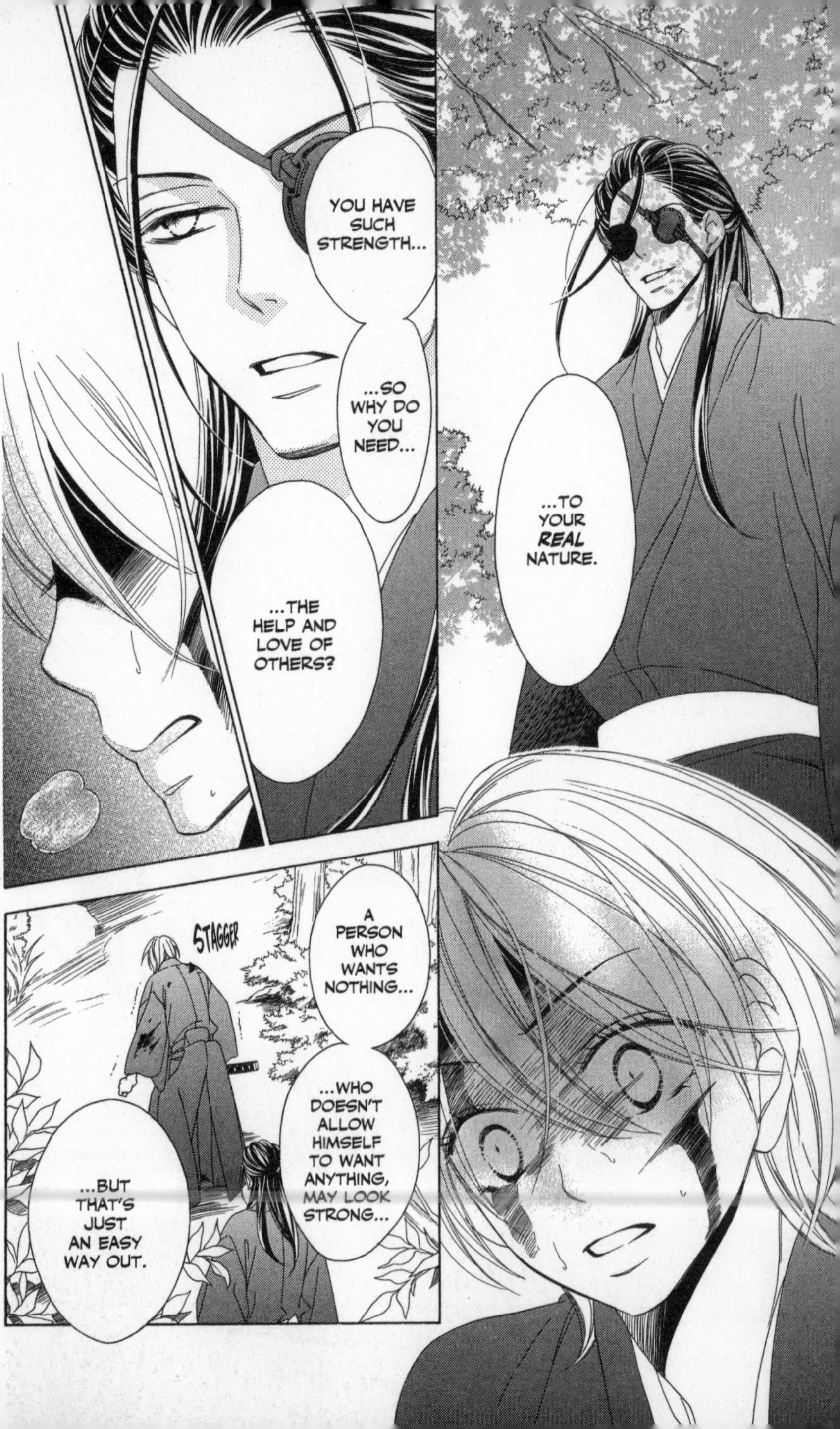
...TO YOUR REAL NATURE.
YOU HAVE SUCH STRENGTH...
...SO WHY DO YOU NEED...
...THE HELP AND LOVE OF OTHERS?
A PERSON WHO WANTS NOTHING...
...WHO DOESN'T ALLOW HIMSELF TO WANT ANYTHING, MAY LOOK STRONG...
STAGGER
...BUT THAT'S JUST AN EASY WAY OUT.

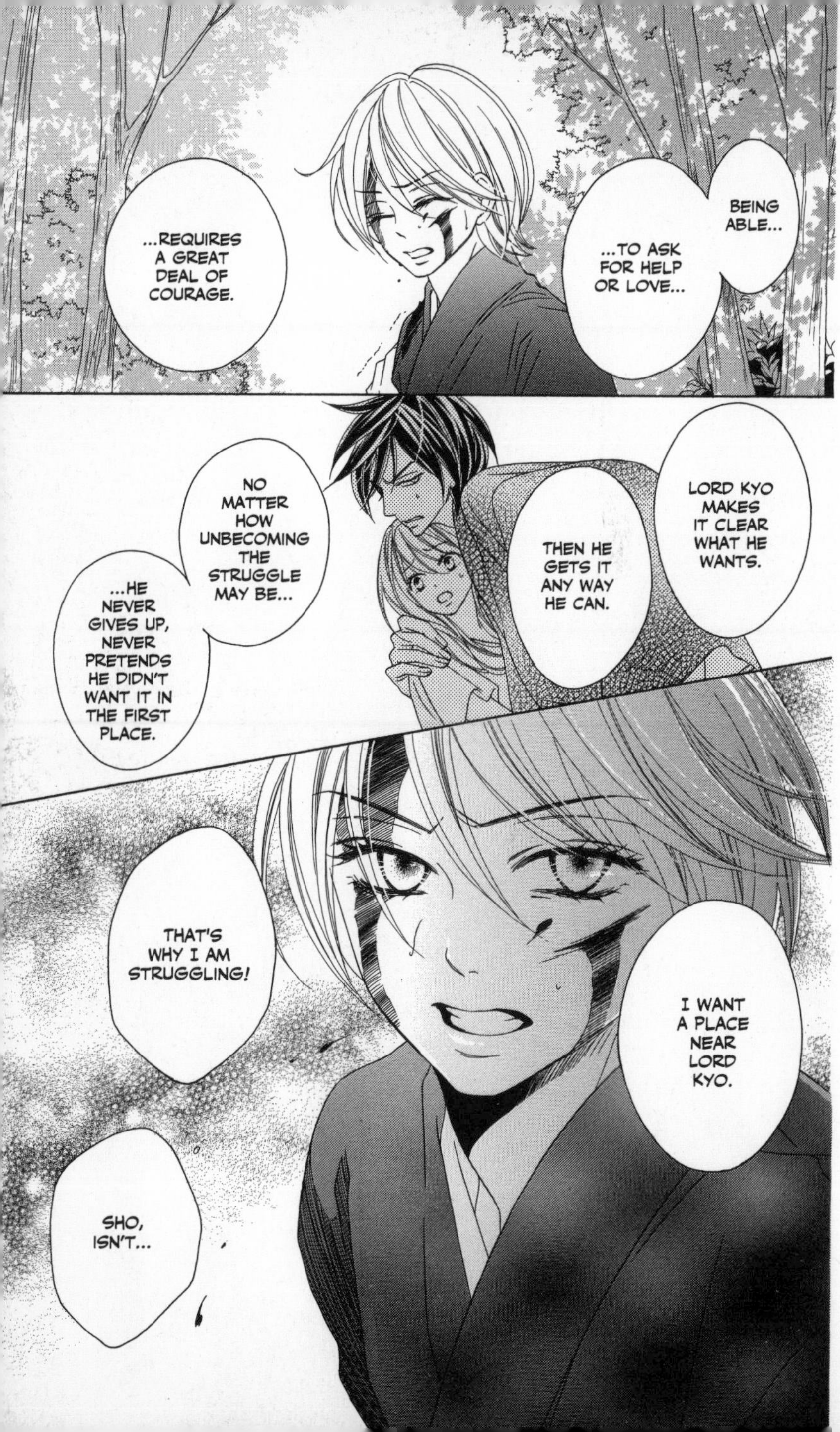
BEING ABLE...
...TO ASK FOR HELP OR LOVE...
...REQUIRES A GREAT DEAL OF COURAGE.
LORD KYO MAKES IT CLEAR WHAT HE WANTS.
THEN HE GETS IT ANY WAY HE CAN.
NO MATTER HOW UNBECOMING THE STRUGGLE MAY BE...
...HE NEVER GIVES UP, NEVER PRETENDS HE DIDN'T WANT IT IN THE FIRST PLACE.
I WANT A PLACE NEAR LORD KYO.
THAT'S WHY I AM STRUGGLING!
SHO, ISN'T...

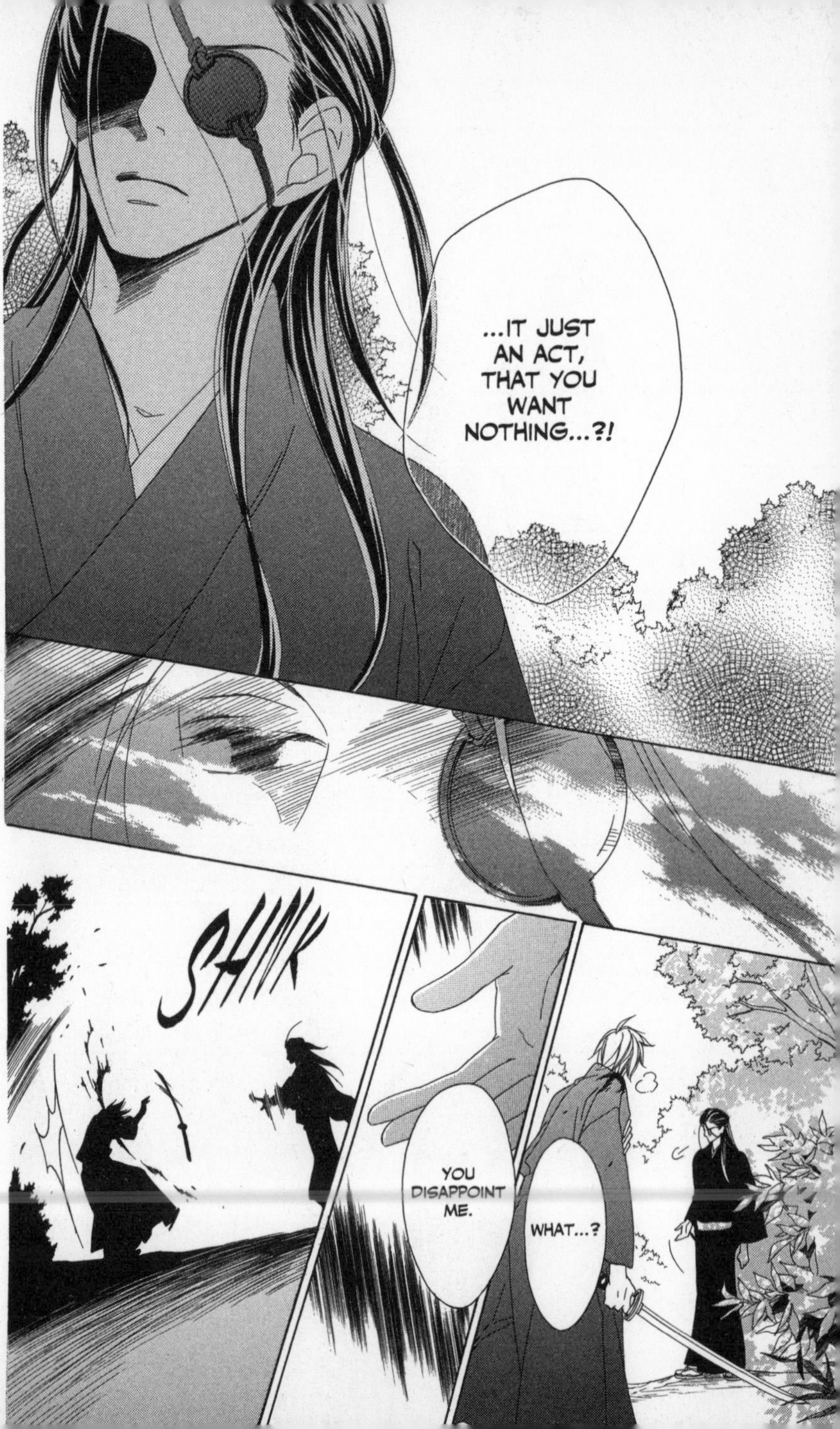
...IT JUST AN ACT, THAT YOU WANT NOTHING...?!
WHAT...?
YOU DISAPPOINT ME.
SHINK

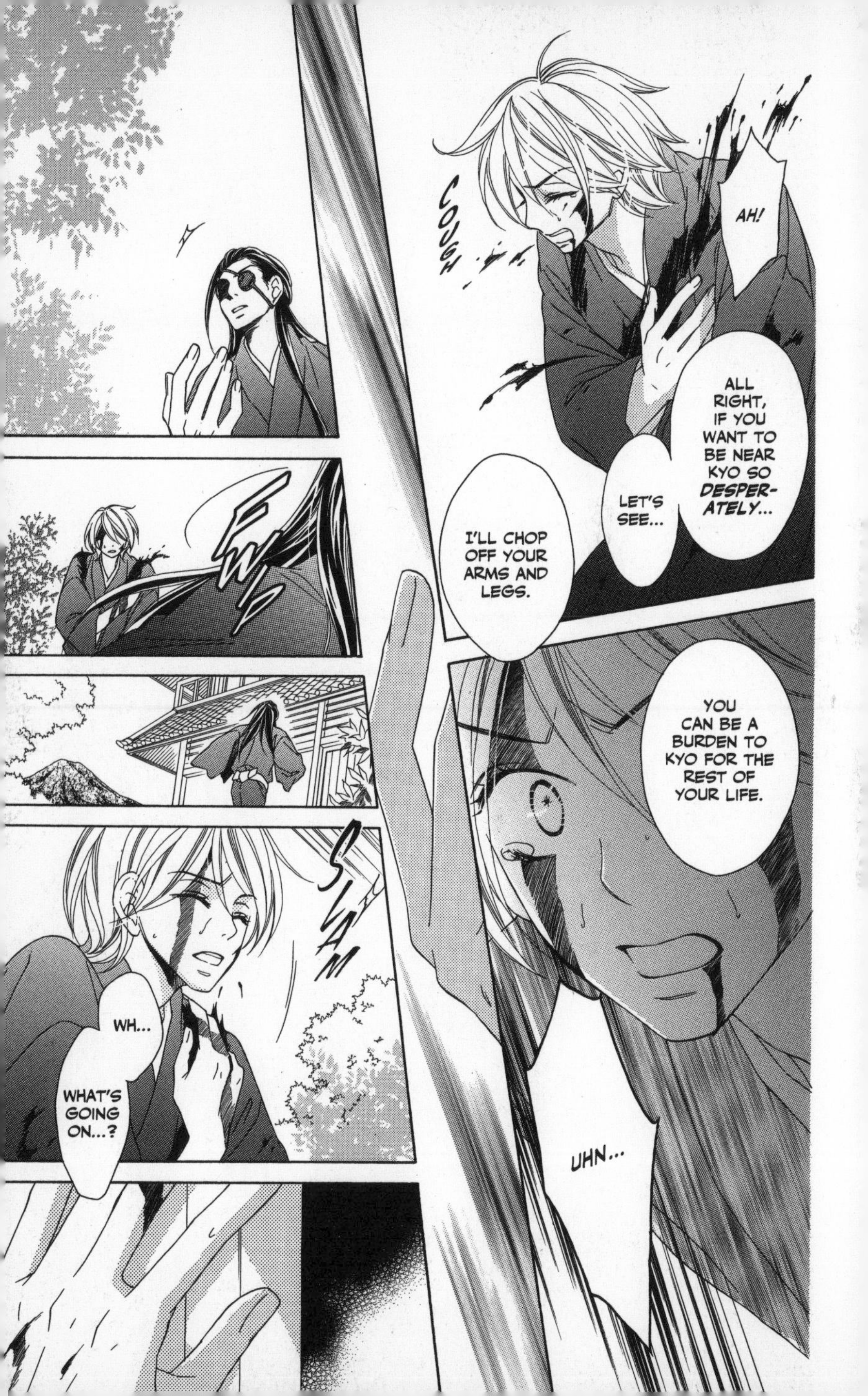
COUGH
AH!
ALL RIGHT, IF YOU WANT TO BE NEAR KYO SO *DESPERATELY*...
LET'S SEE...
I'LL CHOP OFF YOUR ARMS AND LEGS.
YOU CAN BE A BURDEN TO KYO FOR THE REST OF YOUR LIFE.
UHN...
FWIP
SLAM
WH...
WHAT'S GOING ON...?

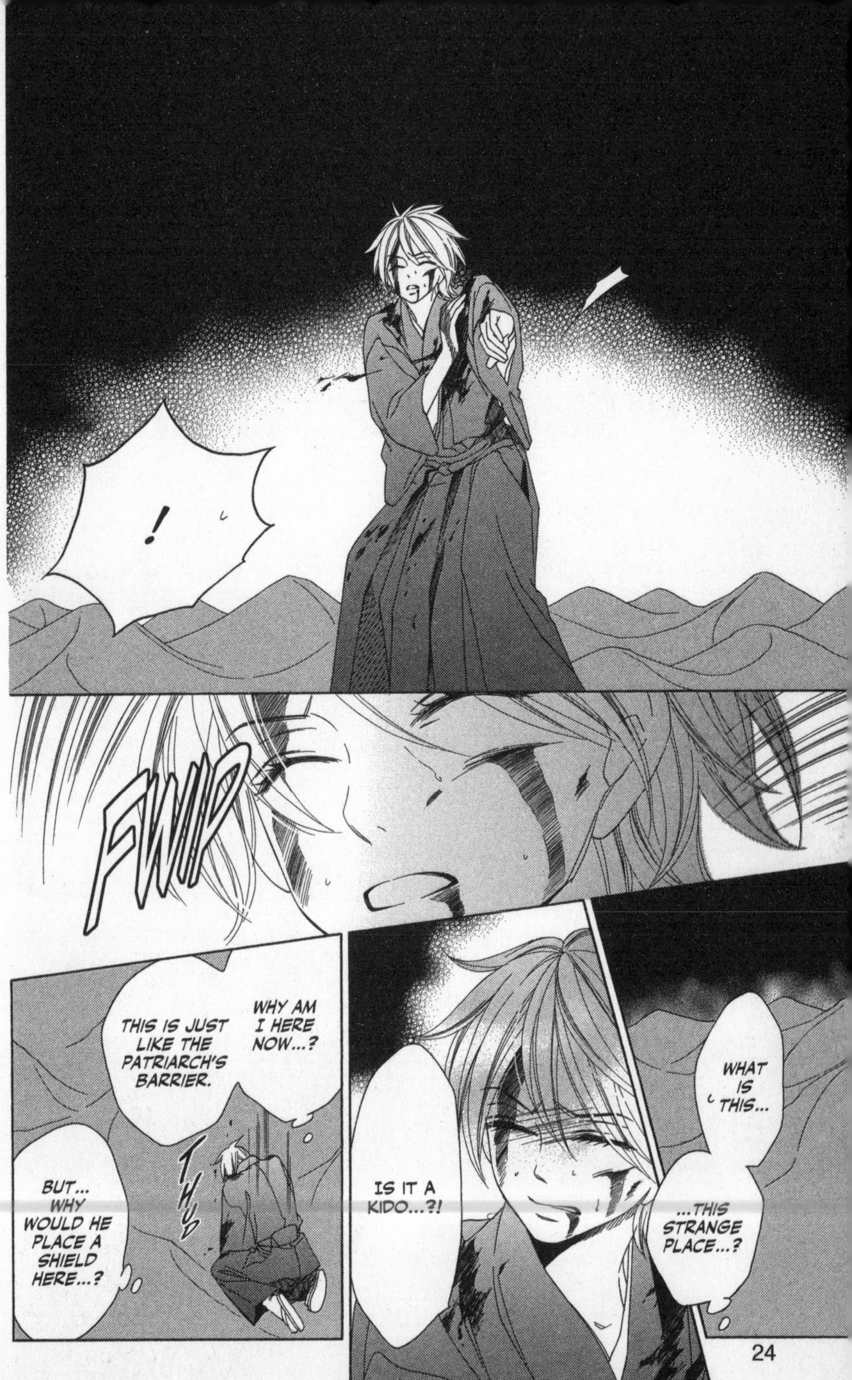
!
FWIP
WHAT IS THIS...
...THIS STRANGE PLACE...?
IS IT A KIDO...?!
WHY AM I HERE NOW...?
THIS IS JUST LIKE THE PATRIARCH'S BARRIER.
THUD
BUT... WHY WOULD HE PLACE A SHIELD HERE...?

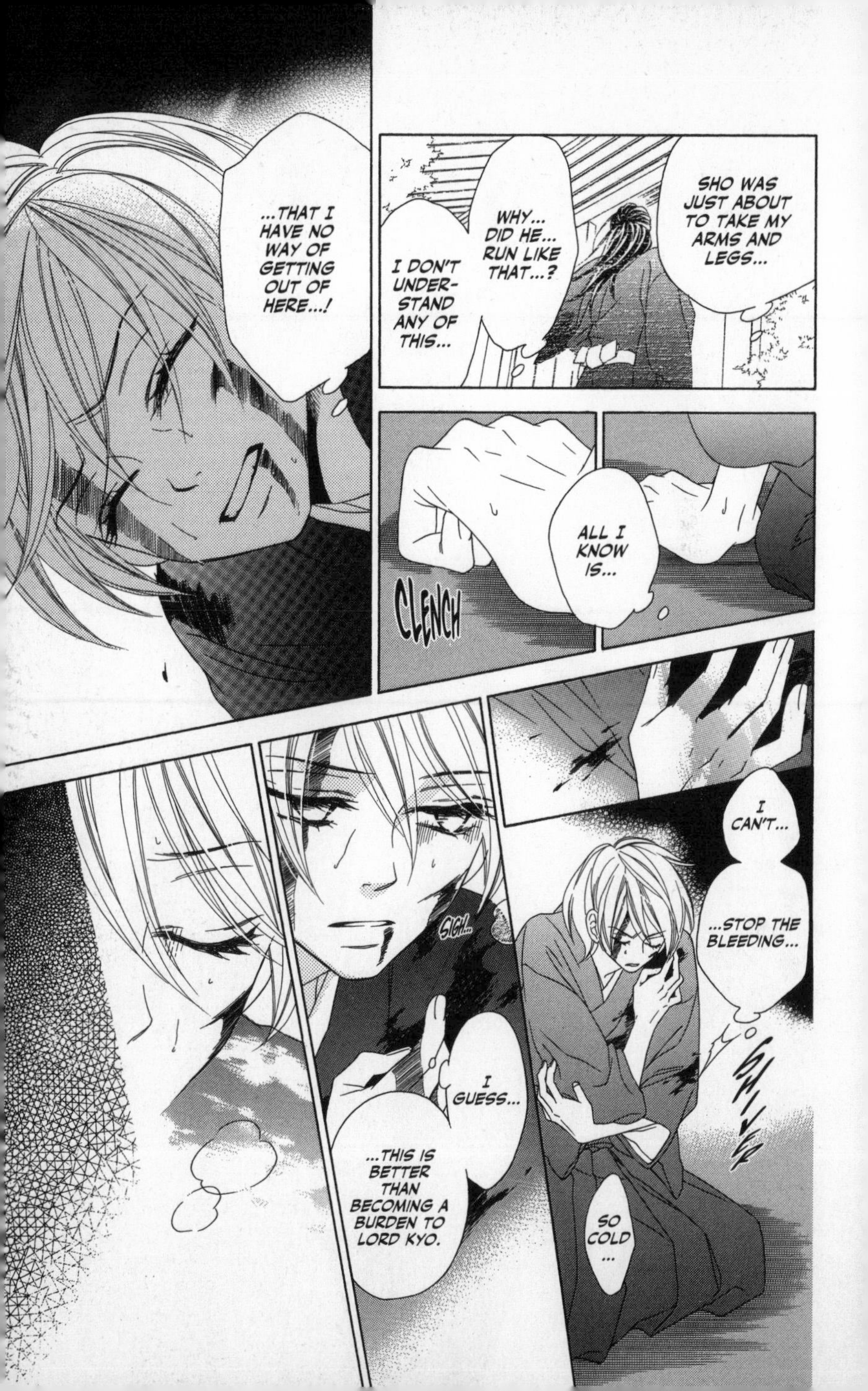
SHO WAS JUST ABOUT TO TAKE MY ARMS AND LEGS...
WHY... DID HE... RUN LIKE THAT...?
I DON'T UNDER-STAND ANY OF THIS...
ALL I KNOW IS...
CLENCH
...THAT I HAVE NO WAY OF GETTING OUT OF HERE...!
I CAN'T...
...STOP THE BLEEDING...
SHIVER
SO COLD...
SIGH...
I GUESS...
...THIS IS BETTER THAN BECOMING A BURDEN TO LORD KYO.

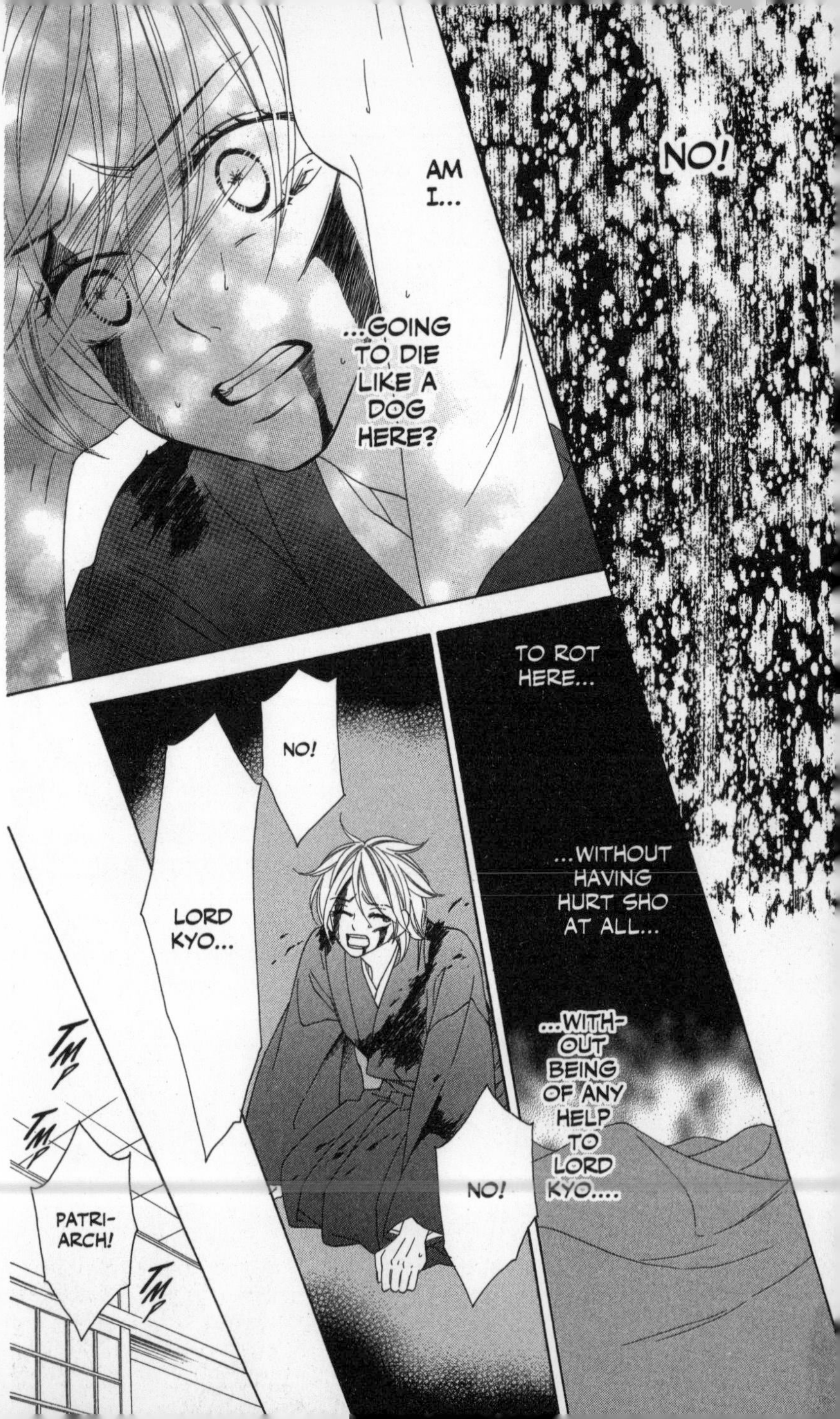
NO!
AM I...
...GOING TO DIE LIKE A DOG HERE?
TO ROT HERE...
...WITHOUT HAVING HURT SHO AT ALL...
...WITH-OUT BEING OF ANY HELP TO LORD KYO....
NO!
LORD KYO...
NO!
TMP
TMP
PATRI-ARCH!
TMP

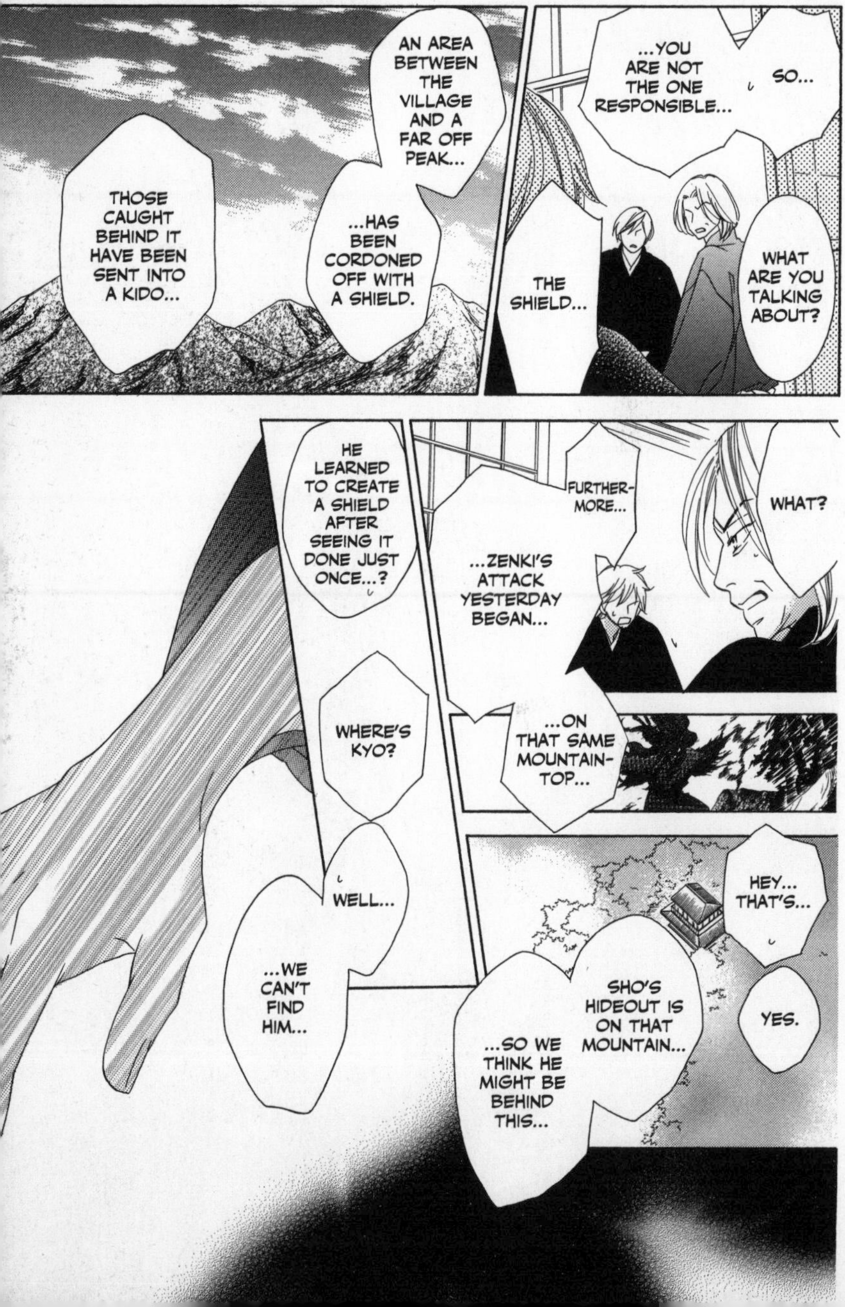
SO...
...YOU ARE NOT THE ONE RESPONSIBLE...
WHAT ARE YOU TALKING ABOUT?
THE SHIELD...
AN AREA BETWEEN THE VILLAGE AND A FAR OFF PEAK...
...HAS BEEN CORDONED OFF WITH A SHIELD.
THOSE CAUGHT BEHIND IT HAVE BEEN SENT INTO A KIDO...
WHAT?
FURTHER-MORE...
...ZENKI'S ATTACK YESTERDAY BEGAN...
...ON THAT SAME MOUNTAIN-TOP...
HEY... THAT'S...
YES.
SHO'S HIDEOUT IS ON THAT MOUNTAIN...
...SO WE THINK HE MIGHT BE BEHIND THIS...
HE LEARNED TO CREATE A SHIELD AFTER SEEING IT DONE JUST ONCE...?
WHERE'S KYO?
WELL...
...WE CAN'T FIND HIM...

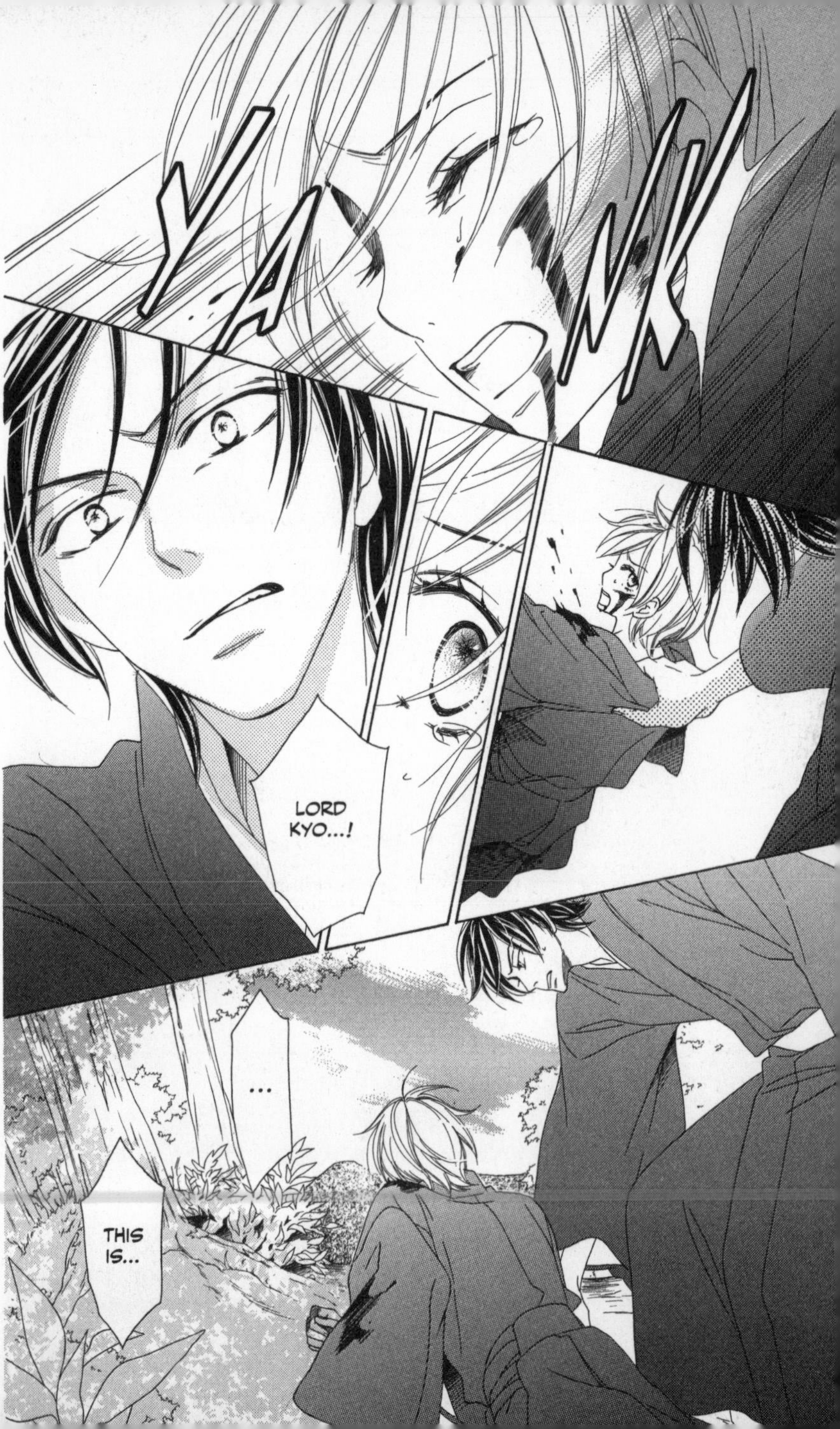
YANK
LORD KYO...!
...
THIS IS...

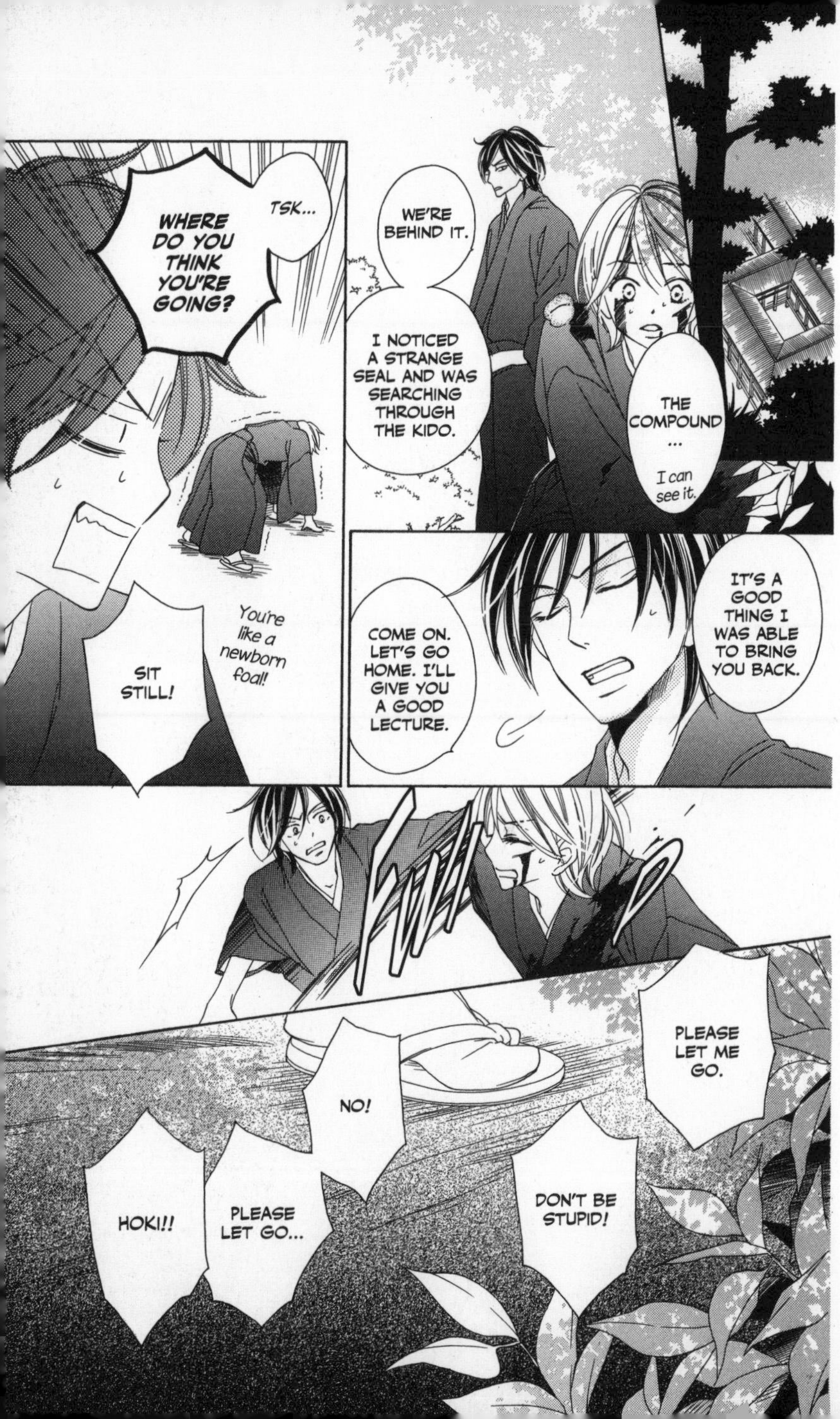
THE COMPOUND ...
I can see it.
WE'RE BEHIND IT.
I NOTICED A STRANGE SEAL AND WAS SEARCHING THROUGH THE KIDO.
IT'S A GOOD THING I WAS ABLE TO BRING YOU BACK.
COME ON. LET'S GO HOME. I'LL GIVE YOU A GOOD LECTURE.
TSK...
WHERE DO YOU THINK YOU'RE GOING?
You're like a newborn foal!
SIT STILL!
PLEASE LET ME GO.
NO!
DON'T BE STUPID!
PLEASE LET GO...
HOKI!!

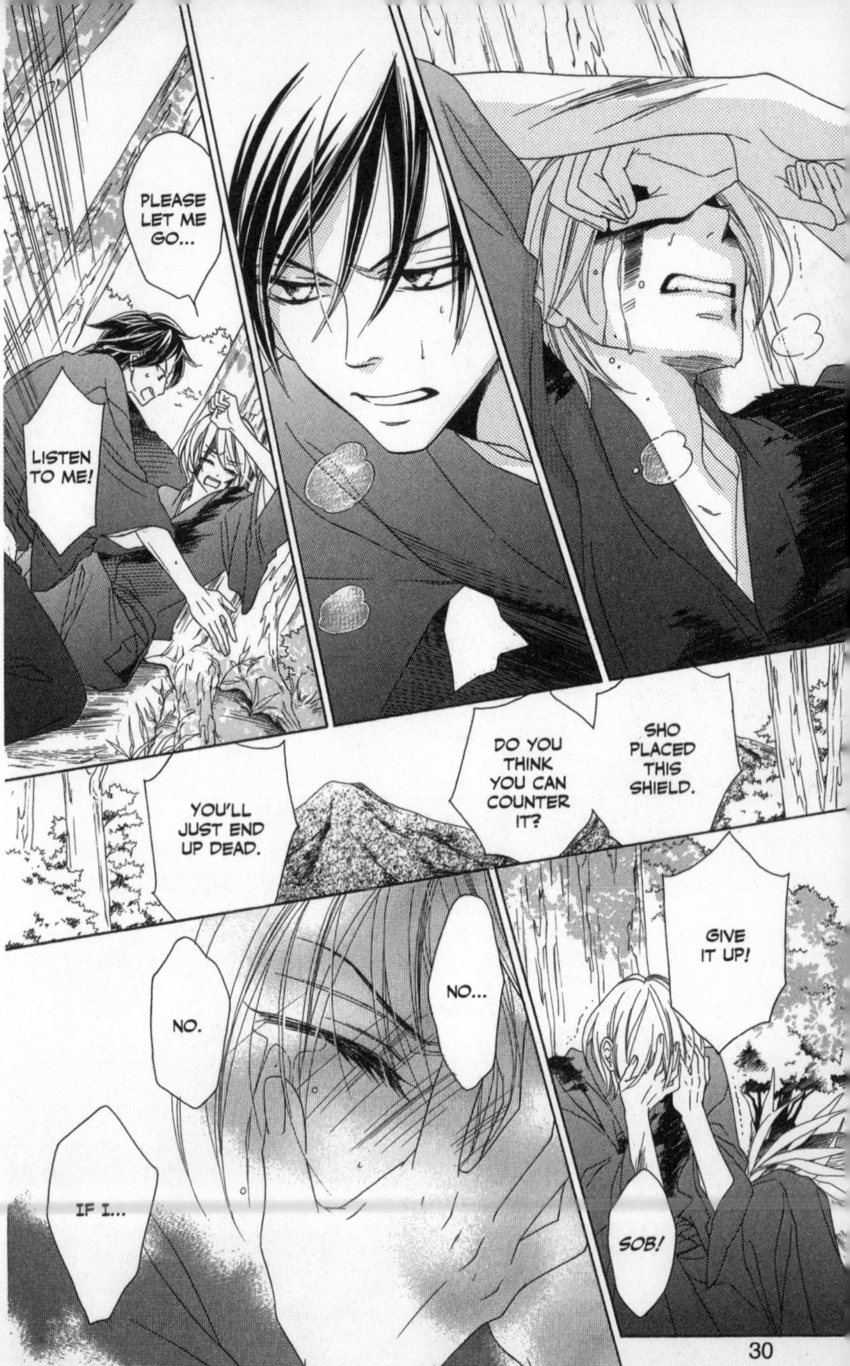
PLEASE LET ME GO...
LISTEN TO ME!
SHO PLACED THIS SHIELD.
DO YOU THINK YOU CAN COUNTER IT?
YOU'LL JUST END UP DEAD.
GIVE IT UP!
SOB!
NO...
NO.
IF I...

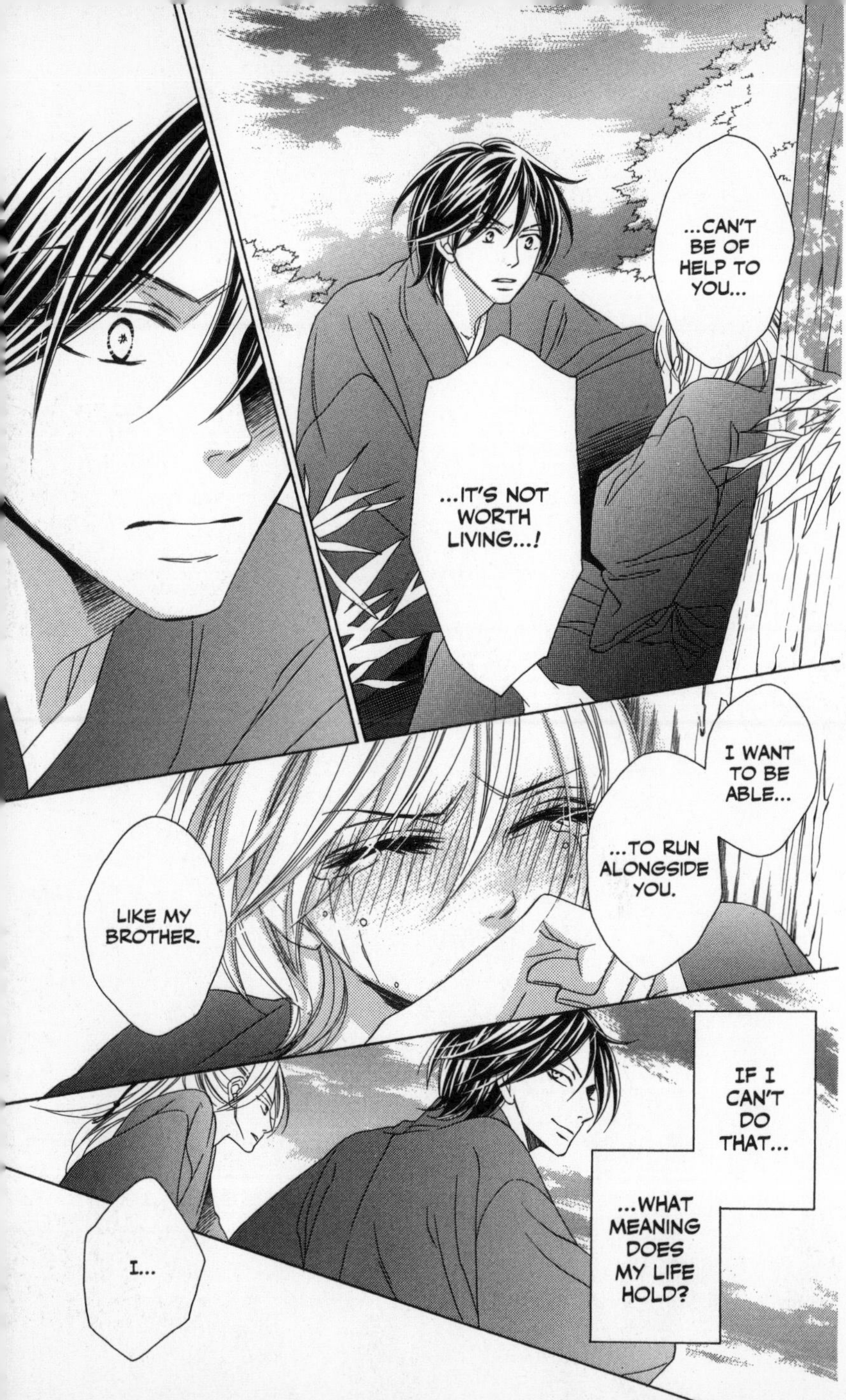
...CAN'T BE OF HELP TO YOU...
...IT'S NOT WORTH LIVING...!
I WANT TO BE ABLE...
...TO RUN ALONGSIDE YOU.
LIKE MY BROTHER.
IF I CAN'T DO THAT...
...WHAT MEANING DOES MY LIFE HOLD?
I...

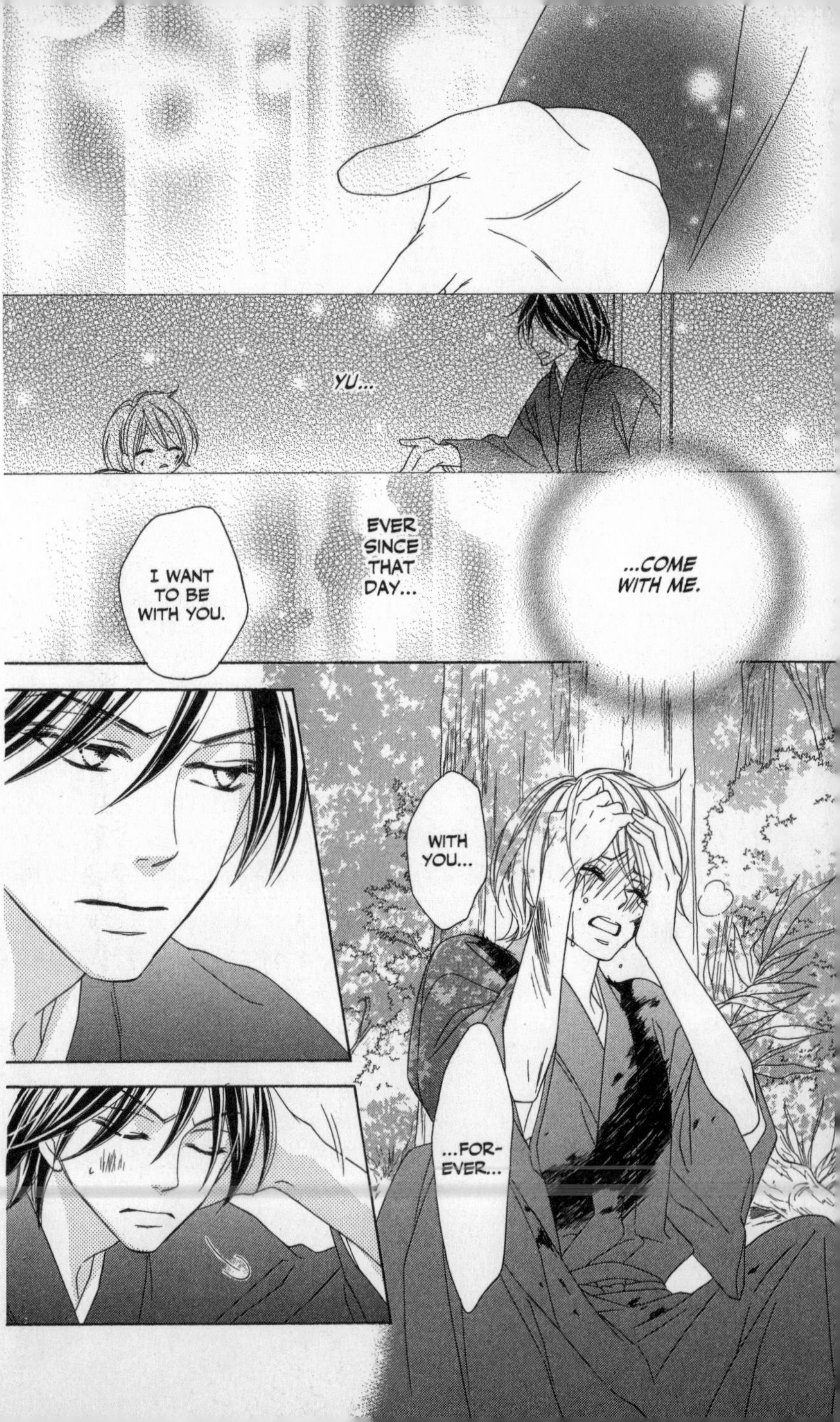
YU...
...COME WITH ME.
EVER SINCE THAT DAY...
I WANT TO BE WITH YOU.
WITH YOU...
...FOR-EVER...

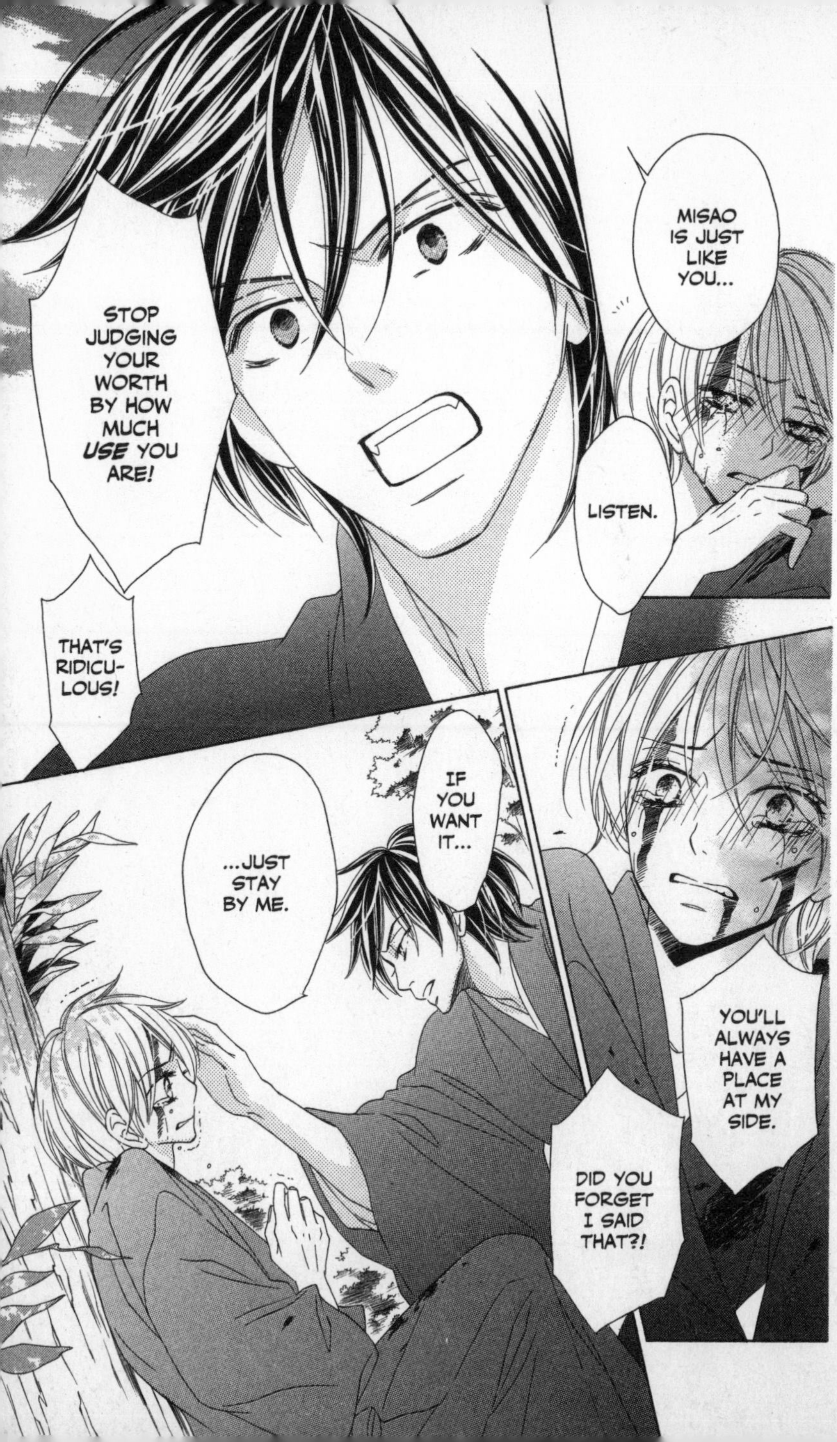
MISAO IS JUST LIKE YOU...
LISTEN.
STOP JUDGING YOUR WORTH BY HOW MUCH *USE* YOU ARE!
THAT'S RIDICULOUS!
YOU'LL ALWAYS HAVE A PLACE AT MY SIDE.
DID YOU FORGET I SAID THAT?!
IF YOU WANT IT...
...JUST STAY BY ME.

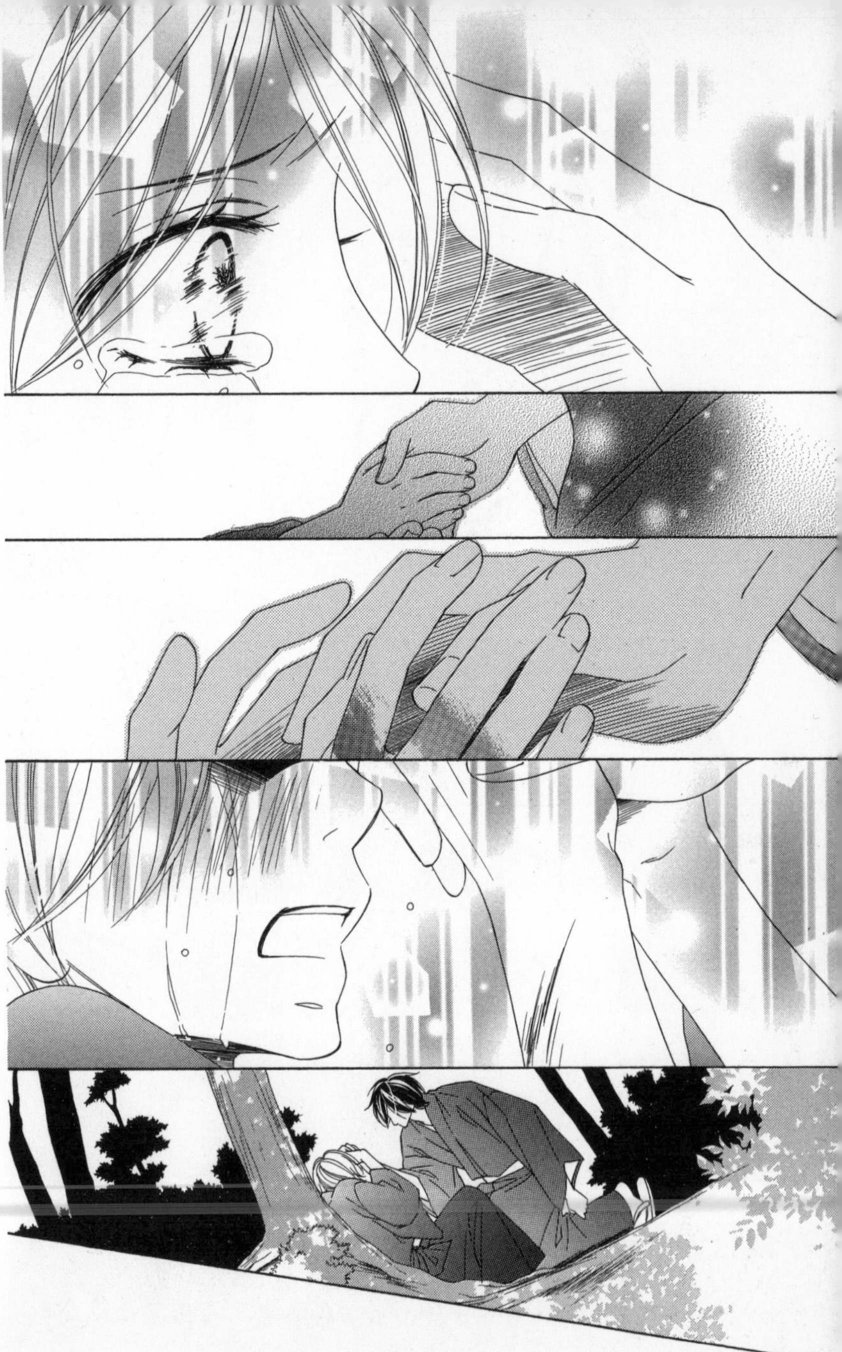

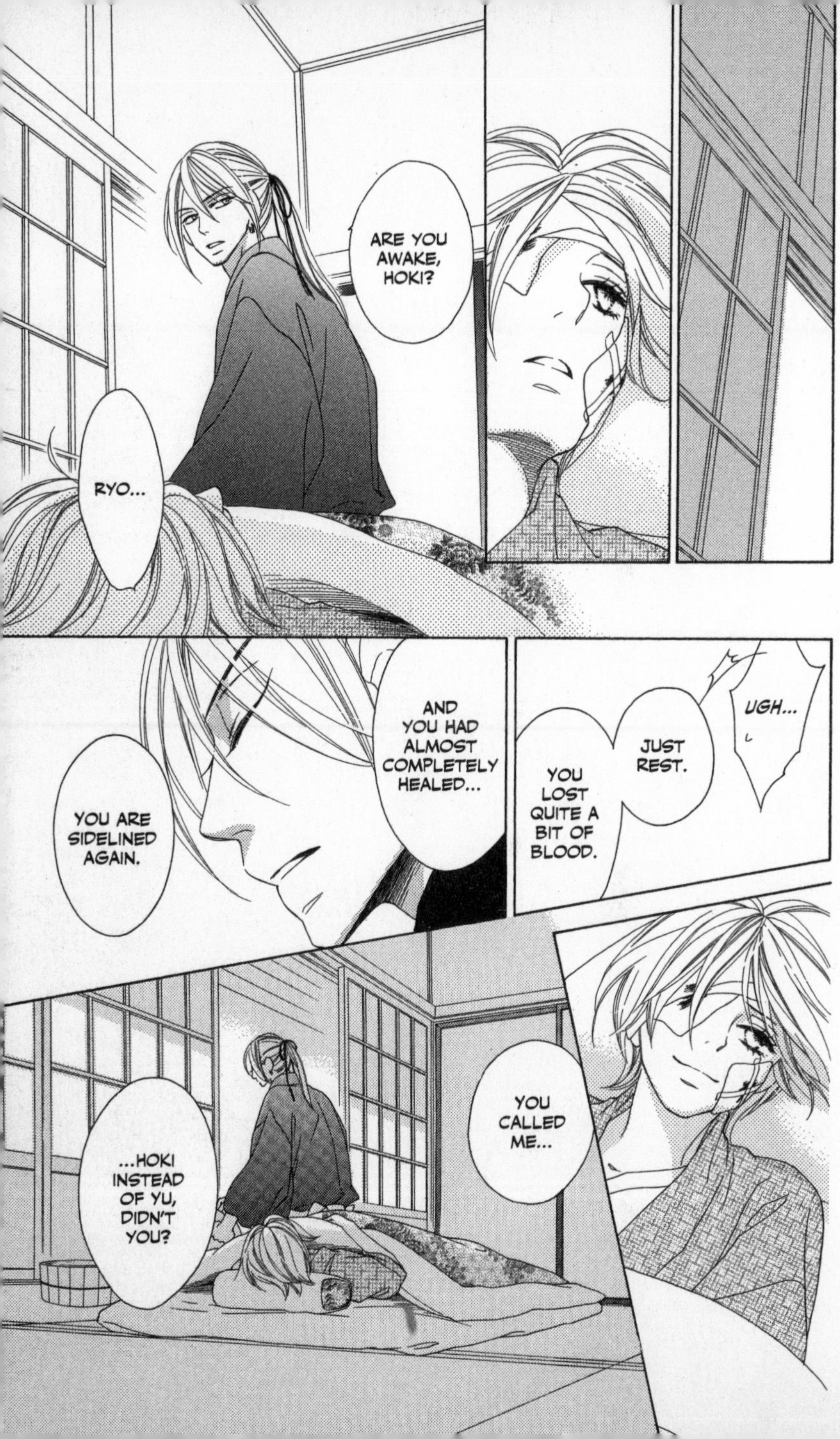
ARE YOU AWAKE, HOKI?
RYO...
UGH...
JUST REST.
YOU LOST QUITE A BIT OF BLOOD.
AND YOU HAD ALMOST COMPLETELY HEALED...
YOU ARE SIDELINED AGAIN.
YOU CALLED ME...
...HOKI INSTEAD OF YU, DIDN'T YOU?

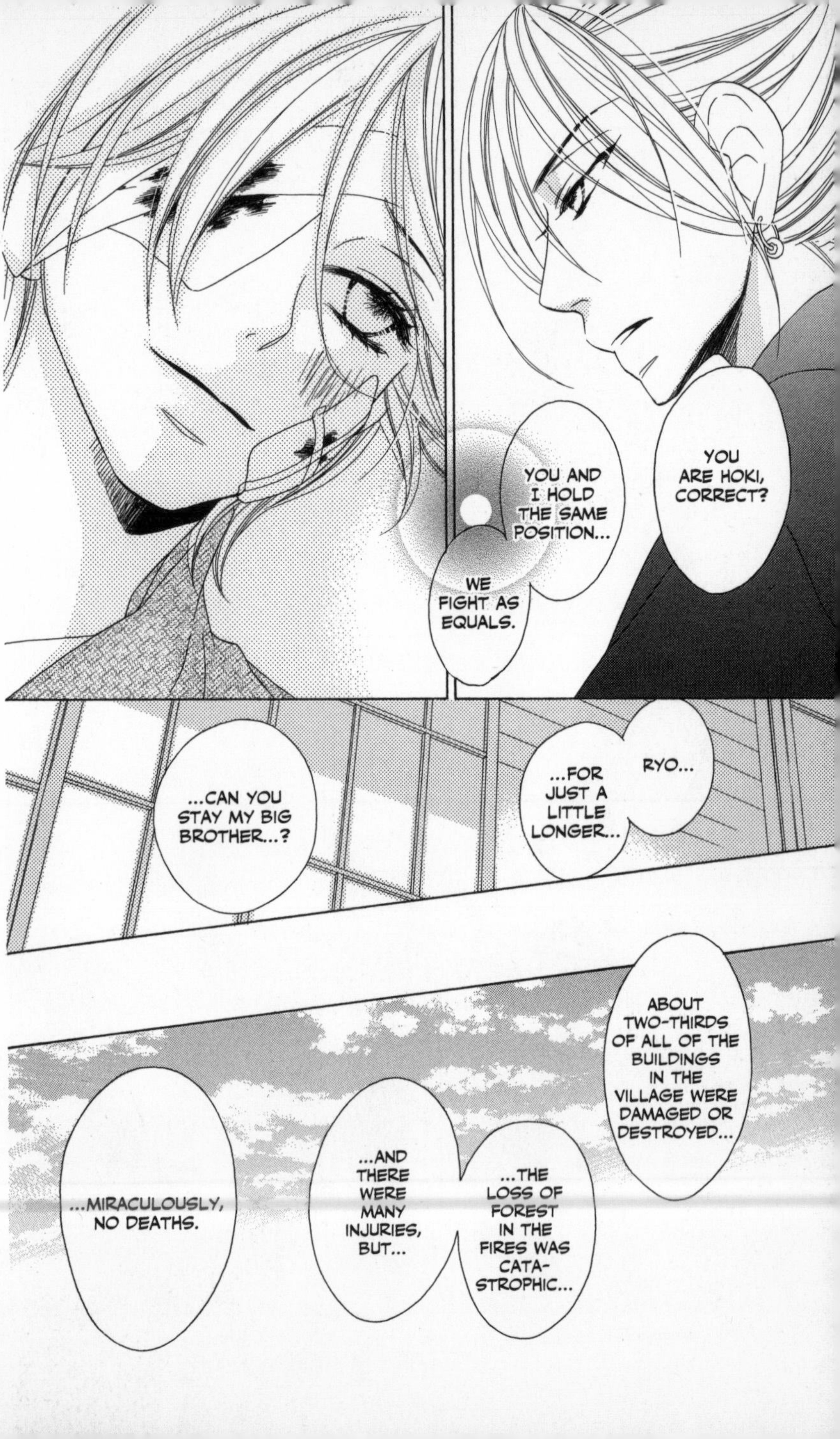
YOU ARE HOKI, CORRECT?
YOU AND I HOLD THE SAME POSITION...
WE FIGHT AS EQUALS.
RYO...
...FOR JUST A LITTLE LONGER...
...CAN YOU STAY MY BIG BROTHER...?
ABOUT TWO-THIRDS OF ALL OF THE BUILDINGS IN THE VILLAGE WERE DAMAGED OR DESTROYED...
...THE LOSS OF FOREST IN THE FIRES WAS CATA-STROPHIC...
...AND THERE WERE MANY INJURIES, BUT...
...MIRACULOUSLY, NO DEATHS.

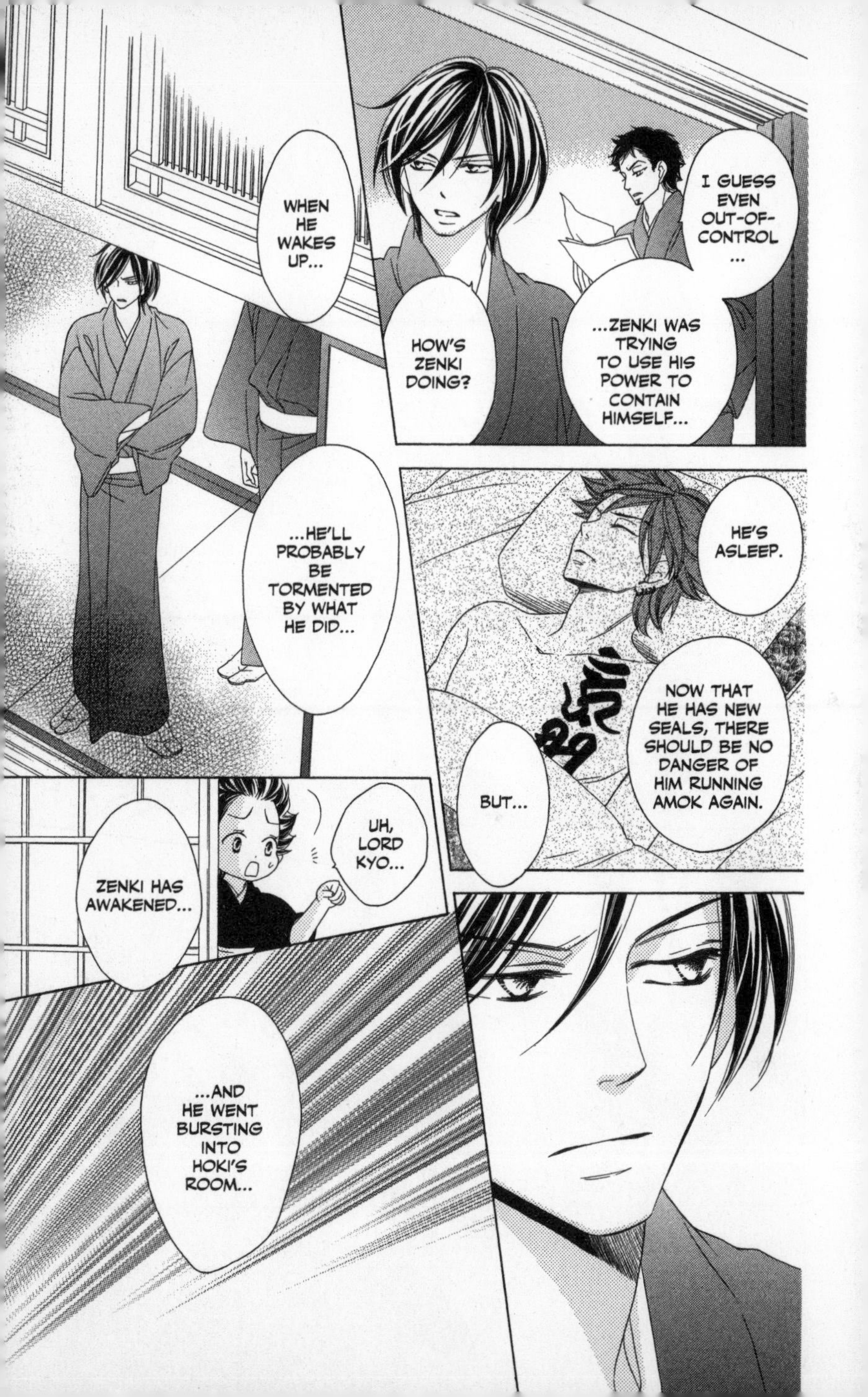

I GUESS EVEN OUT-OF-CONTROL...
...ZENKI WAS TRYING TO USE HIS POWER TO CONTAIN HIMSELF...
HOW'S ZENKI DOING?
HE'S ASLEEP.
NOW THAT HE HAS NEW SEALS, THERE SHOULD BE NO DANGER OF HIM RUNNING AMOK AGAIN.
BUT...
WHEN HE WAKES UP...
...HE'LL PROBABLY BE TORMENTED BY WHAT HE DID...
UH, LORD KYO...
ZENKI HAS AWAKENED...
...AND HE WENT BURSTING INTO HOKI'S ROOM...

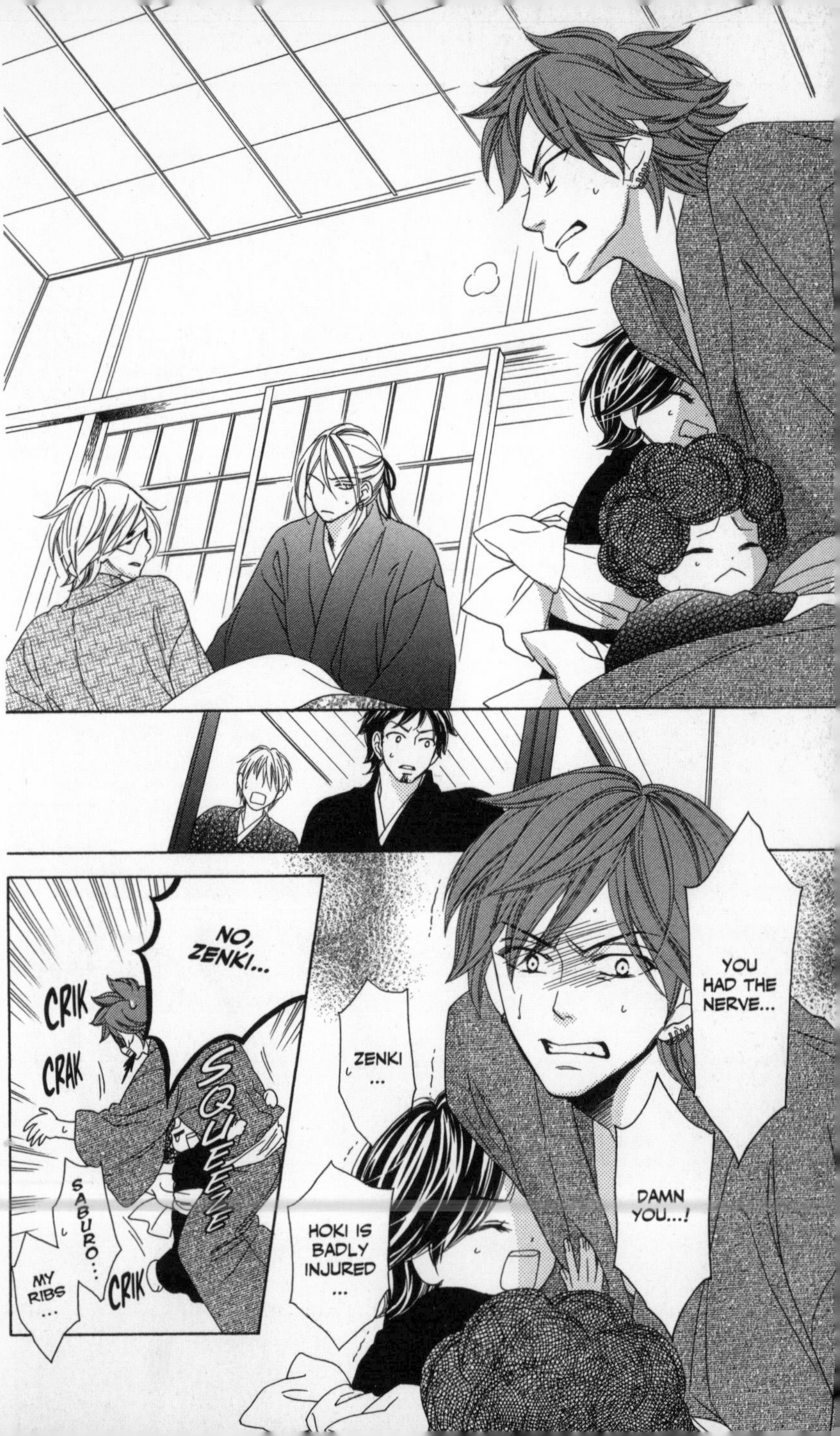
YOU HAD THE NERVE...
ZENKI ...
DAMN YOU...!
HOKI IS BADLY INJURED ...
NO, ZENKI...
CRIK
CRAK
SQUEEZE
SABURO...
CRIK
MY RIBS ...

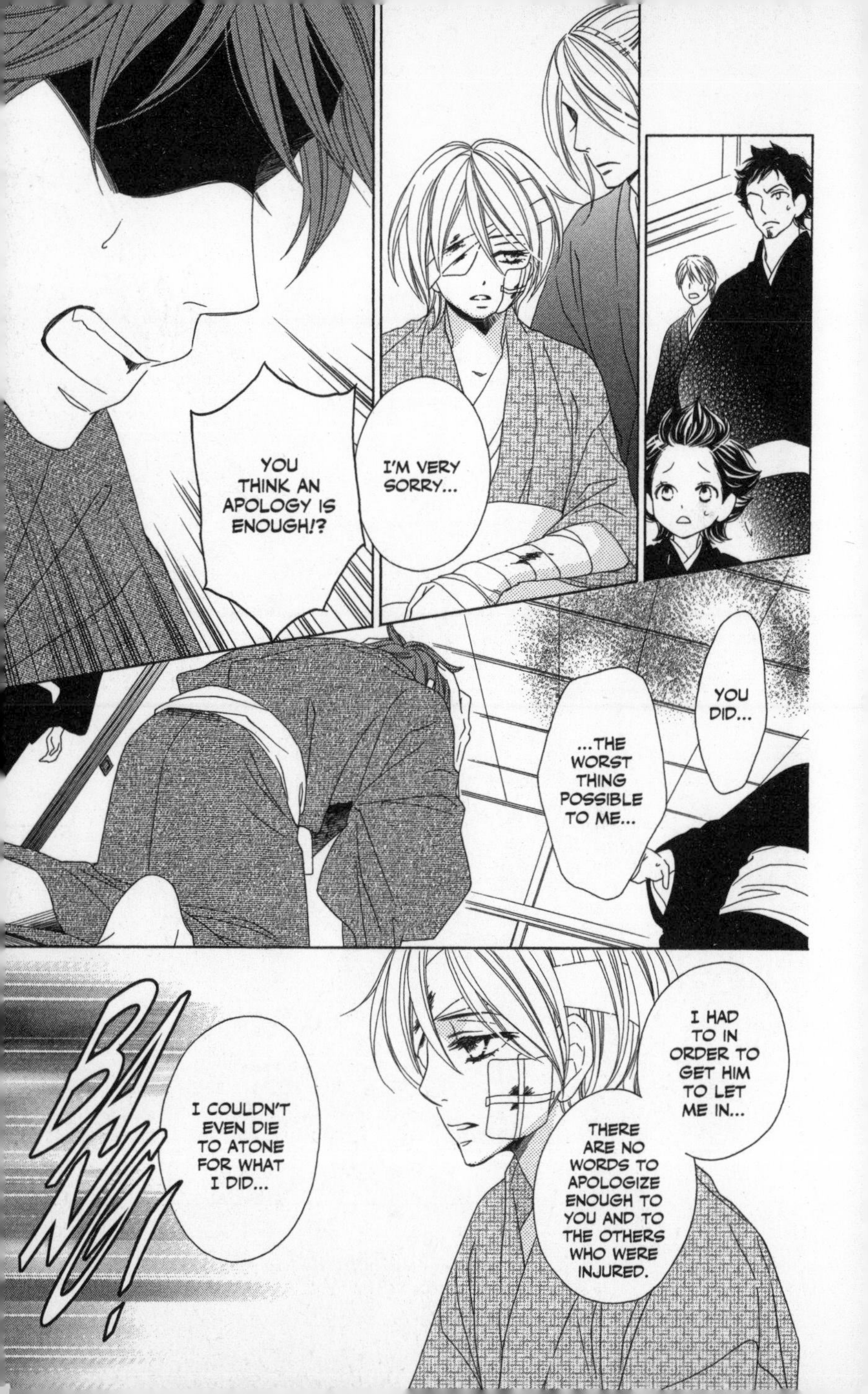
I'M VERY SORRY...
YOU THINK AN APOLOGY IS ENOUGH!?
YOU DID...
...THE WORST THING POSSIBLE TO ME...
I HAD TO IN ORDER TO GET HIM TO LET ME IN...
THERE ARE NO WORDS TO APOLOGIZE ENOUGH TO YOU AND TO THE OTHERS WHO WERE INJURED.
I COULDN'T EVEN DIE TO ATONE FOR WHAT I DID...

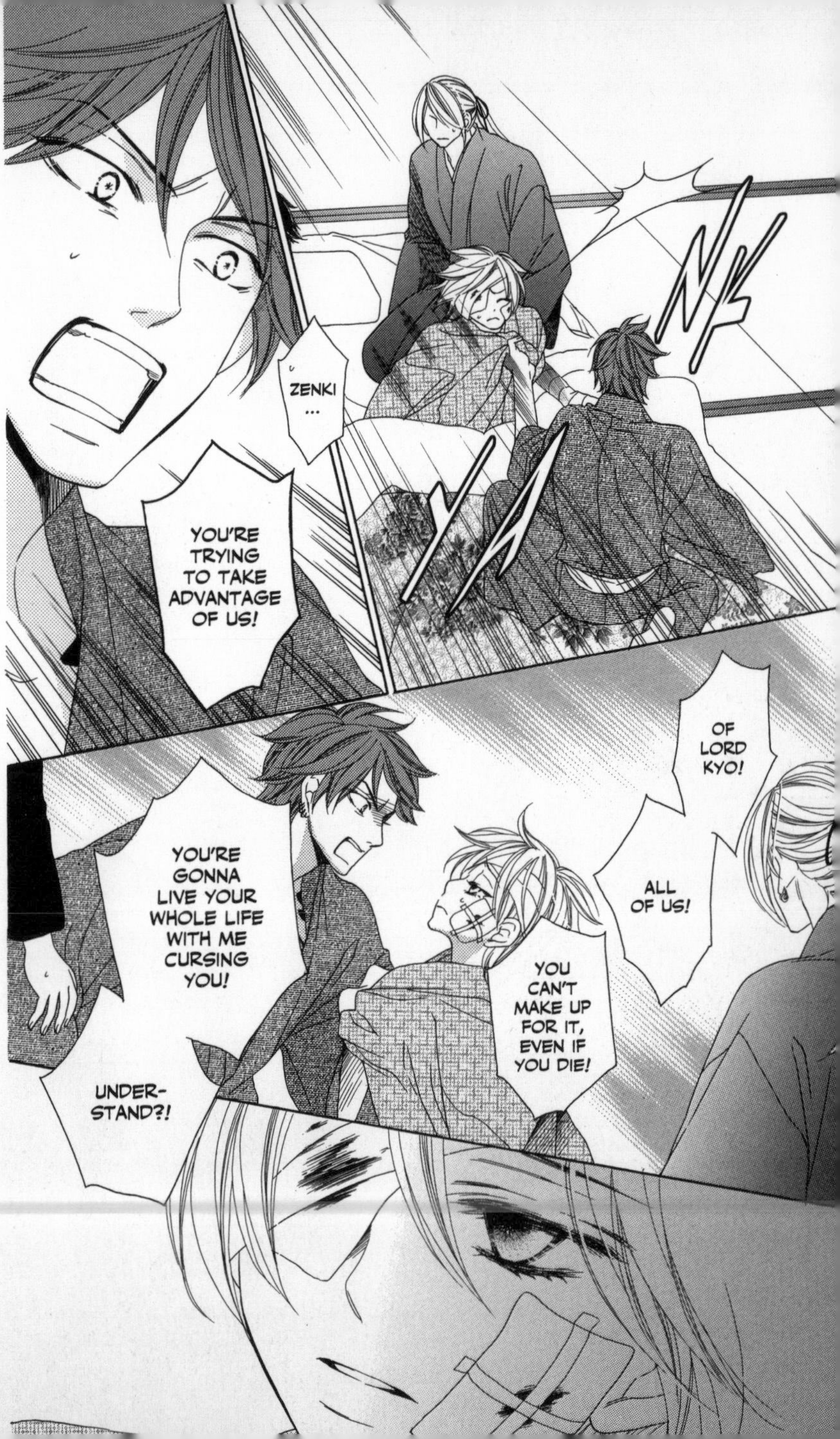
ZENKI ...
YOU'RE TRYING TO TAKE ADVANTAGE OF US!
OF LORD KYO!
ALL OF US!
YOU CAN'T MAKE UP FOR IT, EVEN IF YOU DIE!
YOU'RE GONNA LIVE YOUR WHOLE LIFE WITH ME CURSING YOU!
UNDER-STAND?!

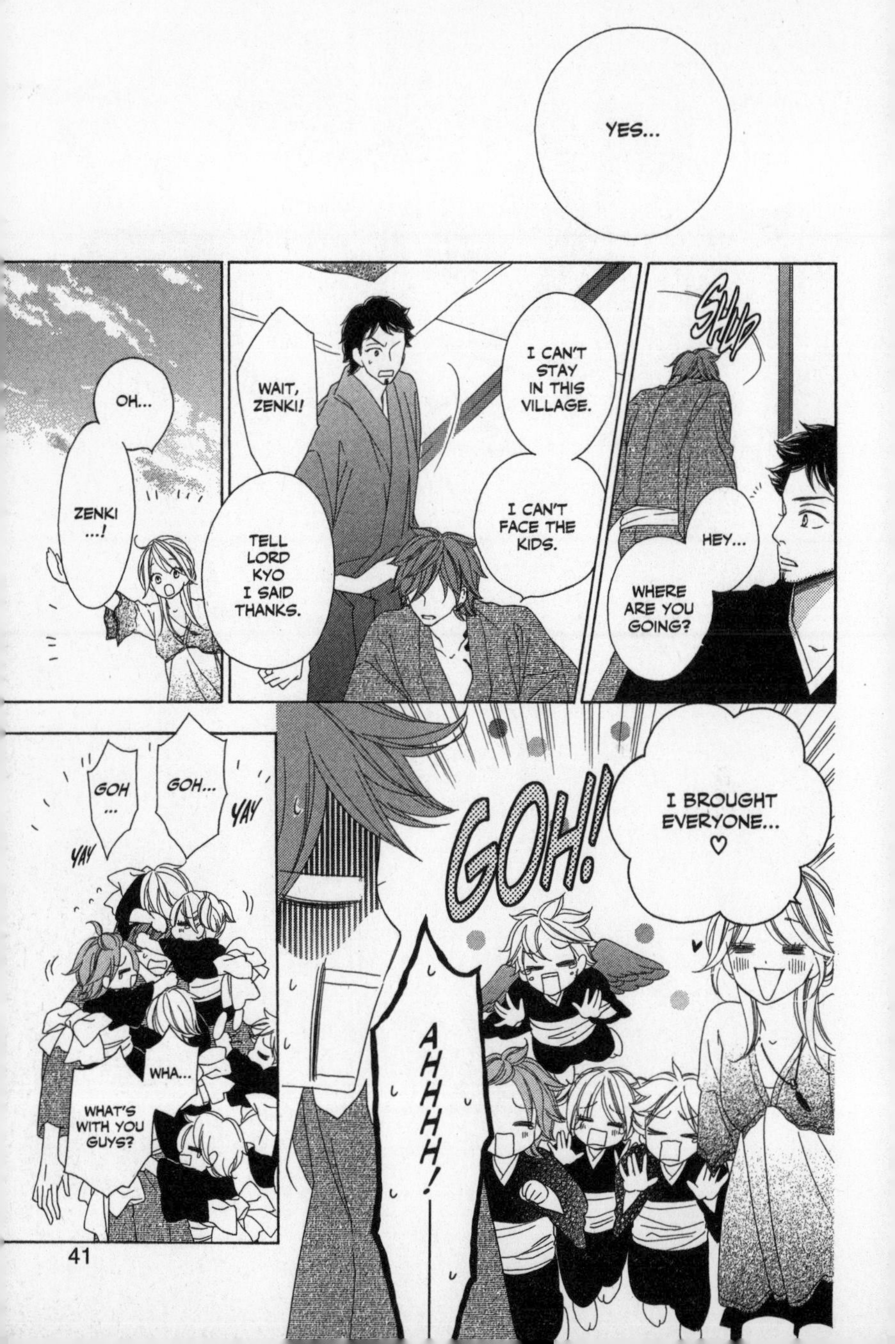
YES...
SHUP
HEY...
WHERE ARE YOU GOING?
I CAN'T STAY IN THIS VILLAGE.
WAIT, ZENKI!
I CAN'T FACE THE KIDS.
TELL LORD KYO I SAID THANKS.
OH...
ZENKI ...!
I BROUGHT EVERYONE... ♡
GOH!
AHHHH!
GOH...
GOH ...
YAY
YAY
WHA...
WHAT'S WITH YOU GUYS?

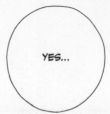

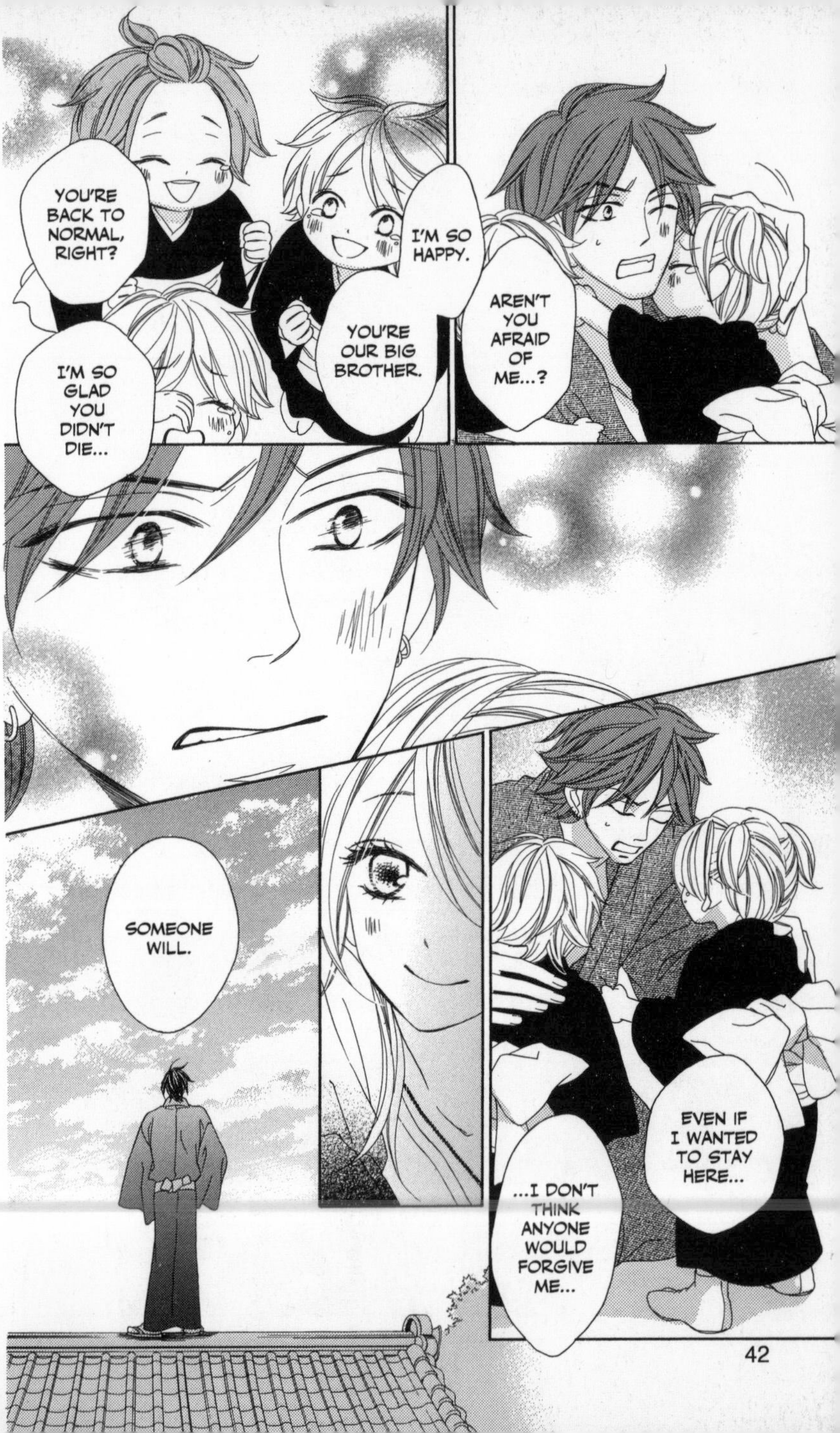
AREN'T YOU AFRAID OF ME...?
I'M SO HAPPY.
YOU'RE BACK TO NORMAL, RIGHT?
YOU'RE OUR BIG BROTHER.
I'M SO GLAD YOU DIDN'T DIE...
EVEN IF I WANTED TO STAY HERE...
...I DON'T THINK ANYONE WOULD FORGIVE ME...
SOMEONE WILL.

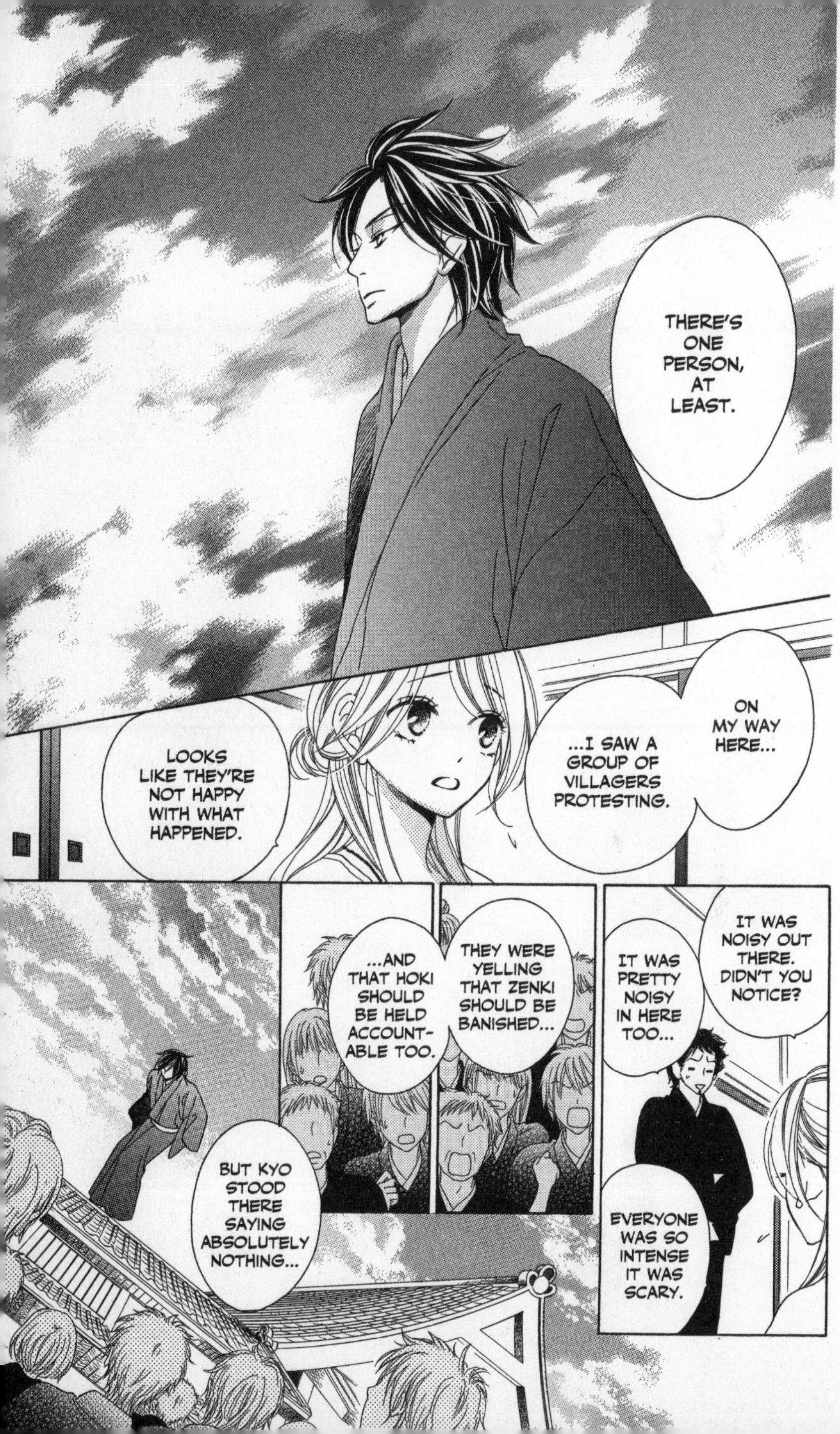

THERE'S ONE PERSON, AT LEAST.
ON MY WAY HERE...
...I SAW A GROUP OF VILLAGERS PROTESTING.
LOOKS LIKE THEY'RE NOT HAPPY WITH WHAT HAPPENED.
IT WAS NOISY OUT THERE. DIDN'T YOU NOTICE?
IT WAS PRETTY NOISY IN HERE TOO...
EVERYONE WAS SO INTENSE IT WAS SCARY.
THEY WERE YELLING THAT ZENKI SHOULD BE BANISHED...
...AND THAT HOKI SHOULD BE HELD ACCOUNT-ABLE TOO.
BUT KYO STOOD THERE SAYING ABSOLUTELY NOTHING...

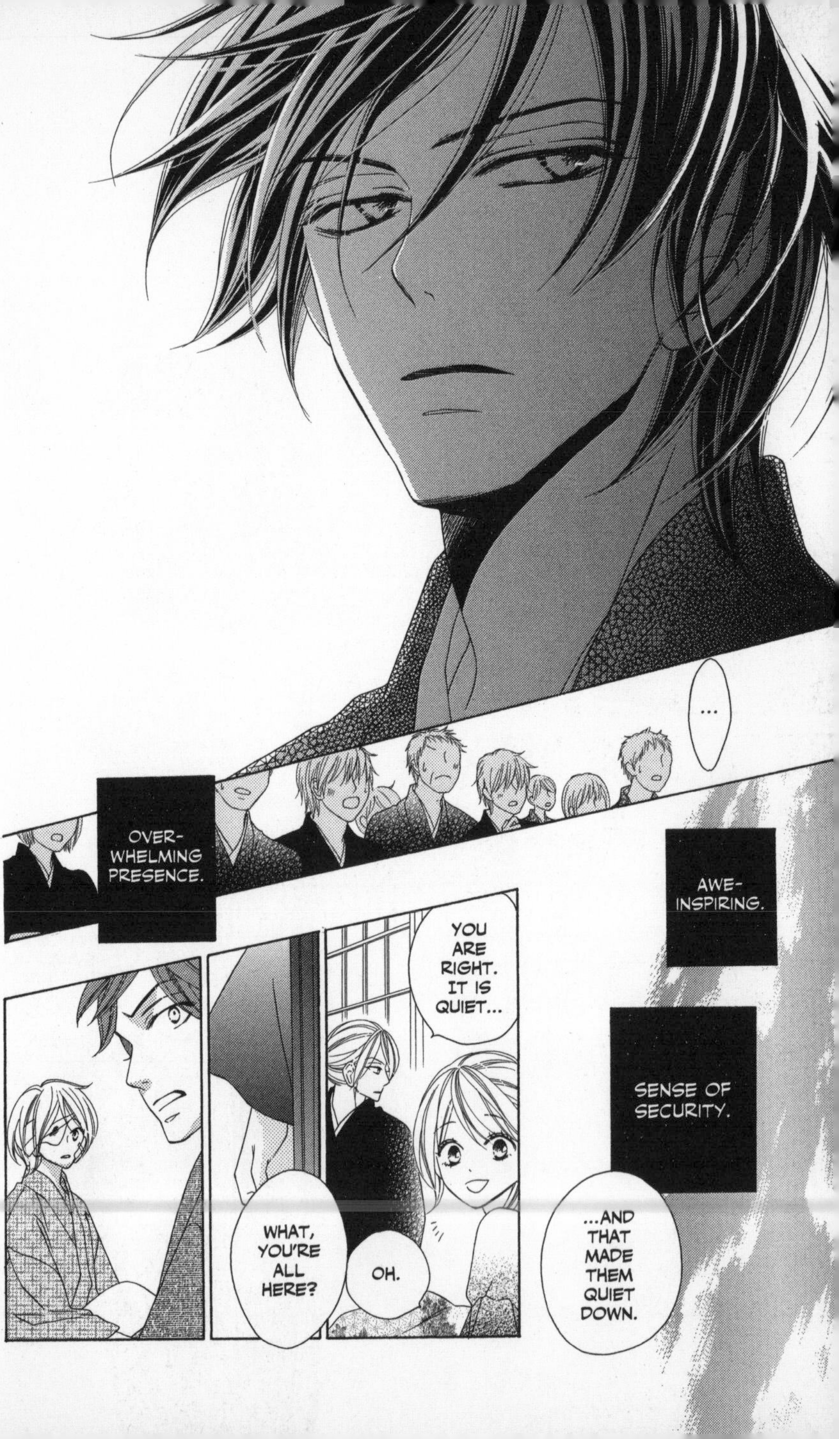
...
OVER-WHELMING PRESENCE.
AWE-INSPIRING.
SENSE OF SECURITY.
...AND THAT MADE THEM QUIET DOWN.
YOU ARE RIGHT. IT IS QUIET...
OH.
WHAT, YOU'RE ALL HERE?

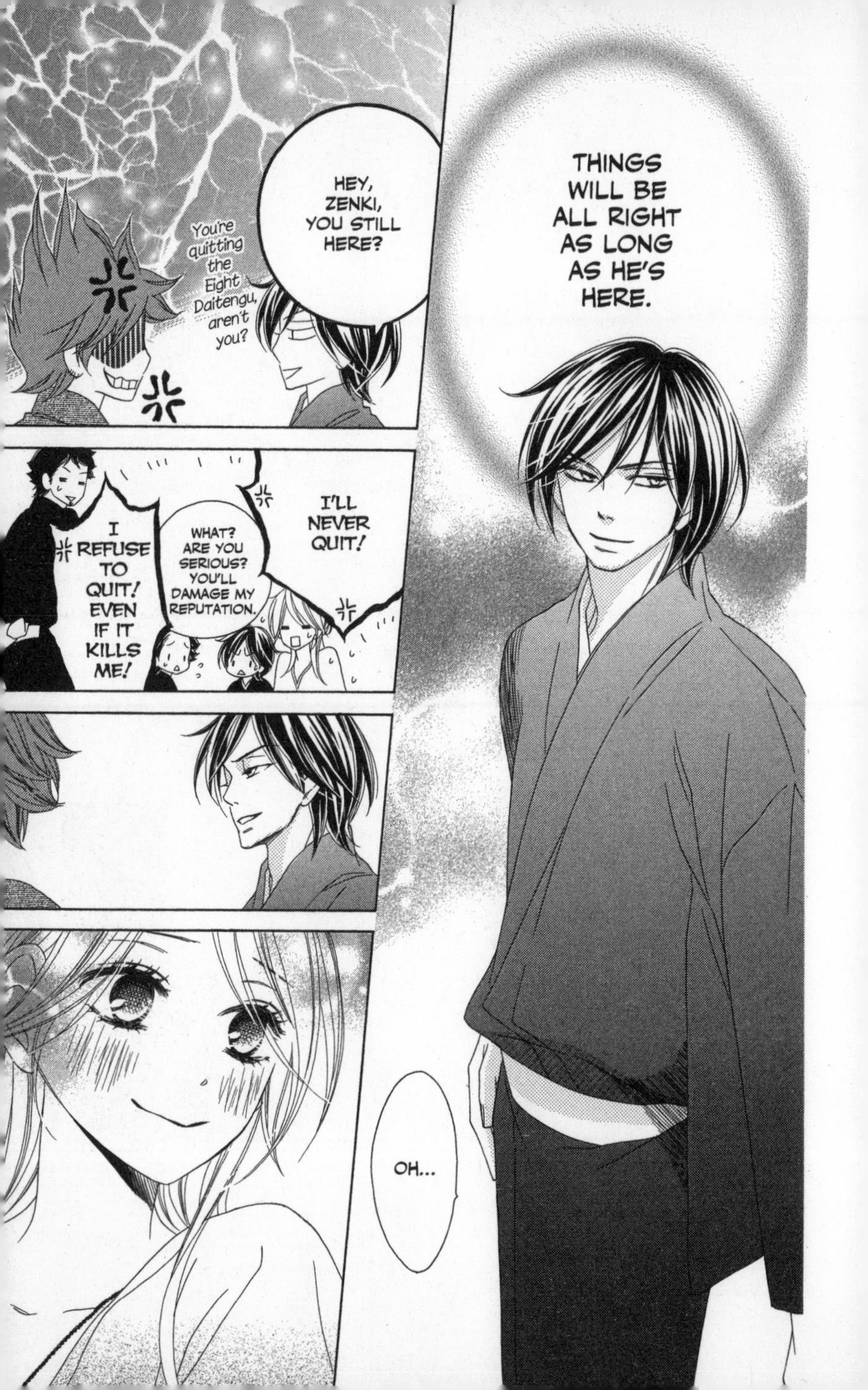
THINGS WILL BE ALL RIGHT AS LONG AS HE'S HERE.
HEY, ZENKI, YOU STILL HERE?
You're quitting the Eight Daitengu, aren't you?
I'LL NEVER QUIT!
WHAT? ARE YOU SERIOUS? YOU'LL DAMAGE MY REPUTATION.
I REFUSE TO QUIT! EVEN IF IT KILLS ME!
OH...

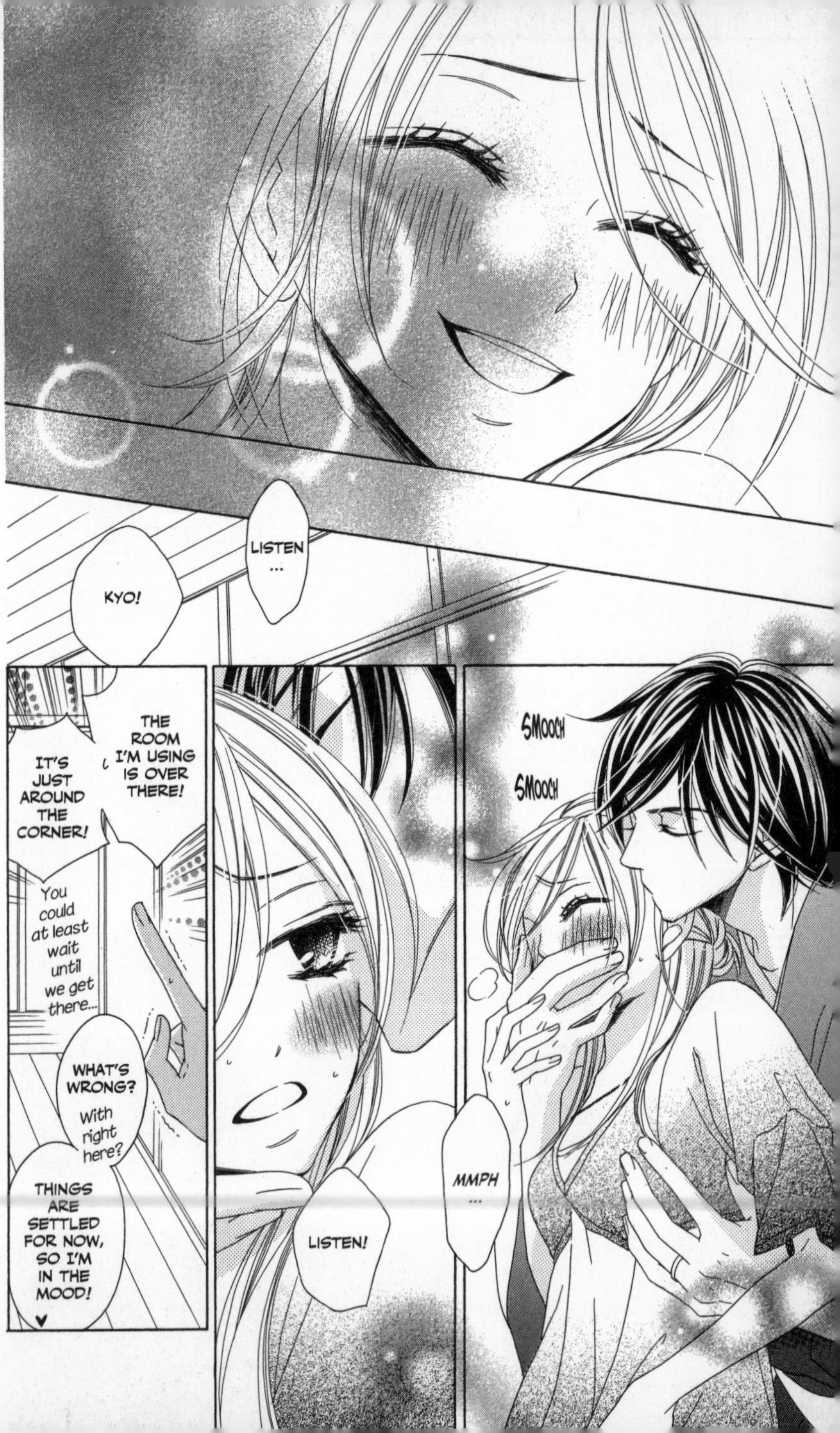
LISTEN ...
KYO!
SMOOCH
SMOOCH
MMPH ...
LISTEN!
THE ROOM I'M USING IS OVER THERE!
IT'S JUST AROUND THE CORNER!
You could at least wait until we get there...
WHAT'S WRONG? With right here?
THINGS ARE SETTLED FOR NOW, SO I'M IN THE MOOD! ♥

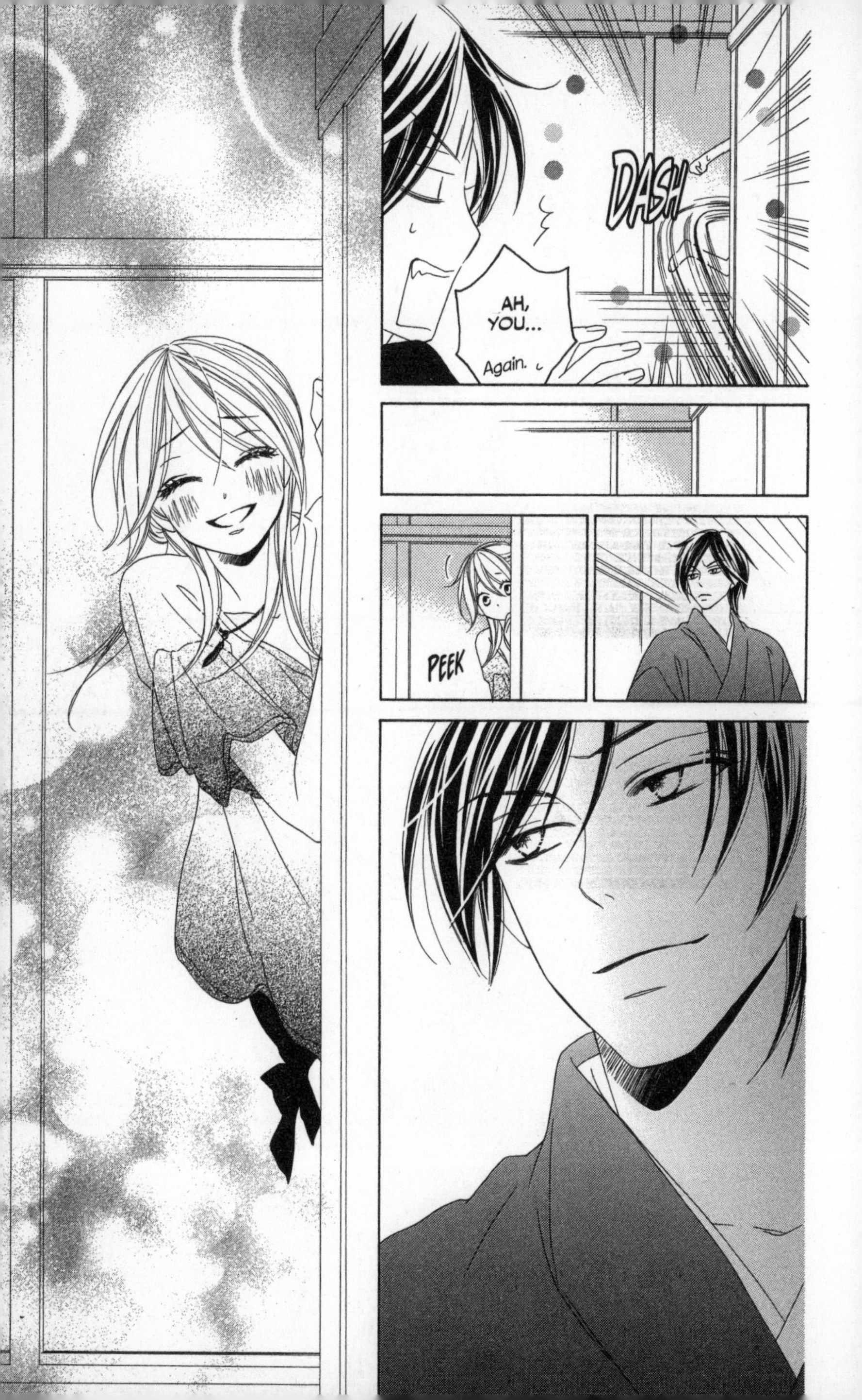
DASH
AH, YOU...
Again.
PEEK

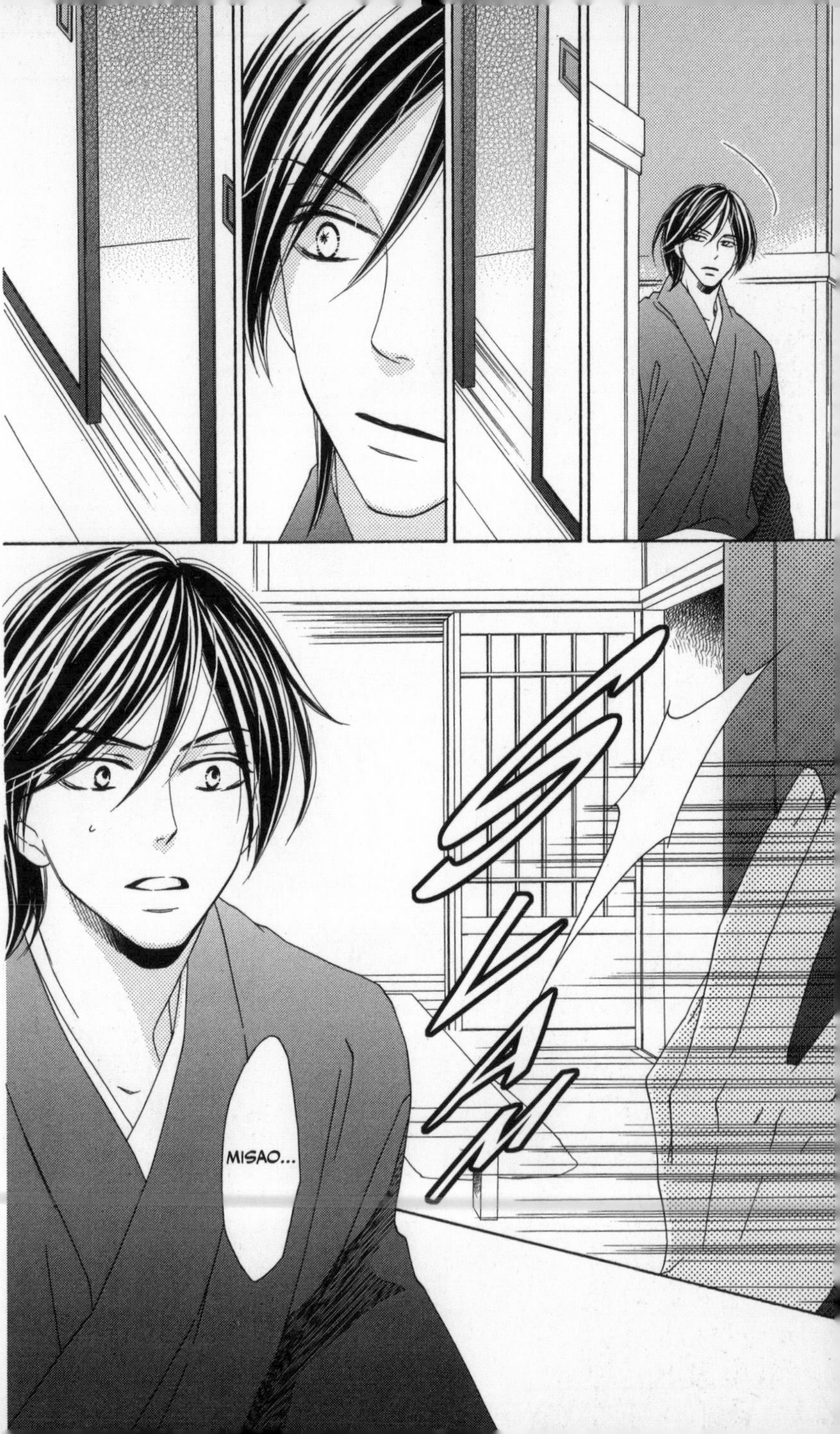
SSWAM
MISAO...

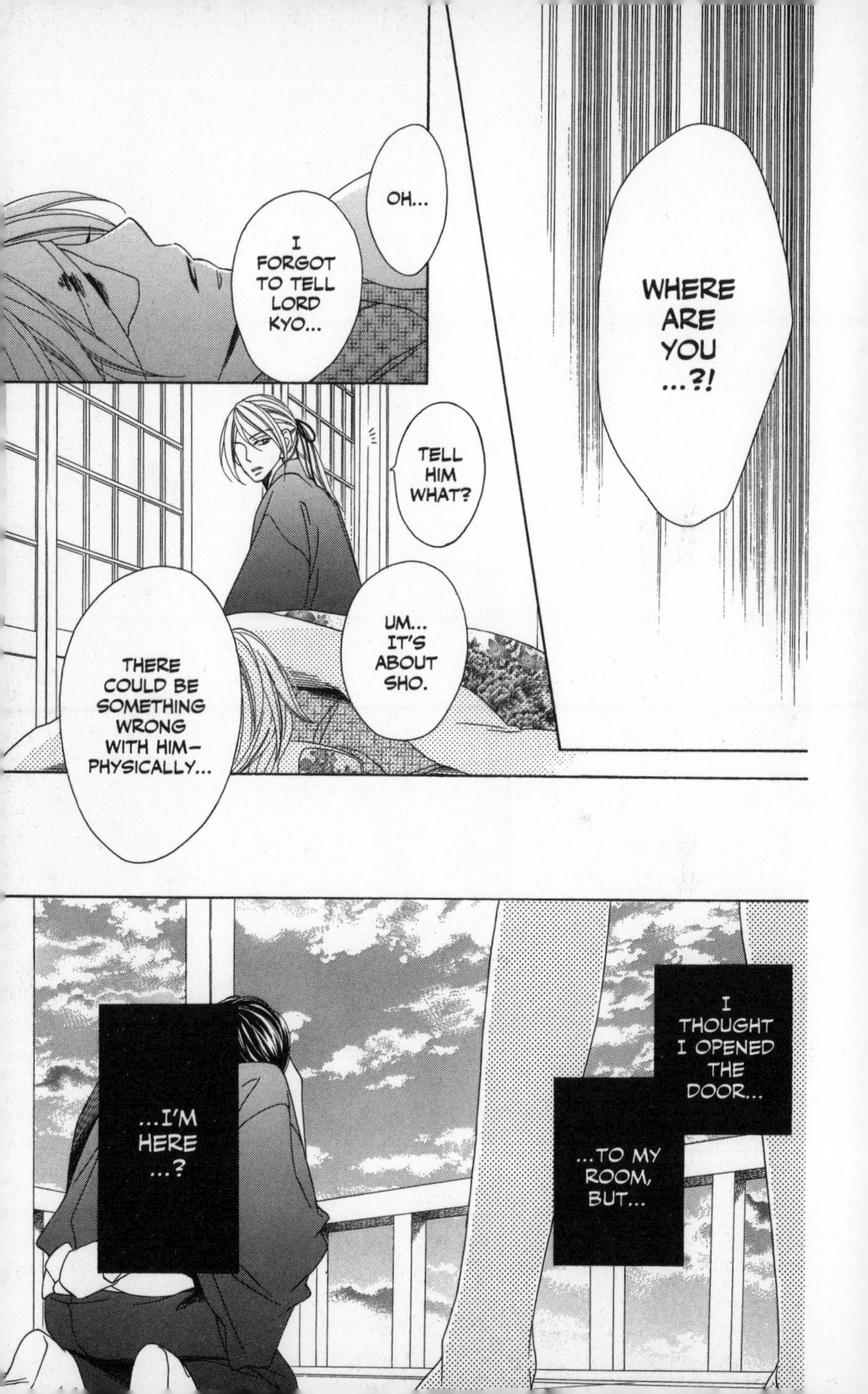
WHERE ARE YOU ...?!
OH...
I FORGOT TO TELL LORD KYO...
TELL HIM WHAT?
UM... IT'S ABOUT SHO.
THERE COULD BE SOMETHING WRONG WITH HIM—PHYSICALLY...
I THOUGHT I OPENED THE DOOR...
...TO MY ROOM, BUT...
...I'M HERE ...?

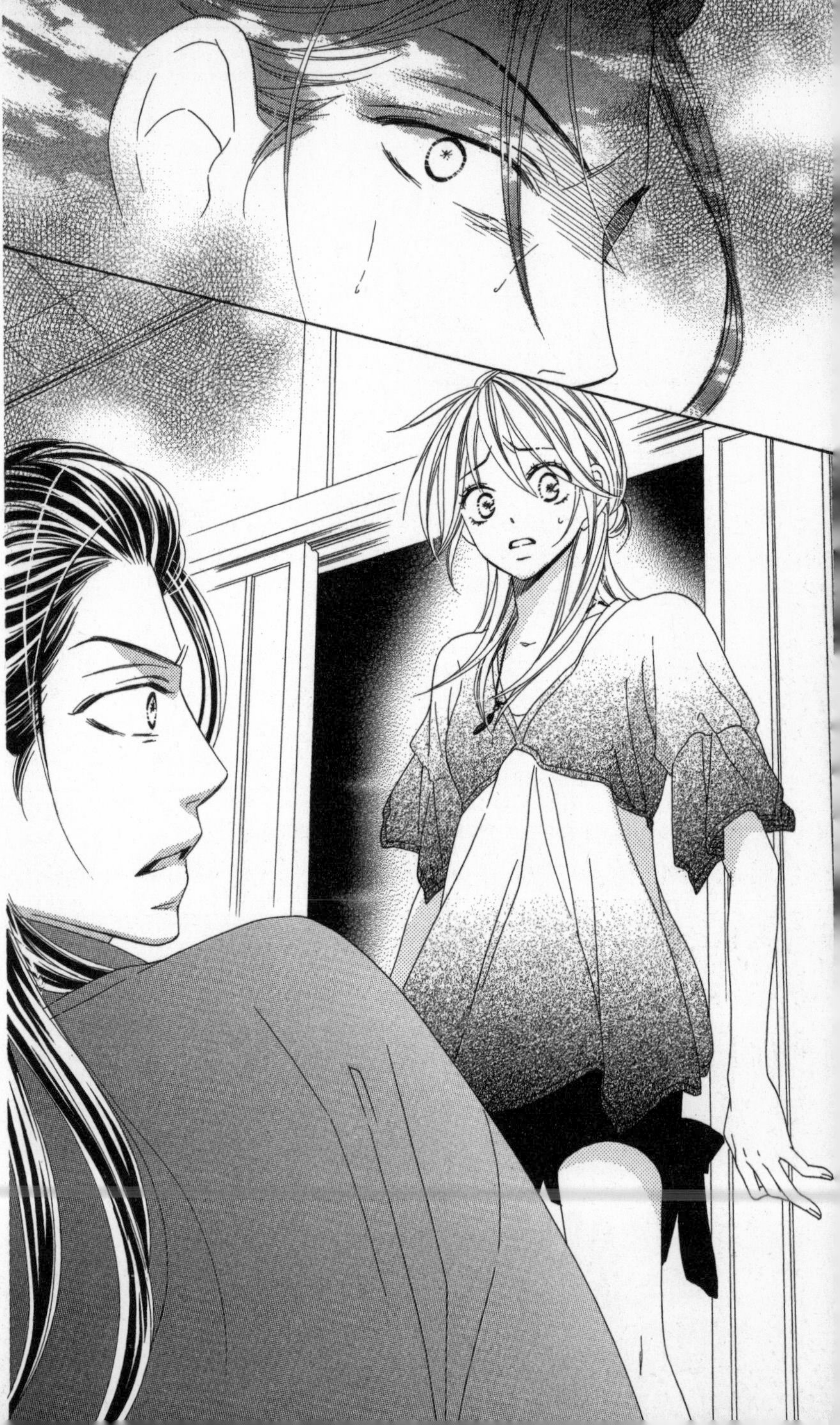

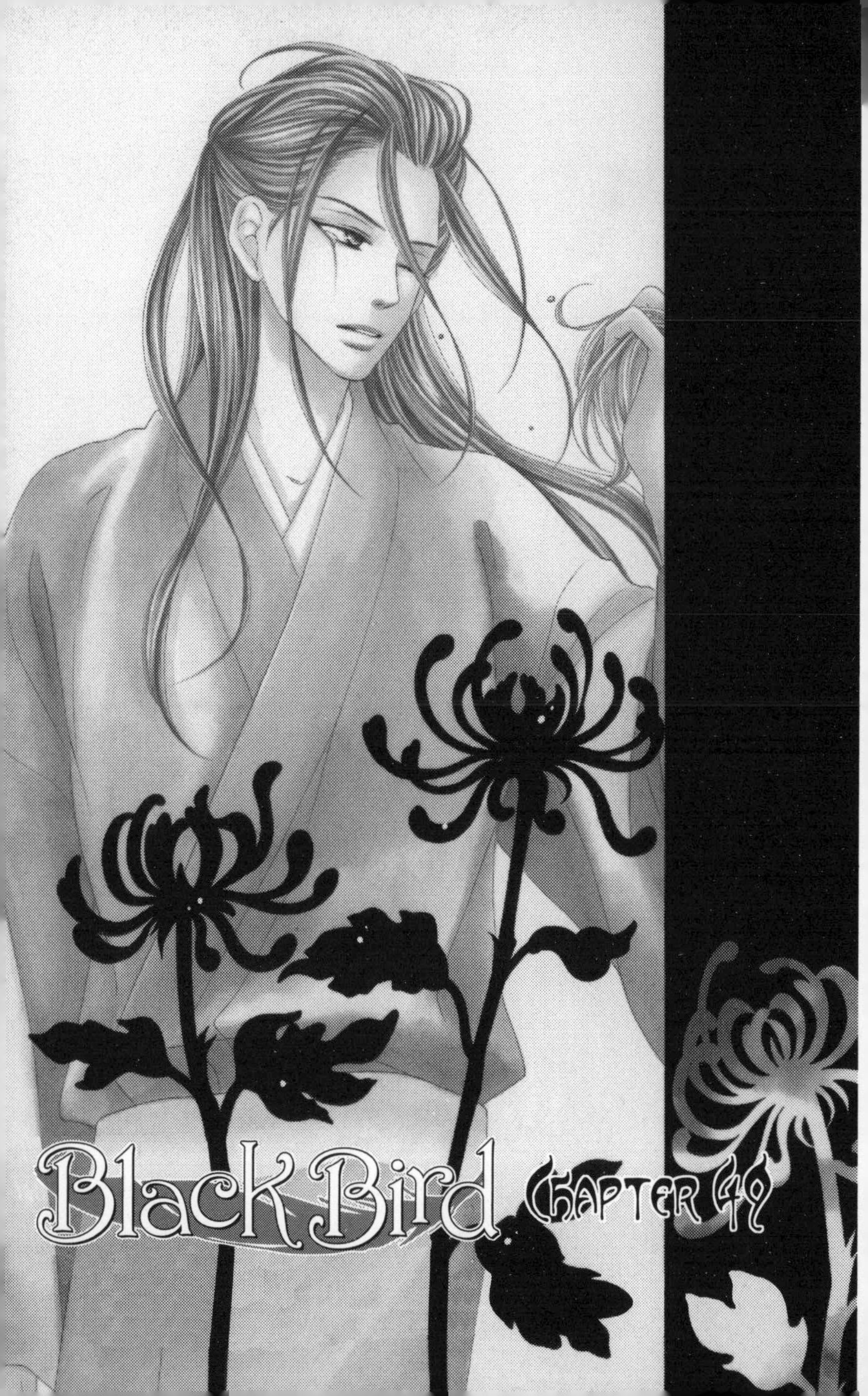
Black Bird
Chapter 49

BLACK BIRD

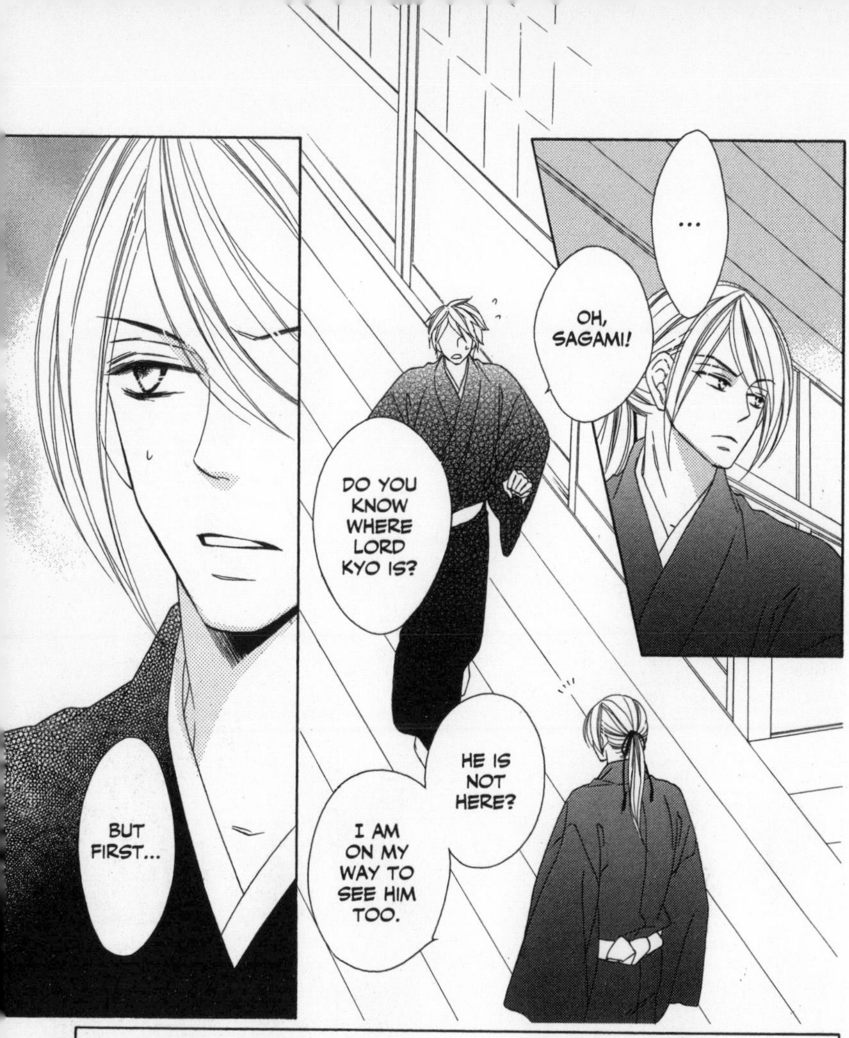
...
OH, SAGAMI!
DO YOU KNOW WHERE LORD KYO IS?
HE IS NOT HERE?
I AM ON MY WAY TO SEE HIM TOO.
BUT FIRST...

I have started a Twitter account.

My blog has sort of fallen by the wayside...

My account is sakurakouji_k (but I may be changing it).

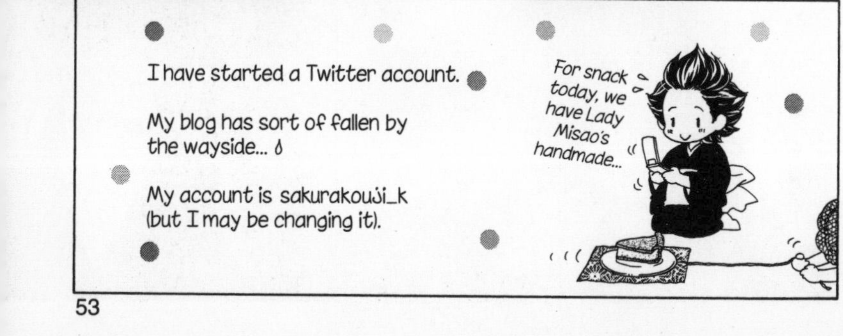
For snack today, we have Lady Misao's handmade...

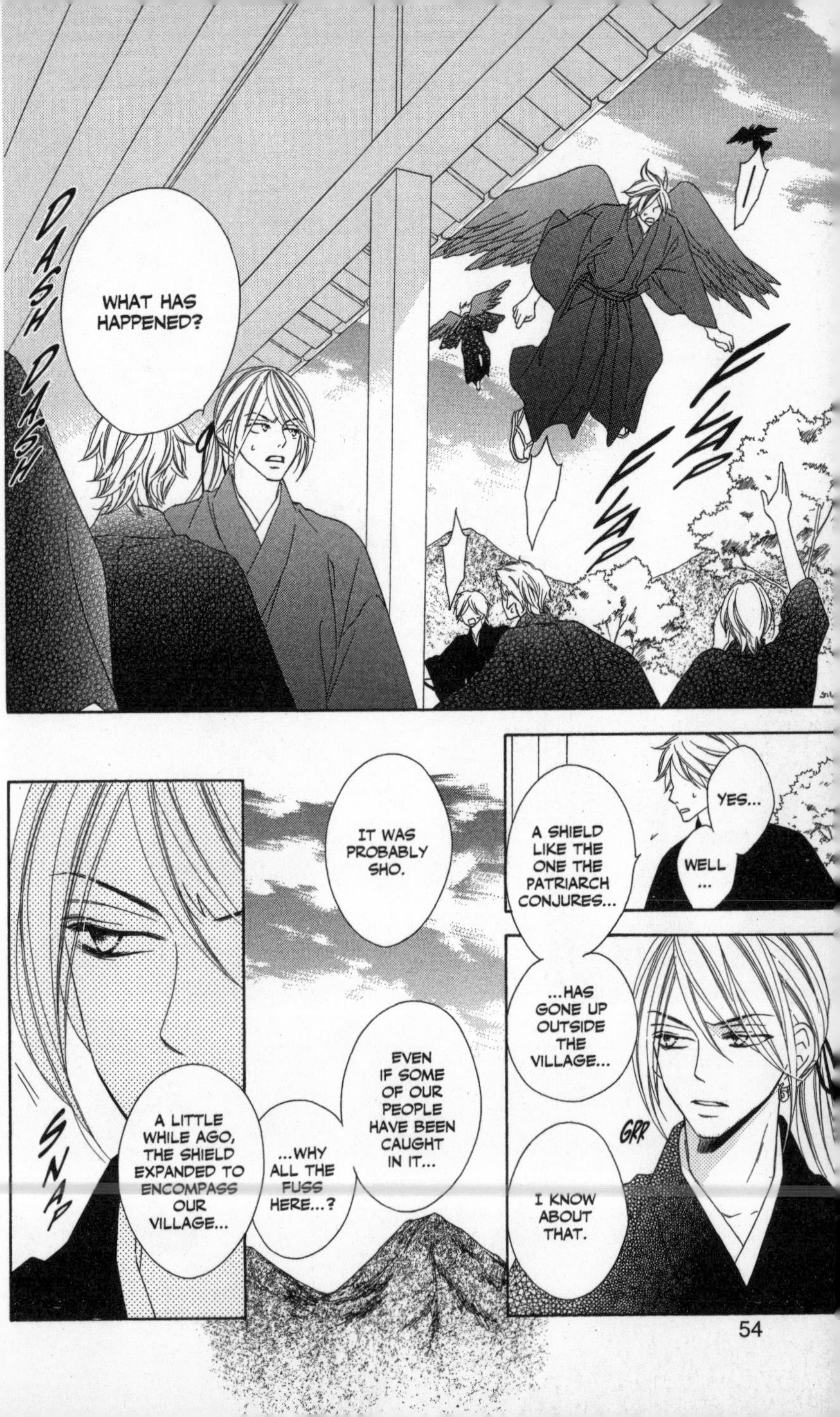
DASH DASH DASH
WHAT HAS HAPPENED?
YES... WELL ...
A SHIELD LIKE THE ONE THE PATRIARCH CONJURES...
...HAS GONE UP OUTSIDE THE VILLAGE...
GRR
I KNOW ABOUT THAT.
IT WAS PROBABLY SHO.
EVEN IF SOME OF OUR PEOPLE HAVE BEEN CAUGHT IN IT...
...WHY ALL THE FUSS HERE...?
A LITTLE WHILE AGO, THE SHIELD EXPANDED TO ENCOMPASS OUR VILLAGE...
SNAP

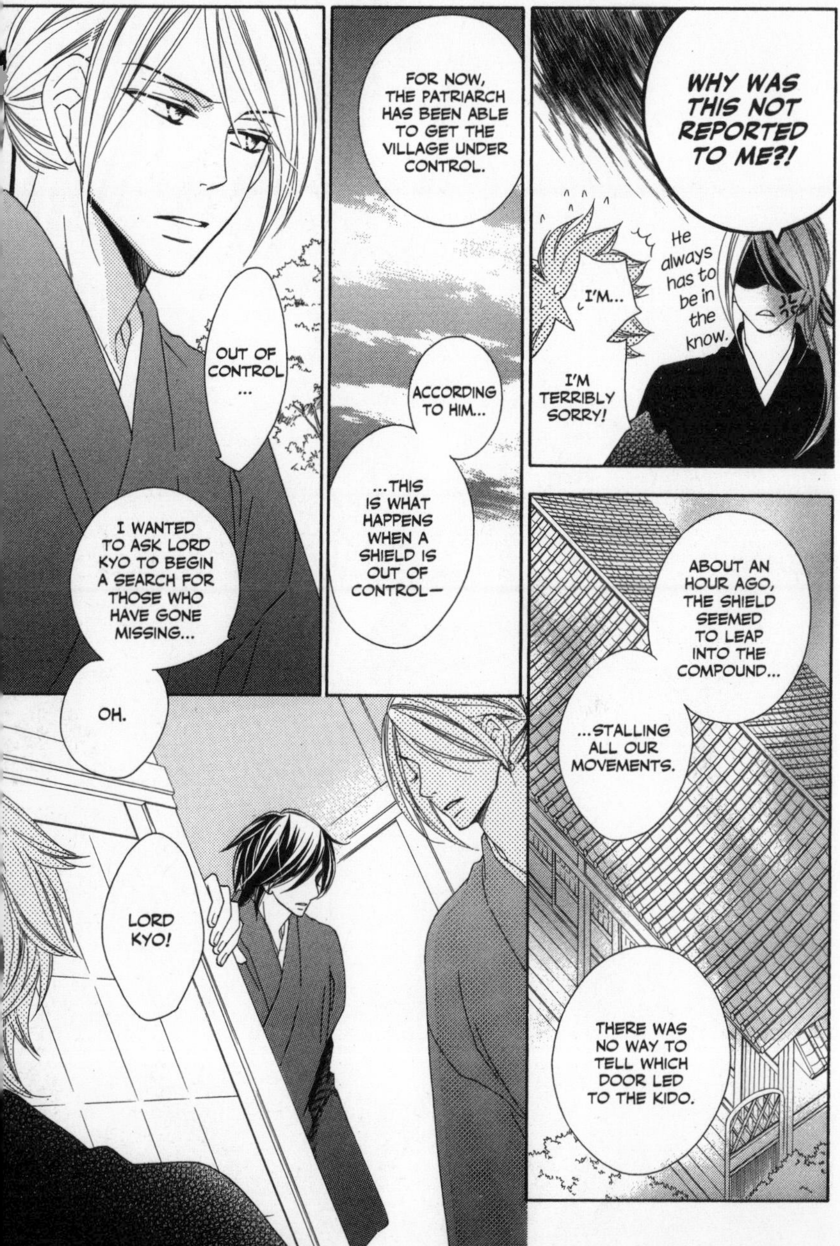
WHY WAS THIS NOT REPORTED TO ME?!
He always has to be in the know.
I'M...
I'M TERRIBLY SORRY!
ABOUT AN HOUR AGO, THE SHIELD SEEMED TO LEAP INTO THE COMPOUND...
...STALLING ALL OUR MOVEMENTS.
THERE WAS NO WAY TO TELL WHICH DOOR LED TO THE KIDO.
FOR NOW, THE PATRIARCH HAS BEEN ABLE TO GET THE VILLAGE UNDER CONTROL.
ACCORDING TO HIM...
...THIS IS WHAT HAPPENS WHEN A SHIELD IS OUT OF CONTROL—
OUT OF CONTROL...
I WANTED TO ASK LORD KYO TO BEGIN A SEARCH FOR THOSE WHO HAVE GONE MISSING...
OH.
LORD KYO!

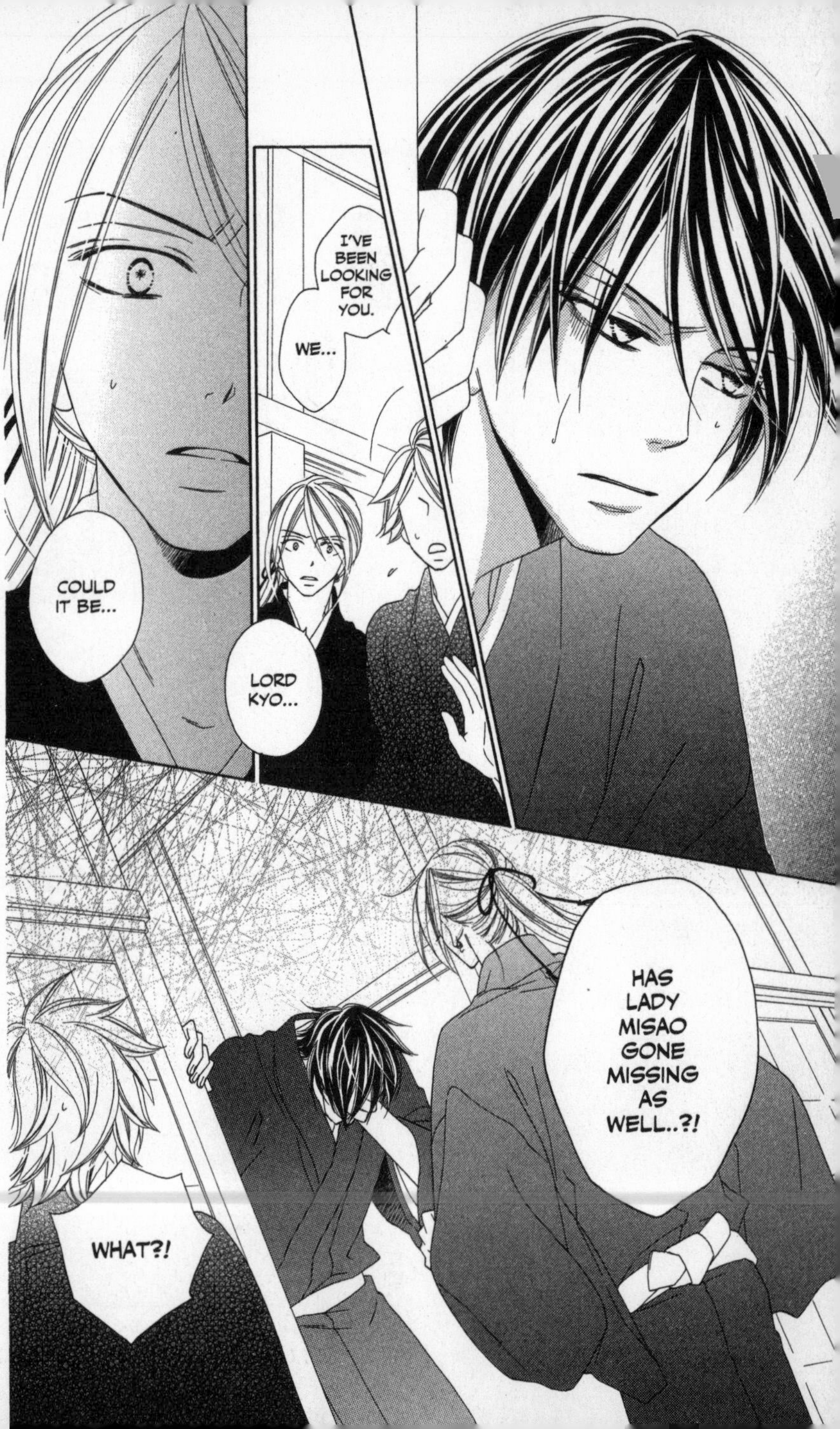
I'VE BEEN LOOKING FOR YOU.
WE...
LORD KYO...
COULD IT BE...
HAS LADY MISAO GONE MISSING AS WELL..?!
WHAT?!

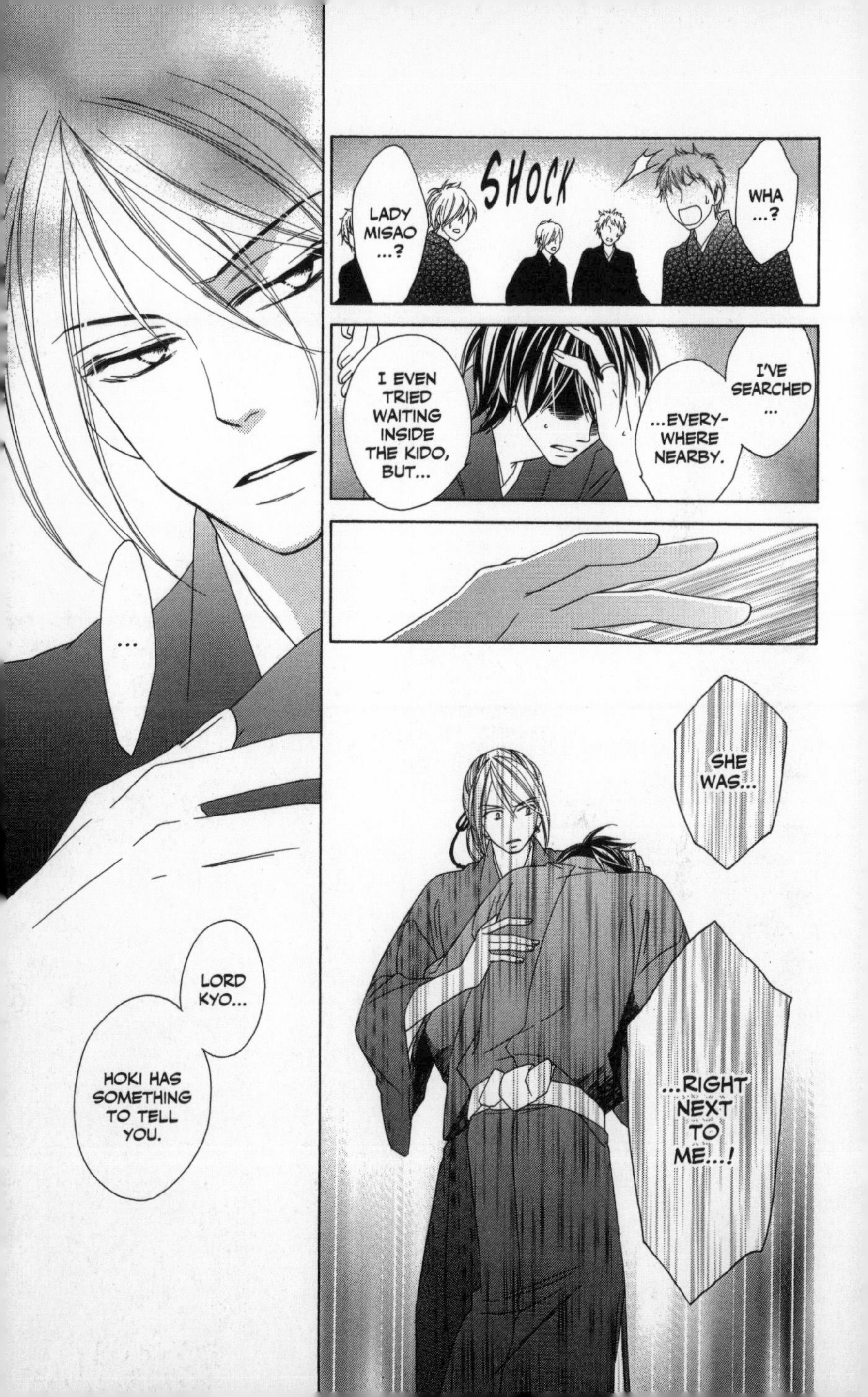
WHA ...?
SHOCK
LADY MISAO ...?
I'VE SEARCHED ...
...EVERY-WHERE NEARBY.
I EVEN TRIED WAITING INSIDE THE KIDO, BUT...
SHE WAS...
...RIGHT NEXT TO ME...!
...
LORD KYO...
HOKI HAS SOMETHING TO TELL YOU.

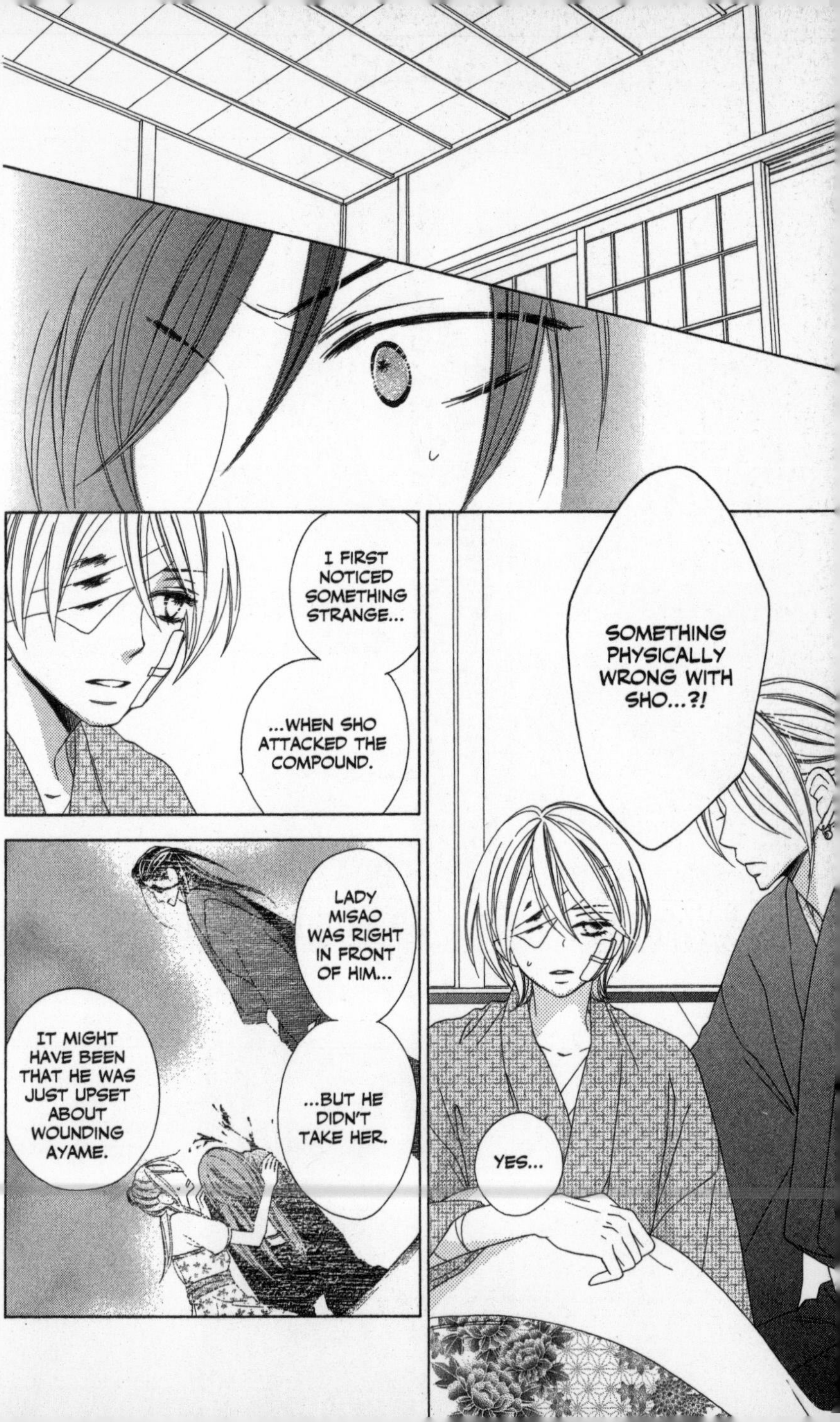
SOMETHING PHYSICALLY WRONG WITH SHO...?!
YES...
I FIRST NOTICED SOMETHING STRANGE...
...WHEN SHO ATTACKED THE COMPOUND.
LADY MISAO WAS RIGHT IN FRONT OF HIM...
...BUT HE DIDN'T TAKE HER.
IT MIGHT HAVE BEEN THAT HE WAS JUST UPSET ABOUT WOUNDING AYAME.

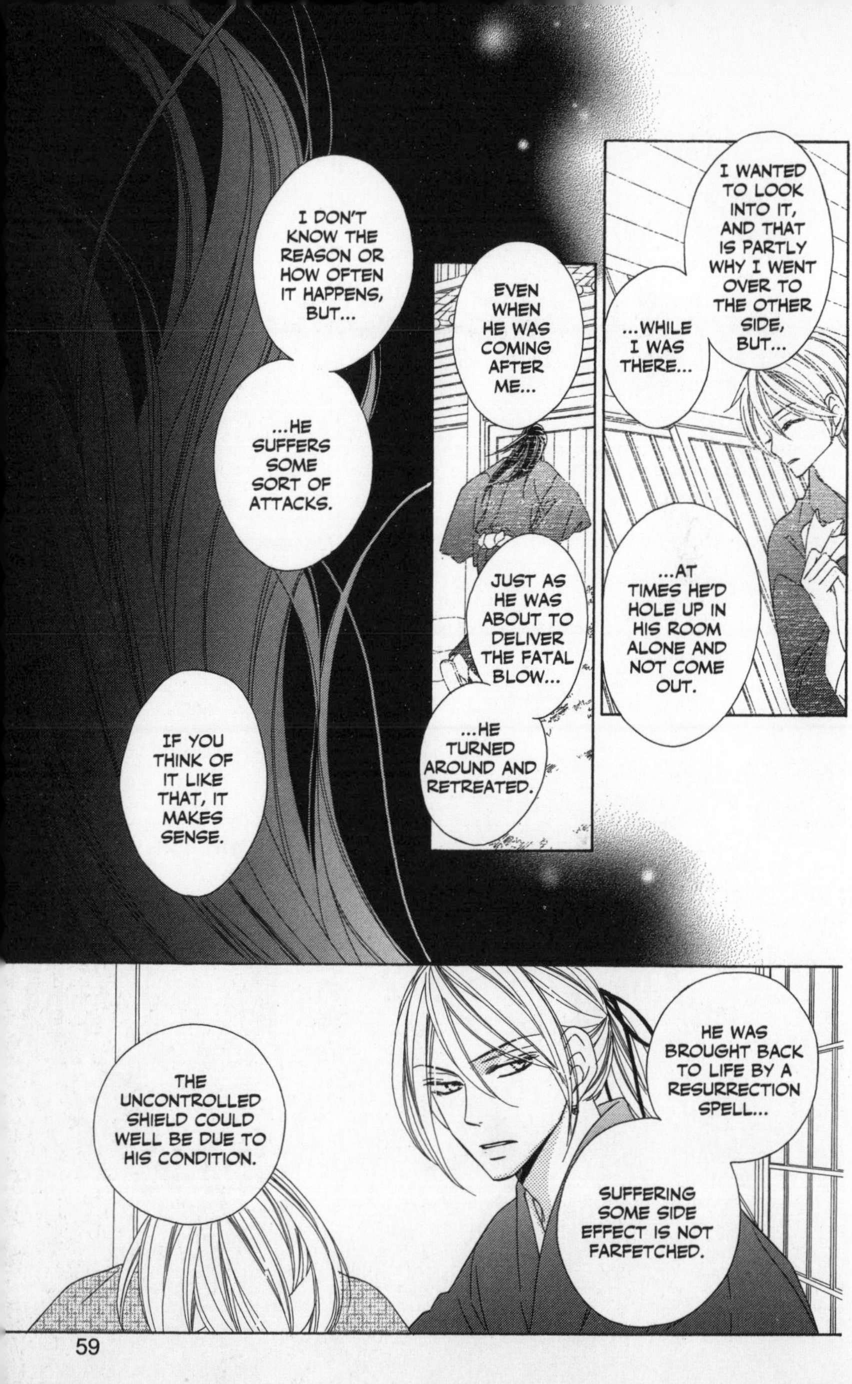
I WANTED TO LOOK INTO IT, AND THAT IS PARTLY WHY I WENT OVER TO THE OTHER SIDE, BUT...
...WHILE I WAS THERE...
...AT TIMES HE'D HOLE UP IN HIS ROOM ALONE AND NOT COME OUT.
EVEN WHEN HE WAS COMING AFTER ME...
JUST AS HE WAS ABOUT TO DELIVER THE FATAL BLOW...
...HE TURNED AROUND AND RETREATED.
I DON'T KNOW THE REASON OR HOW OFTEN IT HAPPENS, BUT...
...HE SUFFERS SOME SORT OF ATTACKS.
IF YOU THINK OF IT LIKE THAT, IT MAKES SENSE.
HE WAS BROUGHT BACK TO LIFE BY A RESURRECTION SPELL...
SUFFERING SOME SIDE EFFECT IS NOT FARFETCHED.
THE UNCONTROLLED SHIELD COULD WELL BE DUE TO HIS CONDITION.

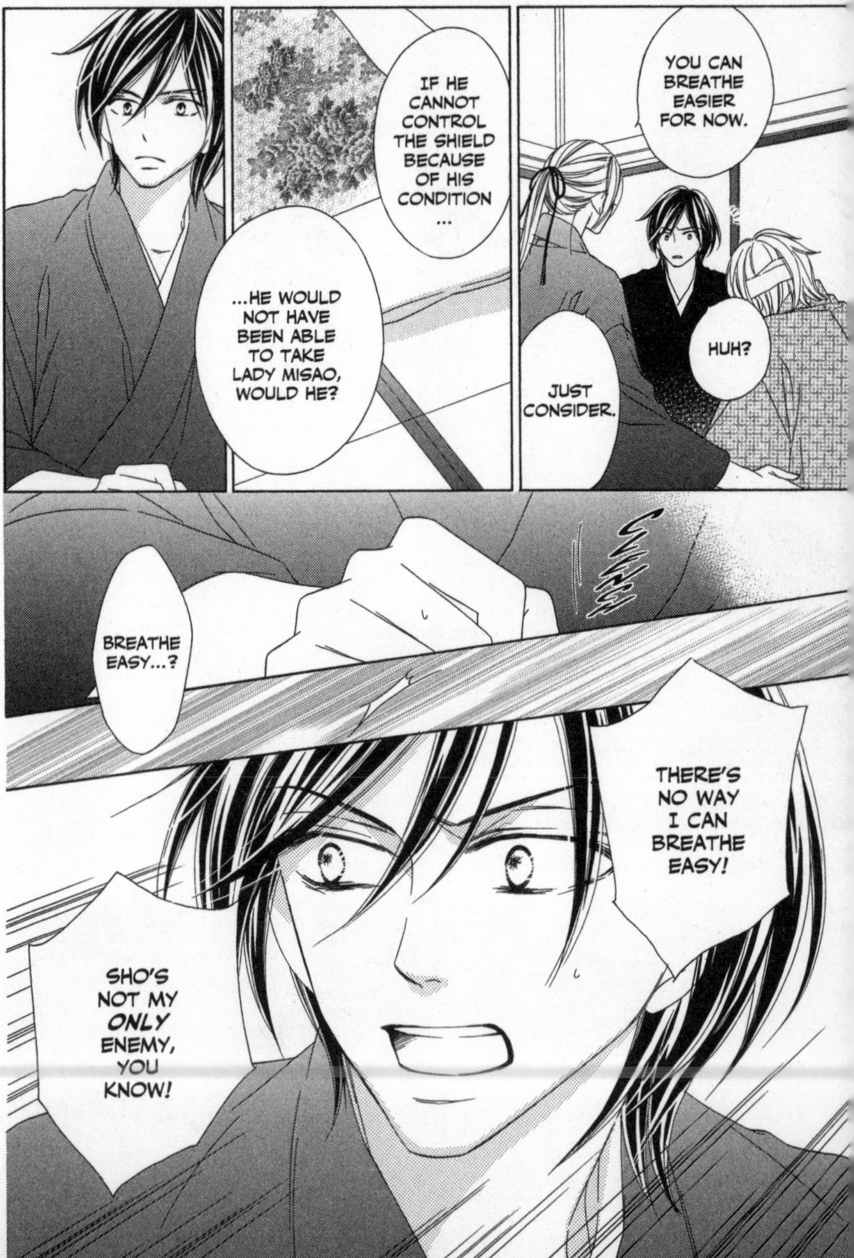
YOU CAN BREATHE EASIER FOR NOW.
HUH?
JUST CONSIDER.
IF HE CANNOT CONTROL THE SHIELD BECAUSE OF HIS CONDITION ...
...HE WOULD NOT HAVE BEEN ABLE TO TAKE LADY MISAO, WOULD HE?
BREATHE EASY...?
THERE'S NO WAY I CAN BREATHE EASY!
SHO'S NOT MY *ONLY* ENEMY, YOU KNOW!

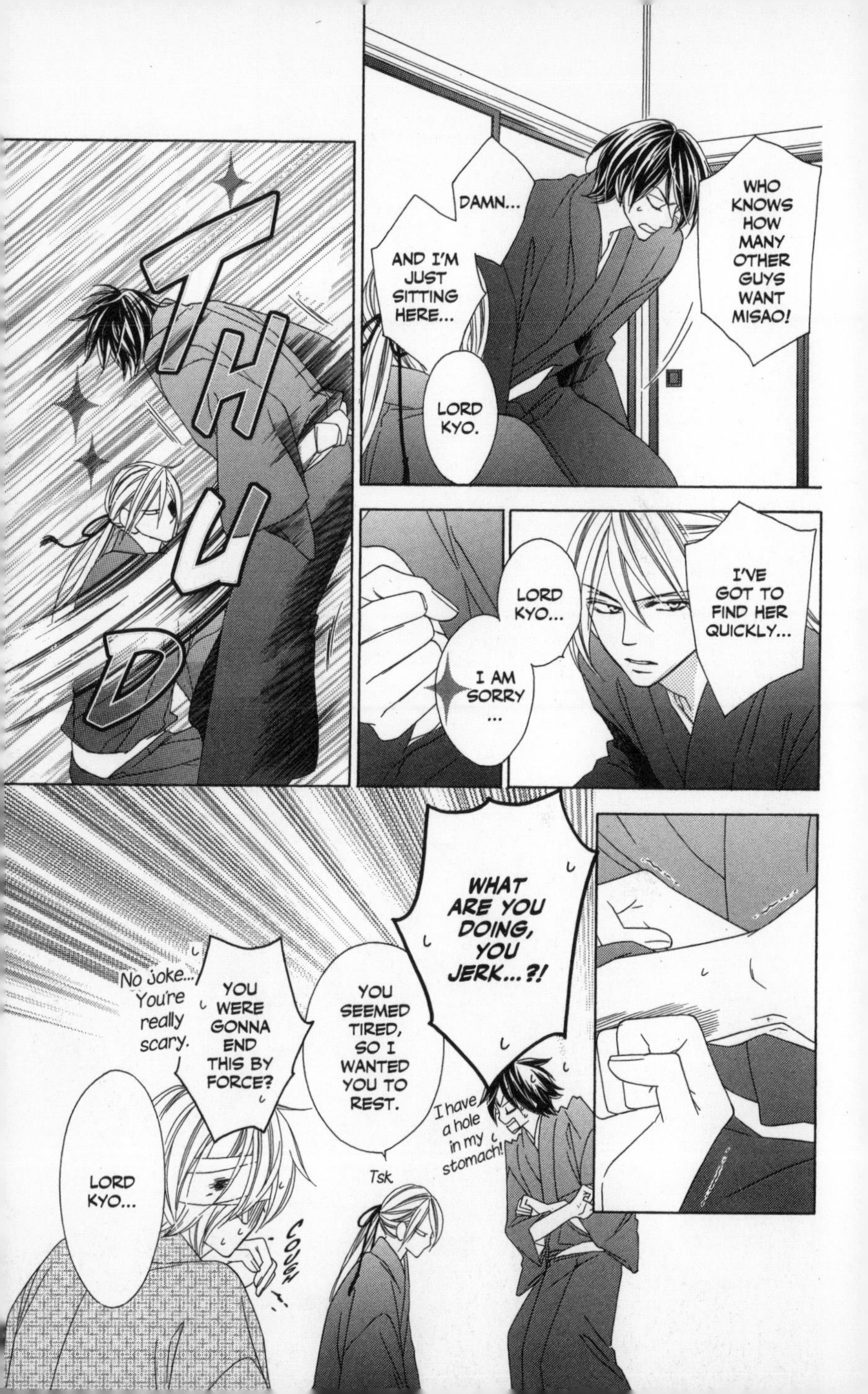
WHO KNOWS HOW MANY OTHER GUYS WANT MISAO!
DAMN...
AND I'M JUST SITTING HERE...
LORD KYO.
I'VE GOT TO FIND HER QUICKLY...
LORD KYO...
I AM SORRY ...
THUD
WHAT ARE YOU DOING, YOU JERK...?!
I have a hole in my stomach!
YOU SEEMED TIRED, SO I WANTED YOU TO REST.
Tsk
YOU WERE GONNA END THIS BY FORCE?
No joke... You're really scary.
LORD KYO...
COUGH

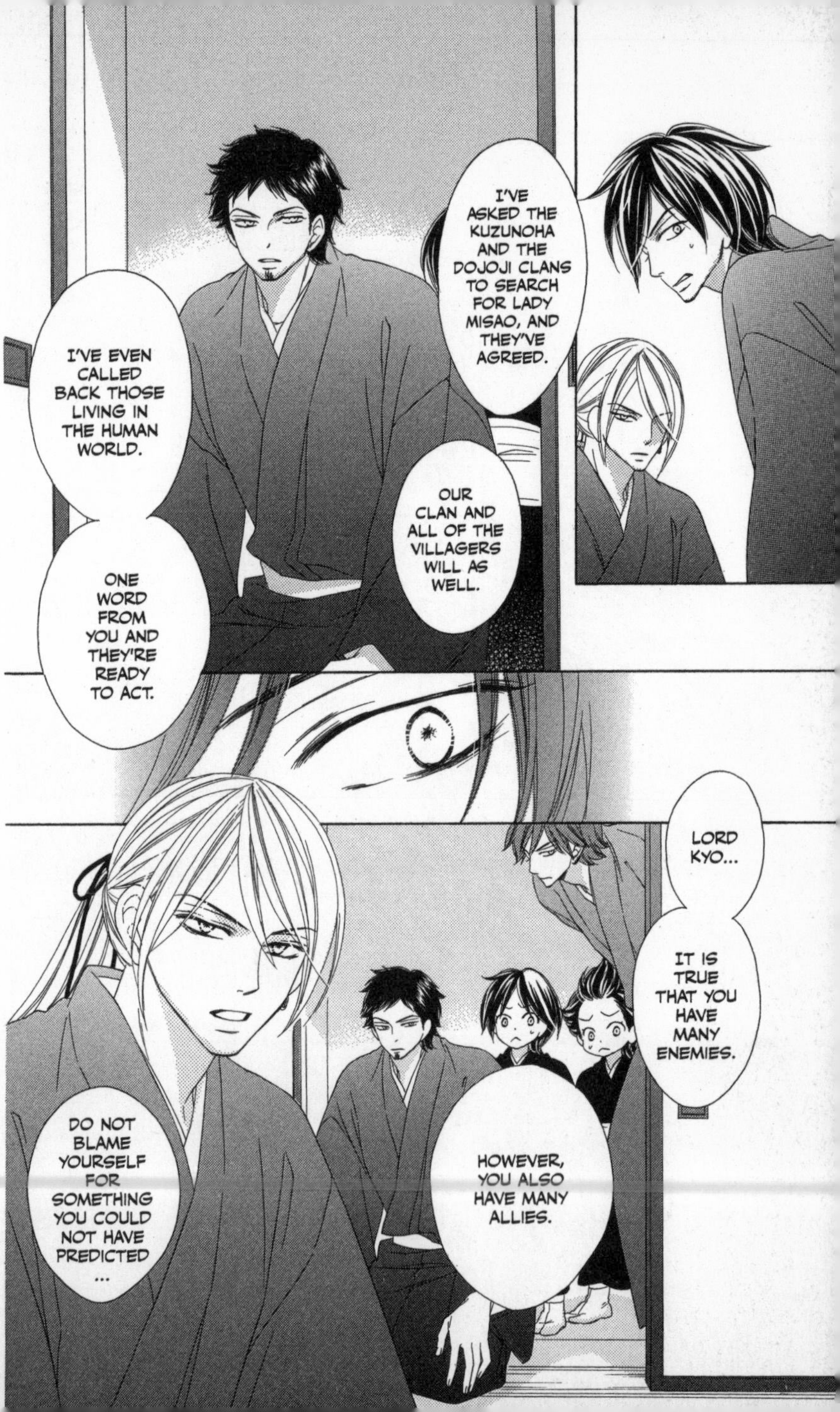
I'VE ASKED THE KUZUNOHA AND THE DOJOJI CLANS TO SEARCH FOR LADY MISAO, AND THEY'VE AGREED.
OUR CLAN AND ALL OF THE VILLAGERS WILL AS WELL.
I'VE EVEN CALLED BACK THOSE LIVING IN THE HUMAN WORLD.
ONE WORD FROM YOU AND THEY'RE READY TO ACT.
LORD KYO...
IT IS TRUE THAT YOU HAVE MANY ENEMIES.
HOWEVER, YOU ALSO HAVE MANY ALLIES.
DO NOT BLAME YOURSELF FOR SOMETHING YOU COULD NOT HAVE PREDICTED ...

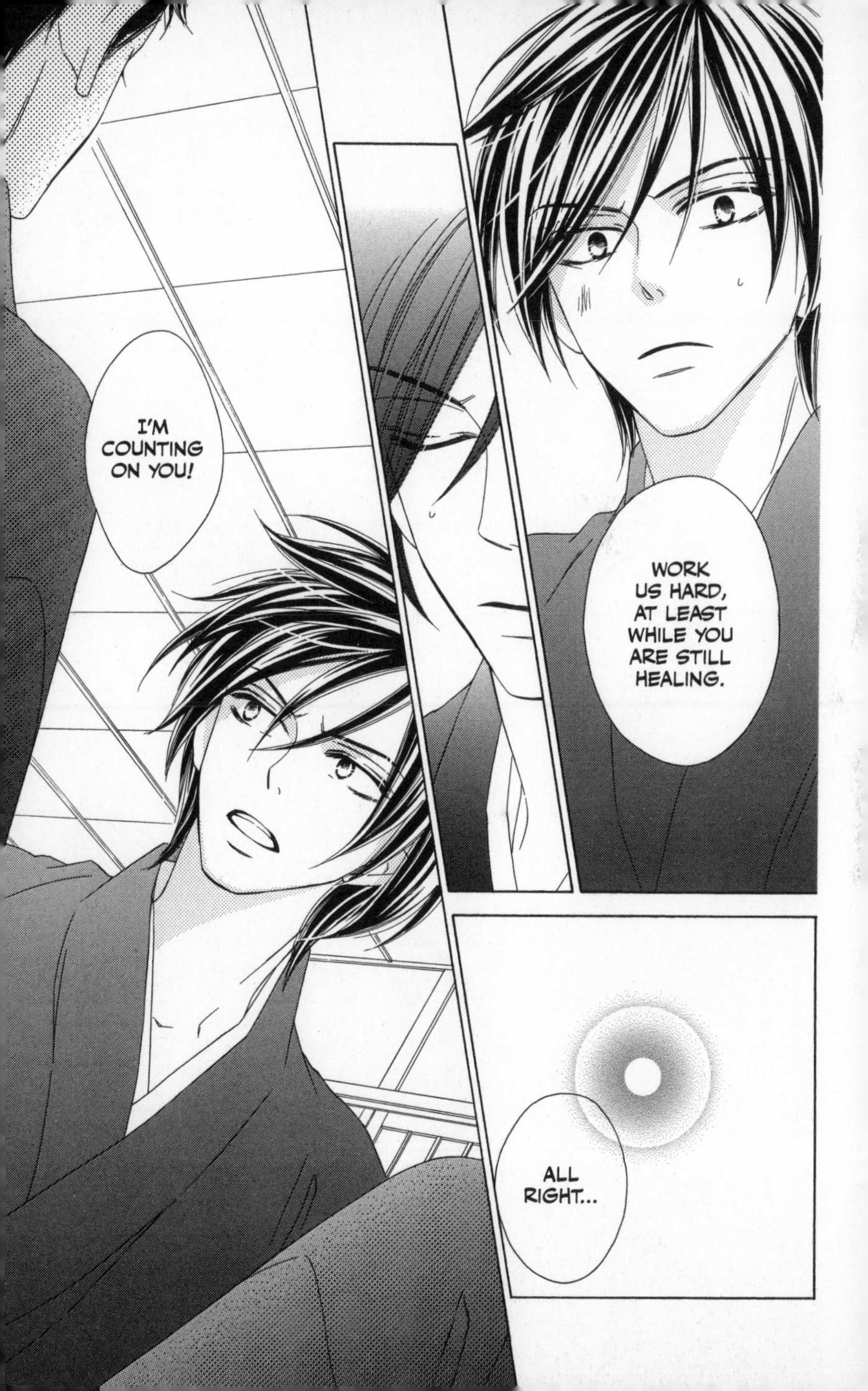
WORK US HARD, AT LEAST WHILE YOU ARE STILL HEALING.
ALL RIGHT...
I'M COUNTING ON YOU!

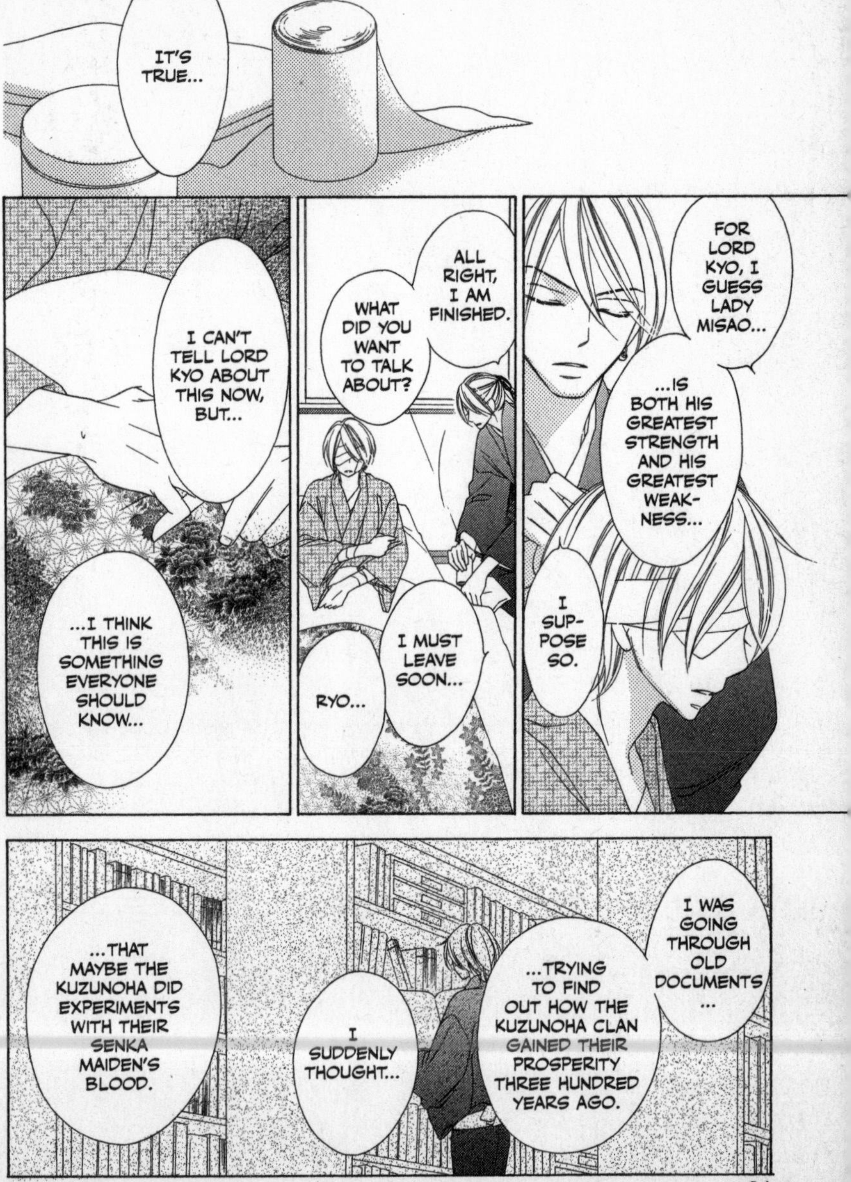
IT'S TRUE...
FOR LORD KYO, I GUESS LADY MISAO...
...IS BOTH HIS GREATEST STRENGTH AND HIS GREATEST WEAKNESS...
I SUPPOSE SO.
ALL RIGHT, I AM FINISHED.
WHAT DID YOU WANT TO TALK ABOUT?
I MUST LEAVE SOON...
RYO...
I CAN'T TELL LORD KYO ABOUT THIS NOW, BUT...
...I THINK THIS IS SOMETHING EVERYONE SHOULD KNOW...
I WAS GOING THROUGH OLD DOCUMENTS...
...TRYING TO FIND OUT HOW THE KUZUNOHA CLAN GAINED THEIR PROSPERITY THREE HUNDRED YEARS AGO.
I SUDDENLY THOUGHT...
...THAT MAYBE THE KUZUNOHA DID EXPERIMENTS WITH THEIR SENKA MAIDEN'S BLOOD.

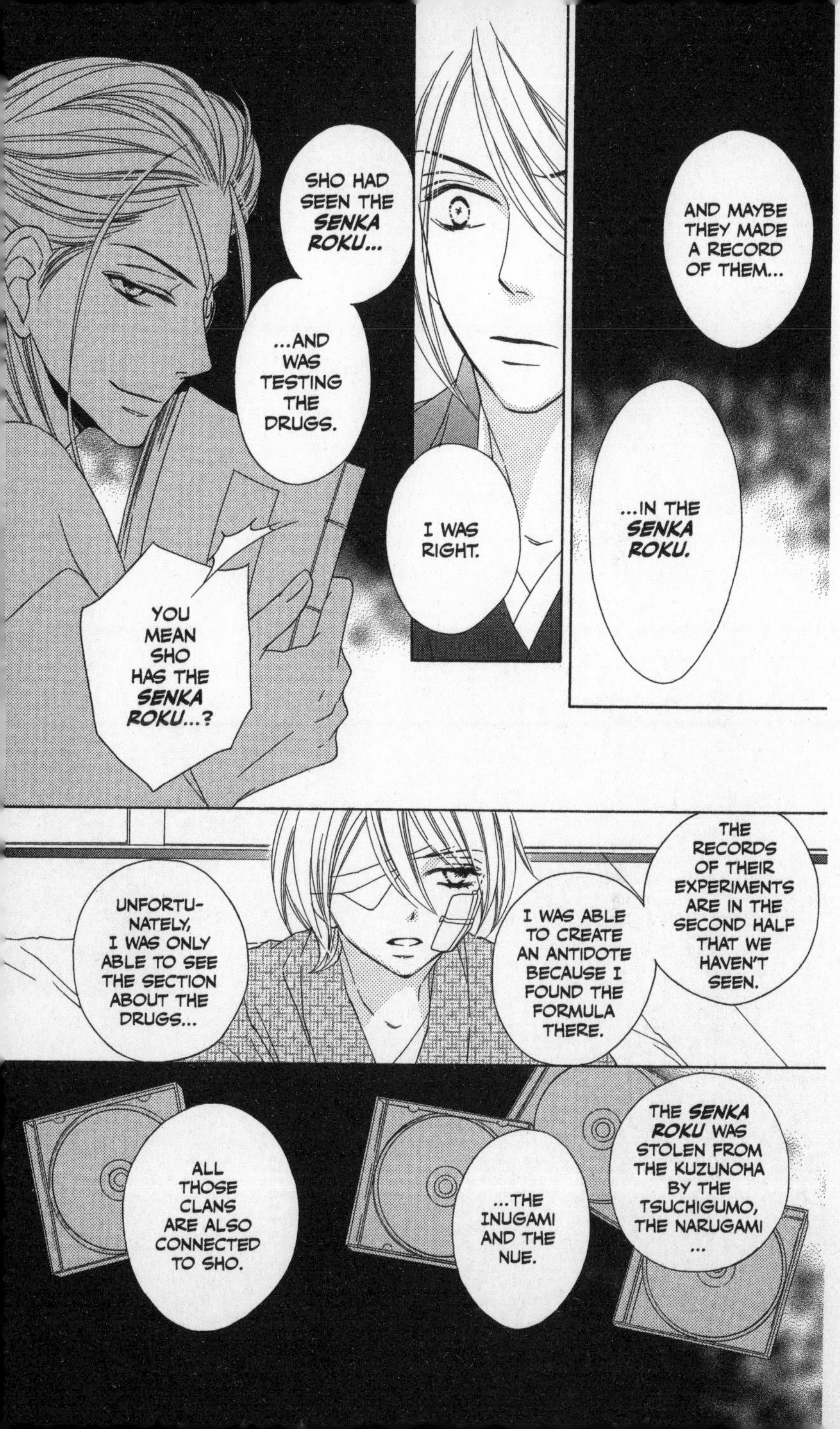
AND MAYBE THEY MADE A RECORD OF THEM...
...IN THE *SENKA ROKU.*
I WAS RIGHT.
SHO HAD SEEN THE *SENKA ROKU*...
...AND WAS TESTING THE DRUGS.
YOU MEAN SHO HAS THE *SENKA ROKU*...?
THE RECORDS OF THEIR EXPERIMENTS ARE IN THE SECOND HALF THAT WE HAVEN'T SEEN.
I WAS ABLE TO CREATE AN ANTIDOTE BECAUSE I FOUND THE FORMULA THERE.
UNFORTU-NATELY, I WAS ONLY ABLE TO SEE THE SECTION ABOUT THE DRUGS...
THE *SENKA ROKU* WAS STOLEN FROM THE KUZUNOHA BY THE TSUCHIGUMO, THE NARUGAMI ...
...THE INUGAMI AND THE NUE.
ALL THOSE CLANS ARE ALSO CONNECTED TO SHO.

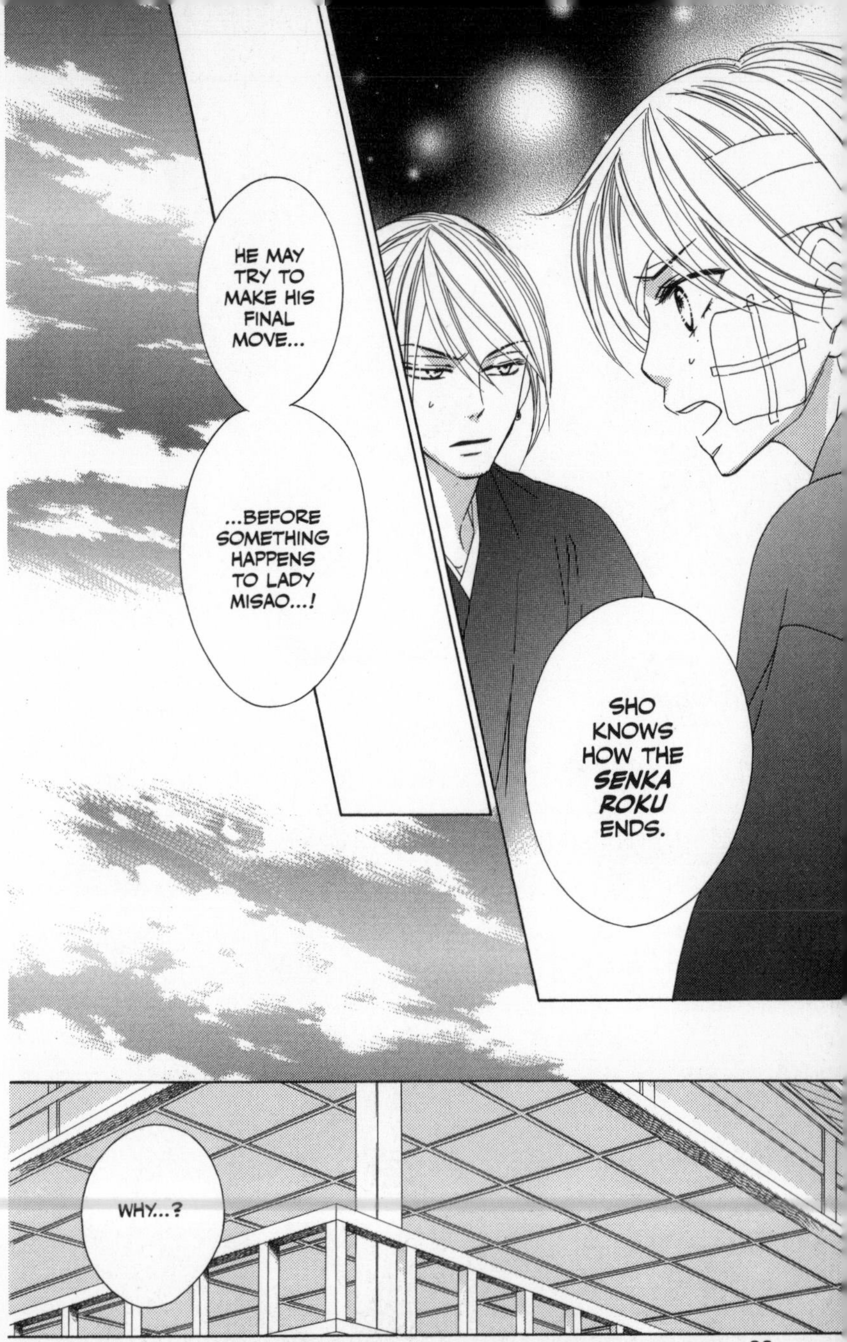
SHO KNOWS HOW THE *SENKA ROKU* ENDS.
HE MAY TRY TO MAKE HIS FINAL MOVE...
...BEFORE SOMETHING HAPPENS TO LADY MISAO...!
WHY...?

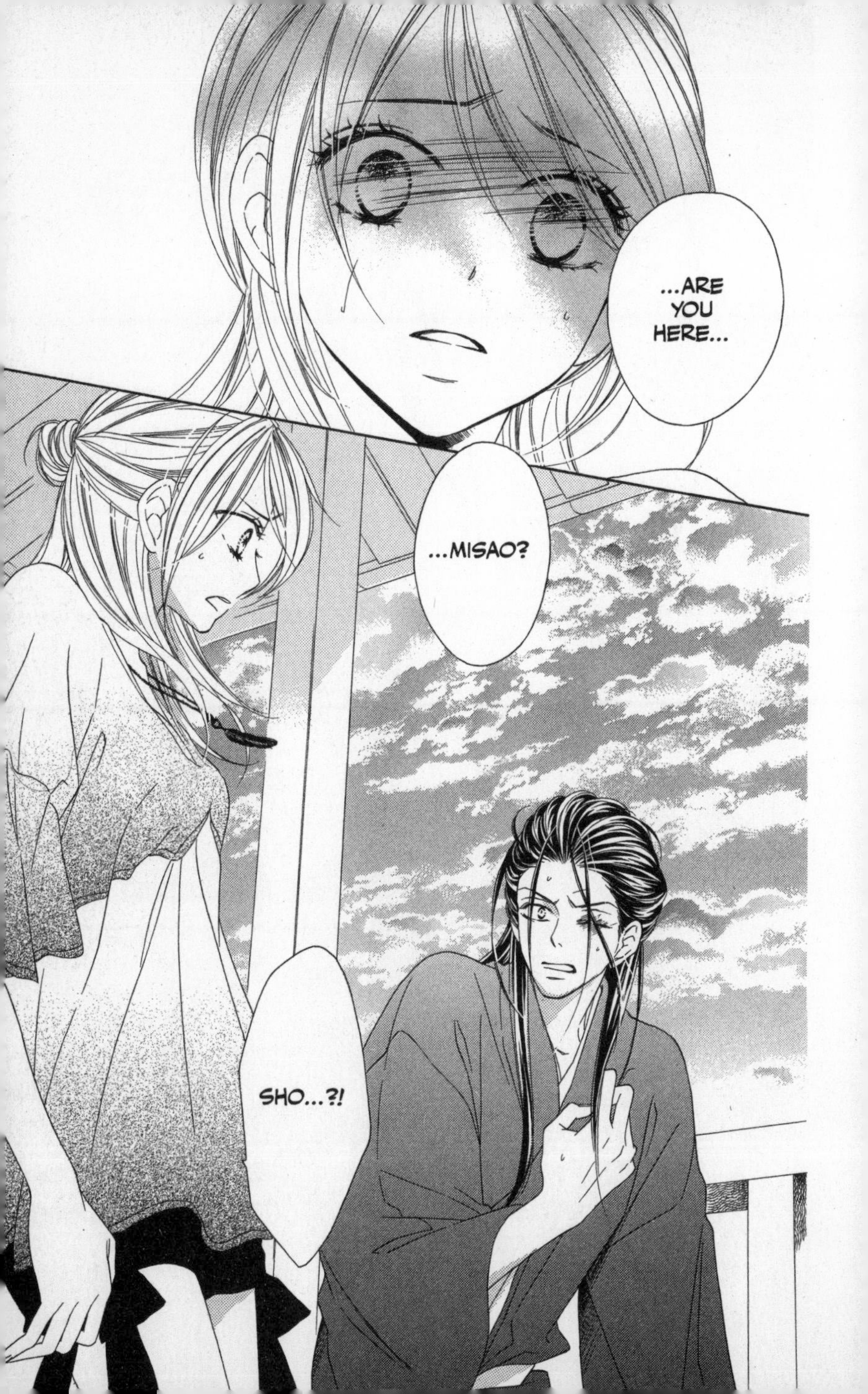
...ARE YOU HERE...
...MISAO?
SHO...?!

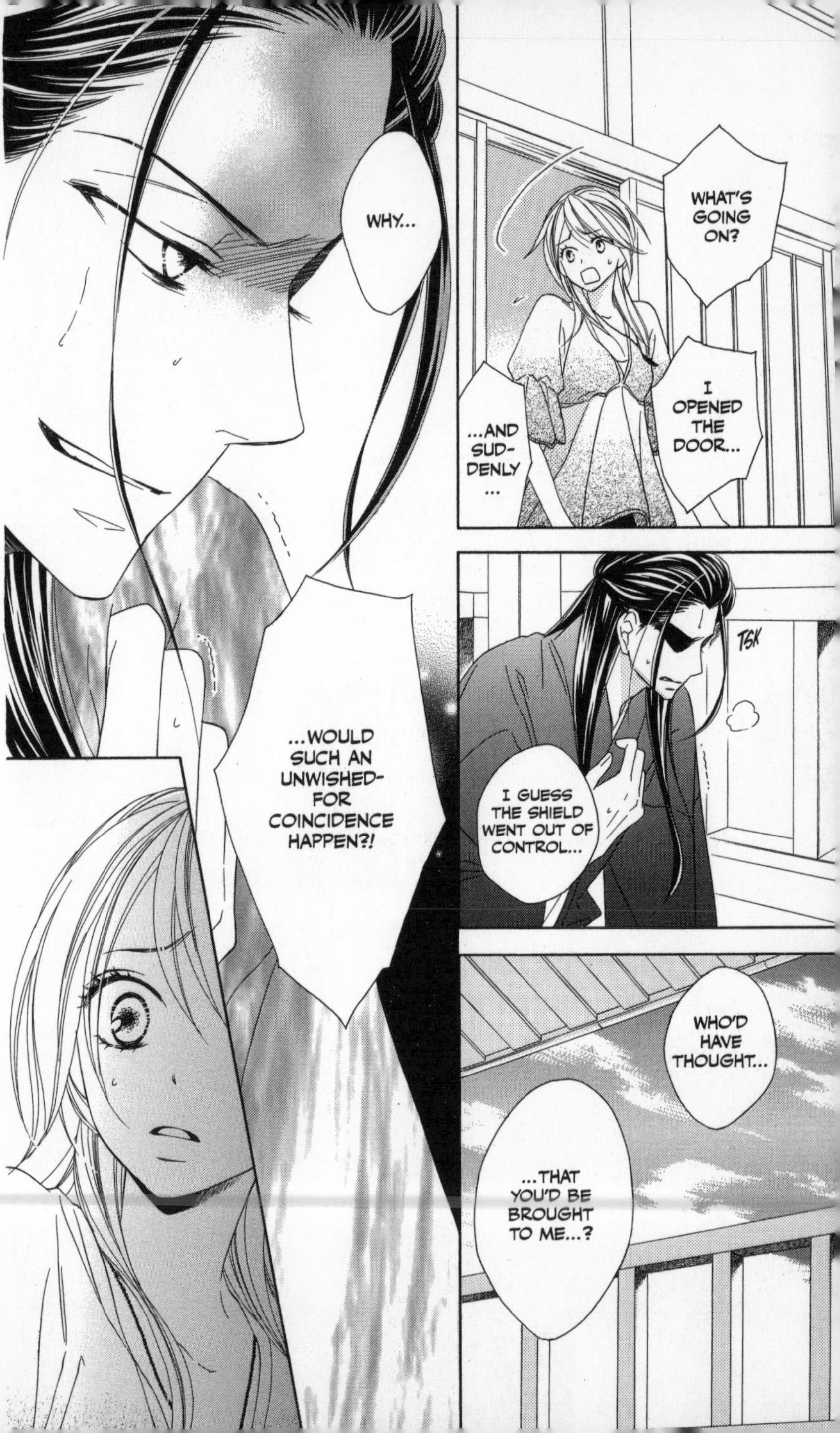
WHAT'S GOING ON?
I OPENED THE DOOR...
...AND SUD-DENLY...
TSK
I GUESS THE SHIELD WENT OUT OF CONTROL...
WHO'D HAVE THOUGHT...
...THAT YOU'D BE BROUGHT TO ME...?
WHY...
...WOULD SUCH AN UNWISHED-FOR COINCIDENCE HAPPEN?!

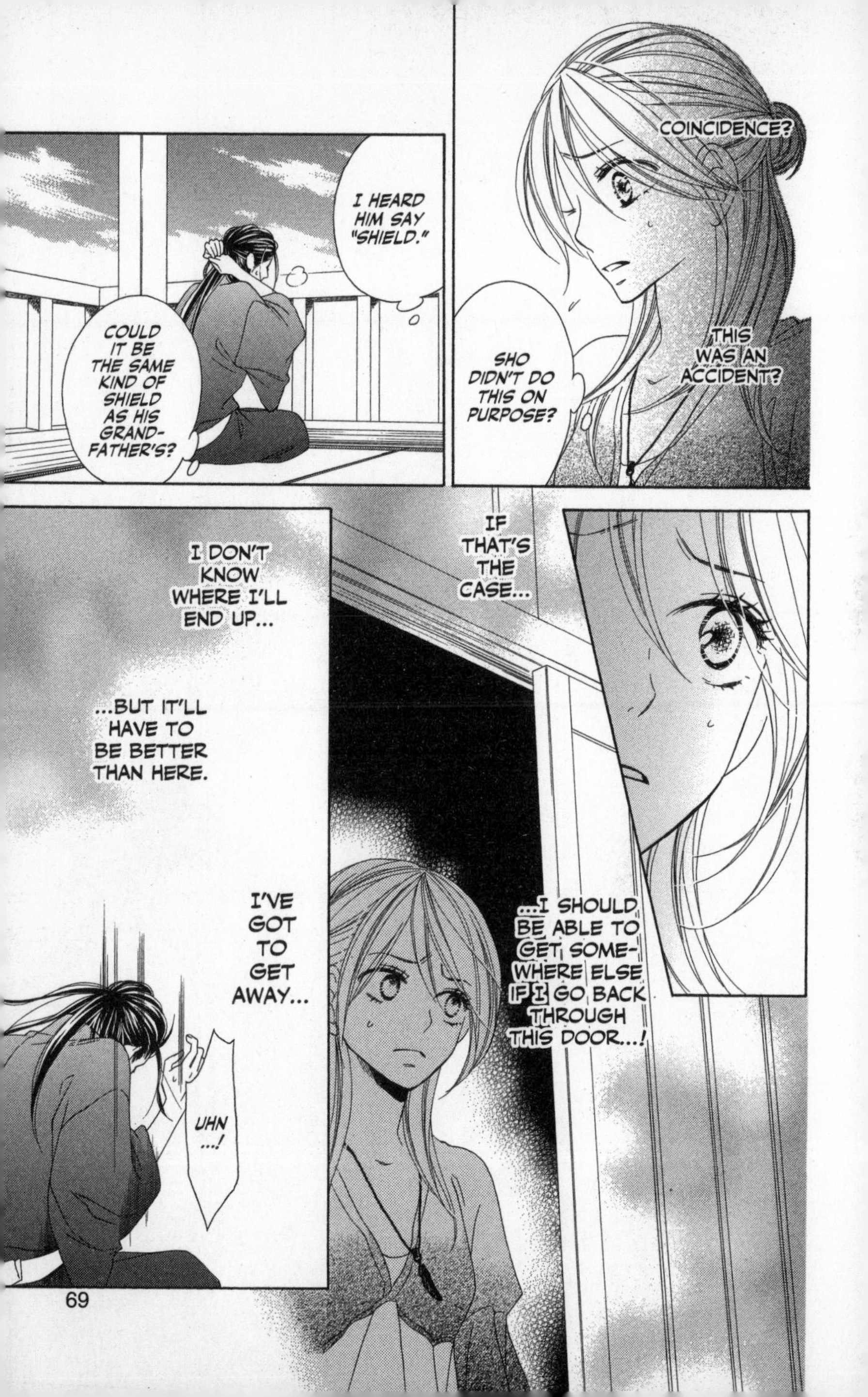

COINCIDENCE?
THIS WAS AN ACCIDENT?
SHO DIDN'T DO THIS ON PURPOSE?
I HEARD HIM SAY "SHIELD."
COULD IT BE THE SAME KIND OF SHIELD AS HIS GRAND-FATHER'S?
IF THAT'S THE CASE...
...I SHOULD BE ABLE TO GET SOME-WHERE ELSE IF I GO BACK THROUGH THIS DOOR...!
I DON'T KNOW WHERE I'LL END UP...
...BUT IT'LL HAVE TO BE BETTER THAN HERE.
I'VE GOT TO GET AWAY...
UHN ...!

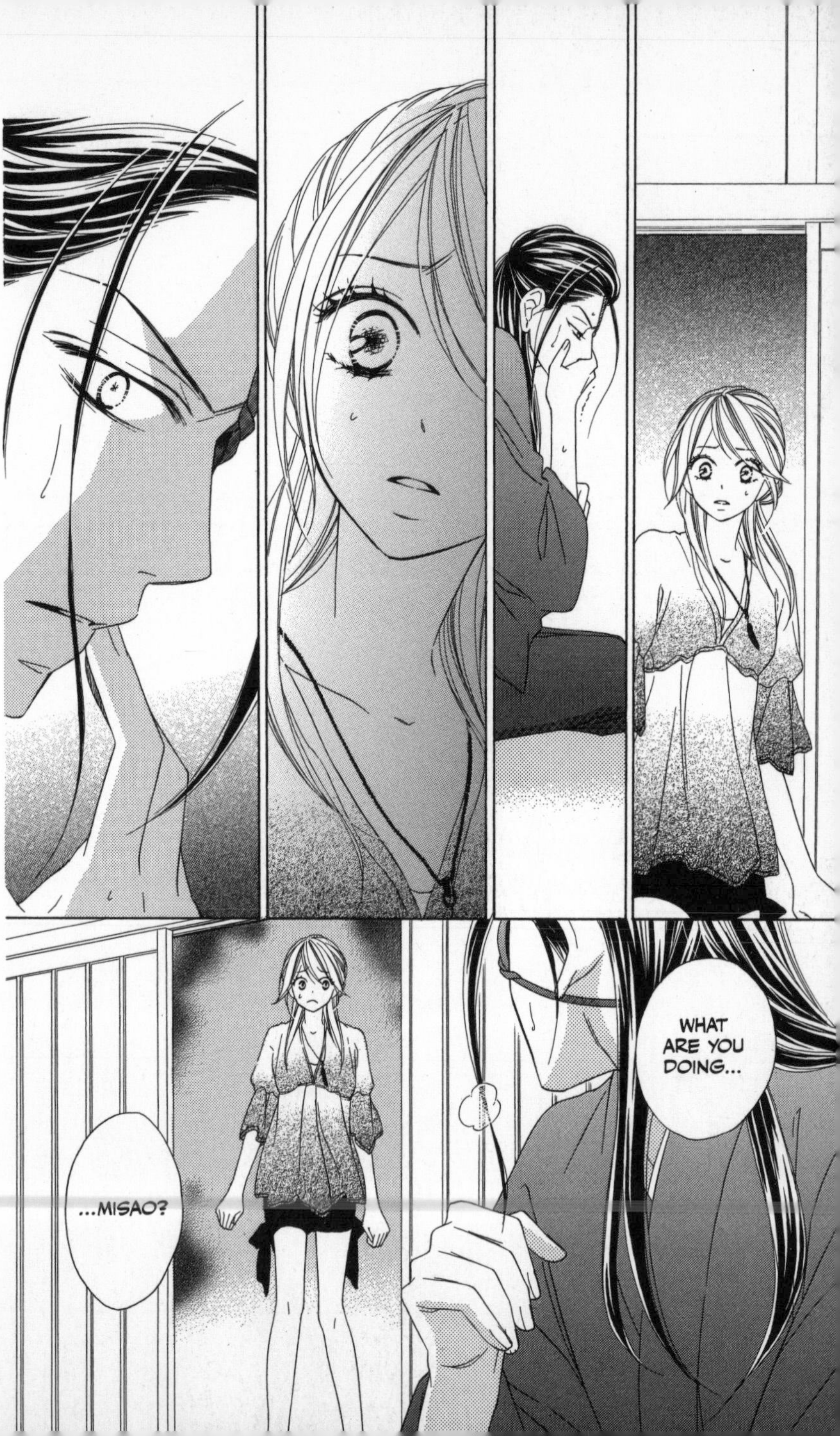
WHAT ARE YOU DOING...
...MISAO?

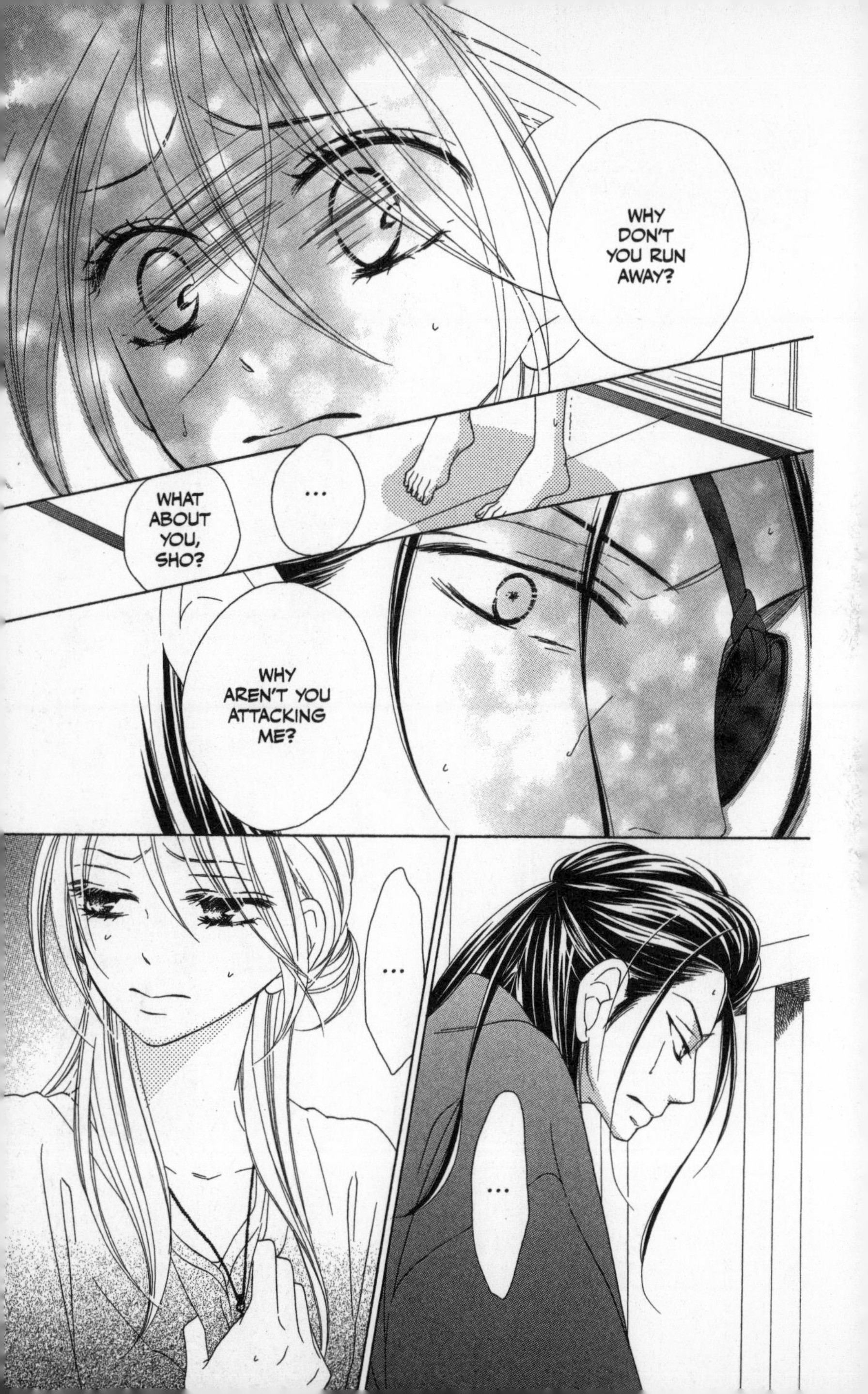
WHY DON'T YOU RUN AWAY?
...
WHAT ABOUT YOU, SHO?
WHY AREN'T YOU ATTACKING ME?
...
...

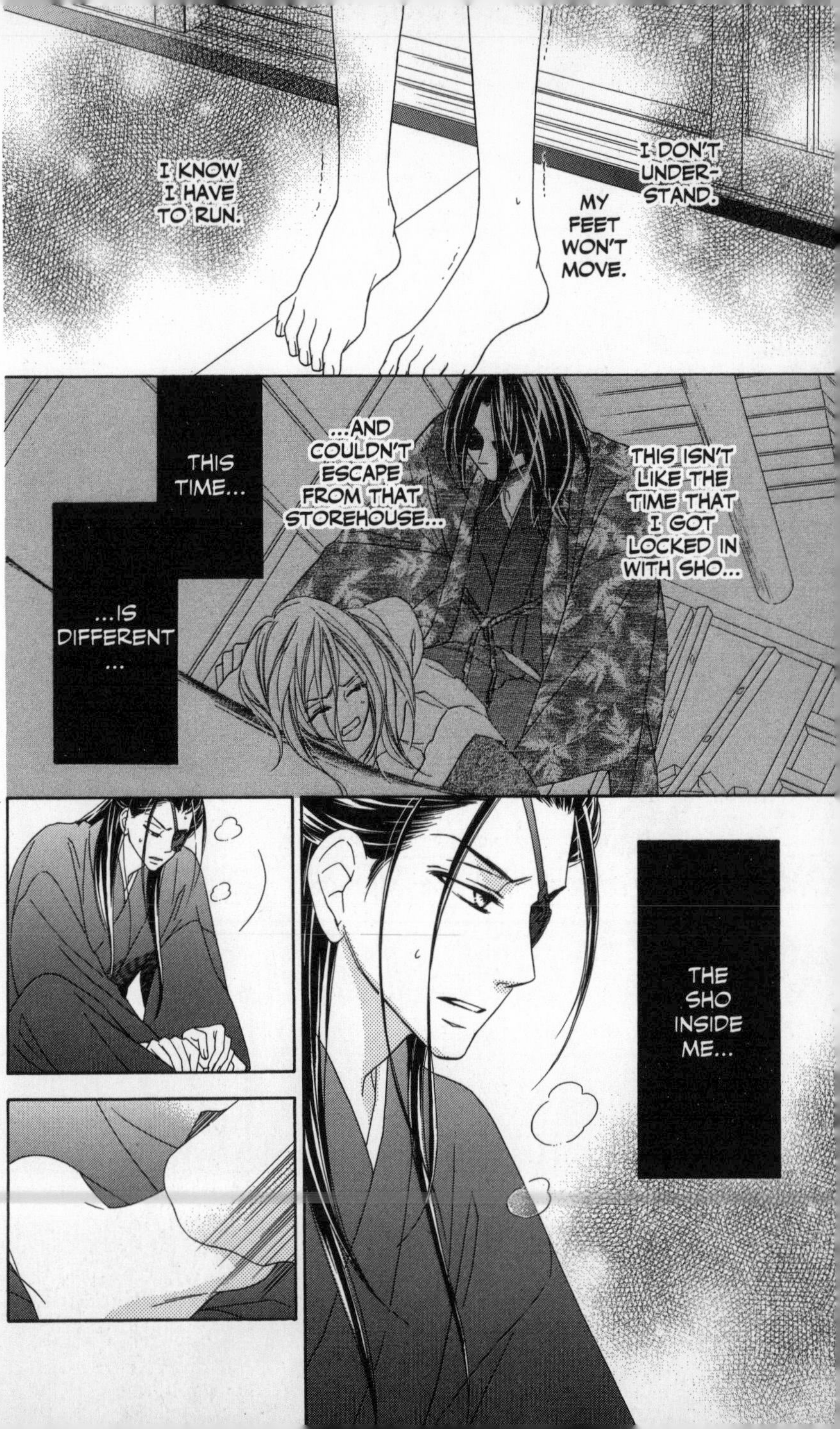
I DON'T UNDER-STAND.
MY FEET WON'T MOVE.
I KNOW I HAVE TO RUN.
THIS ISN'T LIKE THE TIME THAT I GOT LOCKED IN WITH SHO...
...AND COULDN'T ESCAPE FROM THAT STOREHOUSE...
THIS TIME...
...IS DIFFERENT ...
THE SHO INSIDE ME...

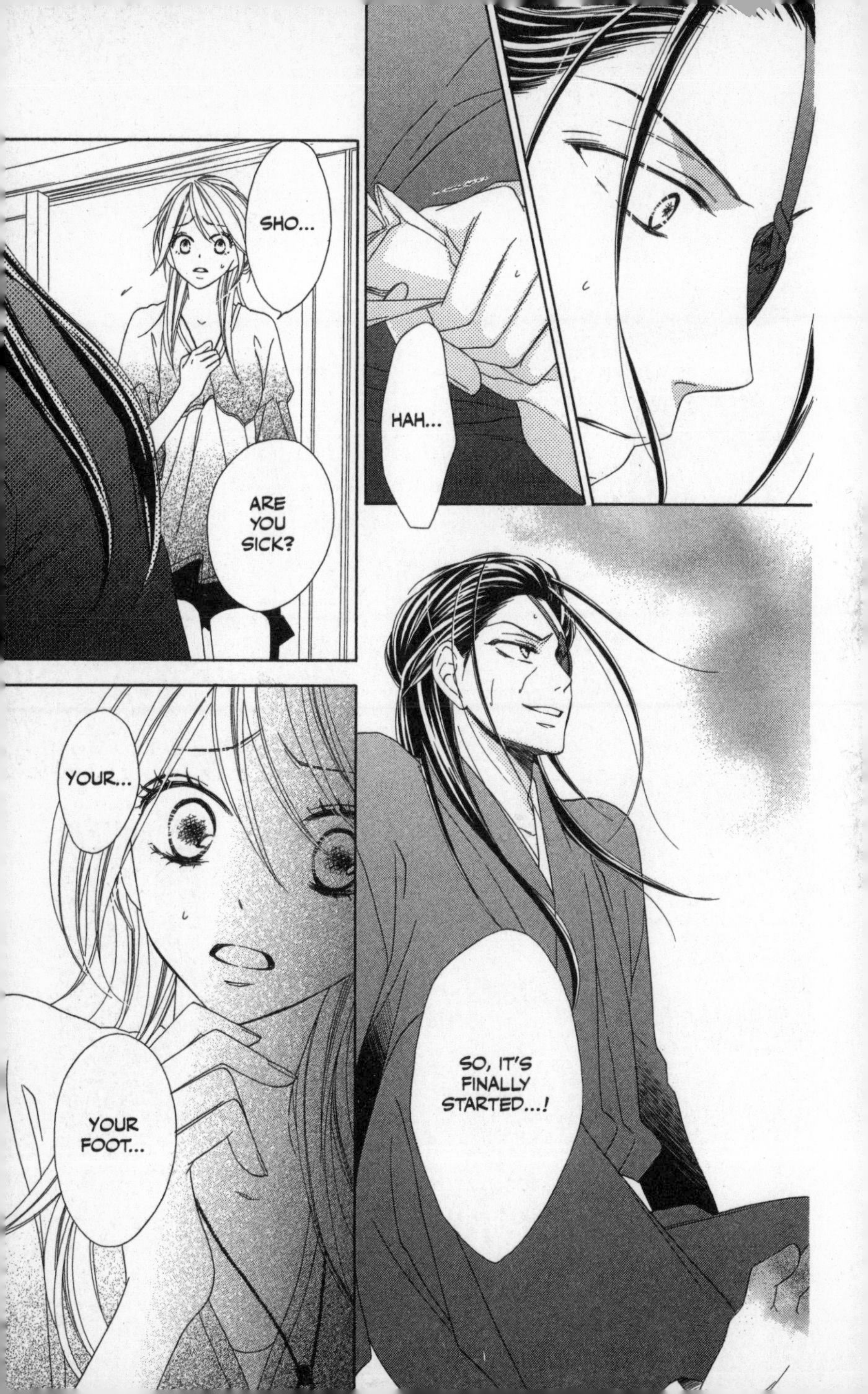
HAH...
SHO...
ARE YOU SICK?
SO, IT'S FINALLY STARTED...!
YOUR...
YOUR FOOT...

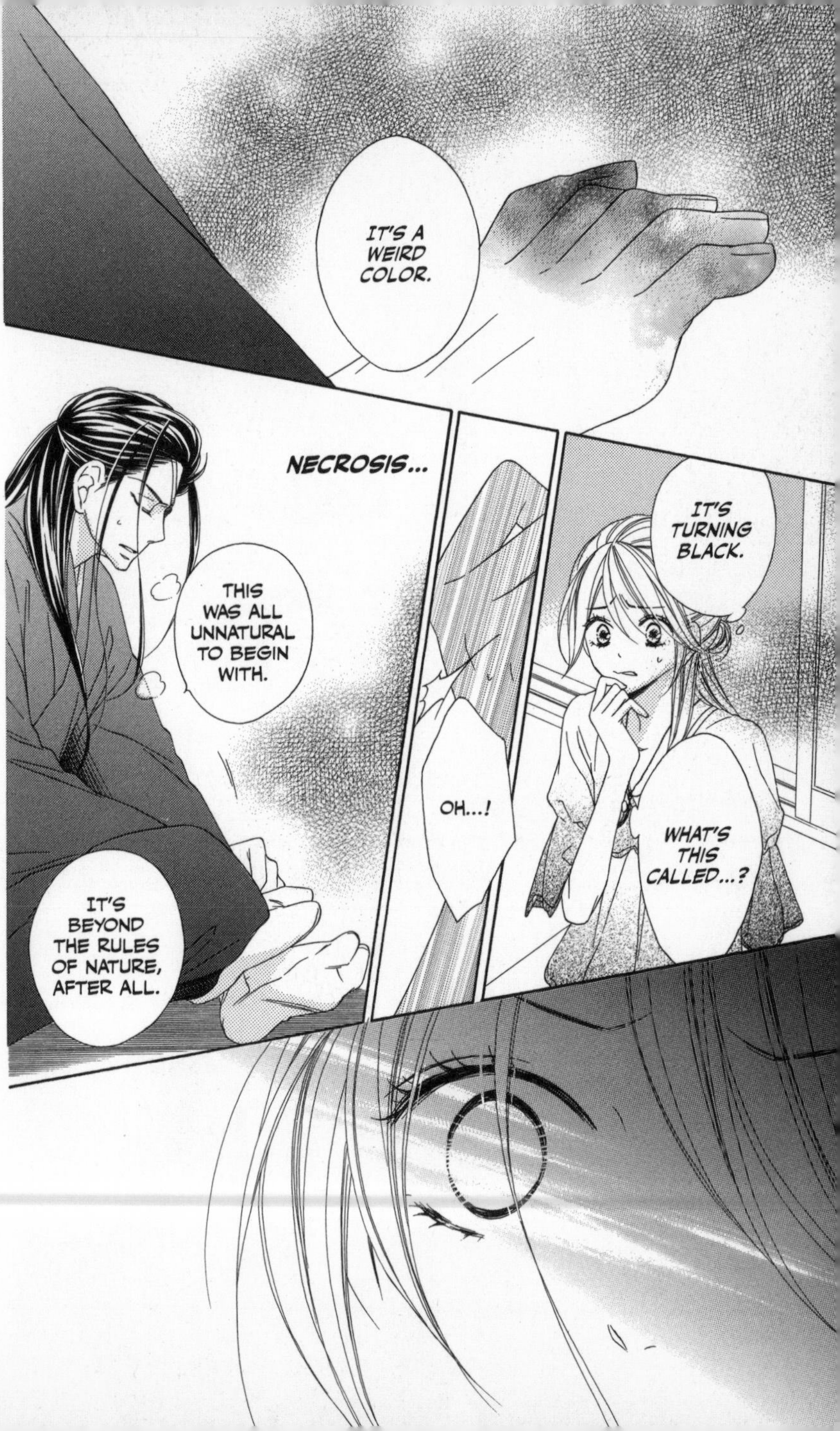
IT'S A WEIRD COLOR.
IT'S TURNING BLACK.
WHAT'S THIS CALLED...?
OH...!
NECROSIS...
THIS WAS ALL UNNATURAL TO BEGIN WITH.
IT'S BEYOND THE RULES OF NATURE, AFTER ALL.

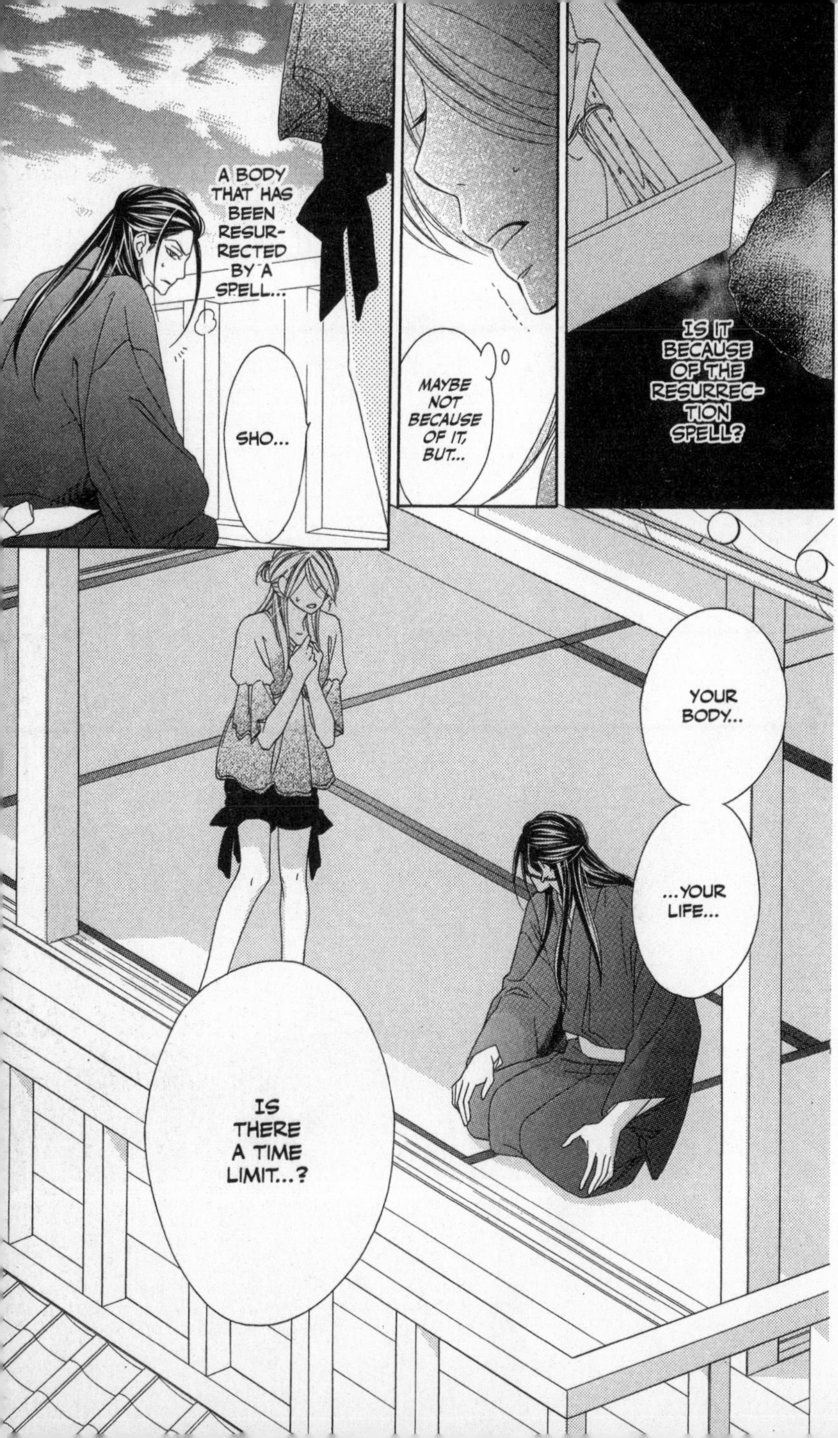
IS IT BECAUSE OF THE RESURRECTION SPELL?
MAYBE NOT BECAUSE OF IT, BUT...
A BODY THAT HAS BEEN RESURRECTED BY A SPELL...
SHO...
YOUR BODY...
...YOUR LIFE...
IS THERE A TIME LIMIT...?

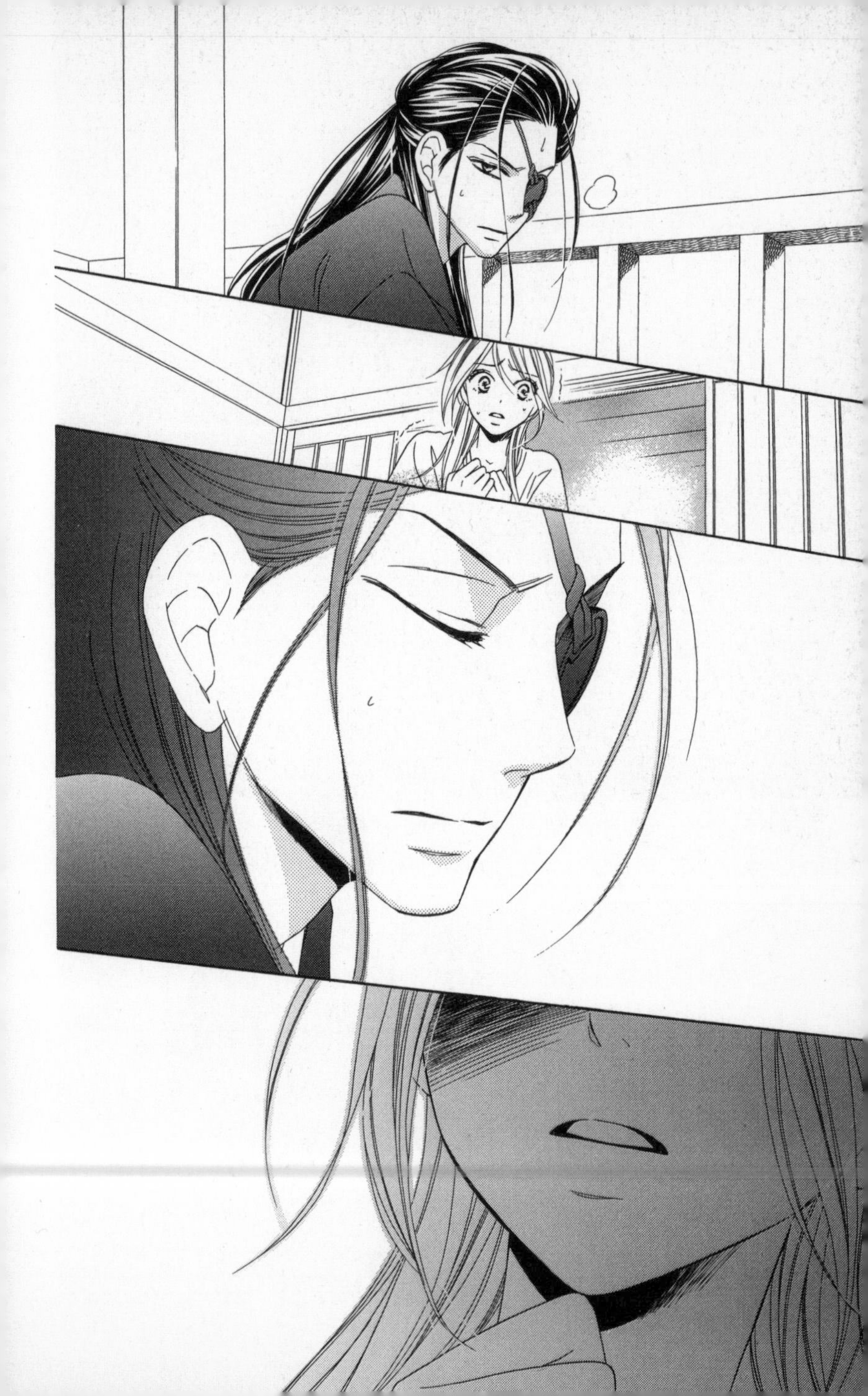

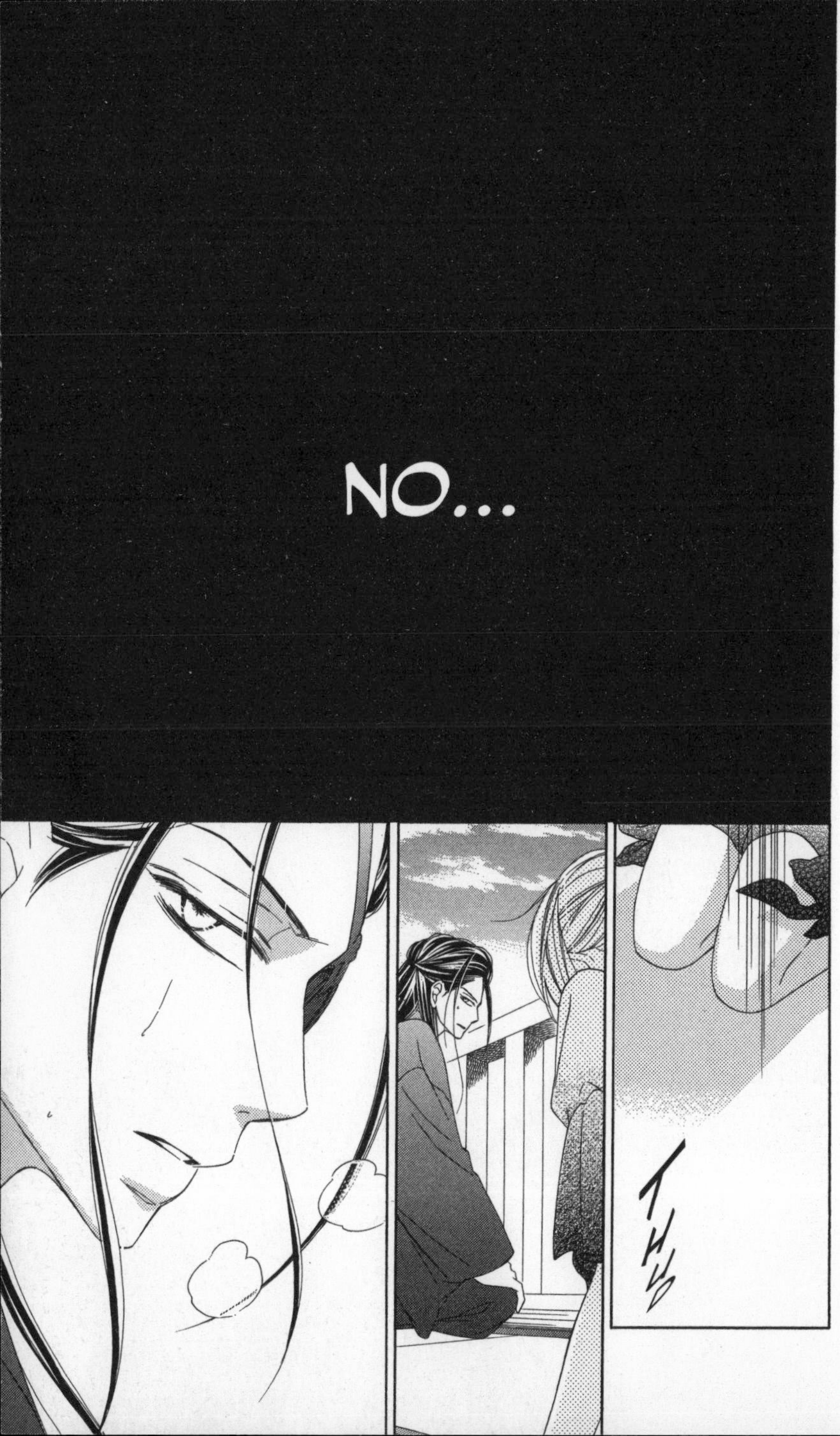
NO...
THUD

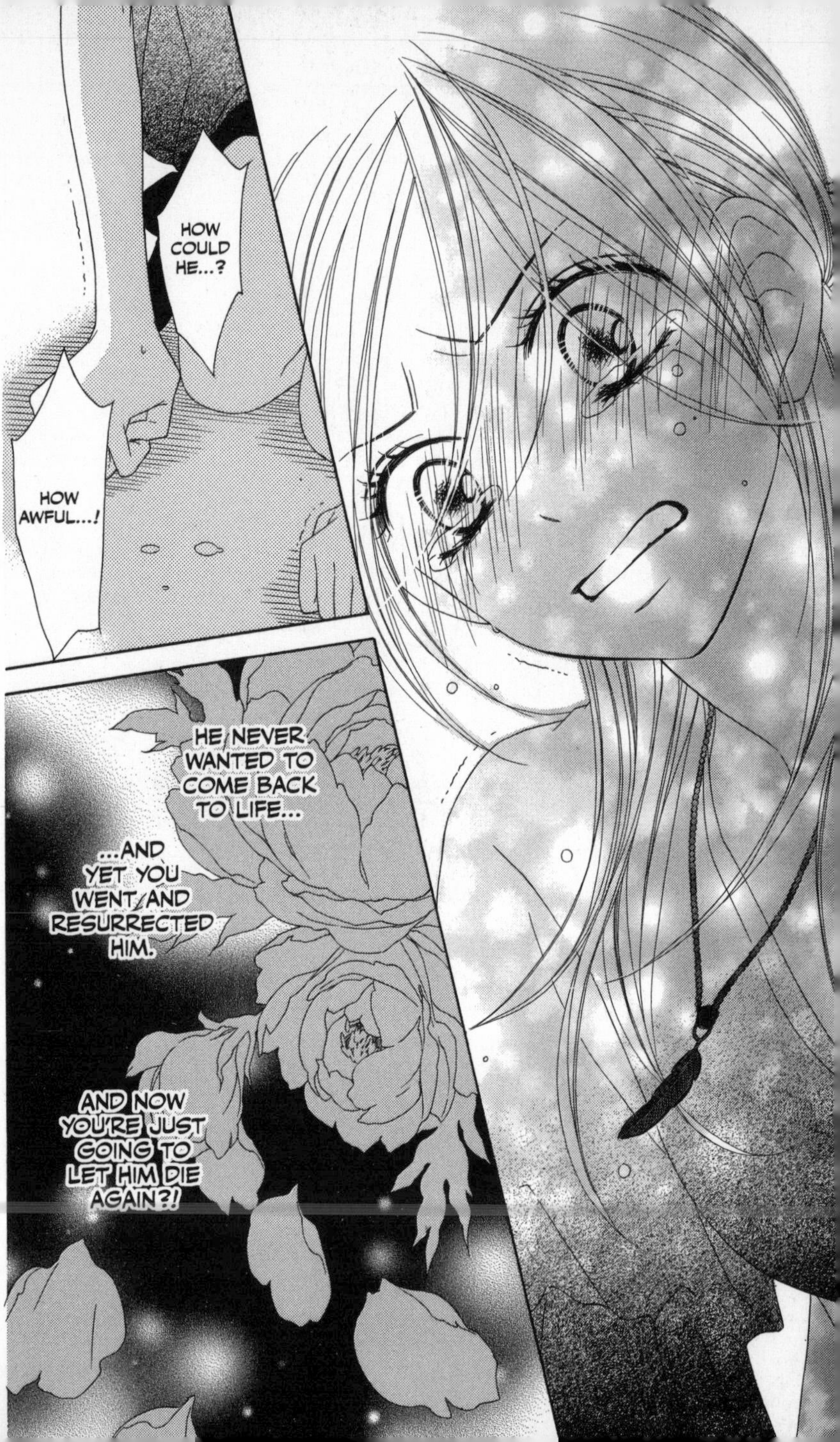
HOW COULD HE...?
HOW AWFUL...!
HE NEVER WANTED TO COME BACK TO LIFE...
...AND YET YOU WENT AND RESURRECTED HIM.
AND NOW YOU'RE JUST GOING TO LET HIM DIE AGAIN?!

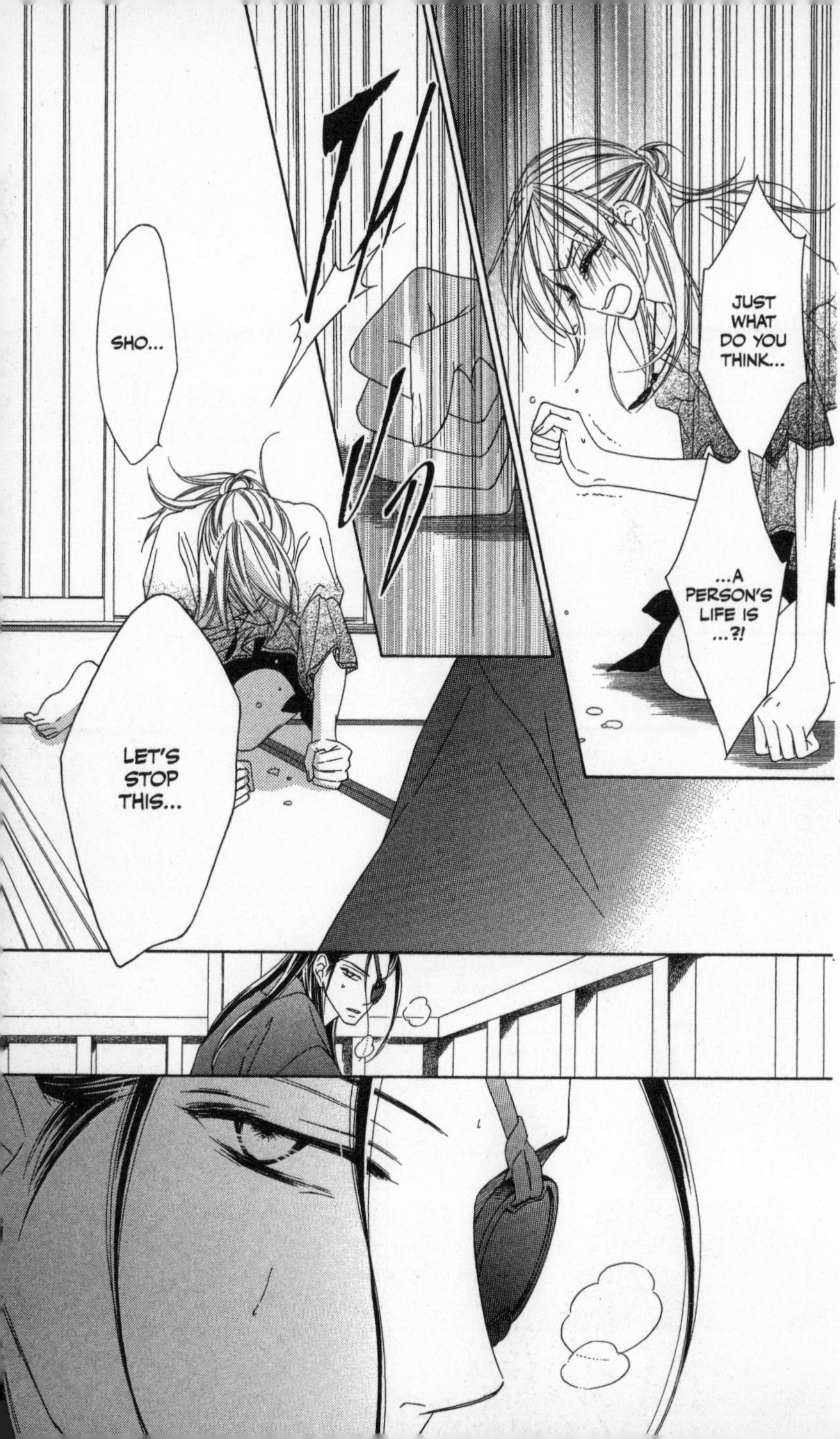
JUST WHAT DO YOU THINK...
...A PERSON'S LIFE IS ...?!
SHO...
LET'S STOP THIS...

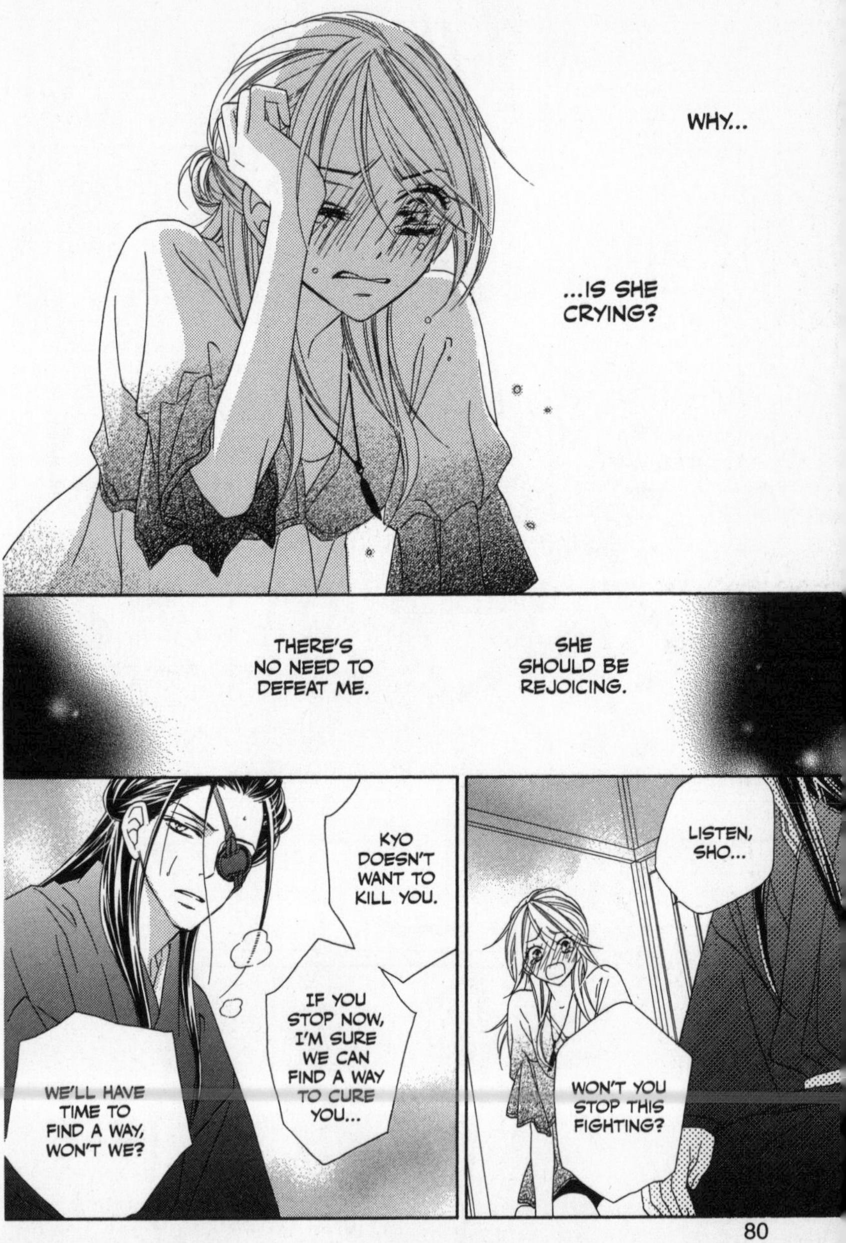
WHY...
...IS SHE CRYING?
SHE SHOULD BE REJOICING.
THERE'S NO NEED TO DEFEAT ME.
LISTEN, SHO...
WON'T YOU STOP THIS FIGHTING?
KYO DOESN'T WANT TO KILL YOU.
IF YOU STOP NOW, I'M SURE WE CAN FIND A WAY TO CURE YOU...
WE'LL HAVE TIME TO FIND A WAY, WON'T WE?

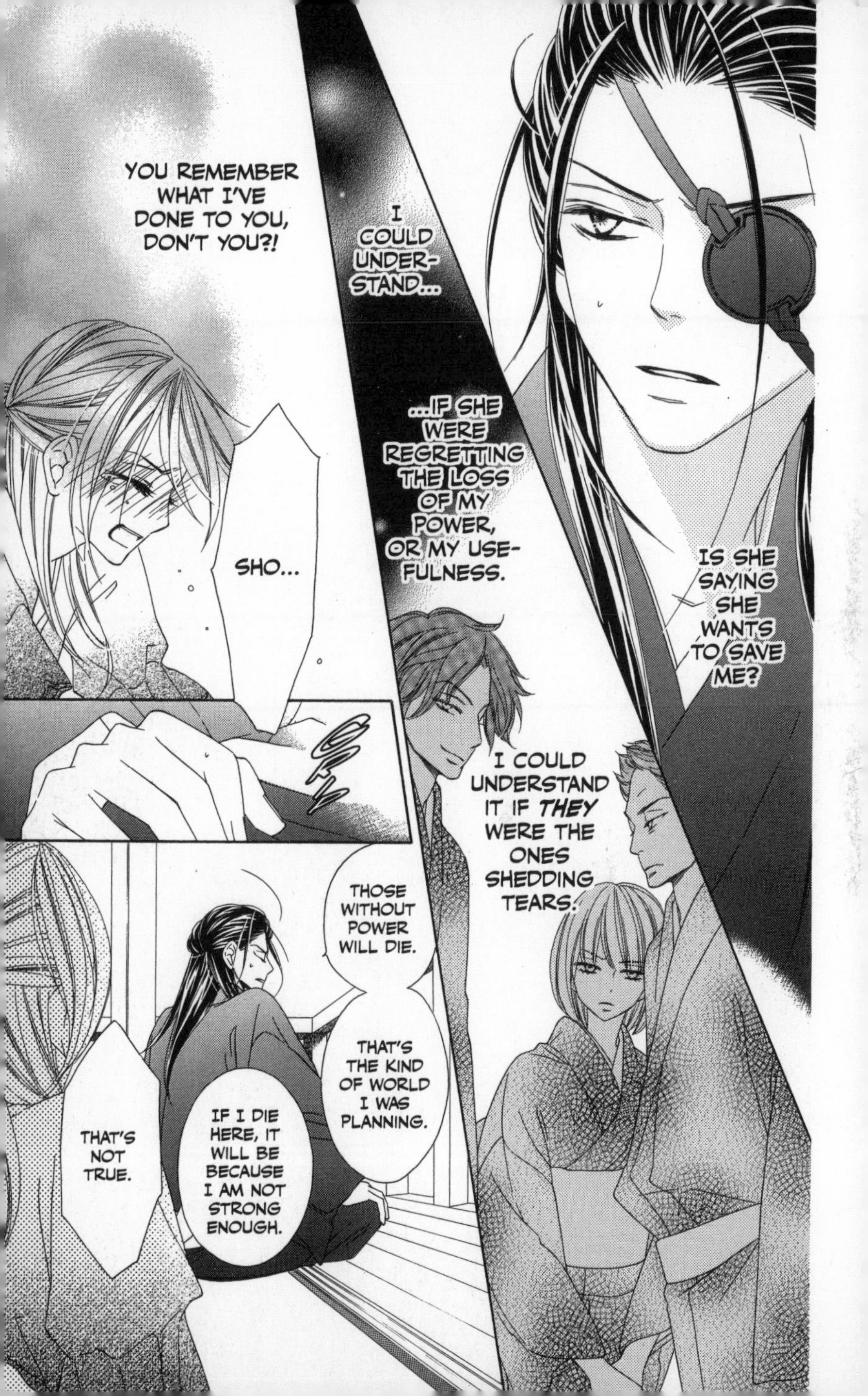
I COULD UNDERSTAND...
...IF SHE WERE REGRETTING THE LOSS OF MY POWER, OR MY USEFULNESS.
IS SHE SAYING SHE WANTS TO SAVE ME?
I COULD UNDERSTAND IT IF *THEY* WERE THE ONES SHEDDING TEARS.
YOU REMEMBER WHAT I'VE DONE TO YOU, DON'T YOU?!
SHO...
THOSE WITHOUT POWER WILL DIE.
THAT'S THE KIND OF WORLD I WAS PLANNING.
IF I DIE HERE, IT WILL BE BECAUSE I AM NOT STRONG ENOUGH.
THAT'S NOT TRUE.

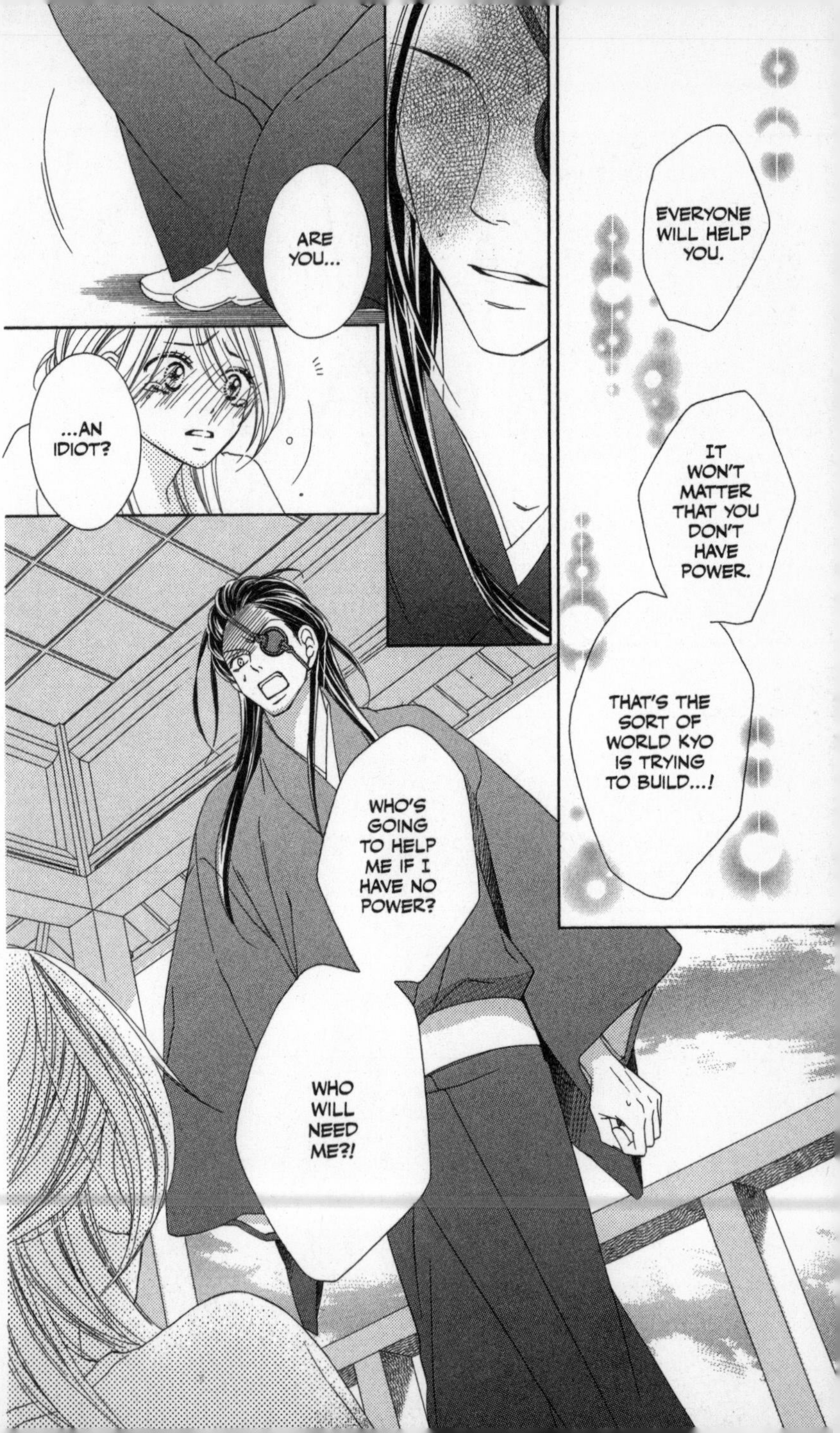
EVERYONE WILL HELP YOU.
IT WON'T MATTER THAT YOU DON'T HAVE POWER.
THAT'S THE SORT OF WORLD KYO IS TRYING TO BUILD...!
ARE YOU...
...AN IDIOT?
WHO'S GOING TO HELP ME IF I HAVE NO POWER?
WHO WILL NEED ME?!

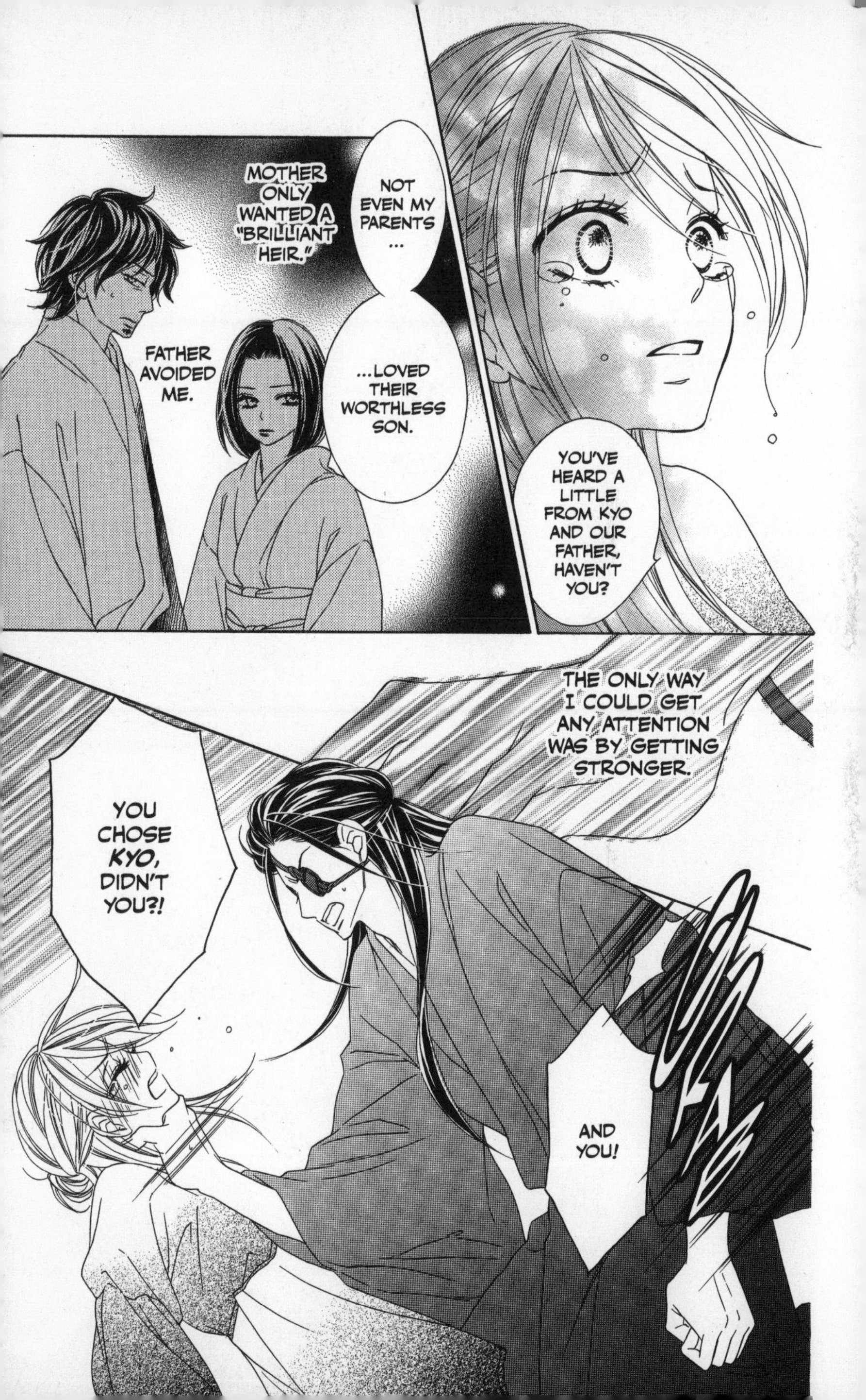

YOU'VE HEARD A LITTLE FROM KYO AND OUR FATHER, HAVEN'T YOU?
NOT EVEN MY PARENTS ...
...LOVED THEIR WORTHLESS SON.
MOTHER ONLY WANTED A "BRILLIANT HEIR."
FATHER AVOIDED ME.
THE ONLY WAY I COULD GET ANY ATTENTION WAS BY GETTING STRONGER.
AND YOU!
YOU CHOSE *KYO*, DIDN'T YOU?!

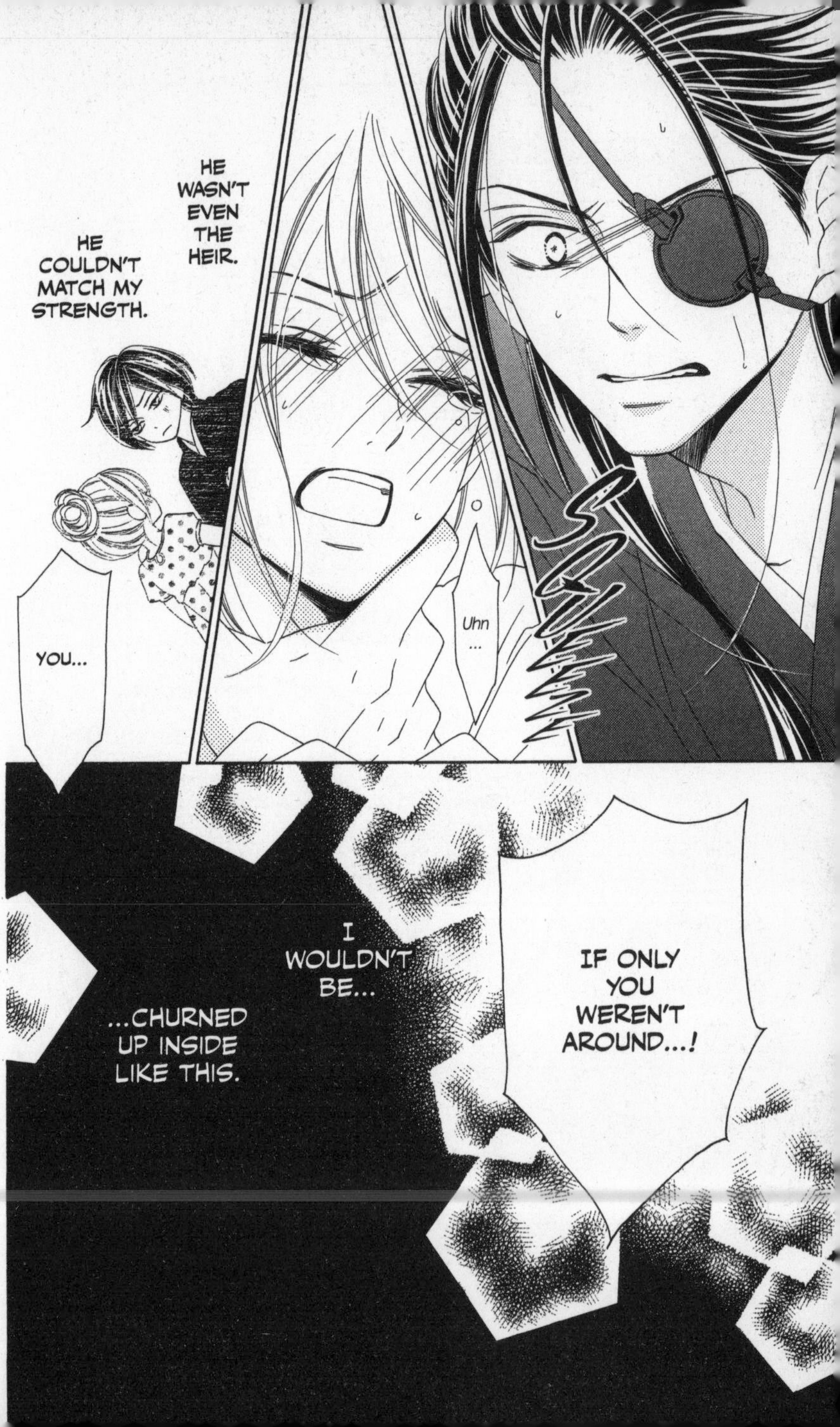
Uhn
...
HE WASN'T EVEN THE HEIR.
HE COULDN'T MATCH MY STRENGTH.
YOU...
IF ONLY YOU WEREN'T AROUND...!
I WOULDN'T BE...
...CHURNED UP INSIDE LIKE THIS.

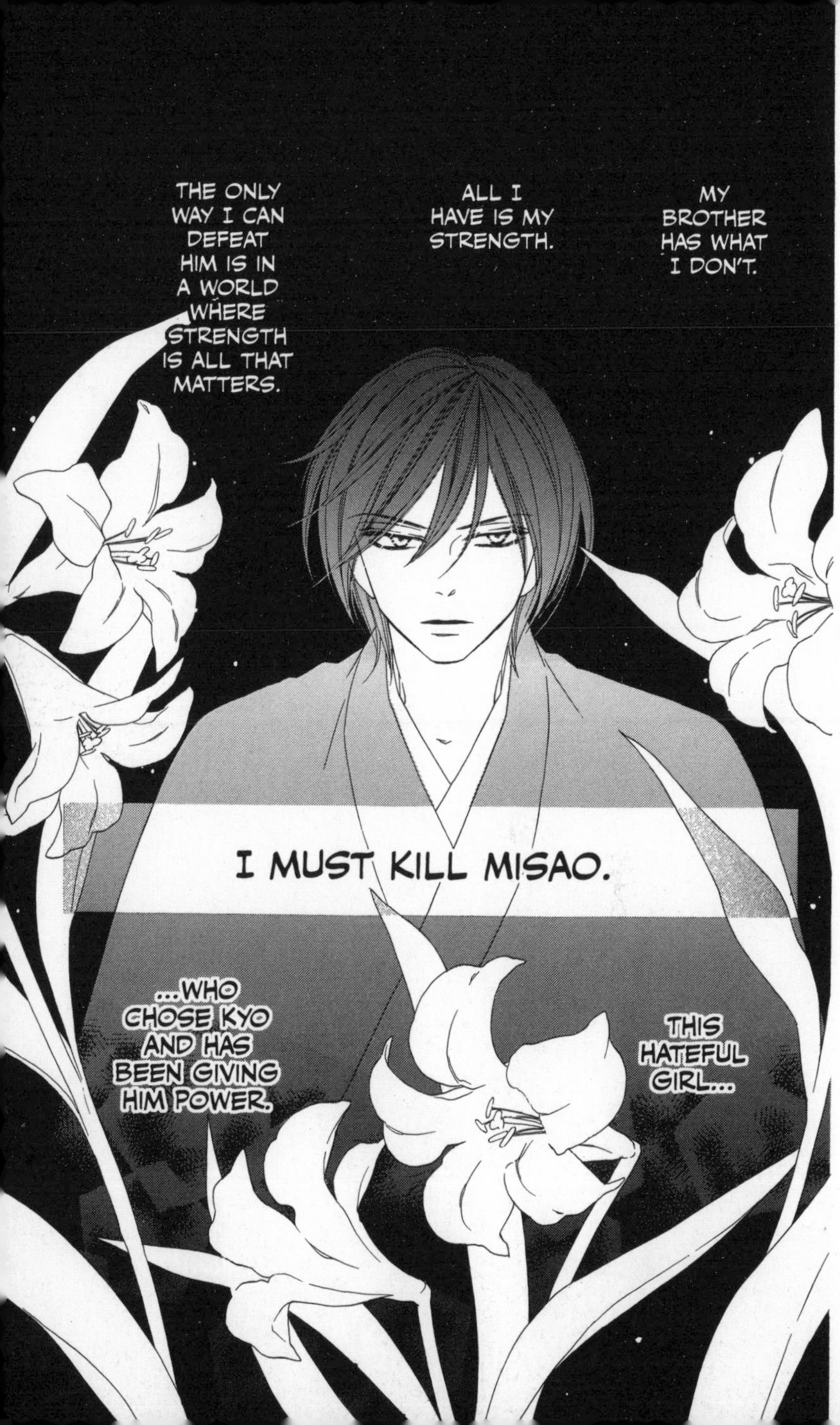
MY BROTHER HAS WHAT I DON'T.
ALL I HAVE IS MY STRENGTH.
THE ONLY WAY I CAN DEFEAT HIM IS IN A WORLD WHERE STRENGTH IS ALL THAT MATTERS.
I MUST KILL MISAO.
THIS HATEFUL GIRL...
...WHO CHOSE KYO AND HAS BEEN GIVING HIM POWER.

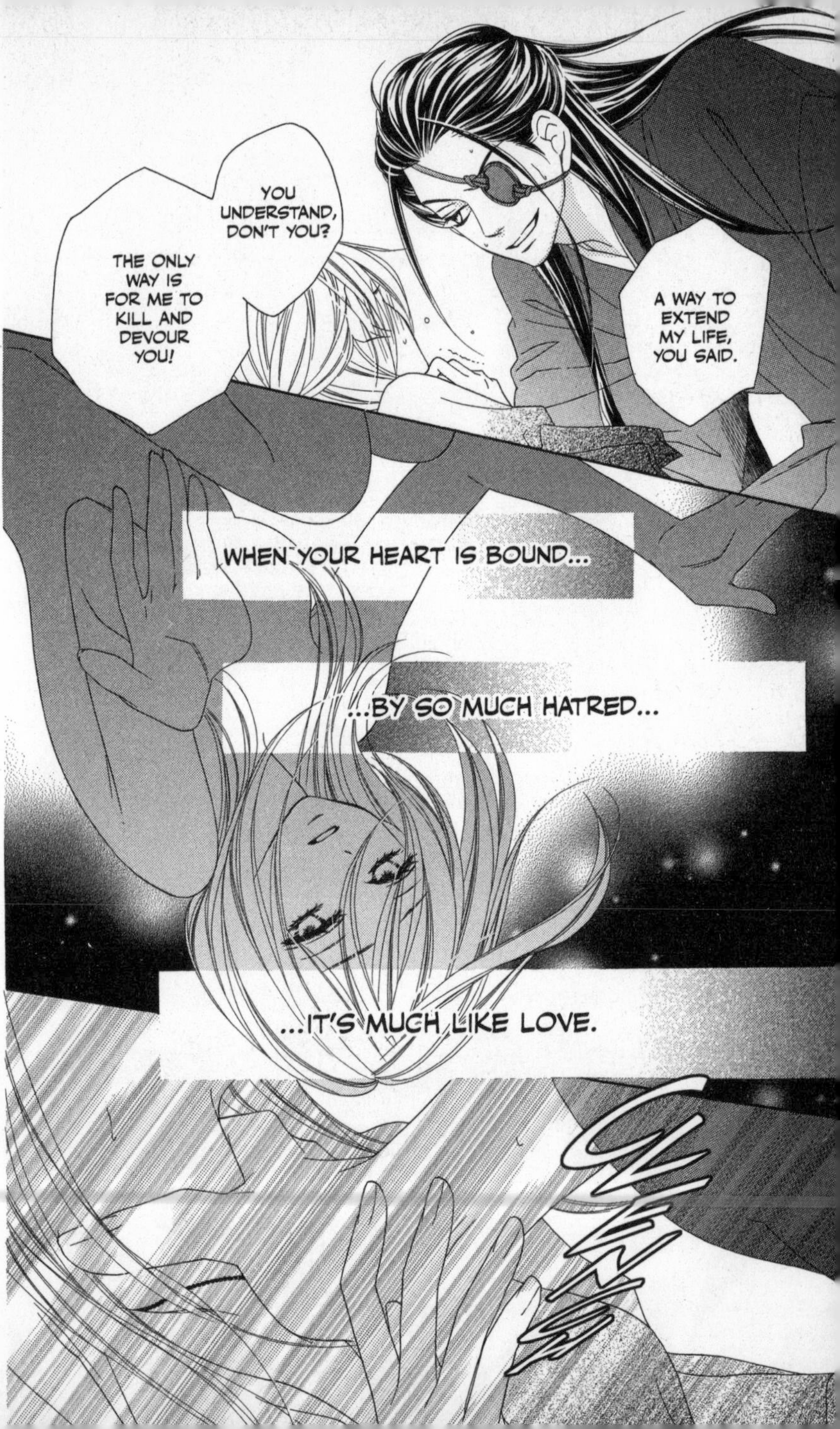
A WAY TO EXTEND MY LIFE, YOU SAID.
YOU UNDERSTAND, DON'T YOU?
THE ONLY WAY IS FOR ME TO KILL AND DEVOUR YOU!
WHEN YOUR HEART IS BOUND...
...BY SO MUCH HATRED...
...IT'S MUCH LIKE LOVE.

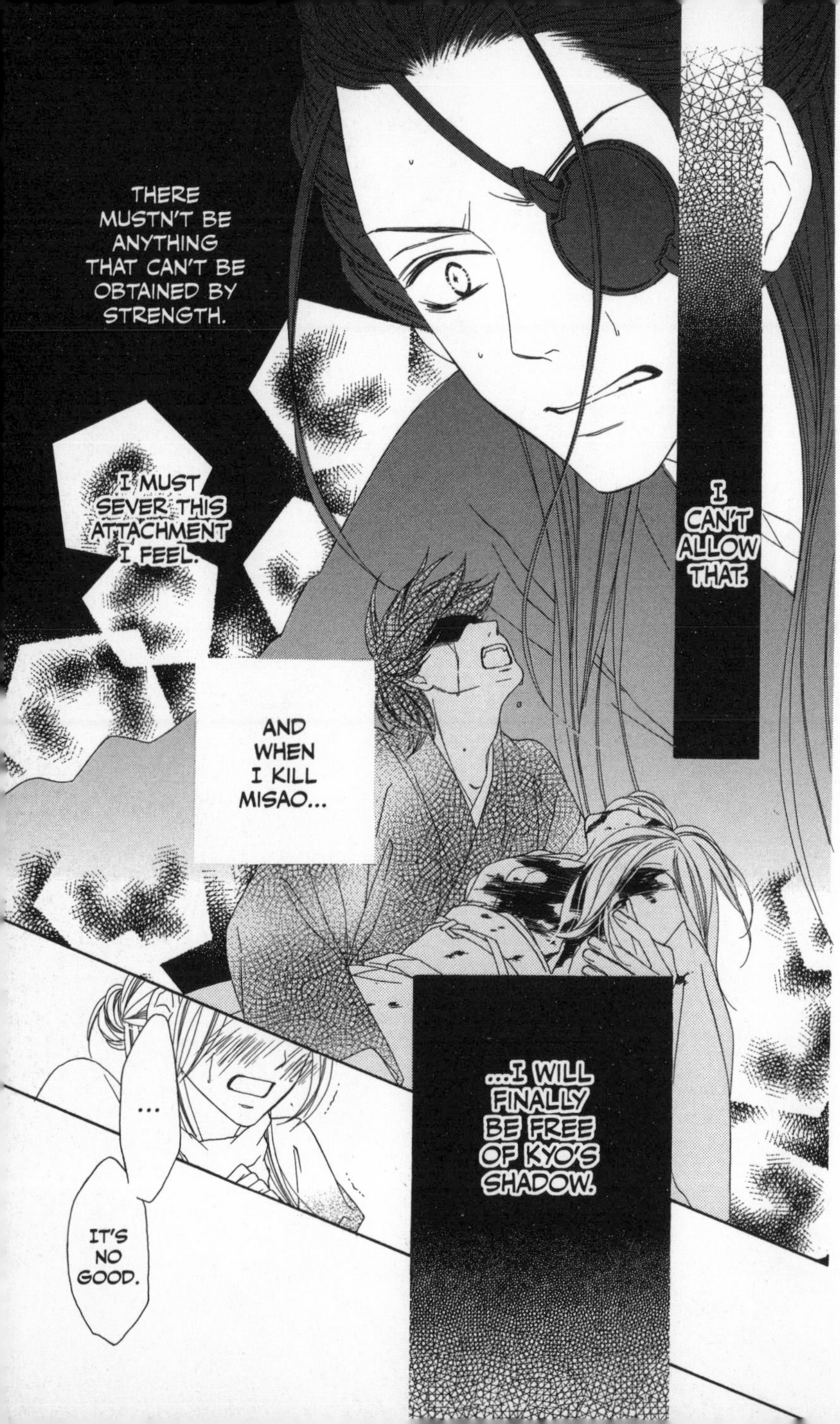
THERE MUSTN'T BE ANYTHING THAT CAN'T BE OBTAINED BY STRENGTH.
I MUST SEVER THIS ATTACHMENT I FEEL.
I CAN'T ALLOW THAT.
AND WHEN I KILL MISAO...
...I WILL FINALLY BE FREE OF KYO'S SHADOW.
...
IT'S NO GOOD.

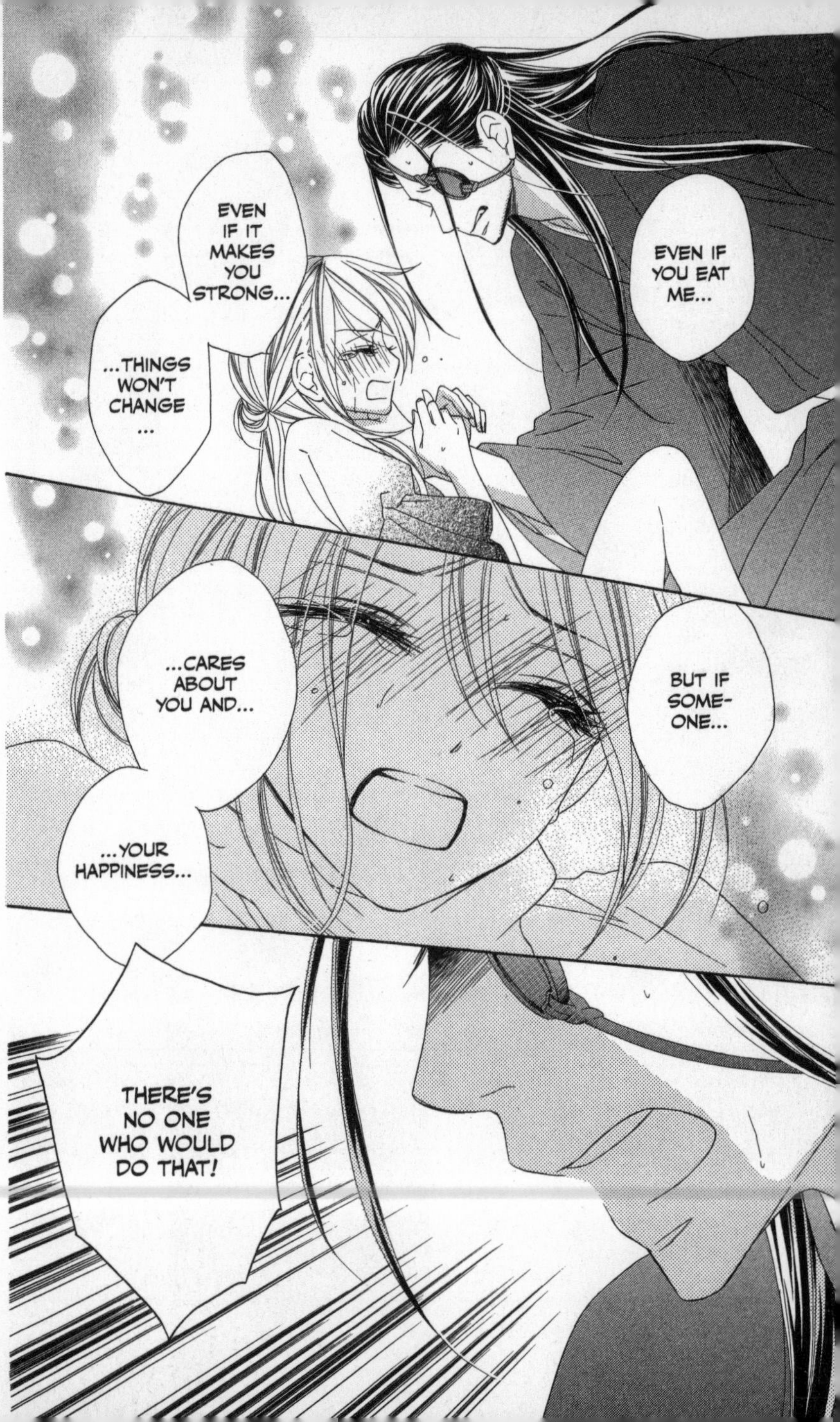
EVEN IF YOU EAT ME...
EVEN IF IT MAKES YOU STRONG...
...THINGS WON'T CHANGE ...
BUT IF SOME-ONE...
...CARES ABOUT YOU AND...
...YOUR HAPPINESS...
THERE'S NO ONE WHO WOULD DO THAT!

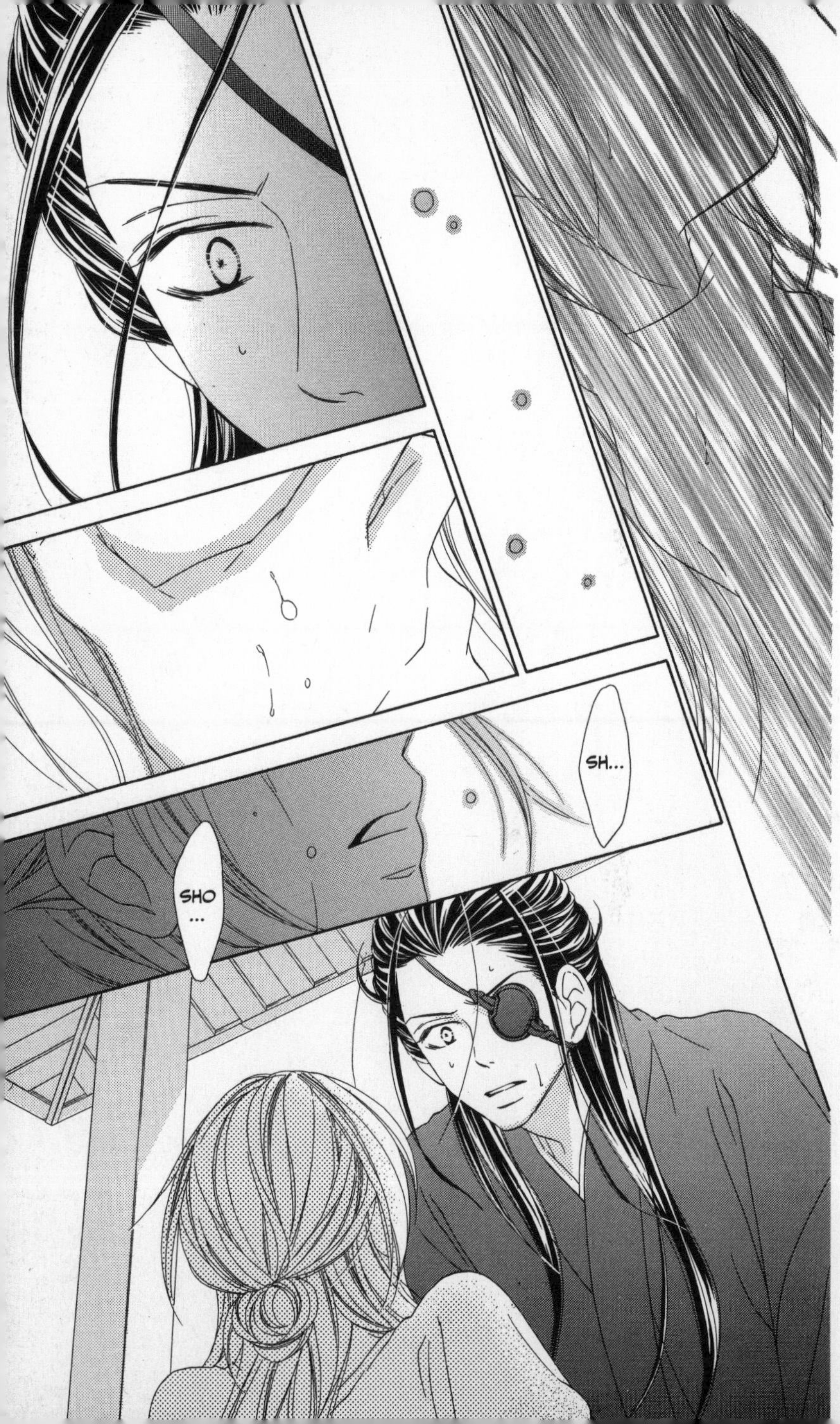
SH...
SHO ...

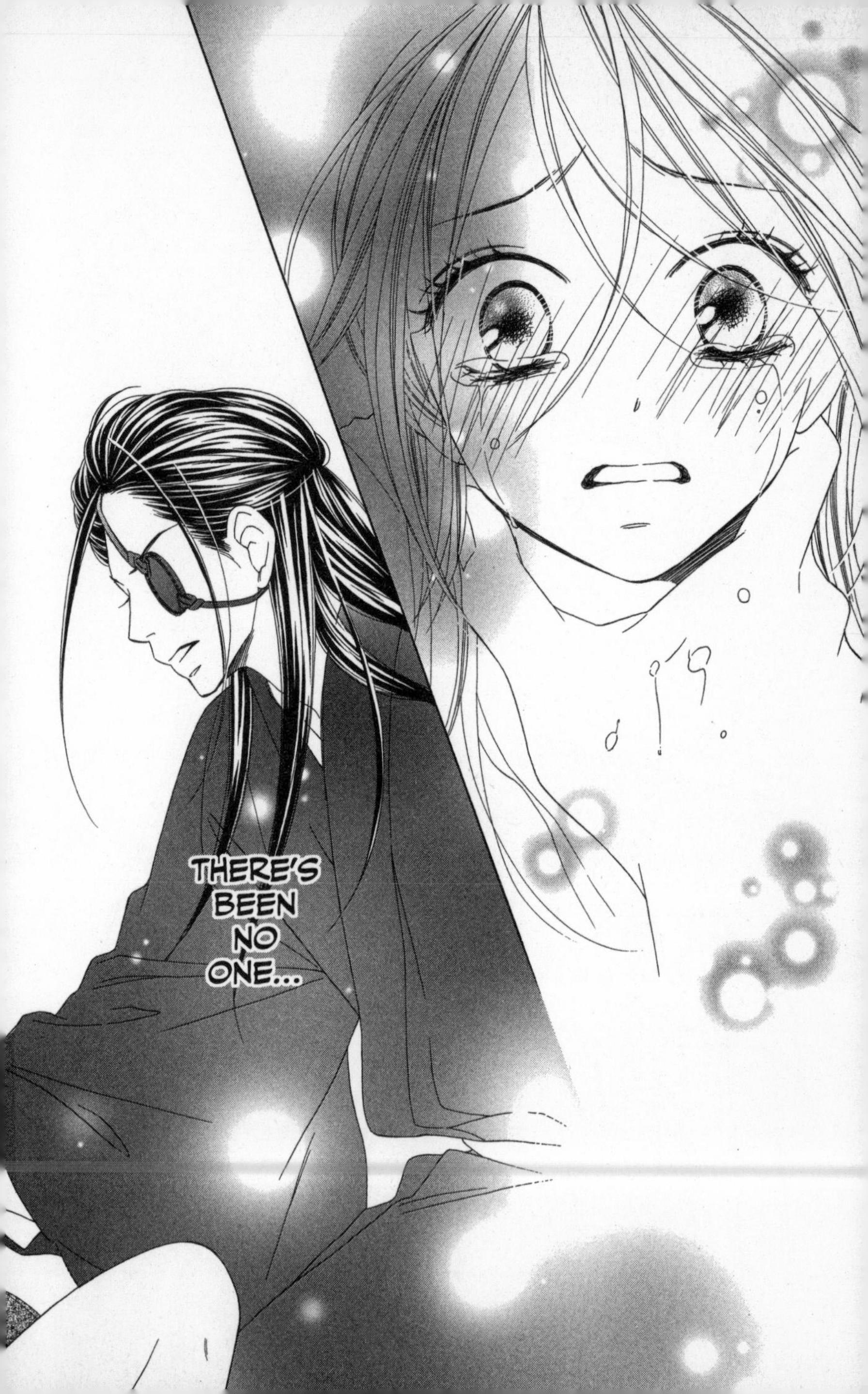
THERE'S BEEN NO ONE...

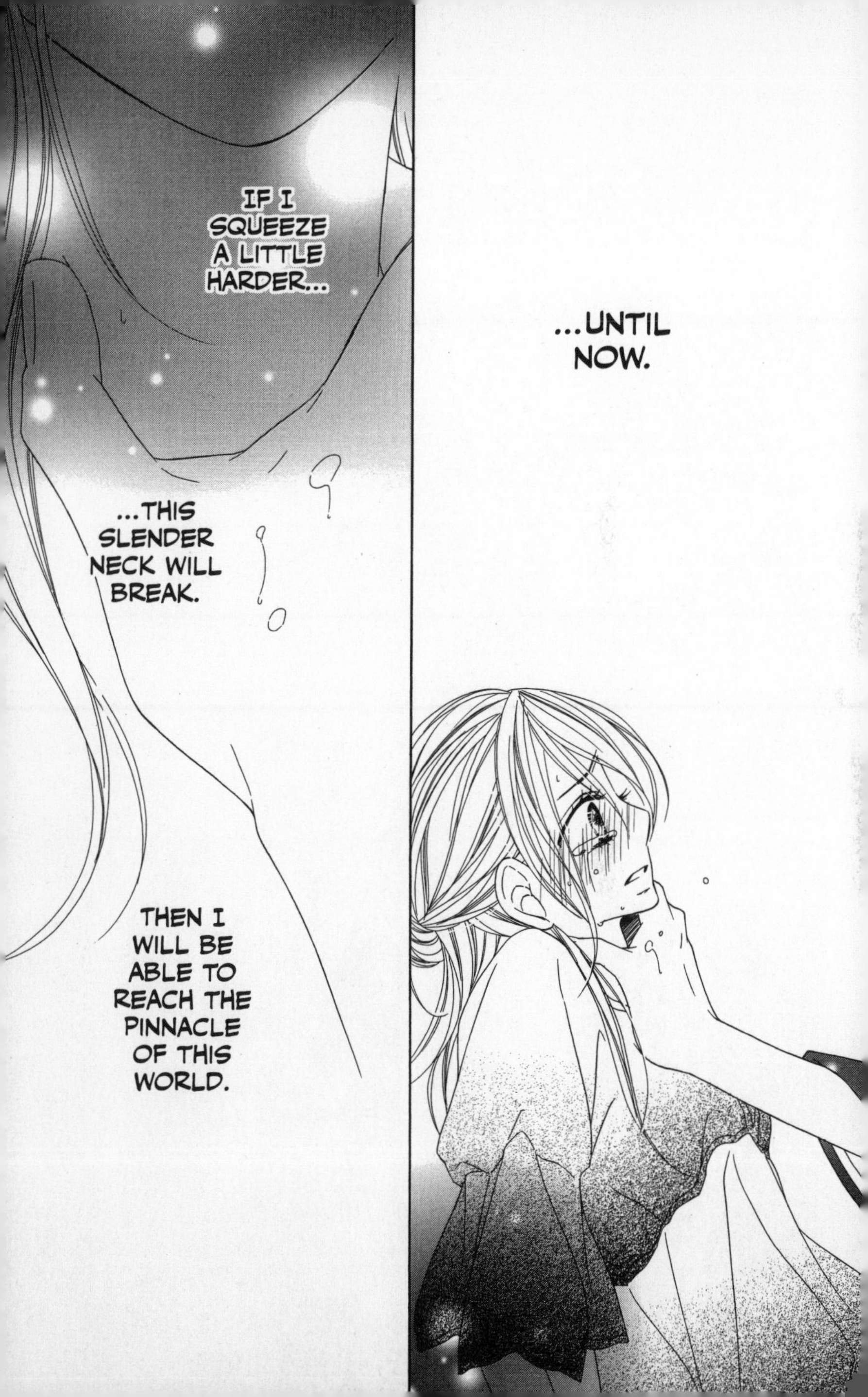
...UNTIL NOW.
IF I SQUEEZE A LITTLE HARDER...
...THIS SLENDER NECK WILL BREAK.
THEN I WILL BE ABLE TO REACH THE PINNACLE OF THIS WORLD.

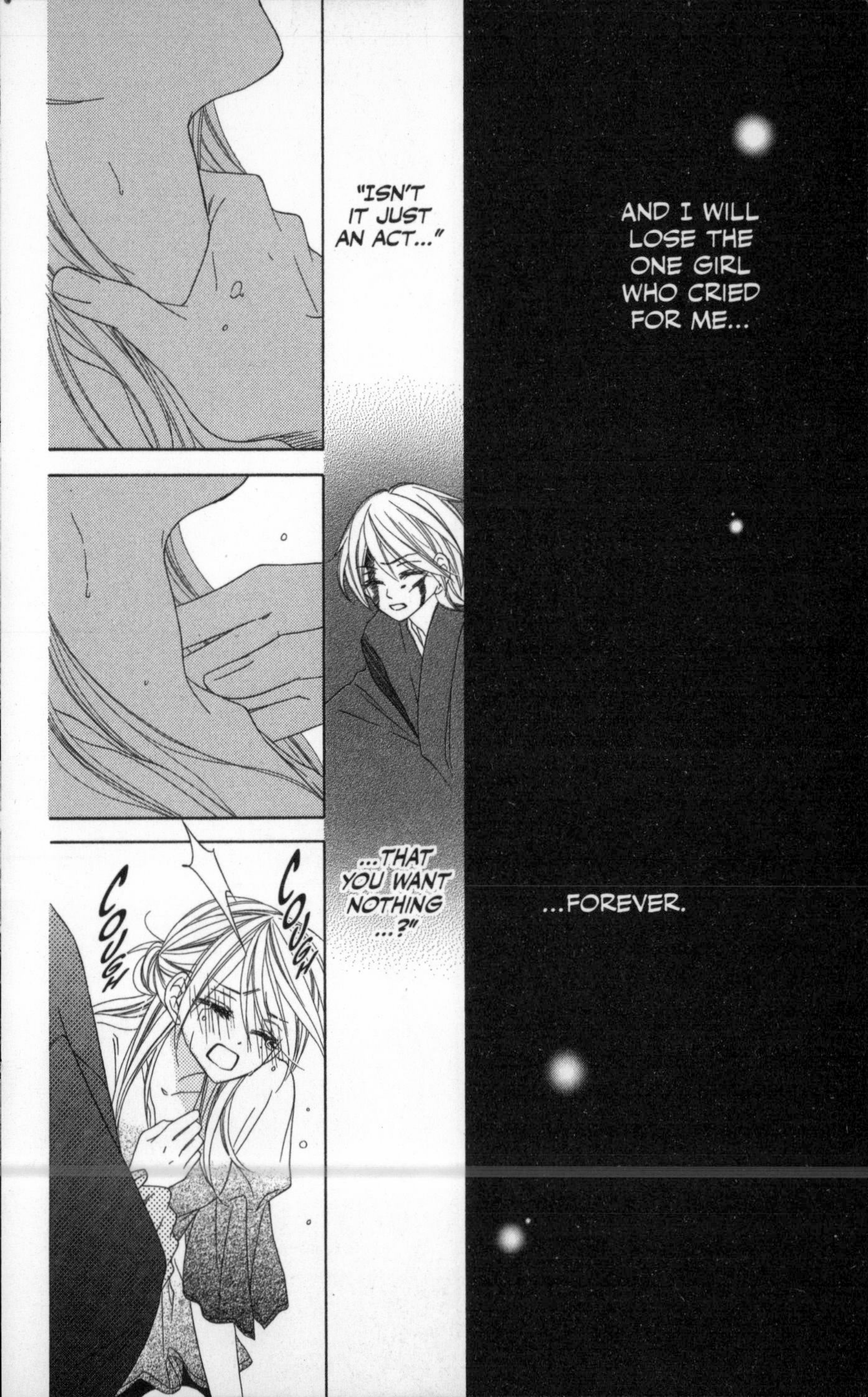
AND I WILL LOSE THE ONE GIRL WHO CRIED FOR ME...
...FOREVER.
"ISN'T IT JUST AN ACT..."
...THAT YOU WANT NOTHING ...?"
COUGH
COUGH

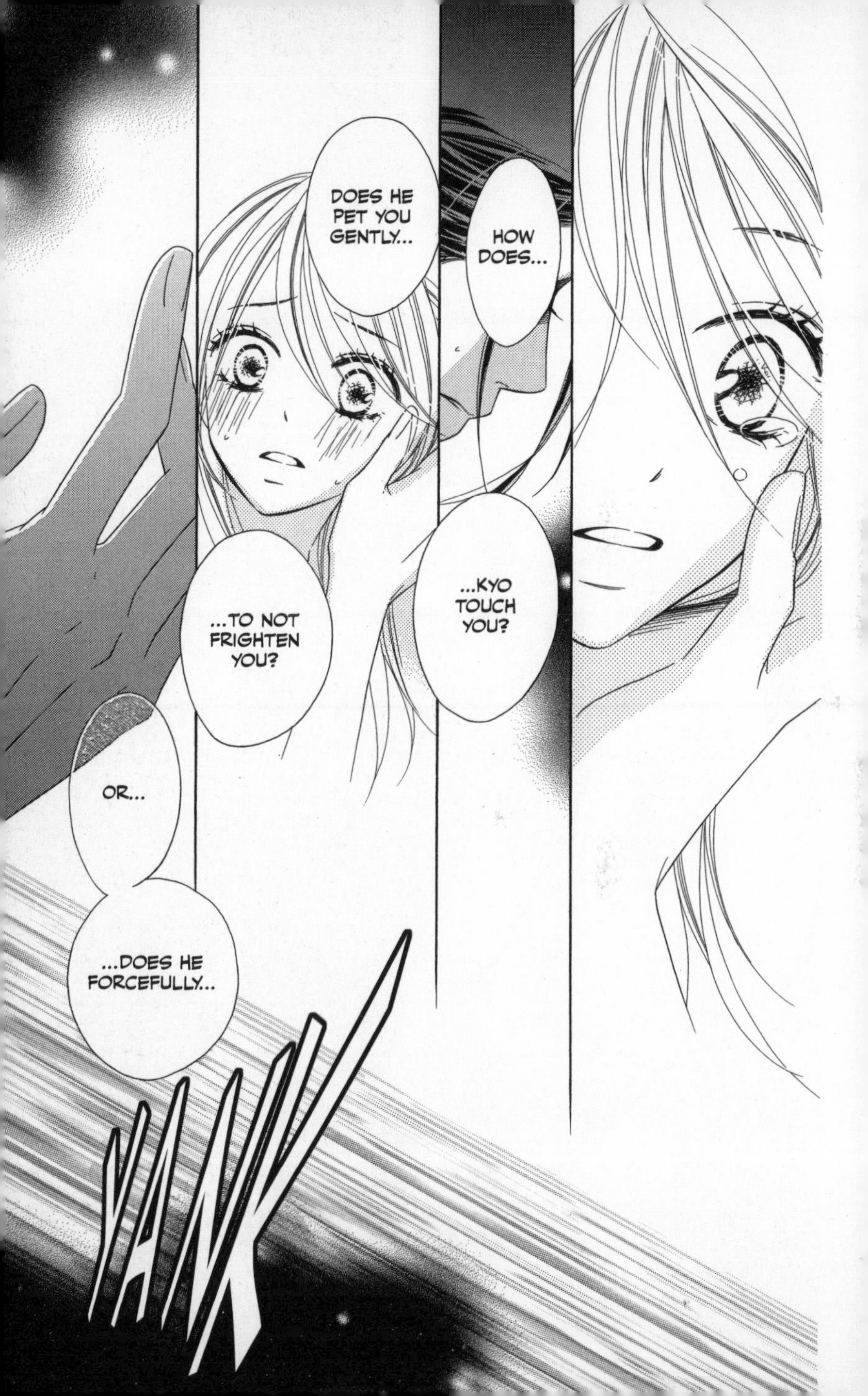
HOW DOES...
...KYO TOUCH YOU?
DOES HE PET YOU GENTLY...
...TO NOT FRIGHTEN YOU?
OR...
...DOES HE FORCEFULLY...
YANK

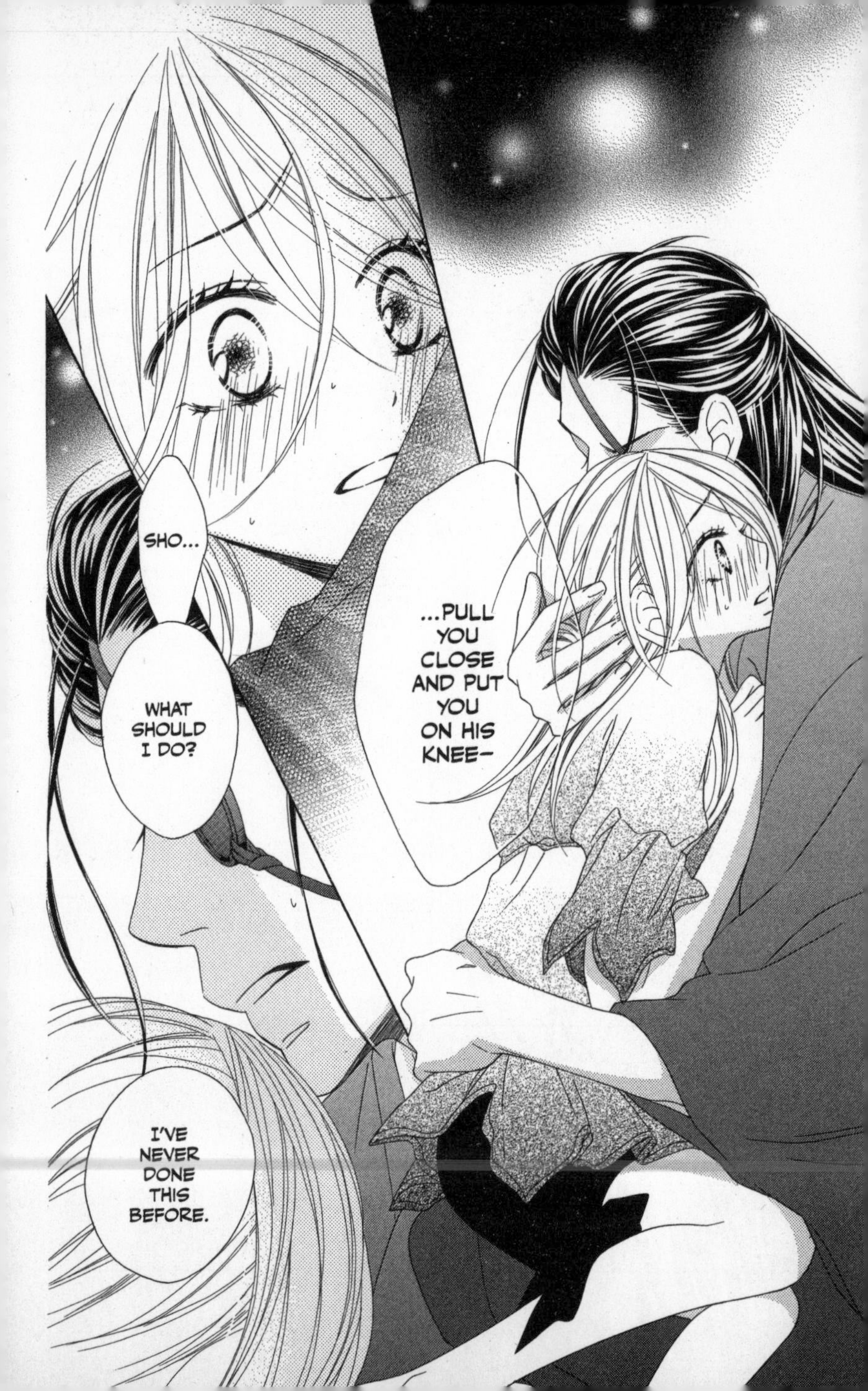
...PULL YOU CLOSE AND PUT YOU ON HIS KNEE–
SHO...
WHAT SHOULD I DO?
I'VE NEVER DONE THIS BEFORE.

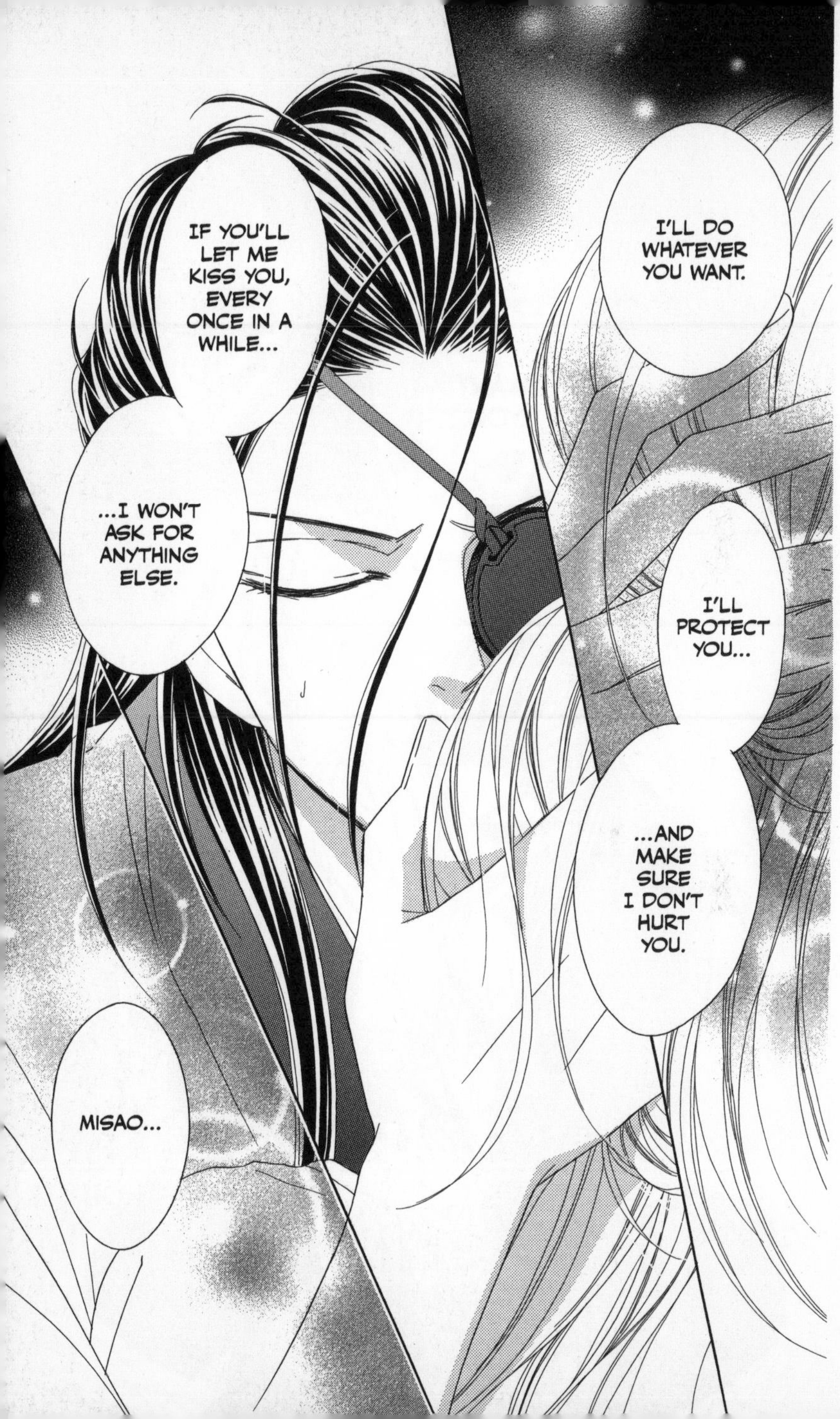
I'LL DO WHATEVER YOU WANT.
I'LL PROTECT YOU...
...AND MAKE SURE I DON'T HURT YOU.
IF YOU'LL LET ME KISS YOU, EVERY ONCE IN A WHILE...
...I WON'T ASK FOR ANYTHING ELSE.
MISAO...

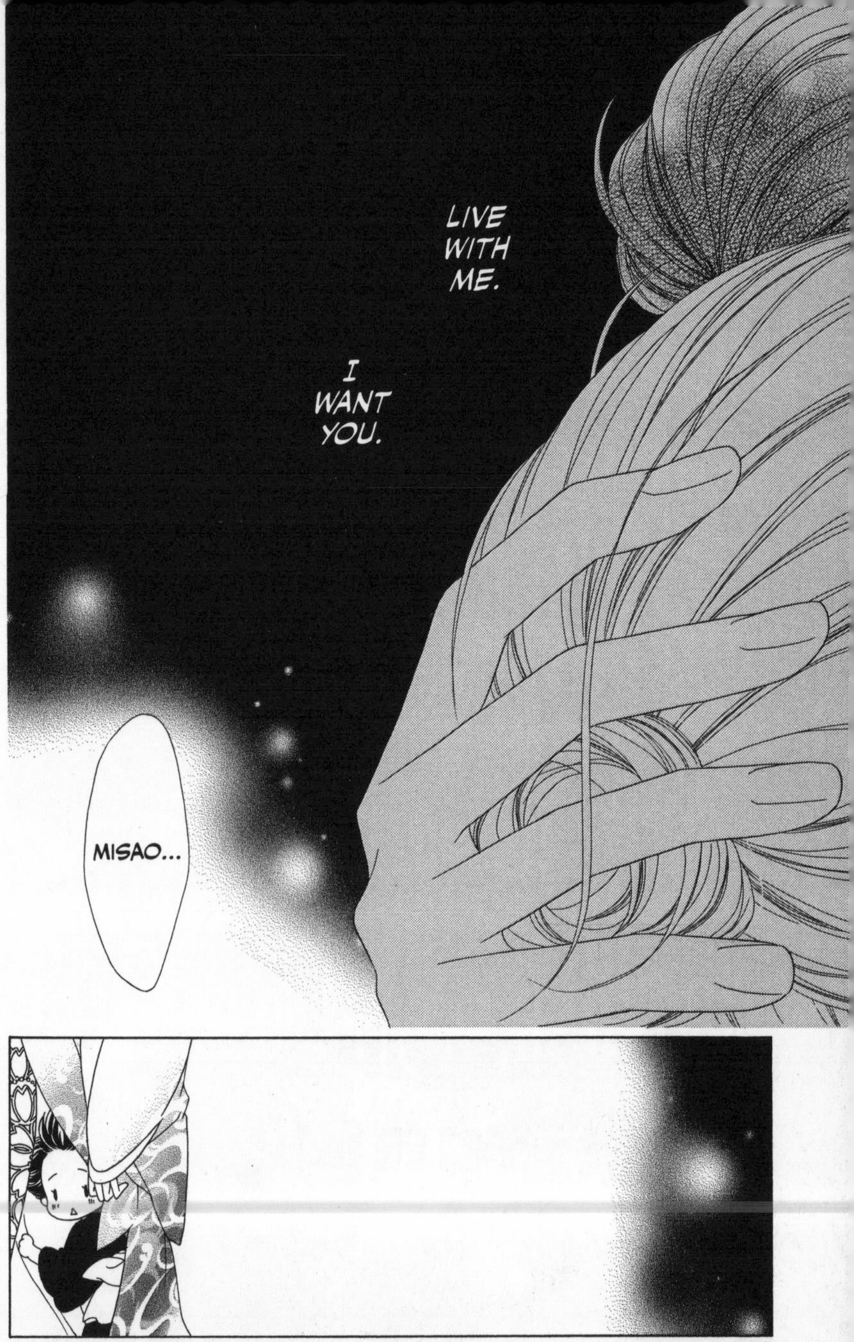
LIVE WITH ME.
I WANT YOU.
MISAO...

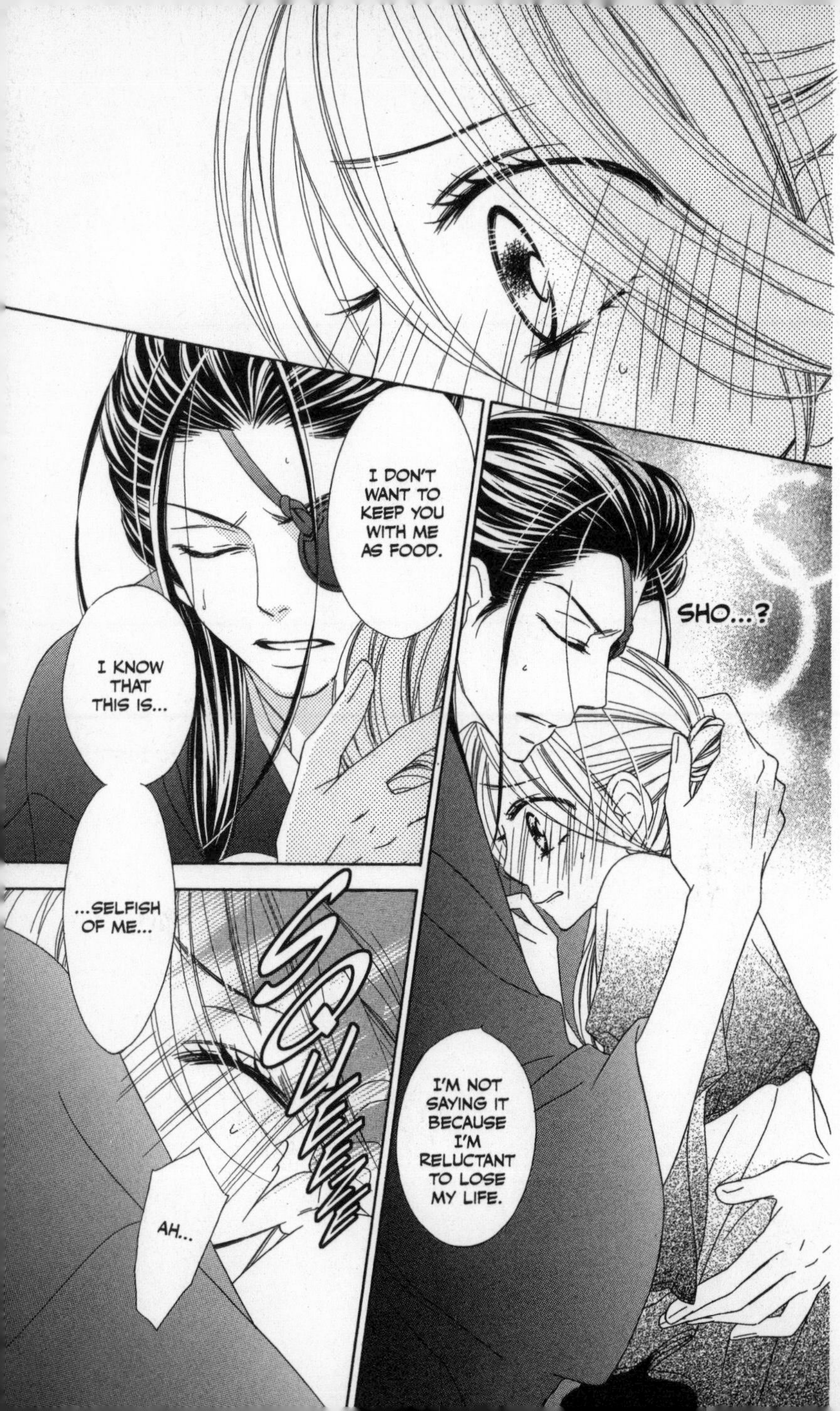
SHO...?
I'M NOT SAYING IT BECAUSE I'M RELUCTANT TO LOSE MY LIFE.
I DON'T WANT TO KEEP YOU WITH ME AS FOOD.
I KNOW THAT THIS IS...
...SELFISH OF ME...
AH...

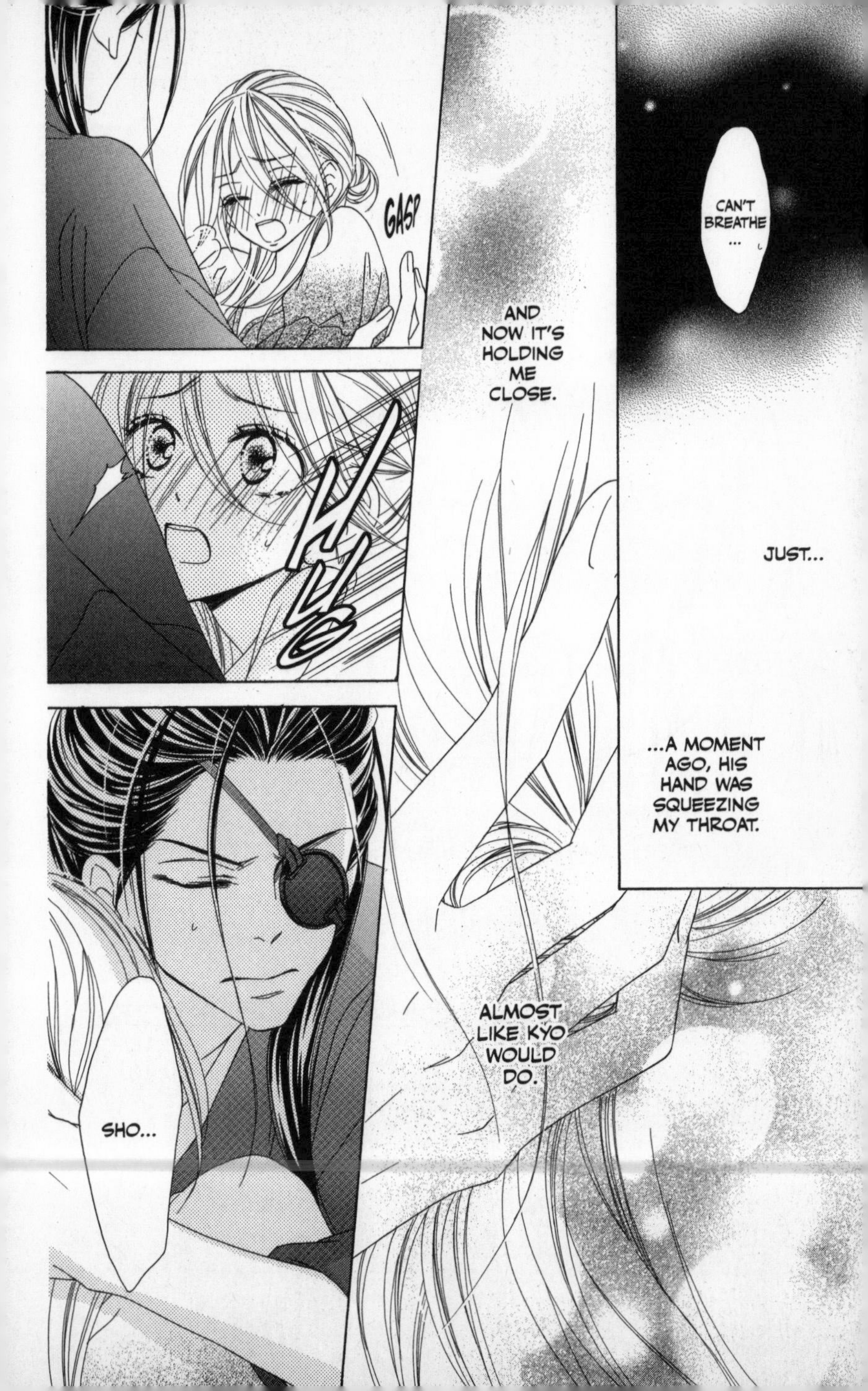
CAN'T BREATHE ...
JUST...
...A MOMENT AGO, HIS HAND WAS SQUEEZING MY THROAT.
AND NOW IT'S HOLDING ME CLOSE.
GASP
ALMOST LIKE KYO WOULD DO.
SHO...

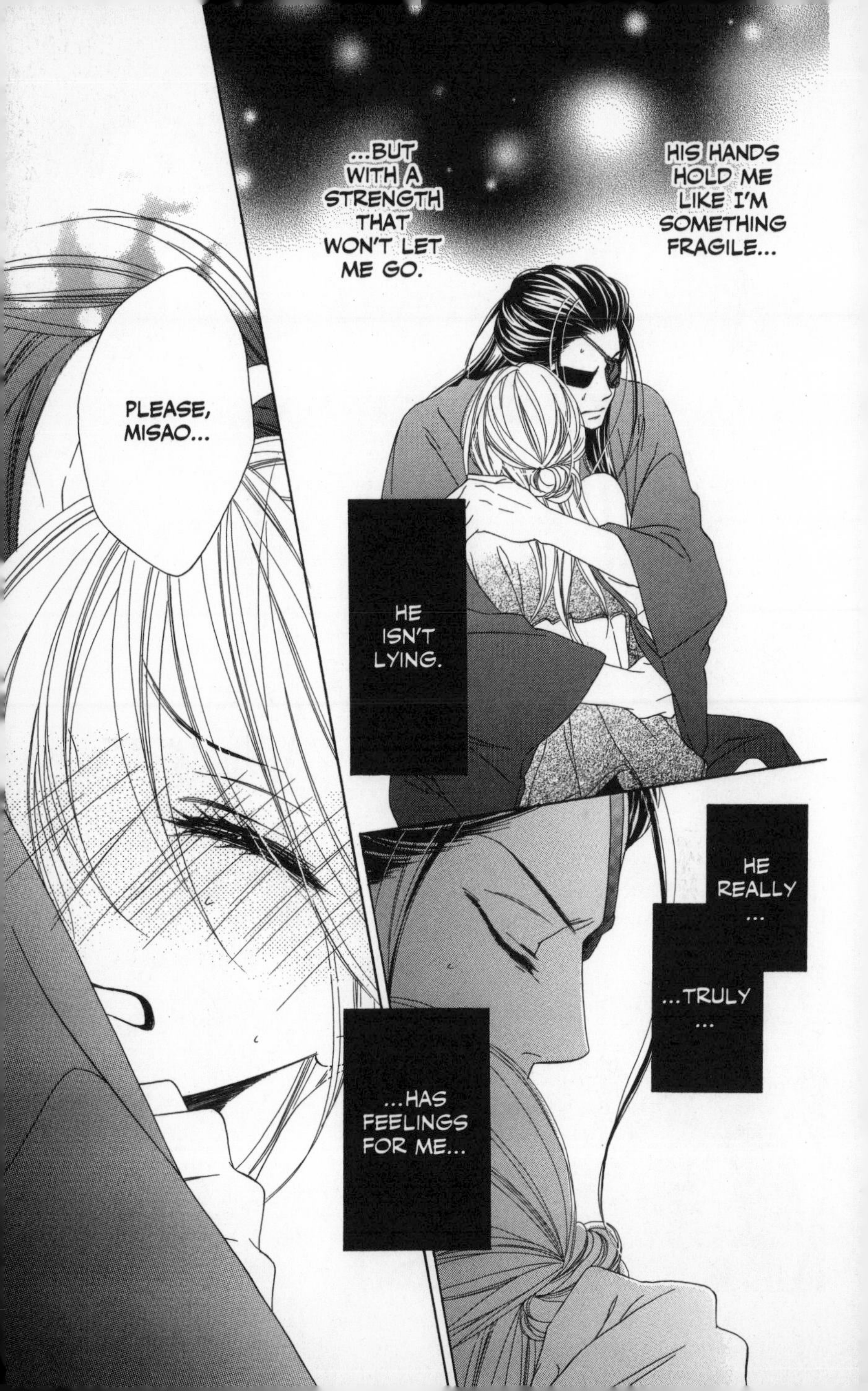
HIS HANDS HOLD ME LIKE I'M SOMETHING FRAGILE...
...BUT WITH A STRENGTH THAT WON'T LET ME GO.
HE ISN'T LYING.
HE REALLY ...
...TRULY ...
...HAS FEELINGS FOR ME...
PLEASE, MISAO...

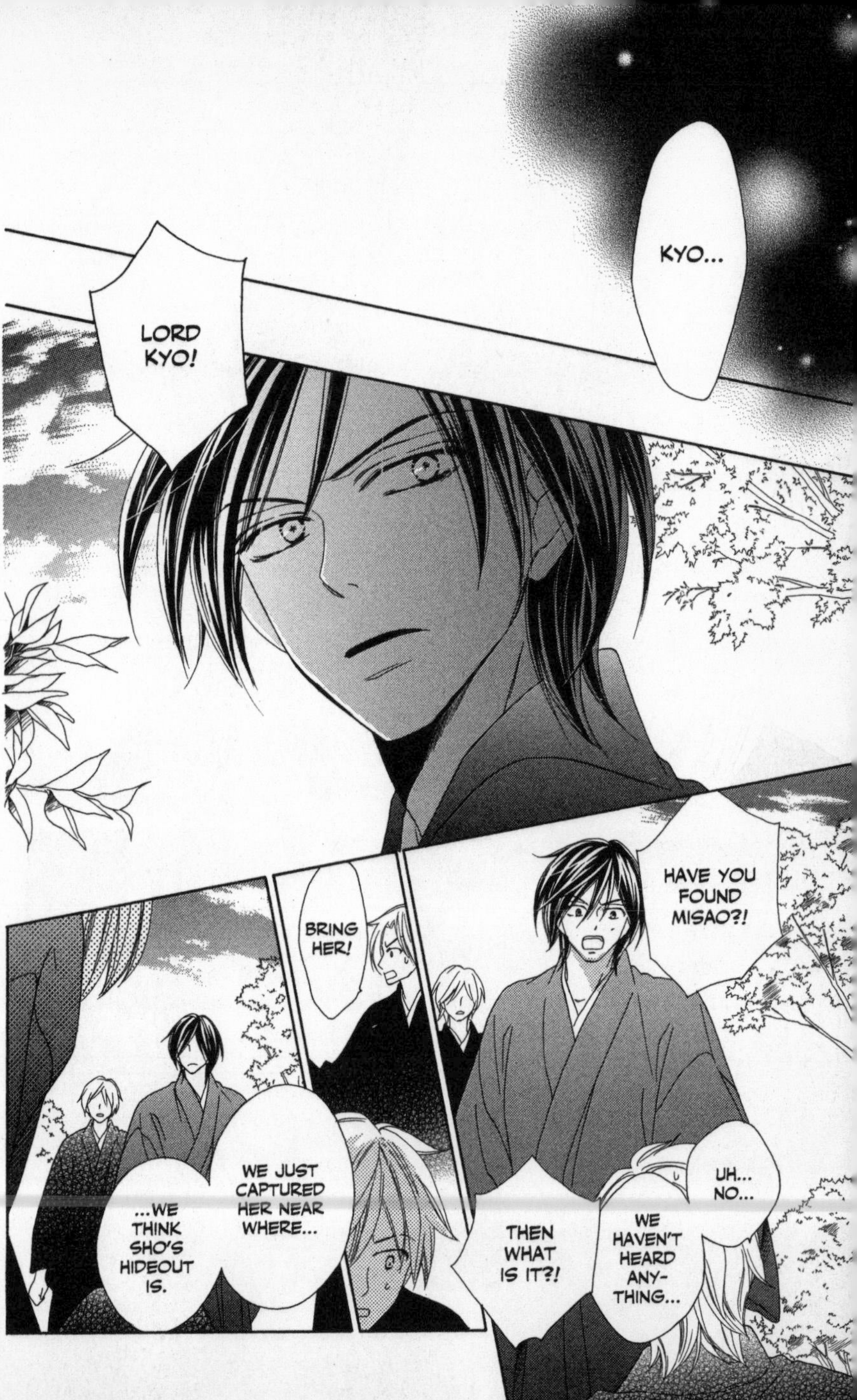
KYO...
LORD KYO!
HAVE YOU FOUND MISAO?!
UH... NO...
WE HAVEN'T HEARD ANY-THING...
THEN WHAT IS IT?!
BRING HER!
WE JUST CAPTURED HER NEAR WHERE...
...WE THINK SHO'S HIDEOUT IS.

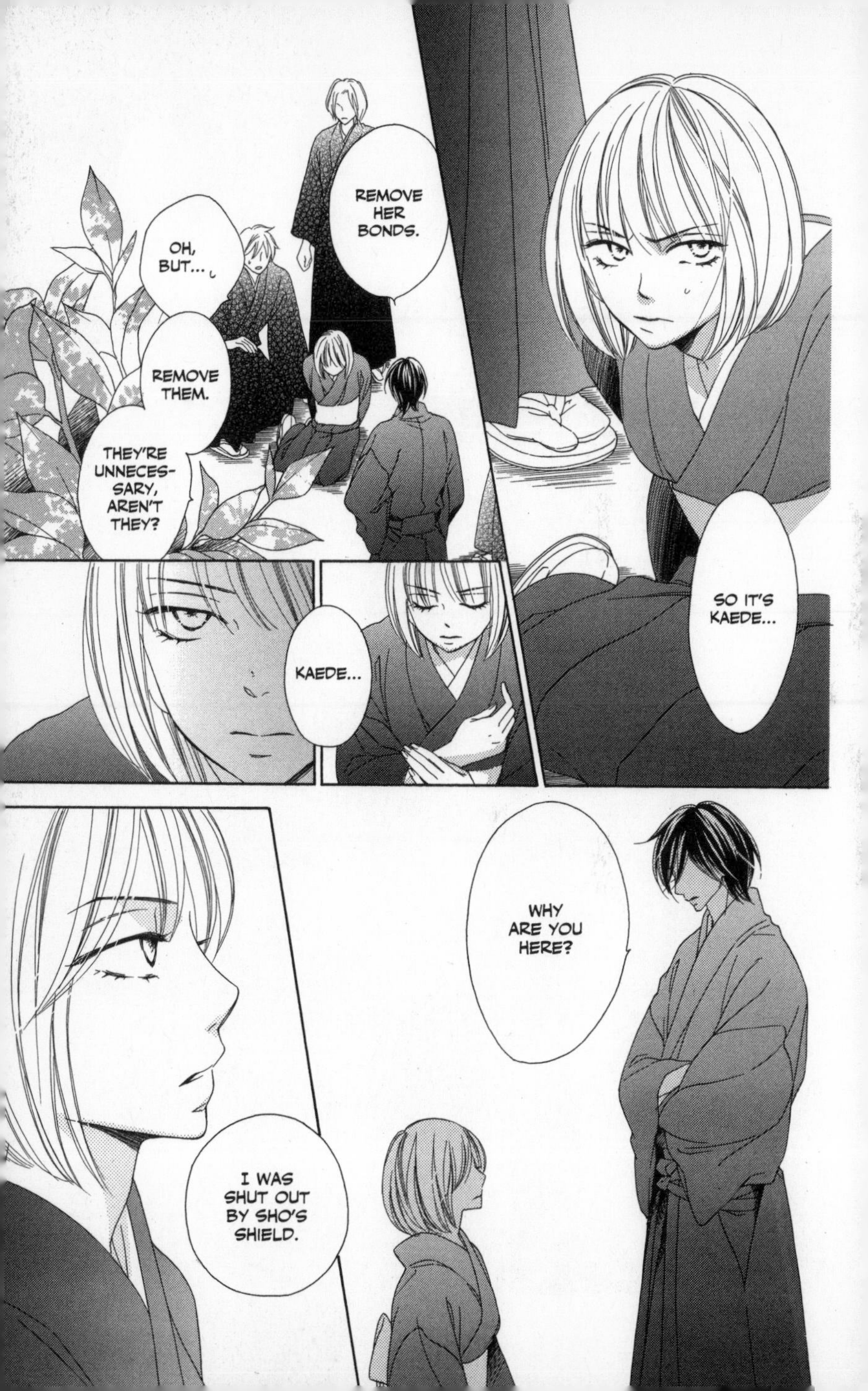
SO IT'S KAEDE...
REMOVE HER BONDS.
OH, BUT...
REMOVE THEM.
THEY'RE UNNECES-SARY, AREN'T THEY?
KAEDE...
WHY ARE YOU HERE?
I WAS SHUT OUT BY SHO'S SHIELD.

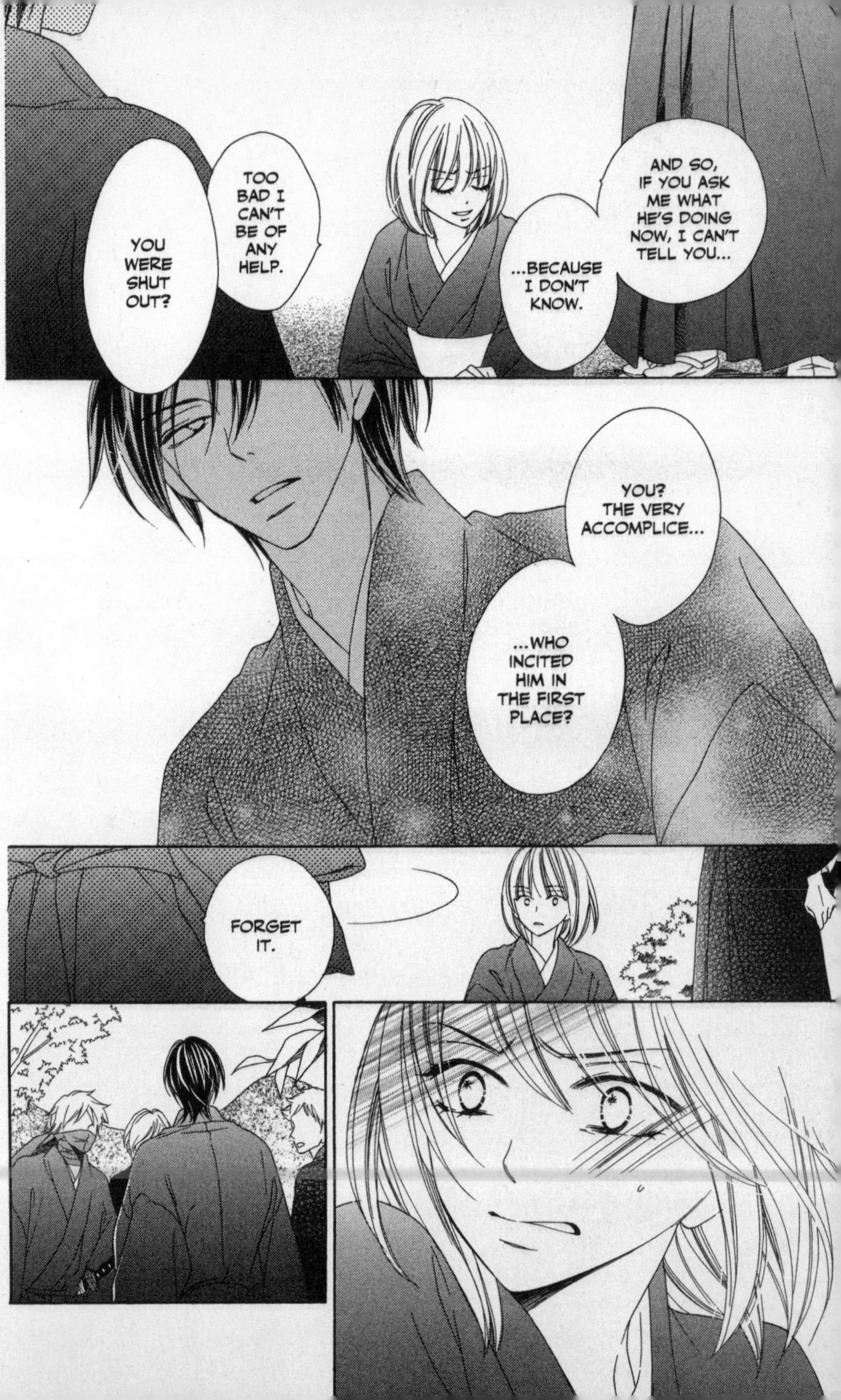
AND SO, IF YOU ASK ME WHAT HE'S DOING NOW, I CAN'T TELL YOU...
...BECAUSE I DON'T KNOW.
TOO BAD I CAN'T BE OF ANY HELP.
YOU WERE SHUT OUT?
YOU? THE VERY ACCOMPLICE...
...WHO INCITED HIM IN THE FIRST PLACE?
FORGET IT.

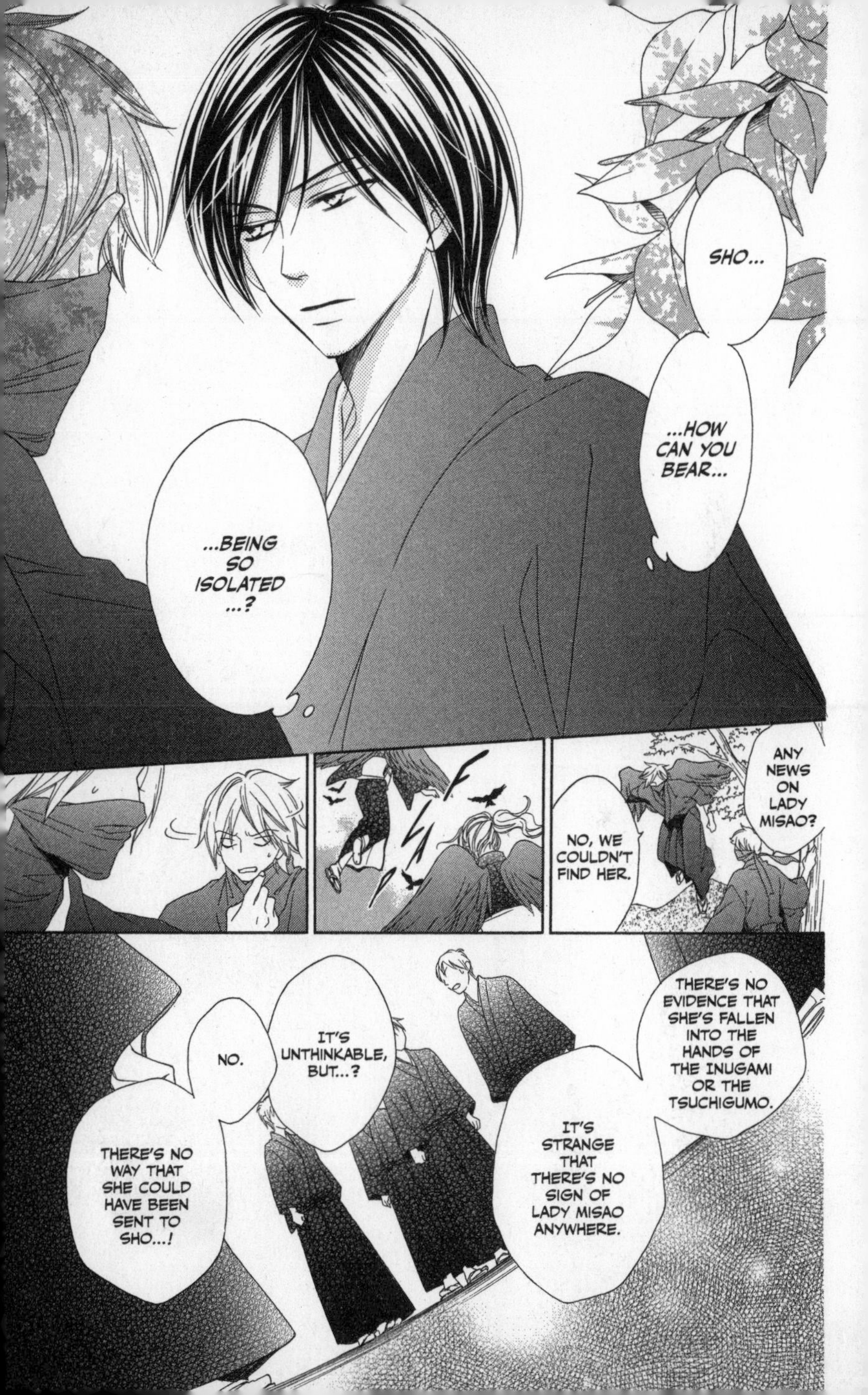
SHO...
...HOW CAN YOU BEAR...
...BEING SO ISOLATED ...?
ANY NEWS ON LADY MISAO?
NO, WE COULDN'T FIND HER.
THERE'S NO EVIDENCE THAT SHE'S FALLEN INTO THE HANDS OF THE INUGAMI OR THE TSUCHIGUMO.
IT'S STRANGE THAT THERE'S NO SIGN OF LADY MISAO ANYWHERE.
IT'S UNTHINKABLE, BUT...?
NO.
THERE'S NO WAY THAT SHE COULD HAVE BEEN SENT TO SHO...!

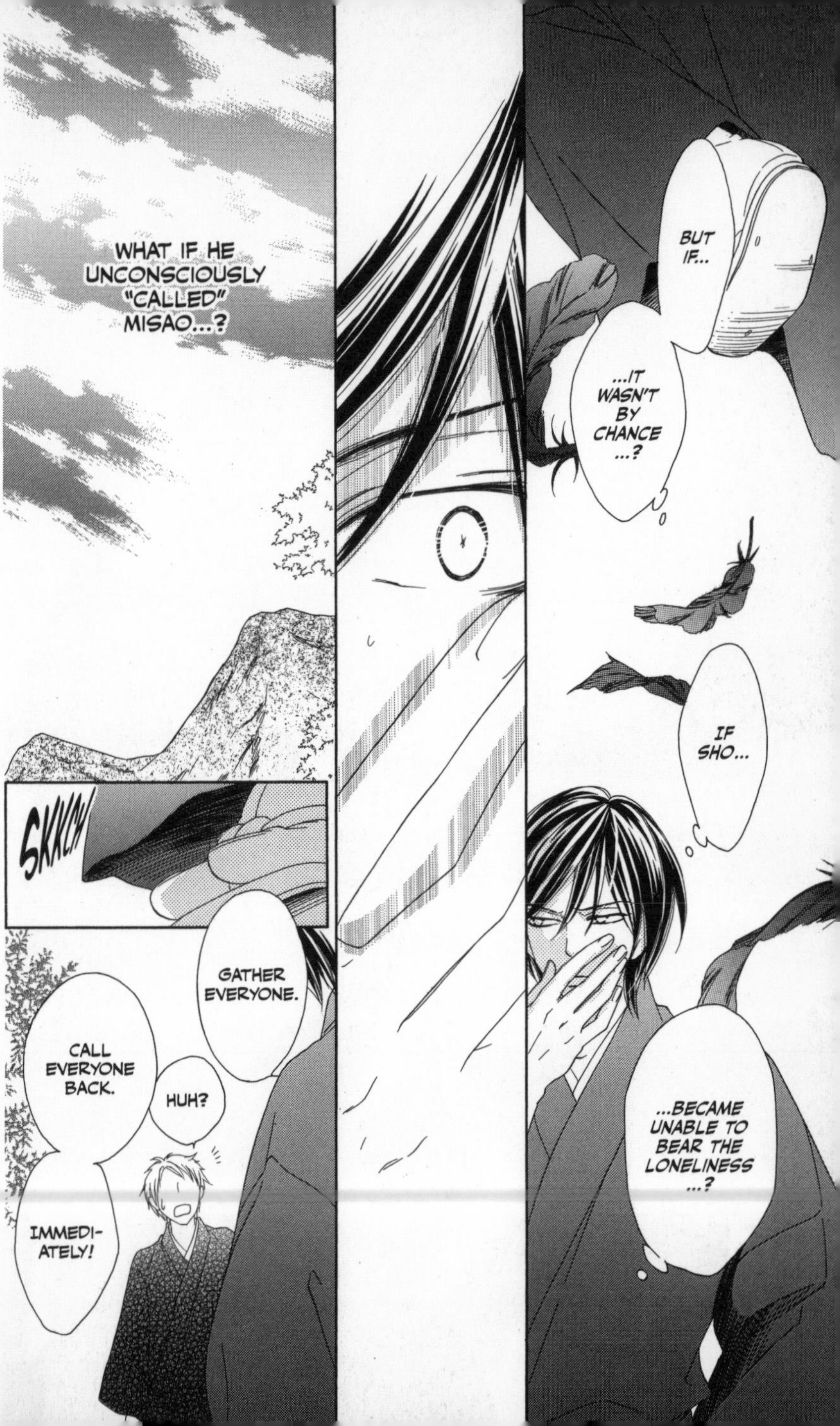
BUT IF...
...IT WASN'T BY CHANCE...?
IF SHO...
...BECAME UNABLE TO BEAR THE LONELINESS...?
WHAT IF HE UNCONSCIOUSLY "CALLED" MISAO...?
SKKCH
GATHER EVERYONE.
HUH?
CALL EVERYONE BACK.
IMMEDI-ATELY!

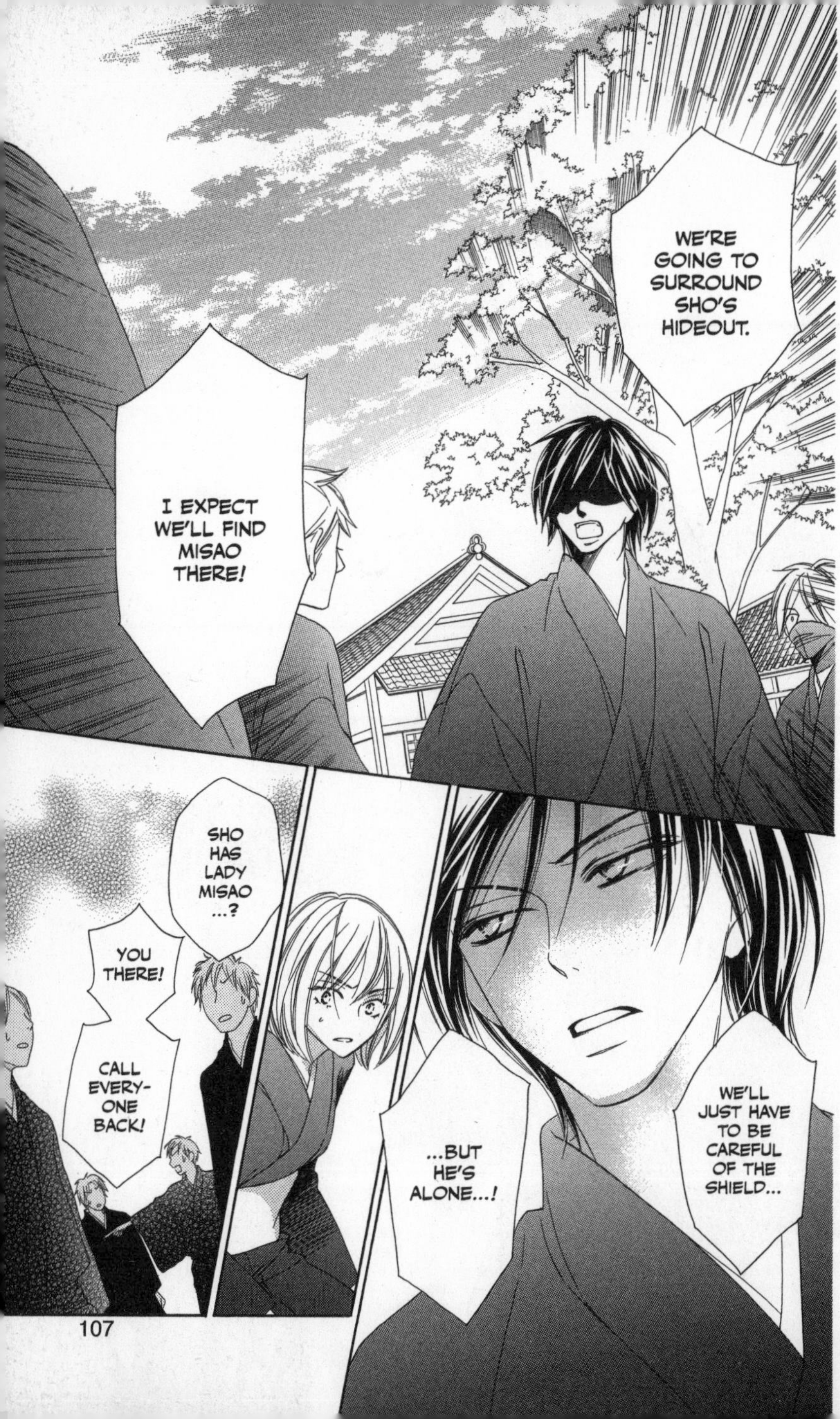
WE'RE GOING TO SURROUND SHO'S HIDEOUT.
I EXPECT WE'LL FIND MISAO THERE!
WE'LL JUST HAVE TO BE CAREFUL OF THE SHIELD...
...BUT HE'S ALONE...!
SHO HAS LADY MISAO ...?
YOU THERE!
CALL EVERY-ONE BACK!

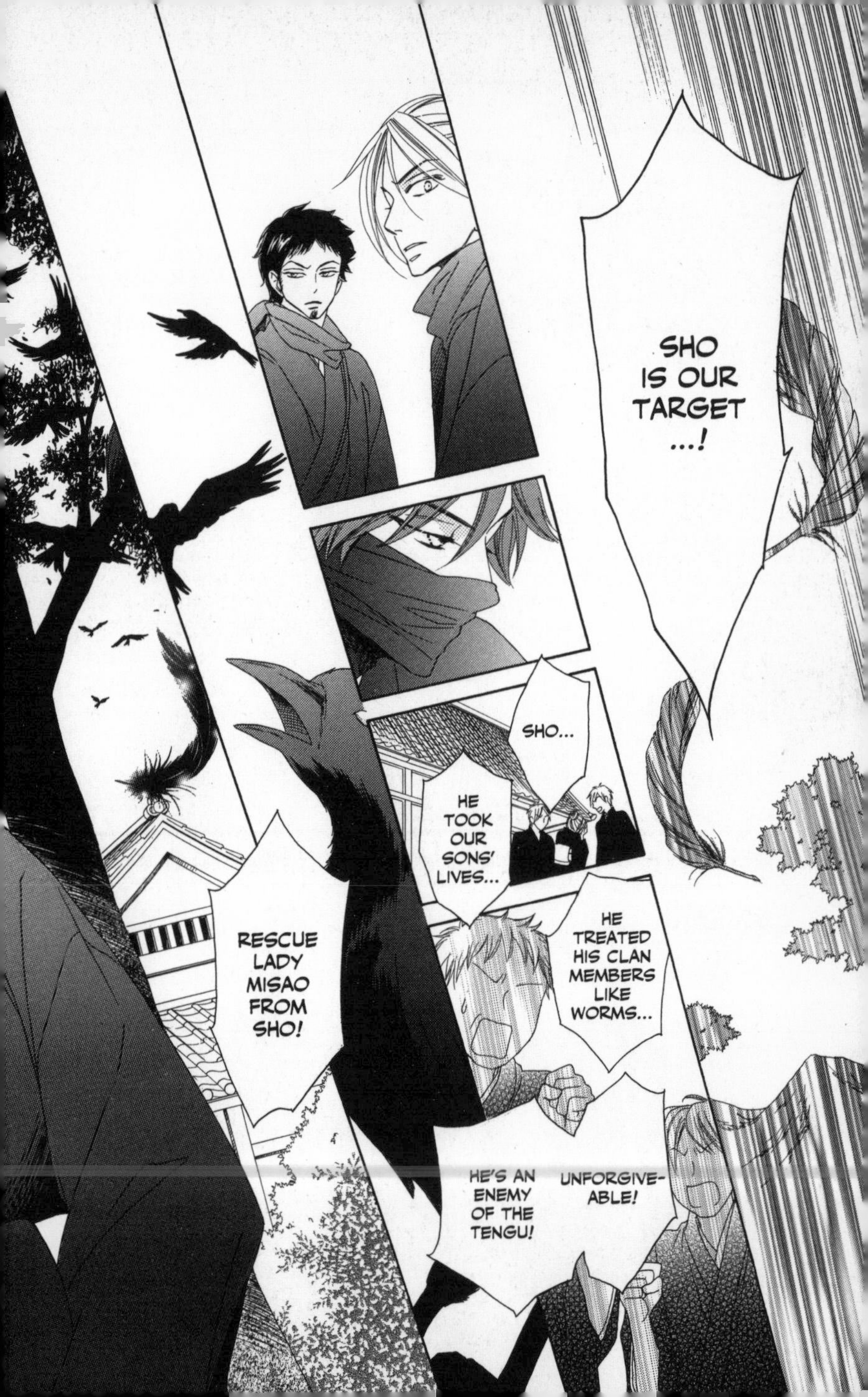
SHO IS OUR TARGET ...!
SHO...
HE TOOK OUR SONS' LIVES...
HE TREATED HIS CLAN MEMBERS LIKE WORMS...
UNFORGIVE-ABLE!
HE'S AN ENEMY OF THE TENGU!
RESCUE LADY MISAO FROM SHO!

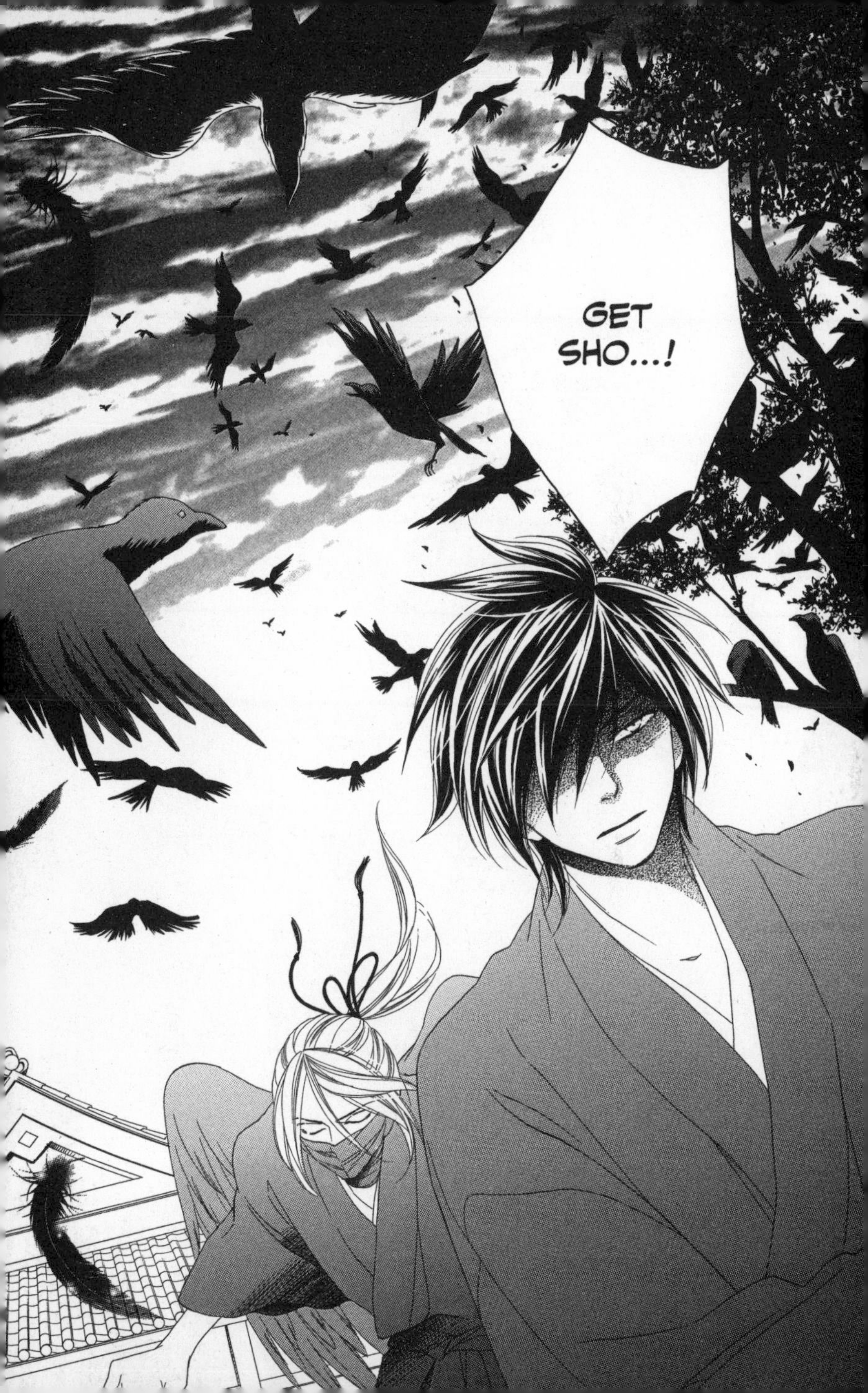
GET SHO...!

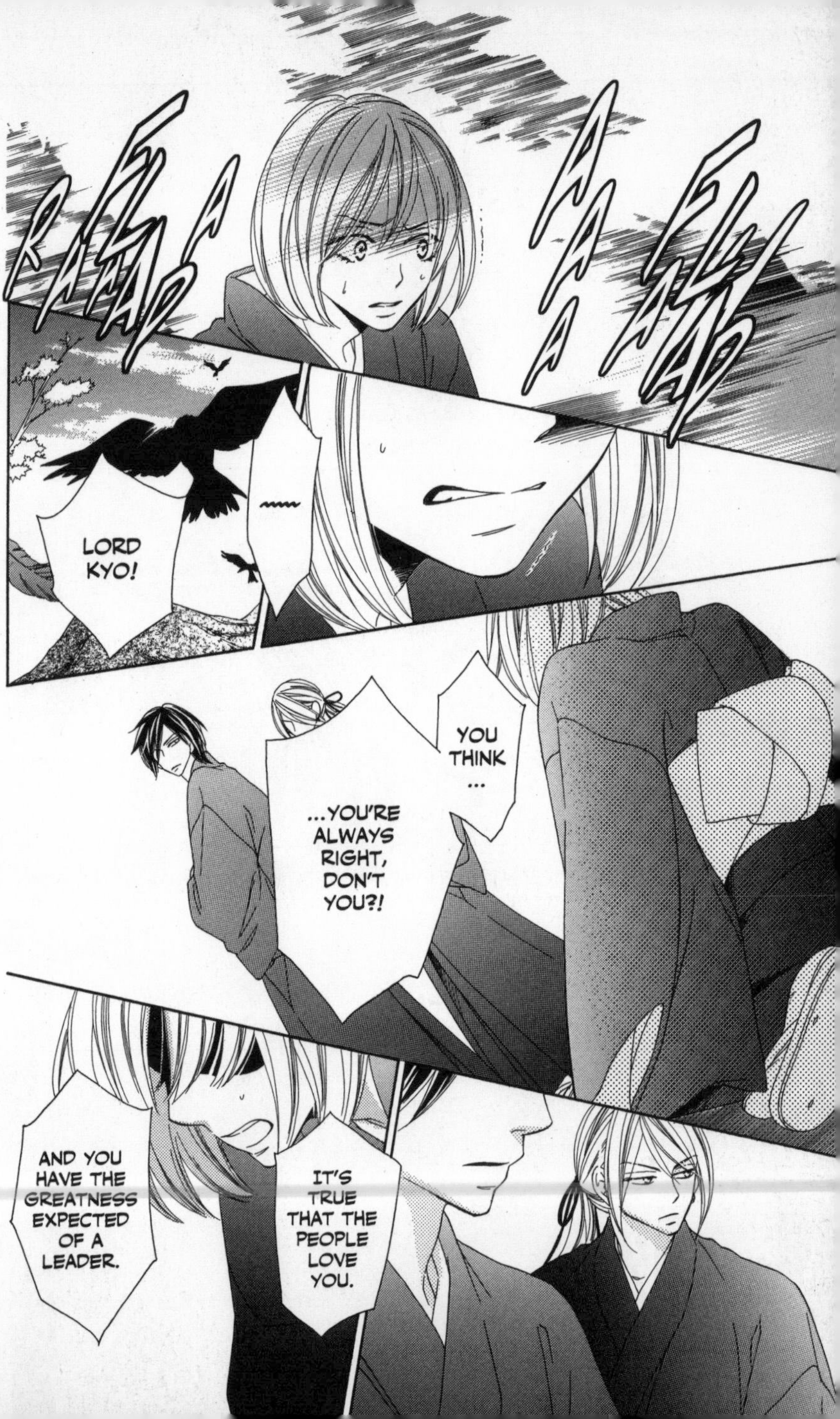
LORD KYO!
YOU THINK ...
...YOU'RE ALWAYS RIGHT, DON'T YOU?!
IT'S TRUE THAT THE PEOPLE LOVE YOU.
AND YOU HAVE THE GREATNESS EXPECTED OF A LEADER.

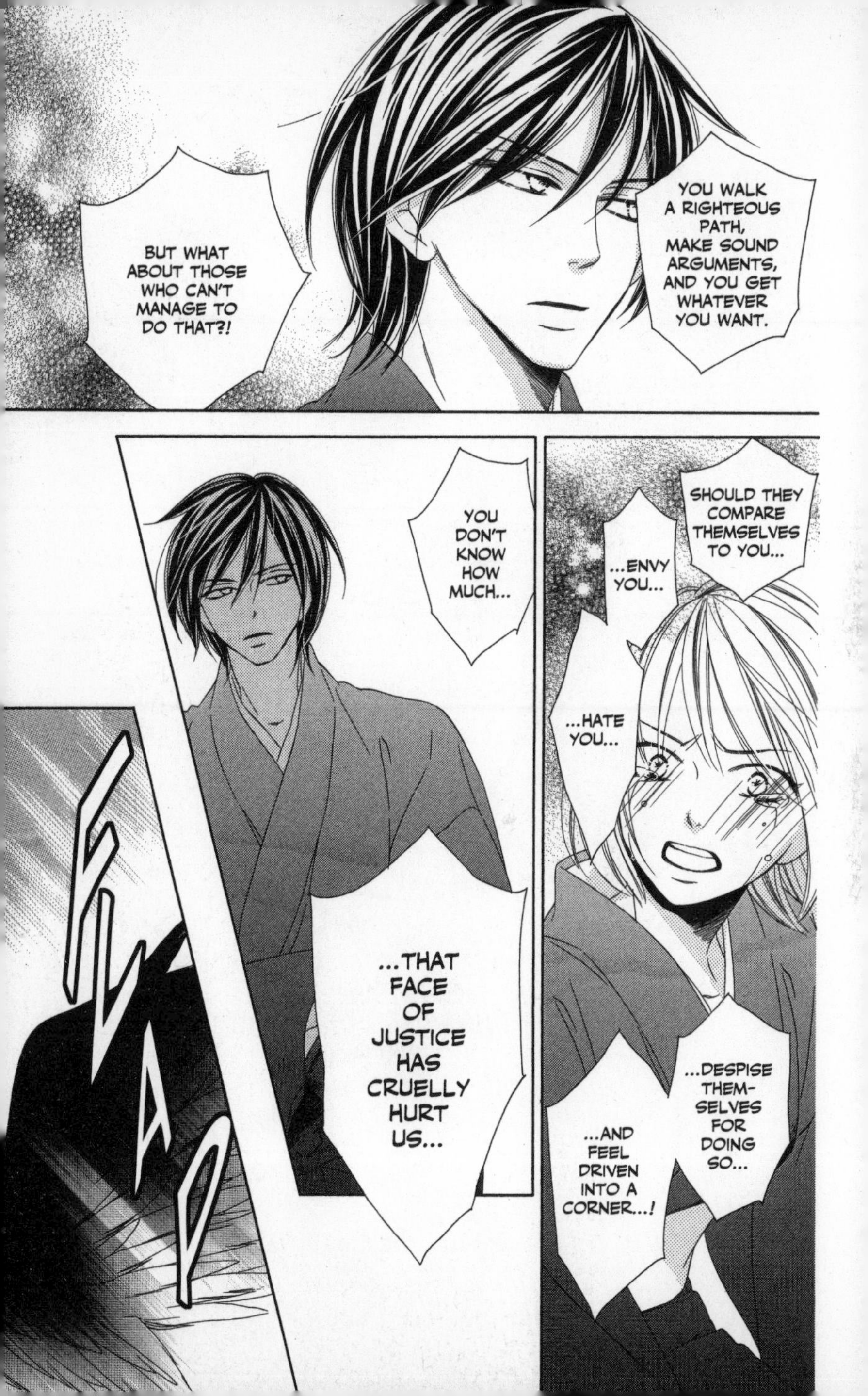
YOU WALK A RIGHTEOUS PATH, MAKE SOUND ARGUMENTS, AND YOU GET WHATEVER YOU WANT.
BUT WHAT ABOUT THOSE WHO CAN'T MANAGE TO DO THAT?!
SHOULD THEY COMPARE THEMSELVES TO YOU...
...ENVY YOU...
...HATE YOU...
...DESPISE THEMSELVES FOR DOING SO...
...AND FEEL DRIVEN INTO A CORNER...!
YOU DON'T KNOW HOW MUCH...
...THAT FACE OF JUSTICE HAS CRUELLY HURT US...

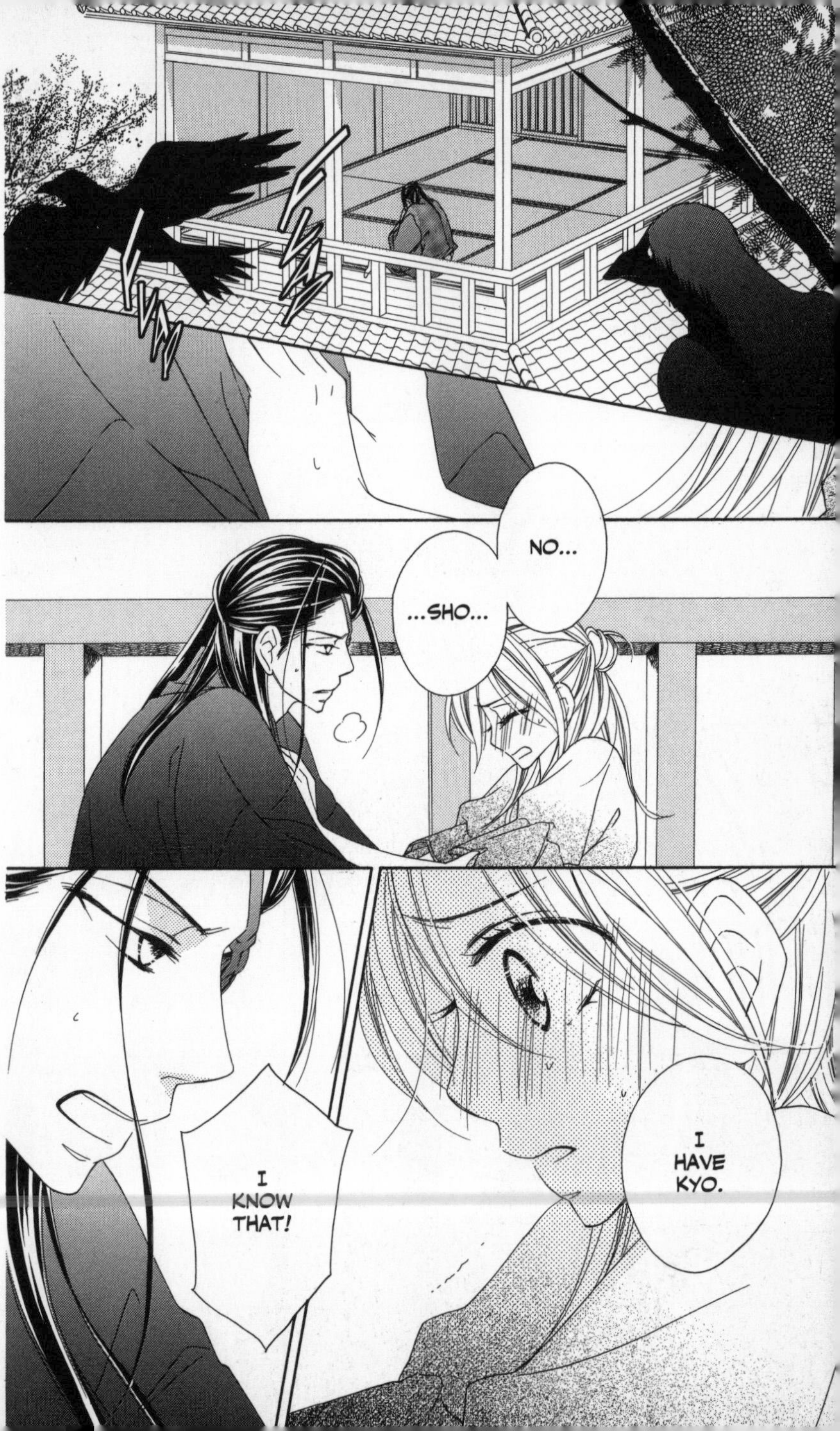
NO...
...SHO...
I HAVE KYO.
I KNOW THAT!

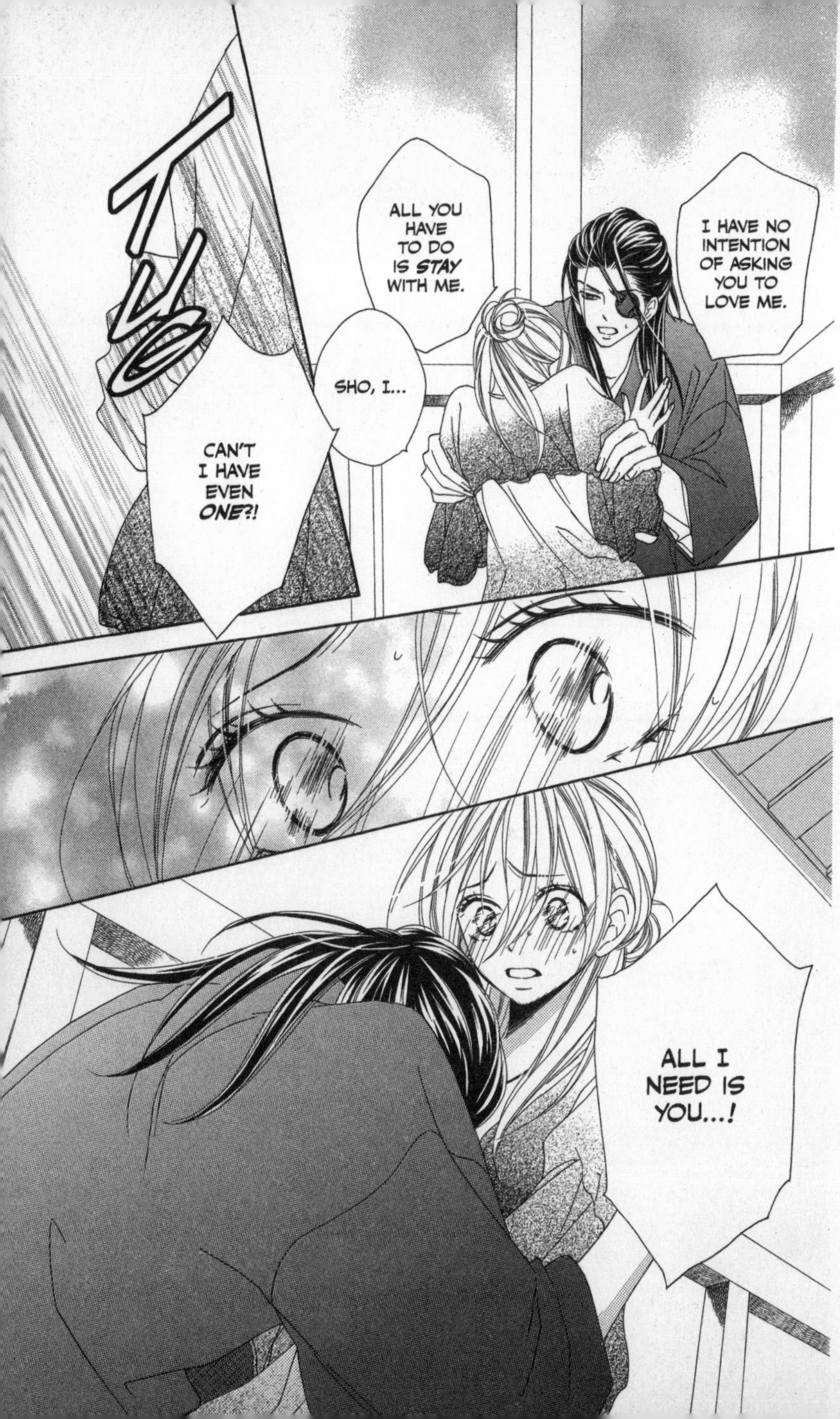
I HAVE NO INTENTION OF ASKING YOU TO LOVE ME.
ALL YOU HAVE TO DO IS *STAY* WITH ME.
SHO, I...
CAN'T I HAVE EVEN *ONE*?!
ALL I NEED IS YOU...!

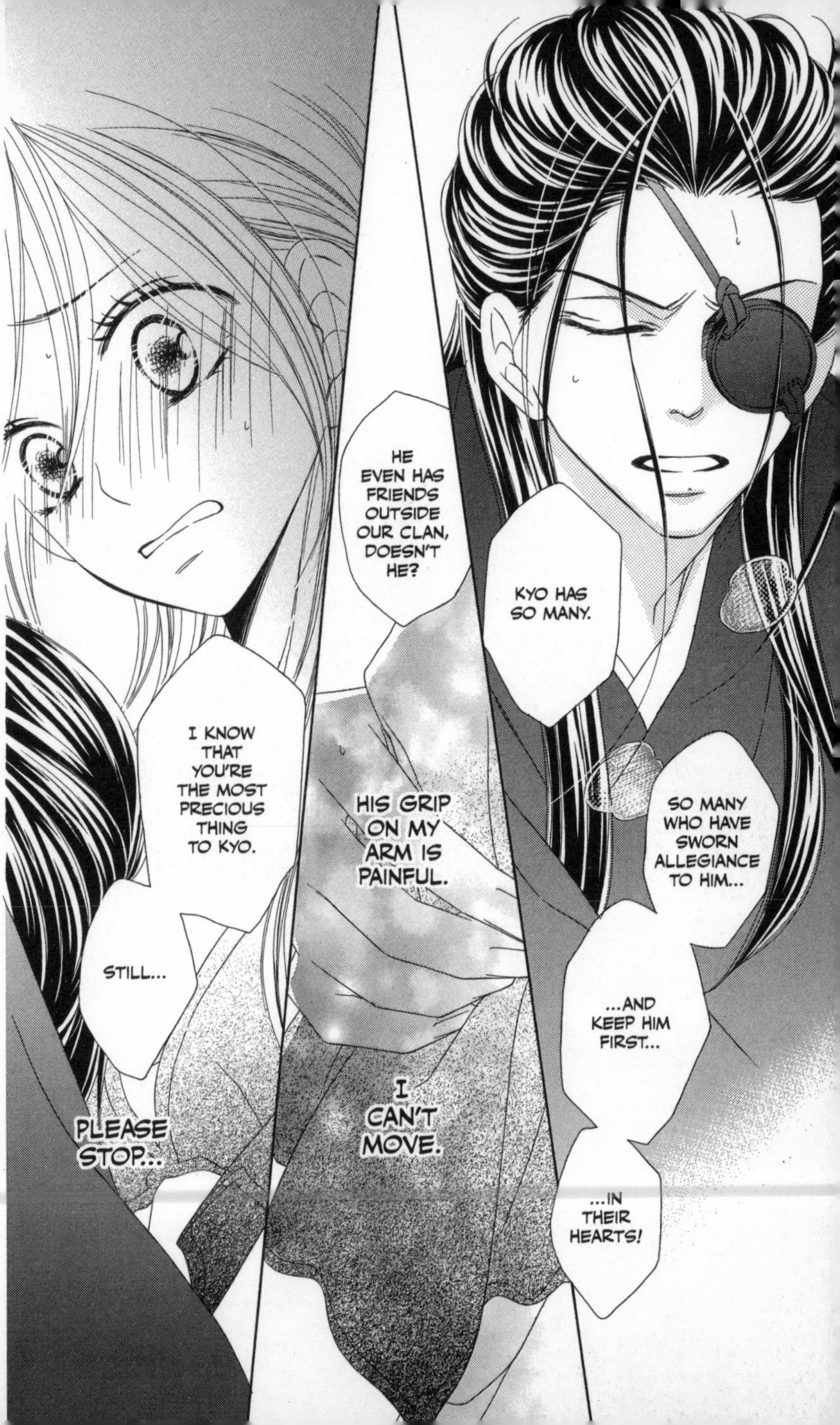

HE EVEN HAS FRIENDS OUTSIDE OUR CLAN, DOESN'T HE?
KYO HAS SO MANY.
SO MANY WHO HAVE SWORN ALLEGIANCE TO HIM...
...AND KEEP HIM FIRST...
...IN THEIR HEARTS!
HIS GRIP ON MY ARM IS PAINFUL.
I CAN'T MOVE.
I KNOW THAT YOU'RE THE MOST PRECIOUS THING TO KYO.
STILL...
PLEASE STOP...

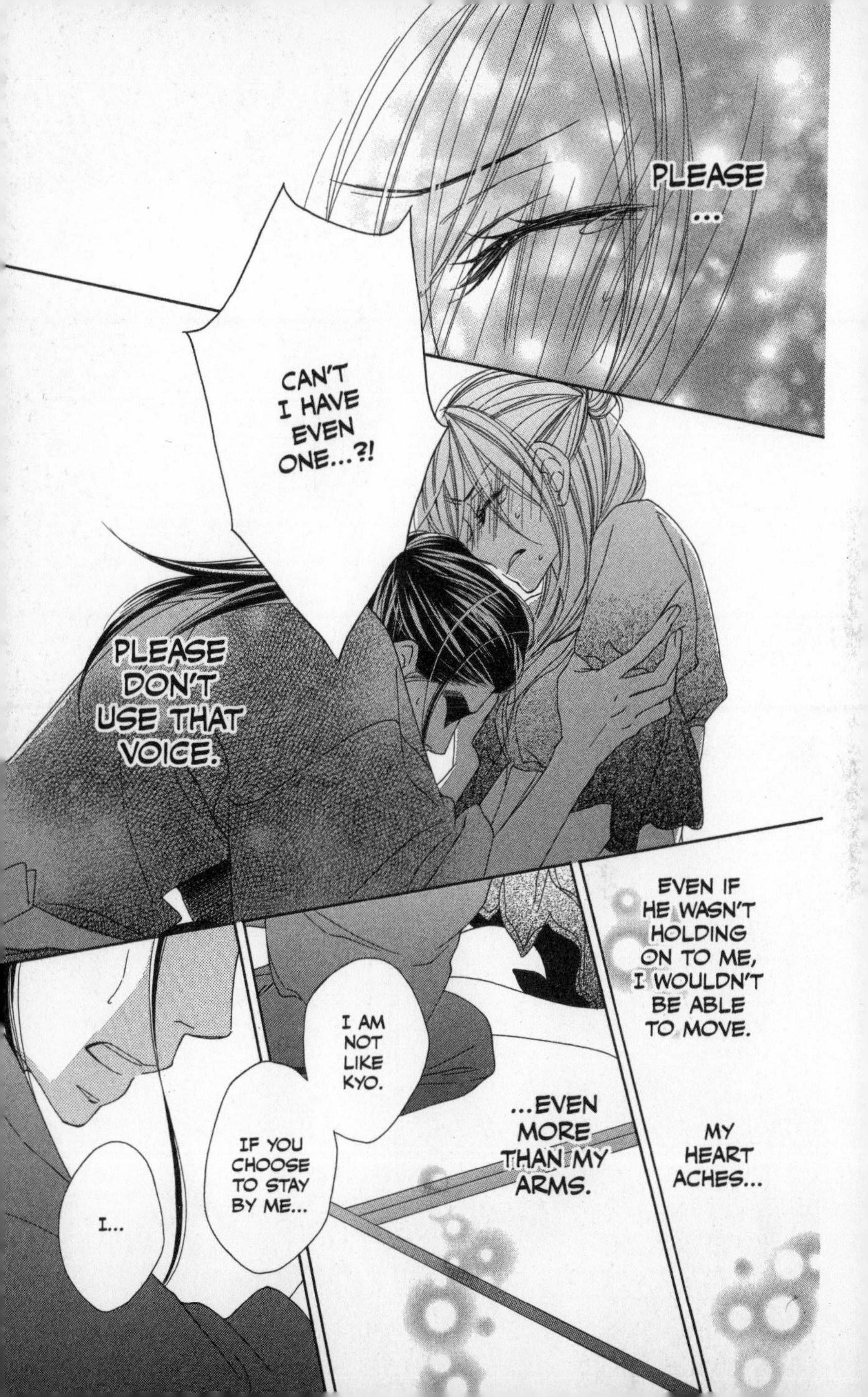
PLEASE...
CAN'T I HAVE EVEN ONE...?!
PLEASE DON'T USE THAT VOICE.
EVEN IF HE WASN'T HOLDING ON TO ME, I WOULDN'T BE ABLE TO MOVE.
MY HEART ACHES...
...EVEN MORE THAN MY ARMS.
I AM NOT LIKE KYO.
IF YOU CHOOSE TO STAY BY ME...
I...

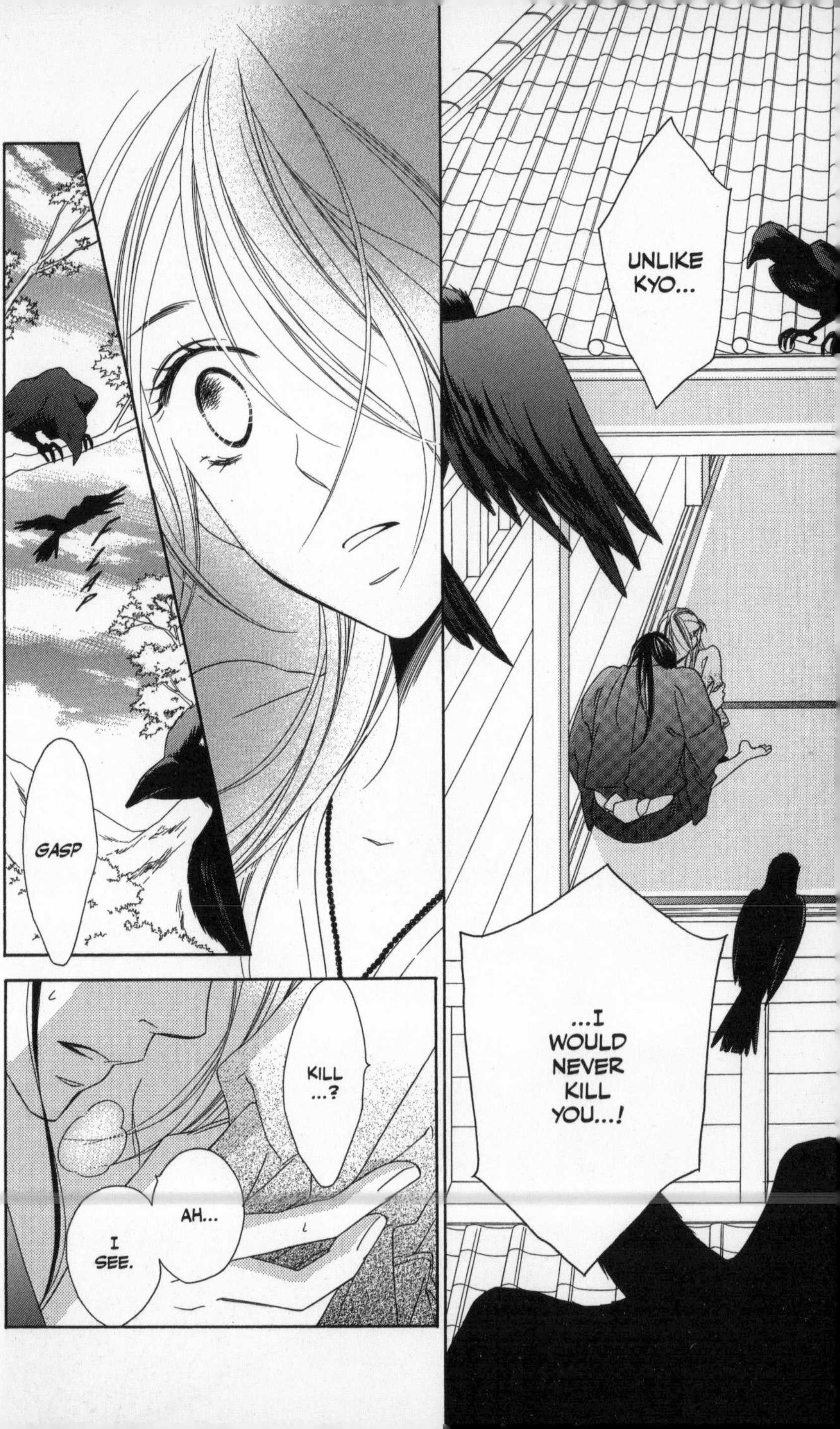
UNLIKE KYO...
...I WOULD NEVER KILL YOU...!
GASP
KILL ...?
AH... I SEE.

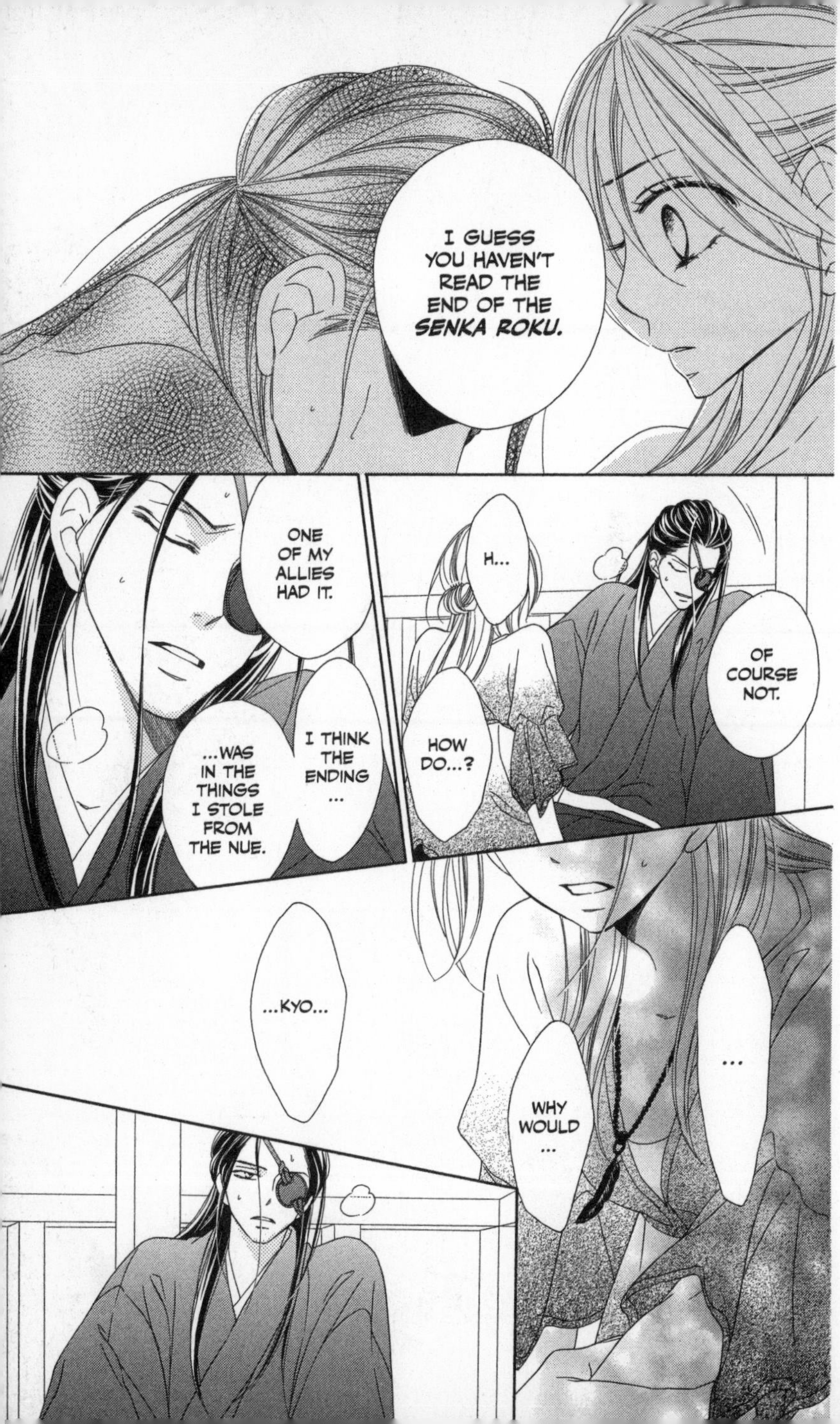
I GUESS YOU HAVEN'T READ THE END OF THE *SENKA ROKU.*
OF COURSE NOT.
H...
HOW DO...?
ONE OF MY ALLIES HAD IT.
I THINK THE ENDING...
...WAS IN THE THINGS I STOLE FROM THE NUE.
...
WHY WOULD...
...KYO...

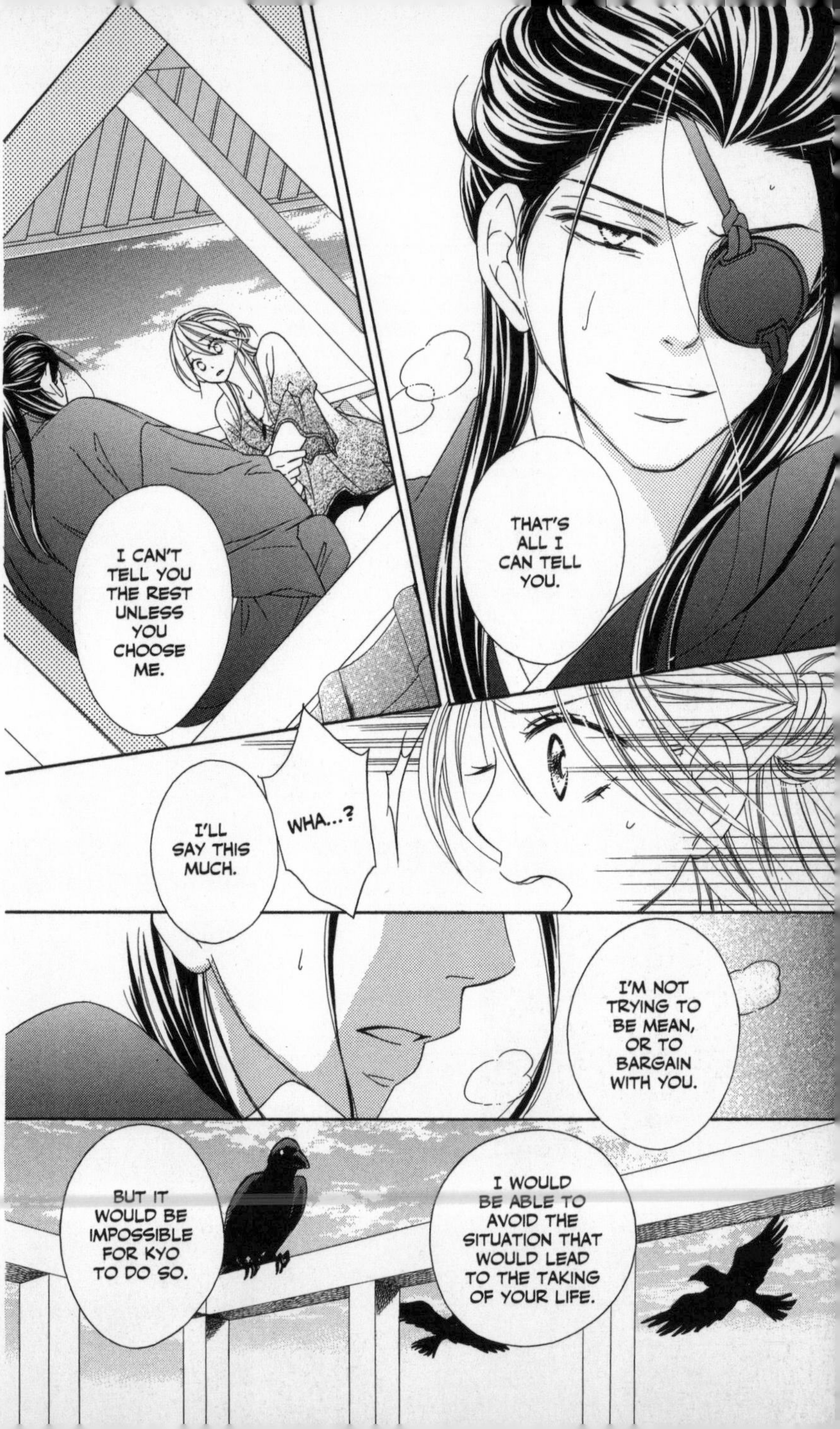
THAT'S ALL I CAN TELL YOU.
I CAN'T TELL YOU THE REST UNLESS YOU CHOOSE ME.
WHA...?
I'LL SAY THIS MUCH.
I'M NOT TRYING TO BE MEAN, OR TO BARGAIN WITH YOU.
I WOULD BE ABLE TO AVOID THE SITUATION THAT WOULD LEAD TO THE TAKING OF YOUR LIFE.
BUT IT WOULD BE IMPOSSIBLE FOR KYO TO DO SO.

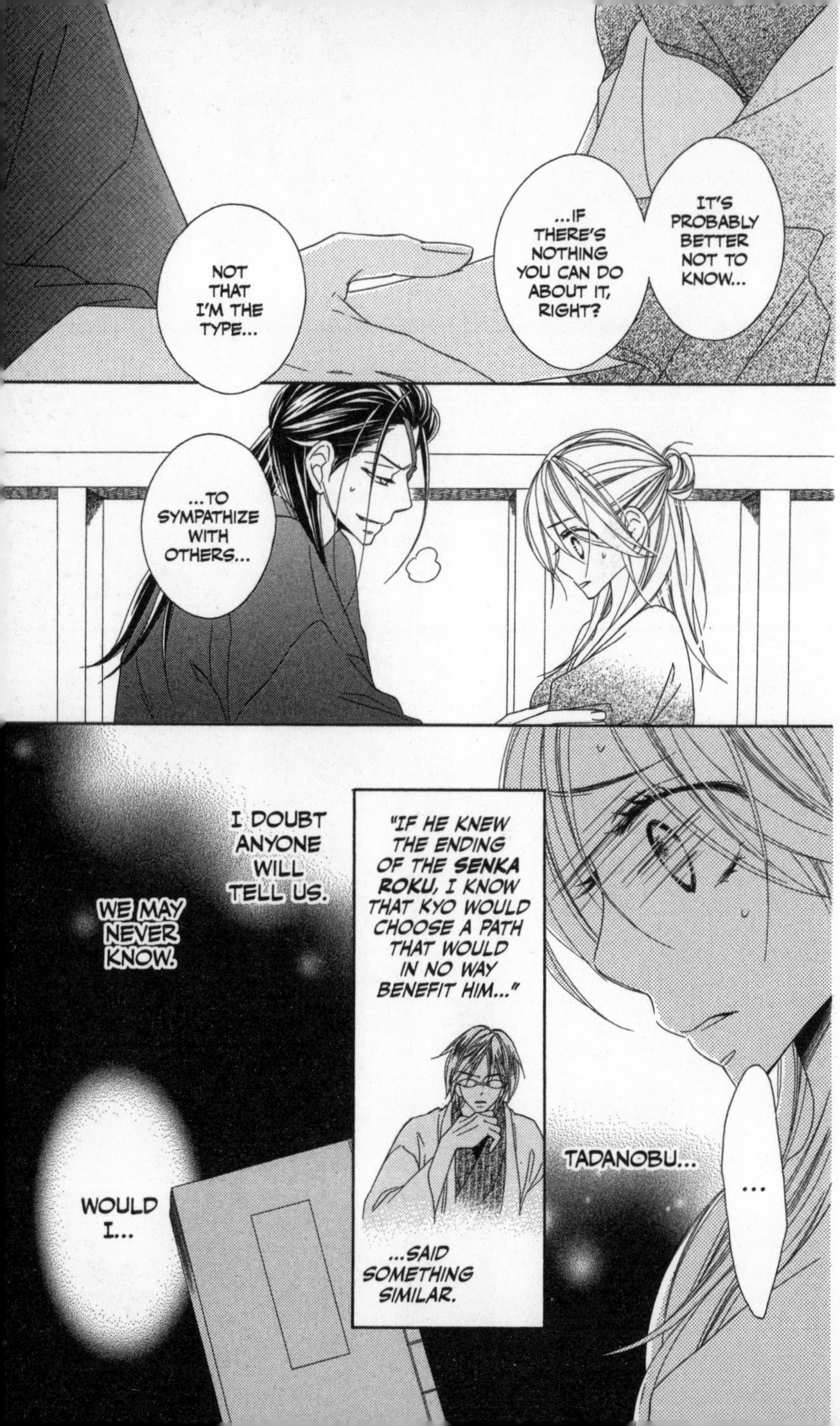
IT'S PROBABLY BETTER NOT TO KNOW...
...IF THERE'S NOTHING YOU CAN DO ABOUT IT, RIGHT?
NOT THAT I'M THE TYPE...
...TO SYMPATHIZE WITH OTHERS...
...
TADANOBU...
"IF HE KNEW THE ENDING OF THE **SENKA ROKU**, I KNOW THAT KYO WOULD CHOOSE A PATH THAT WOULD IN NO WAY BENEFIT HIM..."
...SAID SOMETHING SIMILAR.
I DOUBT ANYONE WILL TELL US.
WE MAY NEVER KNOW.
WOULD I...

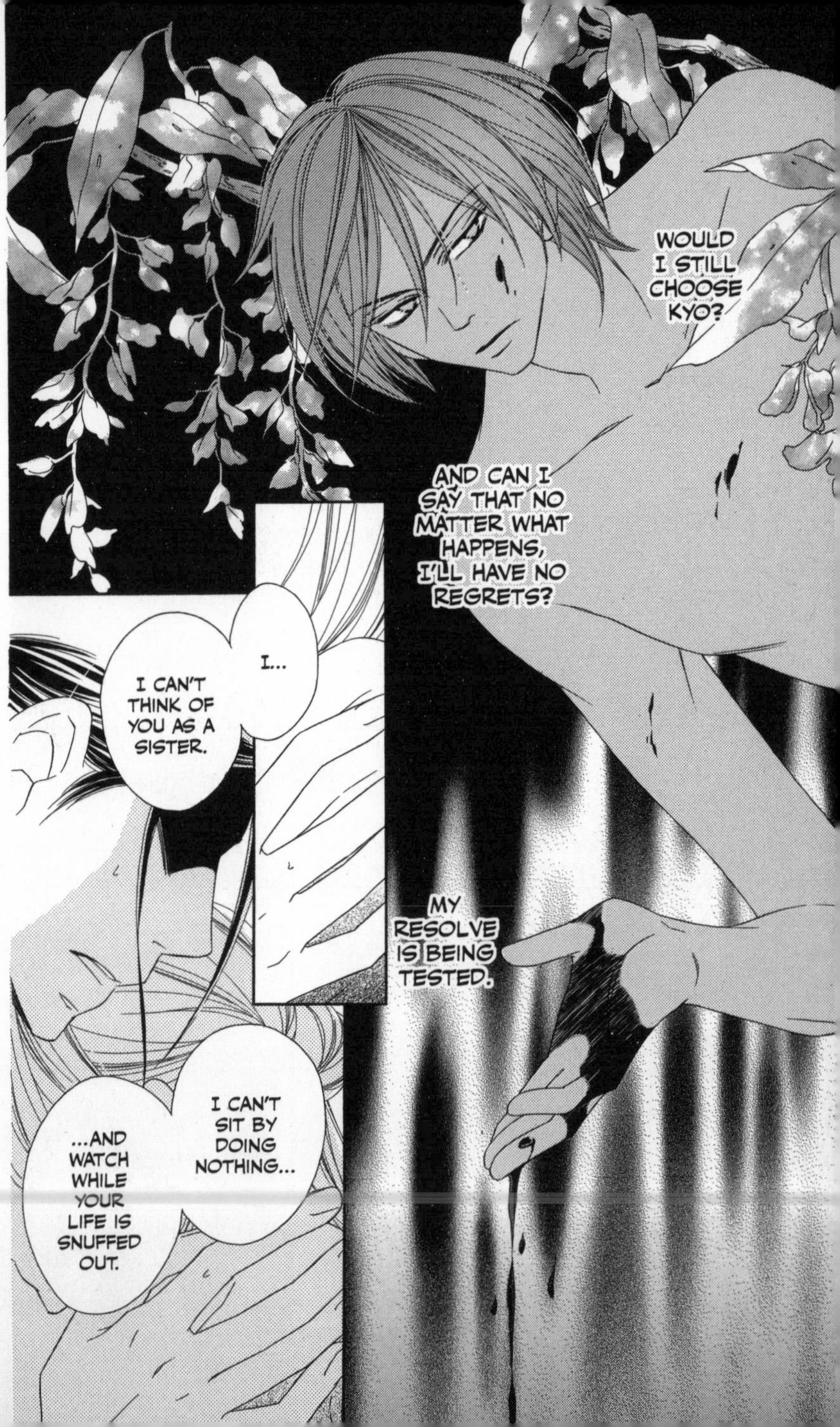
WOULD I STILL CHOOSE KYO?
AND CAN I SAY THAT NO MATTER WHAT HAPPENS, I'LL HAVE NO REGRETS?
MY RESOLVE IS BEING TESTED.
I...
I CAN'T THINK OF YOU AS A SISTER.
I CAN'T SIT BY DOING NOTHING...
...AND WATCH WHILE YOUR LIFE IS SNUFFED OUT.

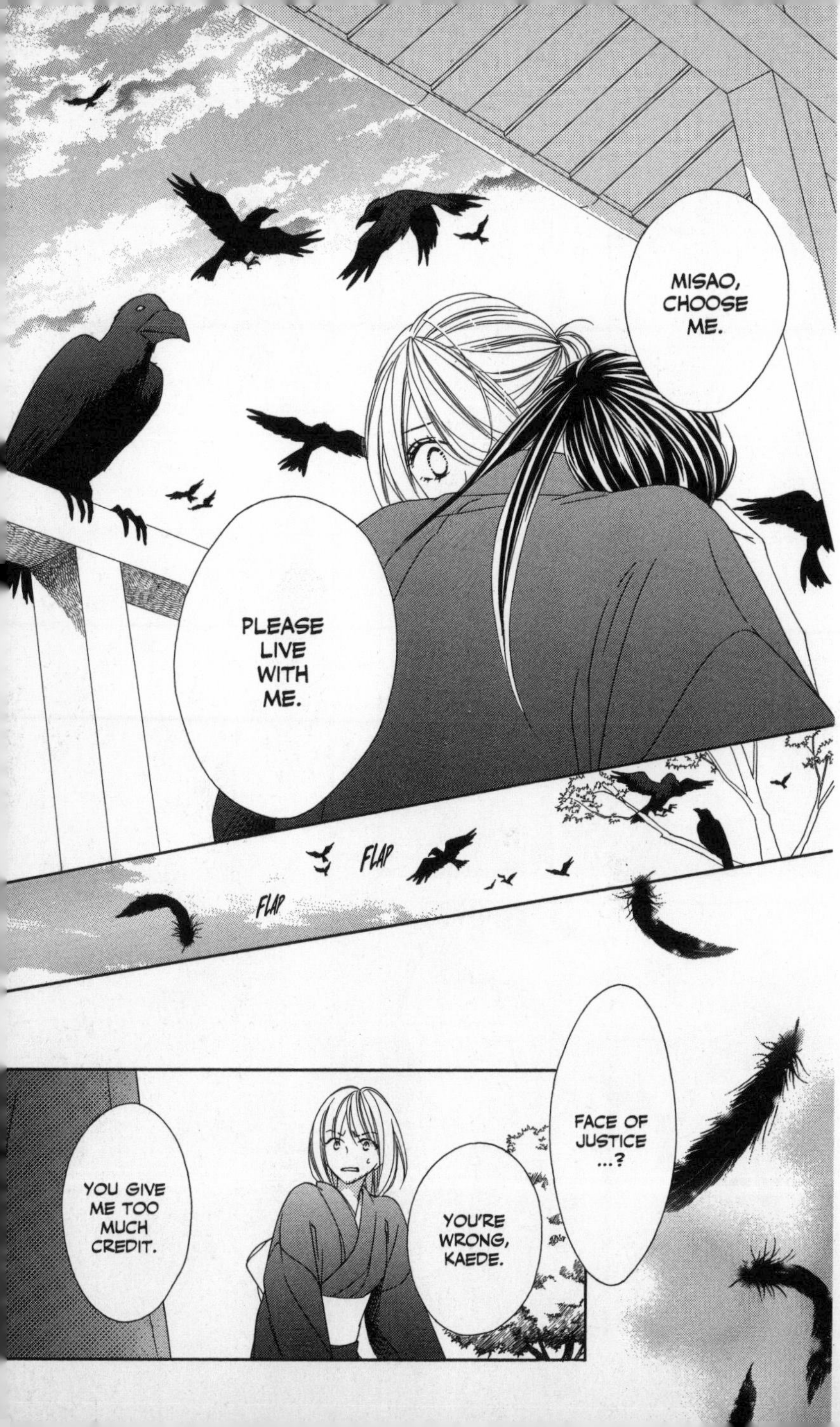
MISAO, CHOOSE ME.
PLEASE LIVE WITH ME.
FLAP
FLAP
FACE OF JUSTICE ...?
YOU'RE WRONG, KAEDE.
YOU GIVE ME TOO MUCH CREDIT.

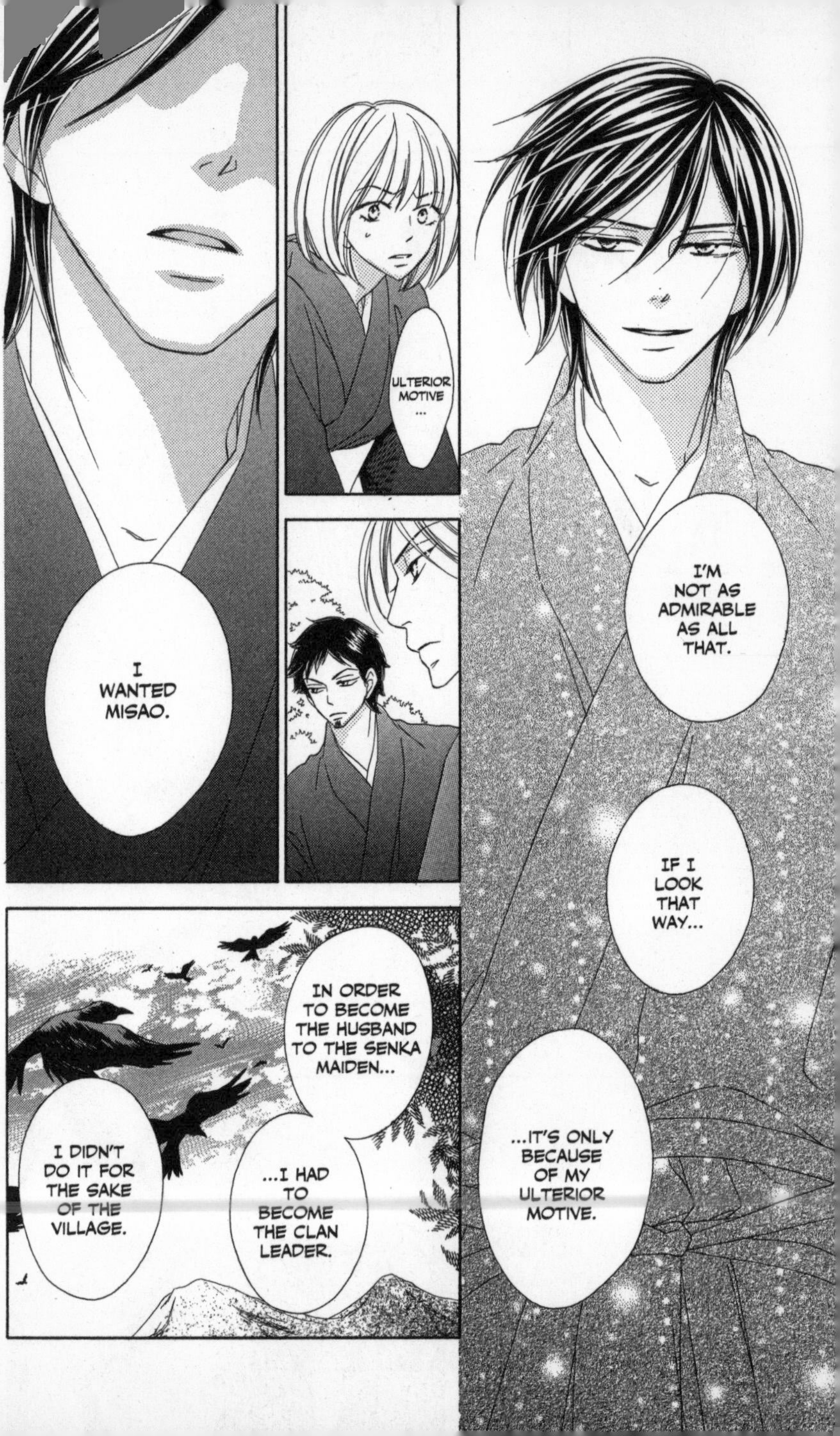
I'M NOT AS ADMIRABLE AS ALL THAT.
IF I LOOK THAT WAY...
...IT'S ONLY BECAUSE OF MY ULTERIOR MOTIVE.
ULTERIOR MOTIVE...
I WANTED MISAO.
IN ORDER TO BECOME THE HUSBAND TO THE SENKA MAIDEN...
...I HAD TO BECOME THE CLAN LEADER.
I DIDN'T DO IT FOR THE SAKE OF THE VILLAGE.

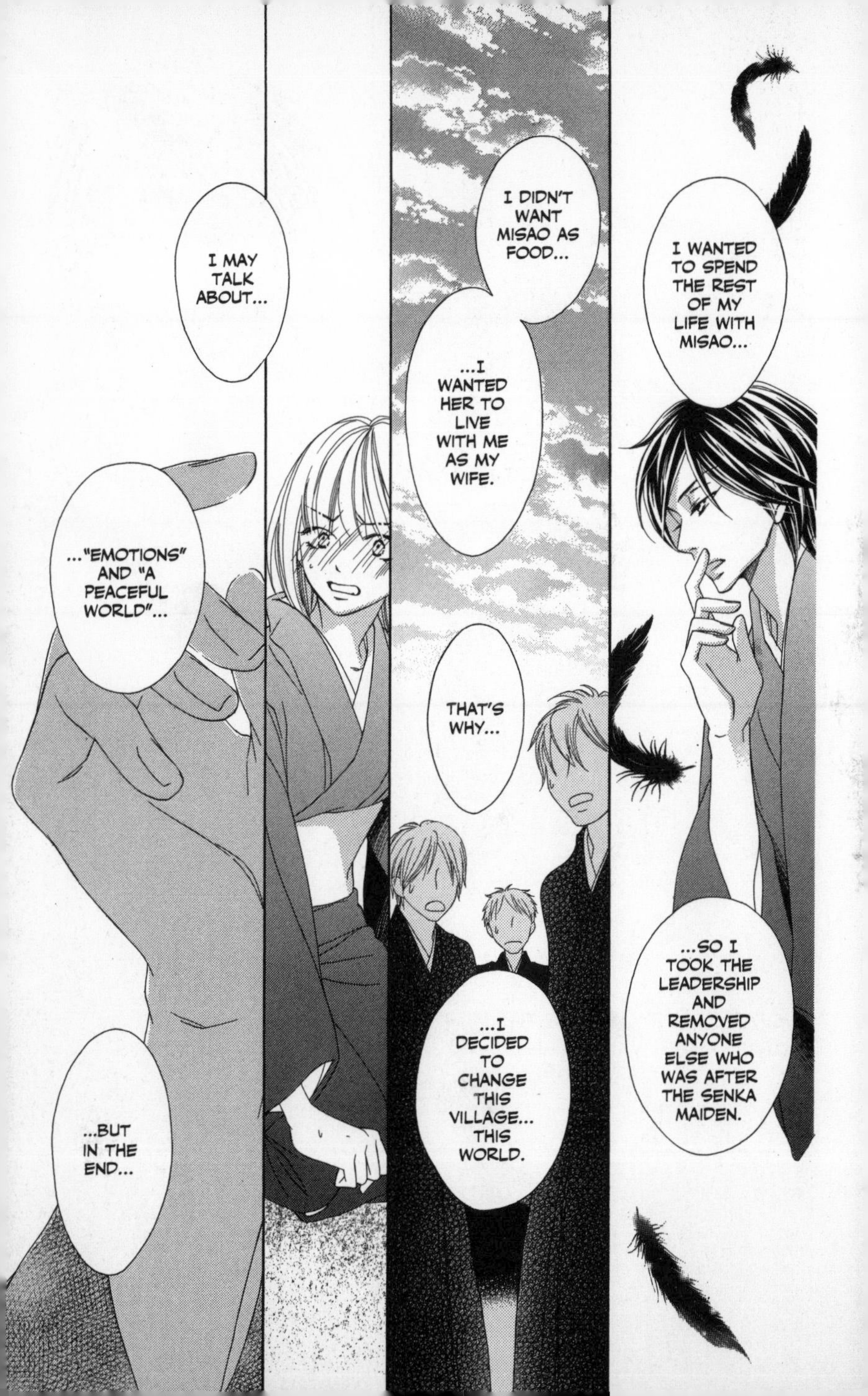
I WANTED TO SPEND THE REST OF MY LIFE WITH MISAO...
...SO I TOOK THE LEADERSHIP AND REMOVED ANYONE ELSE WHO WAS AFTER THE SENKA MAIDEN.
I DIDN'T WANT MISAO AS FOOD...
...I WANTED HER TO LIVE WITH ME AS MY WIFE.
THAT'S WHY...
...I DECIDED TO CHANGE THIS VILLAGE... THIS WORLD.
I MAY TALK ABOUT...
..."EMOTIONS" AND "A PEACEFUL WORLD"...
...BUT IN THE END...

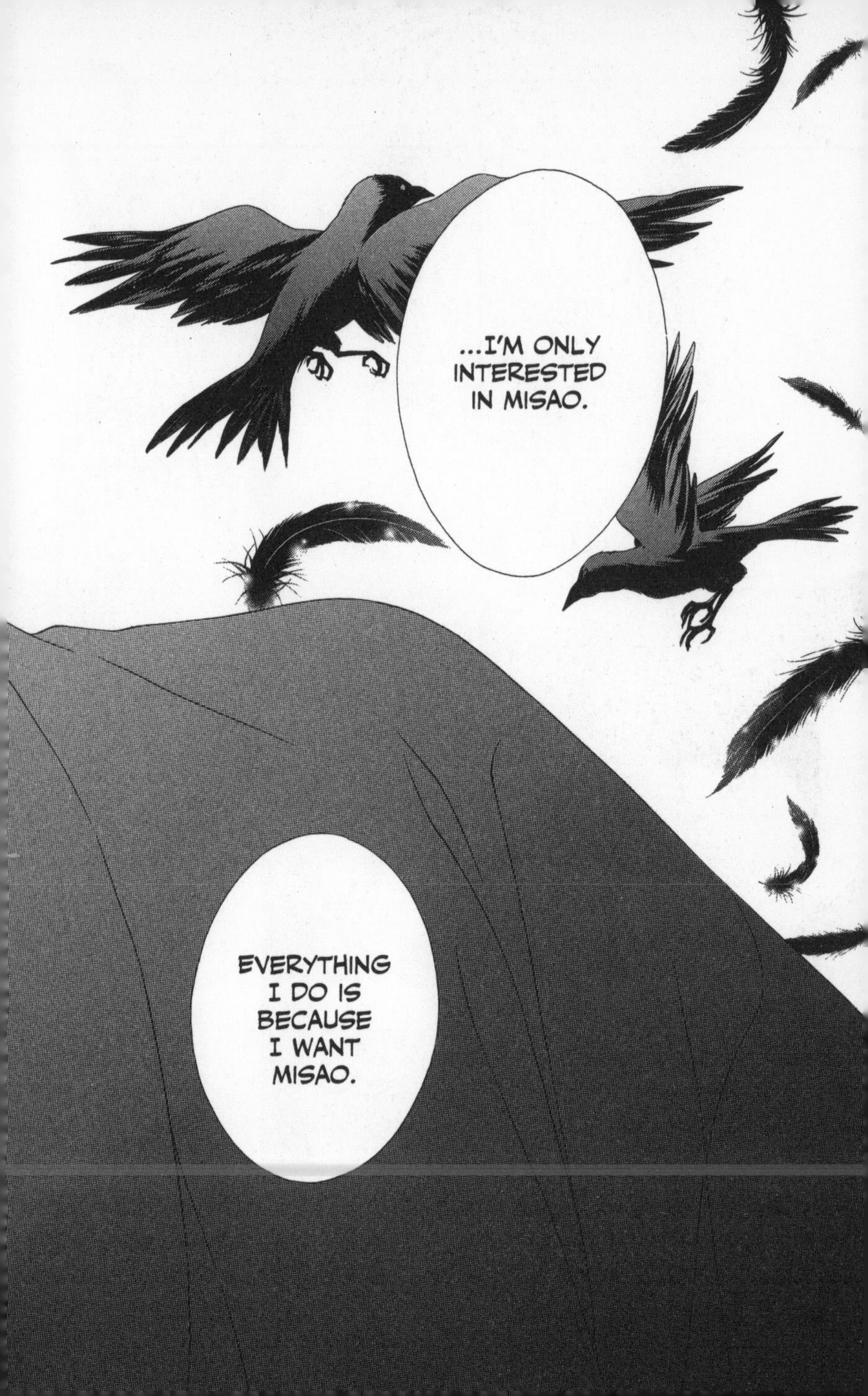
...I'M ONLY INTERESTED IN MISAO.
EVERYTHING I DO IS BECAUSE I WANT MISAO.

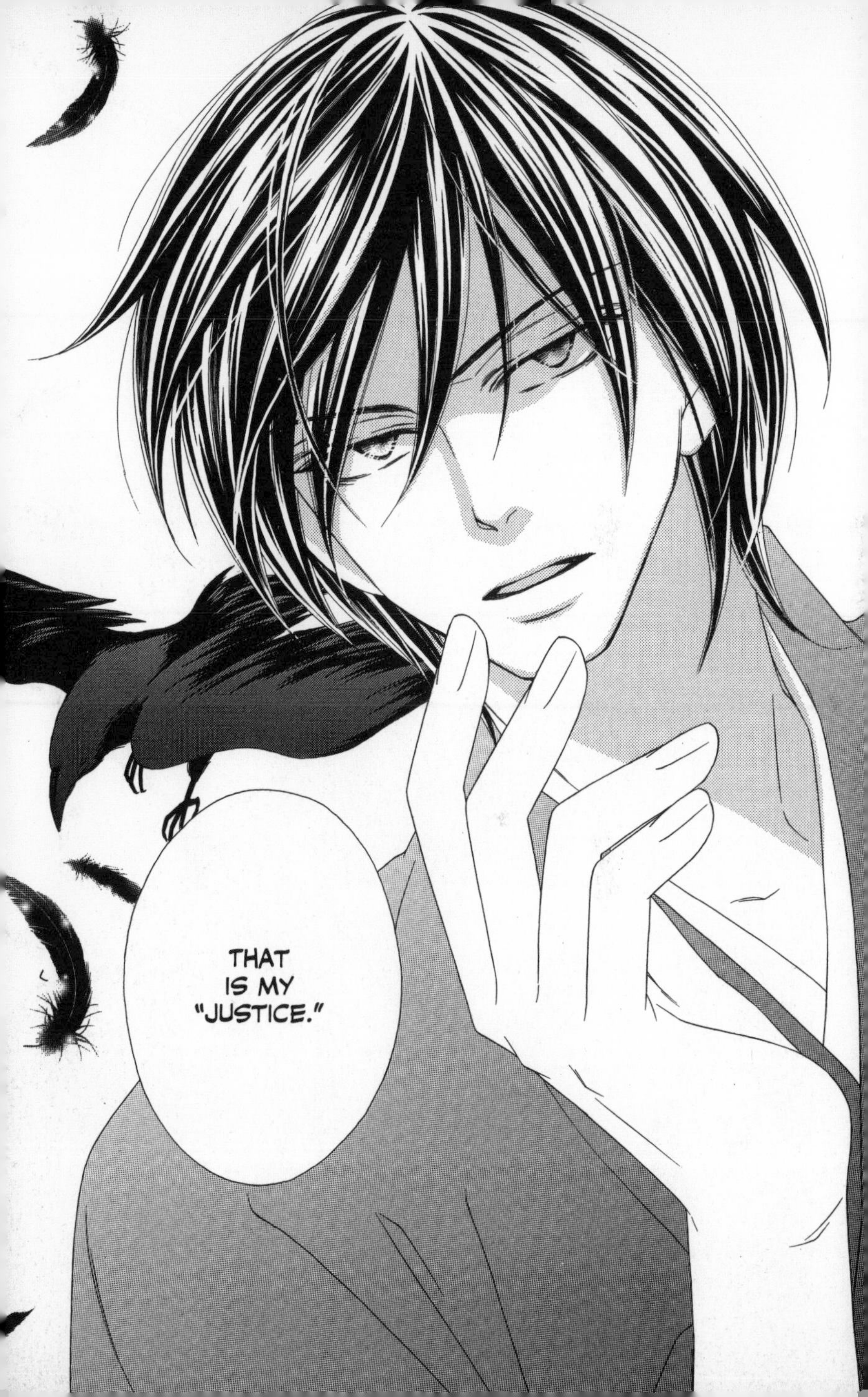
THAT IS MY "JUSTICE."

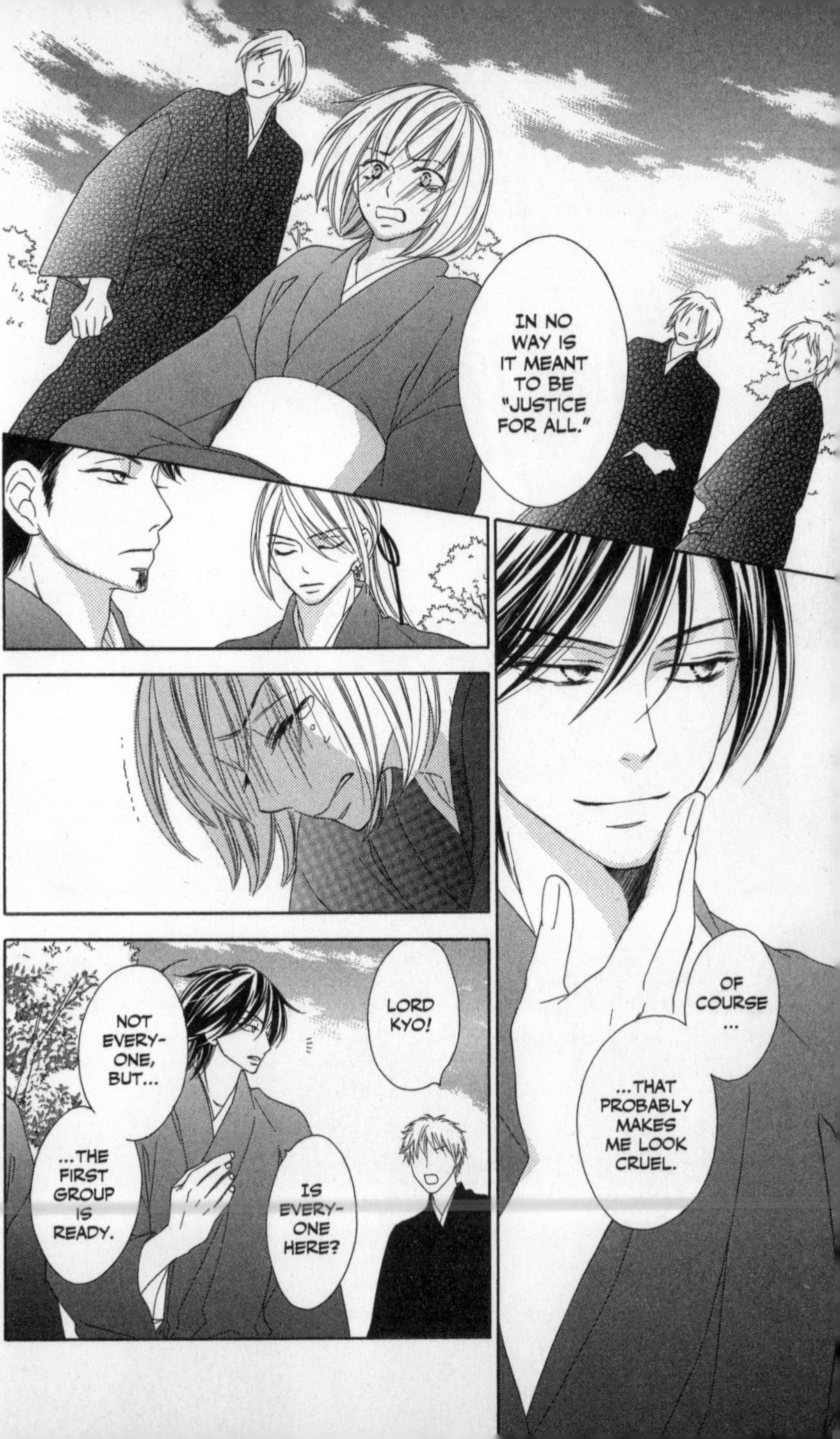
IN NO WAY IS IT MEANT TO BE "JUSTICE FOR ALL."
OF COURSE...
...THAT PROBABLY MAKES ME LOOK CRUEL.
LORD KYO!
IS EVERY-ONE HERE?
NOT EVERY-ONE, BUT...
...THE FIRST GROUP IS READY.

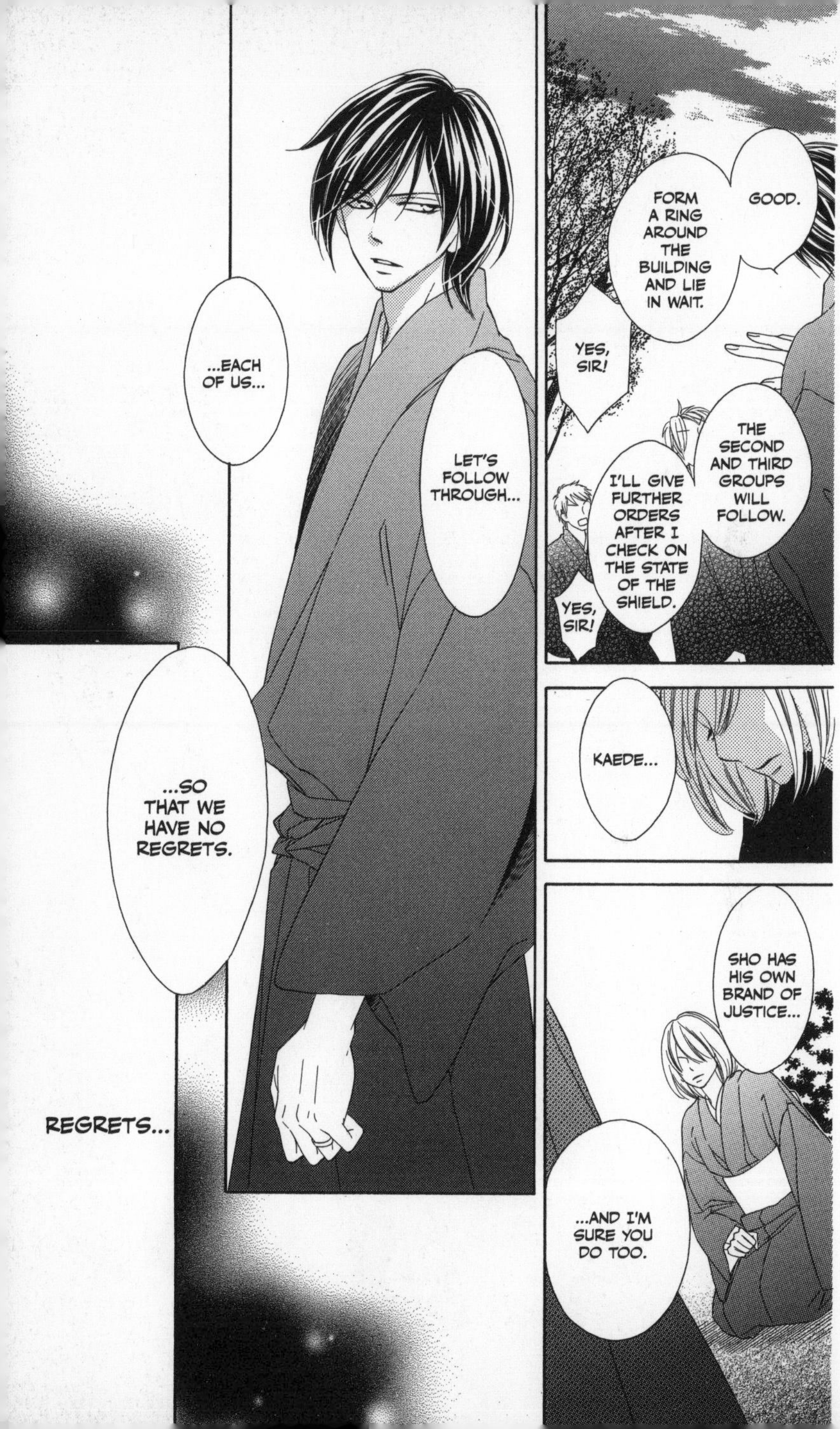
GOOD.
FORM A RING AROUND THE BUILDING AND LIE IN WAIT.
YES, SIR!
THE SECOND AND THIRD GROUPS WILL FOLLOW.
I'LL GIVE FURTHER ORDERS AFTER I CHECK ON THE STATE OF THE SHIELD.
YES, SIR!
KAEDE...
SHO HAS HIS OWN BRAND OF JUSTICE...
...AND I'M SURE YOU DO TOO.
LET'S FOLLOW THROUGH...
...EACH OF US...
...SO THAT WE HAVE NO REGRETS.
REGRETS...

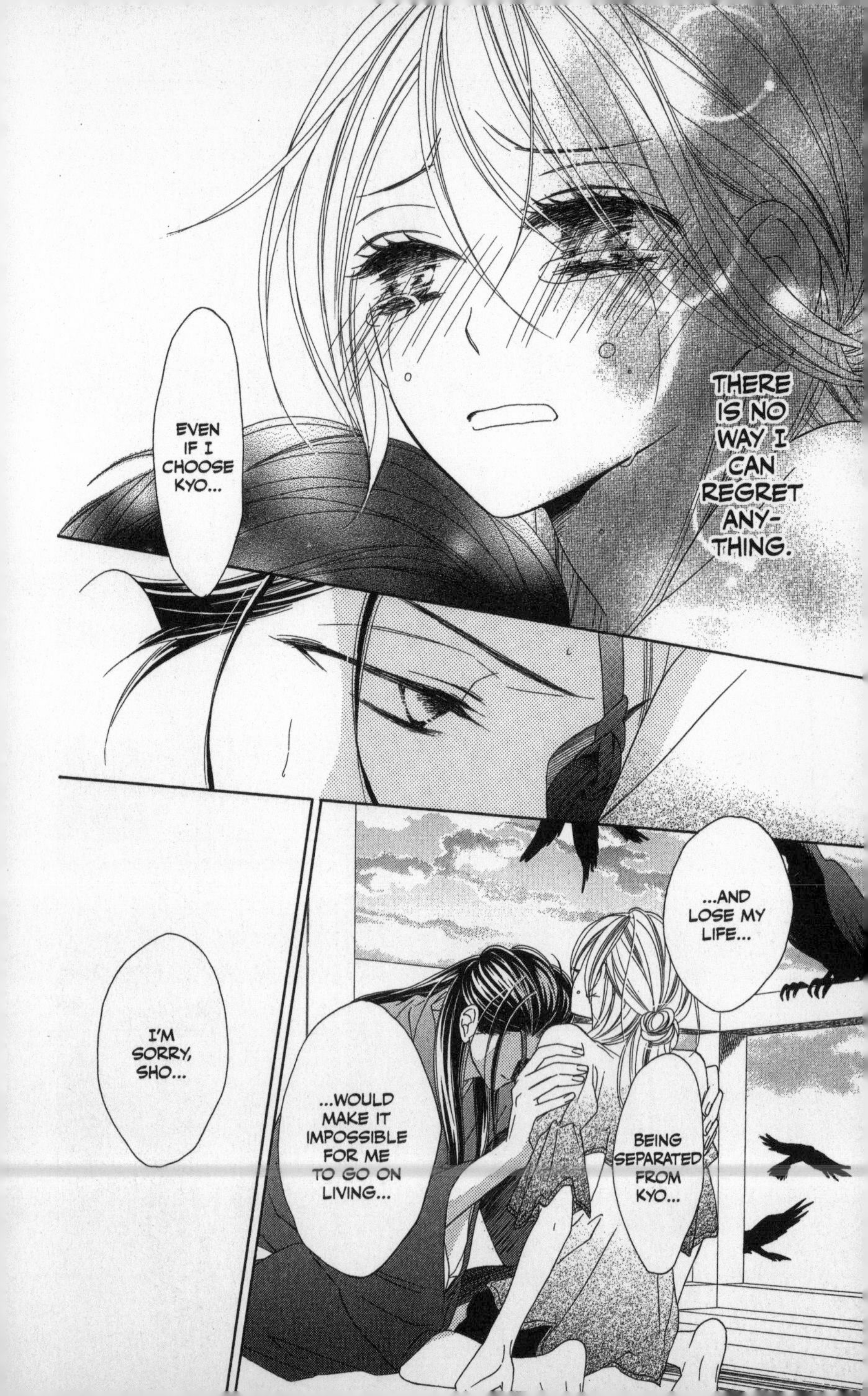
THERE IS NO WAY I CAN REGRET ANYTHING.
EVEN IF I CHOOSE KYO...
...AND LOSE MY LIFE...
BEING SEPARATED FROM KYO...
...WOULD MAKE IT IMPOSSIBLE FOR ME TO GO ON LIVING...
I'M SORRY, SHO...

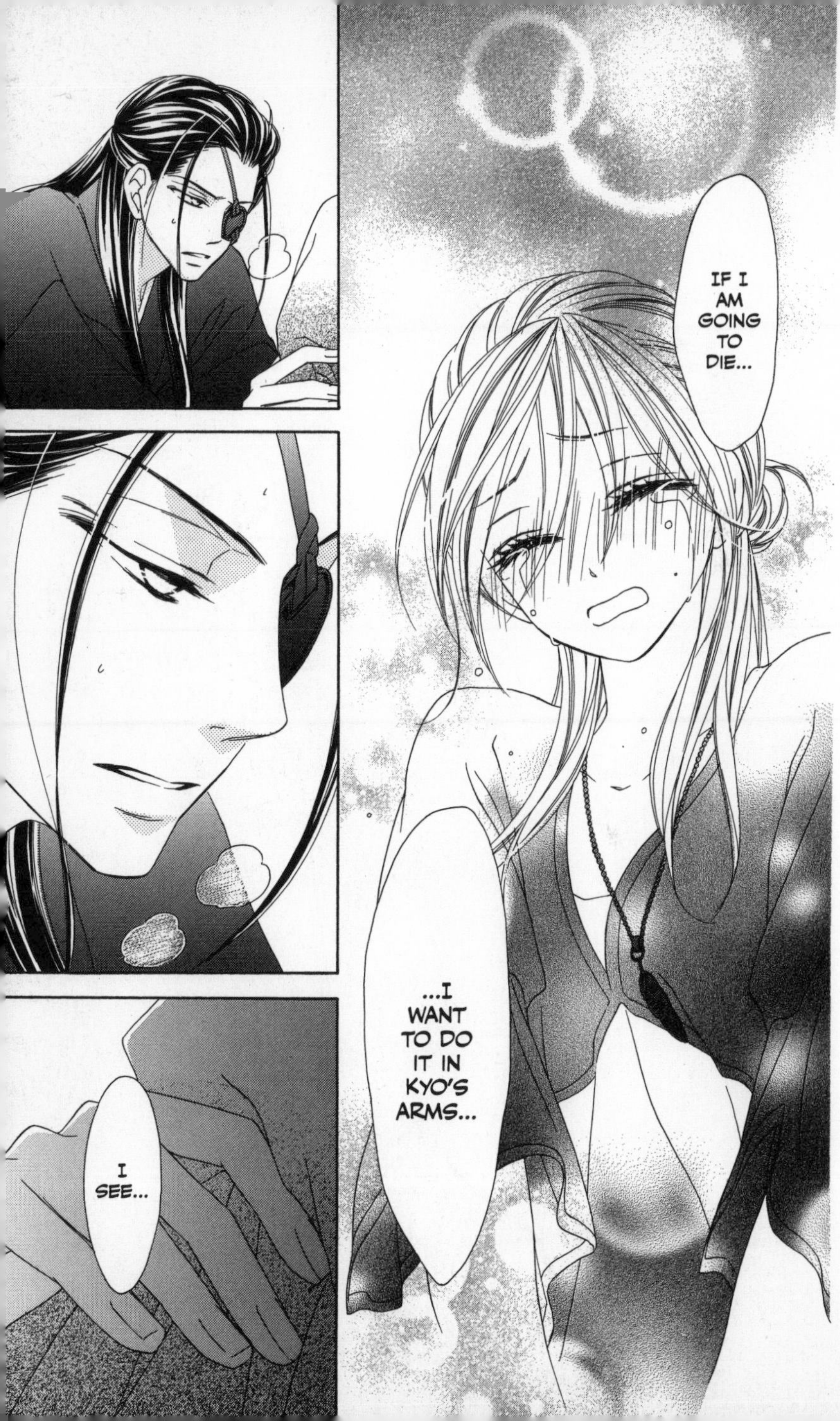
IF I AM GOING TO DIE...
...I WANT TO DO IT IN KYO'S ARMS...
I SEE...

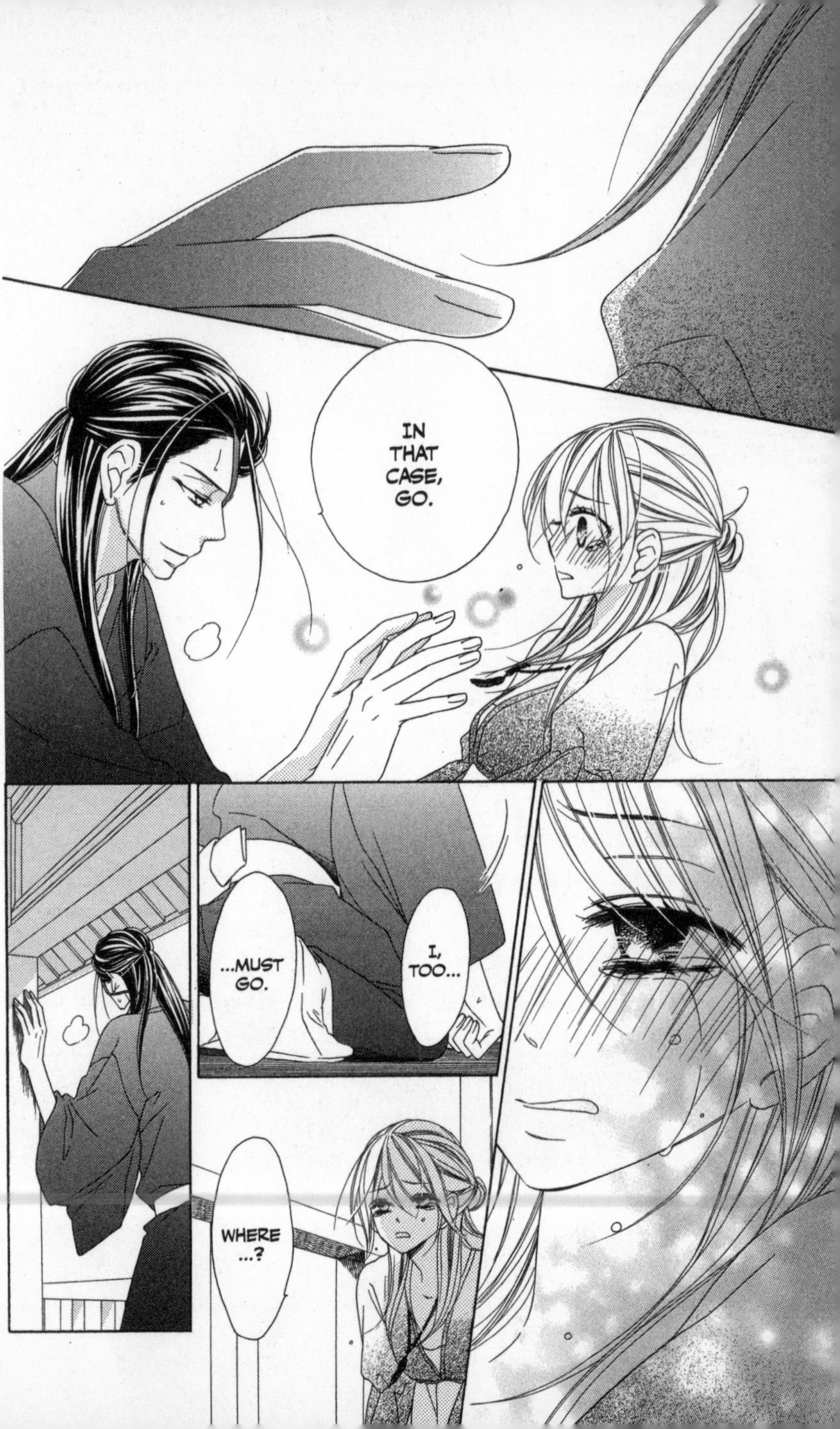
IN THAT CASE, GO.
I, TOO...
...MUST GO.
WHERE ...?

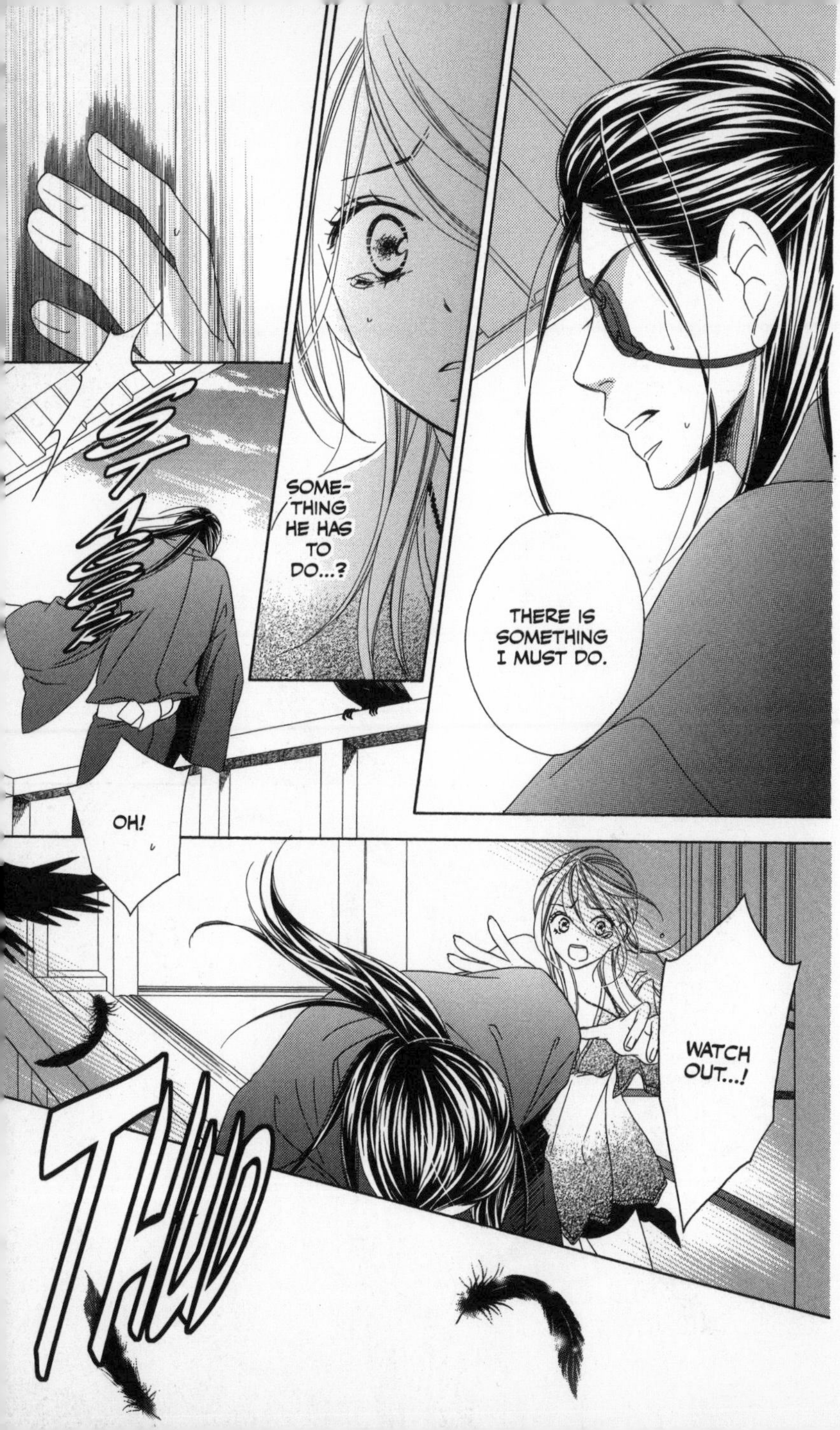
THERE IS SOMETHING I MUST DO.
SOME-THING HE HAS TO DO...?
OH!
WATCH OUT...!
THUD

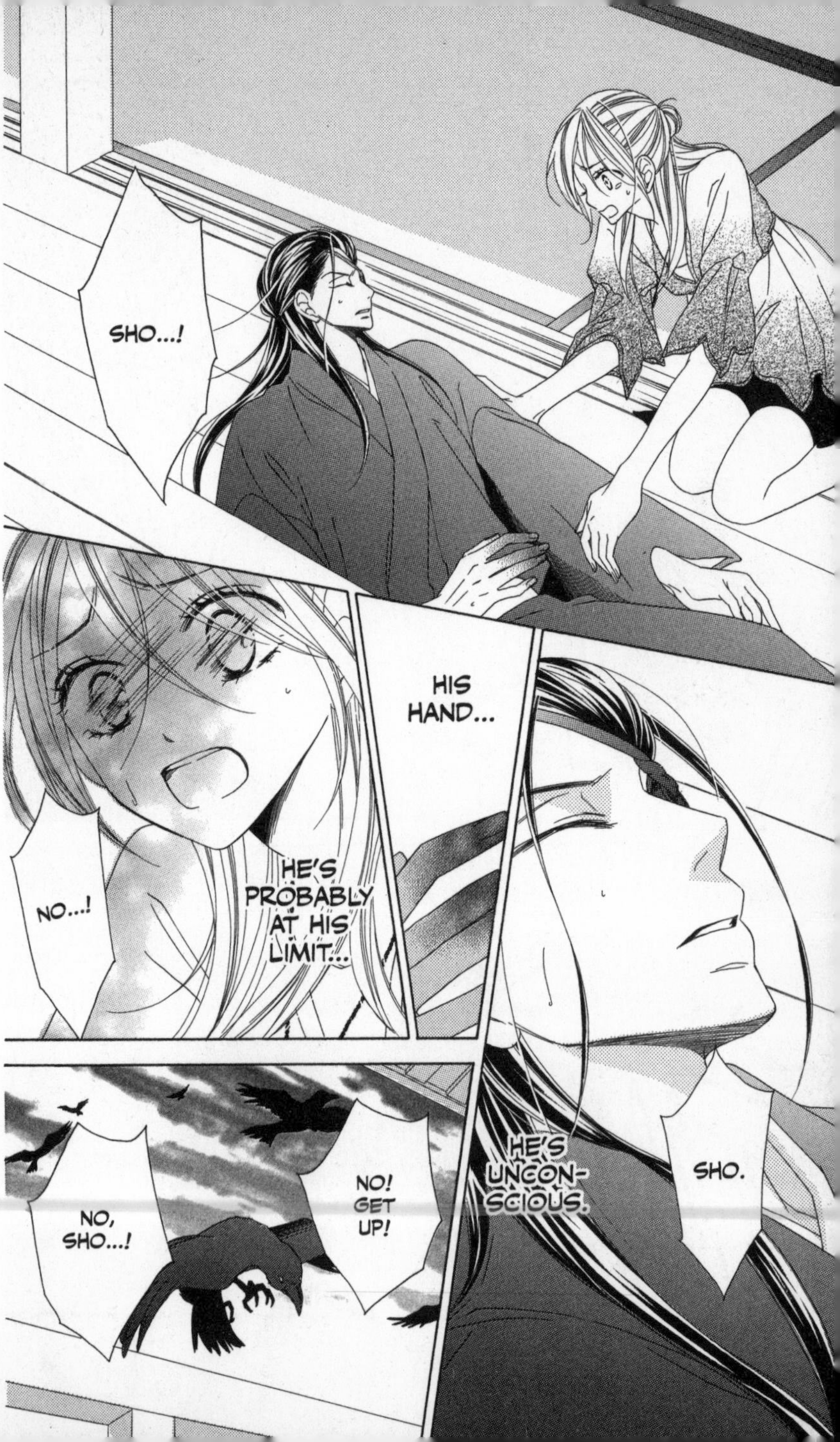
SHO...!
SHO.
HE'S UNCON-SCIOUS.
HIS HAND...
HE'S PROBABLY AT HIS LIMIT...
NO...!
NO! GET UP!
NO, SHO...!

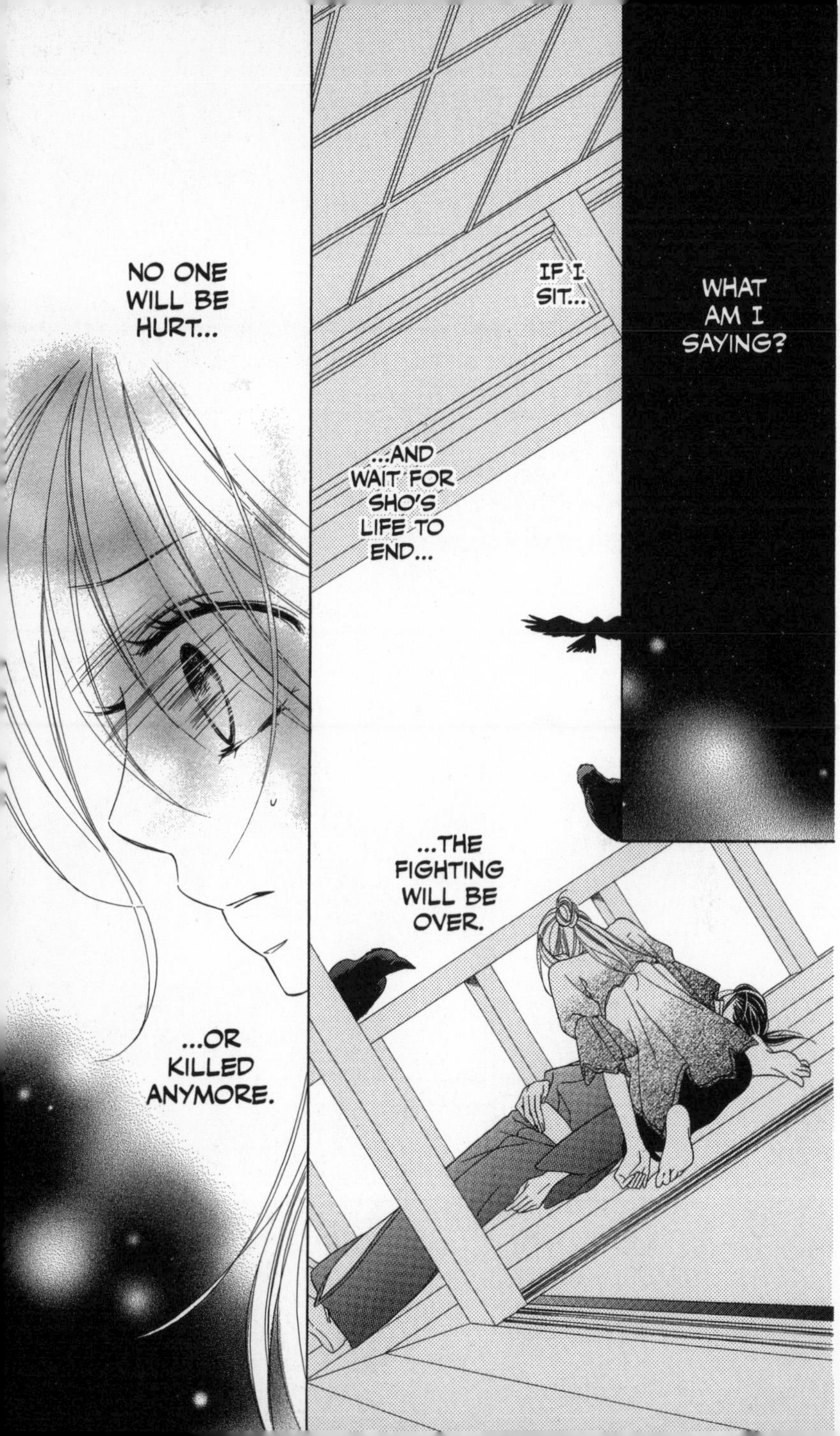
WHAT AM I SAYING?
IF I SIT...
...AND WAIT FOR SHO'S LIFE TO END...
...THE FIGHTING WILL BE OVER.
NO ONE WILL BE HURT...
...OR KILLED ANYMORE.

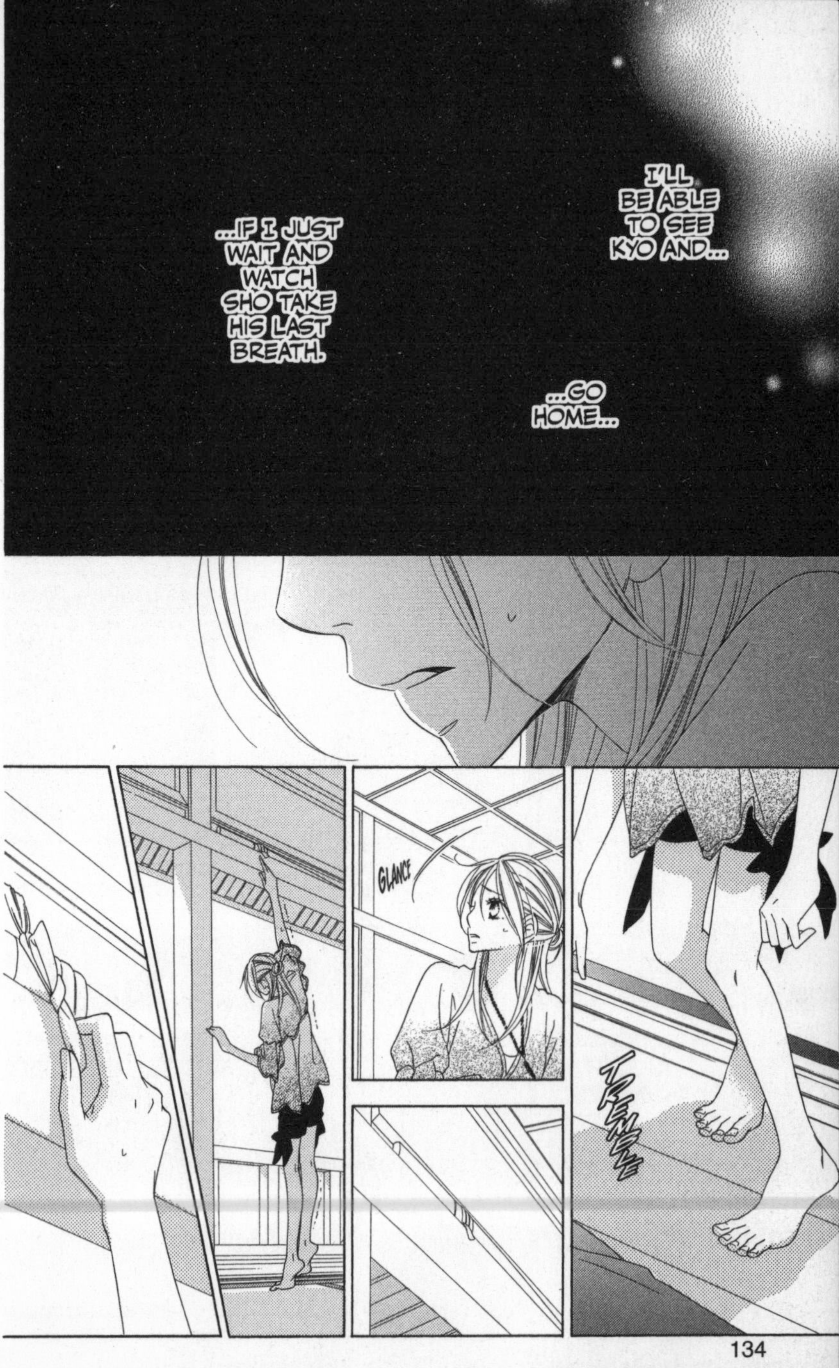
I'LL BE ABLE TO SEE KYO AND...
...GO HOME...
...IF I JUST WAIT AND WATCH SHO TAKE HIS LAST BREATH.
TREMBLE
GLANCE

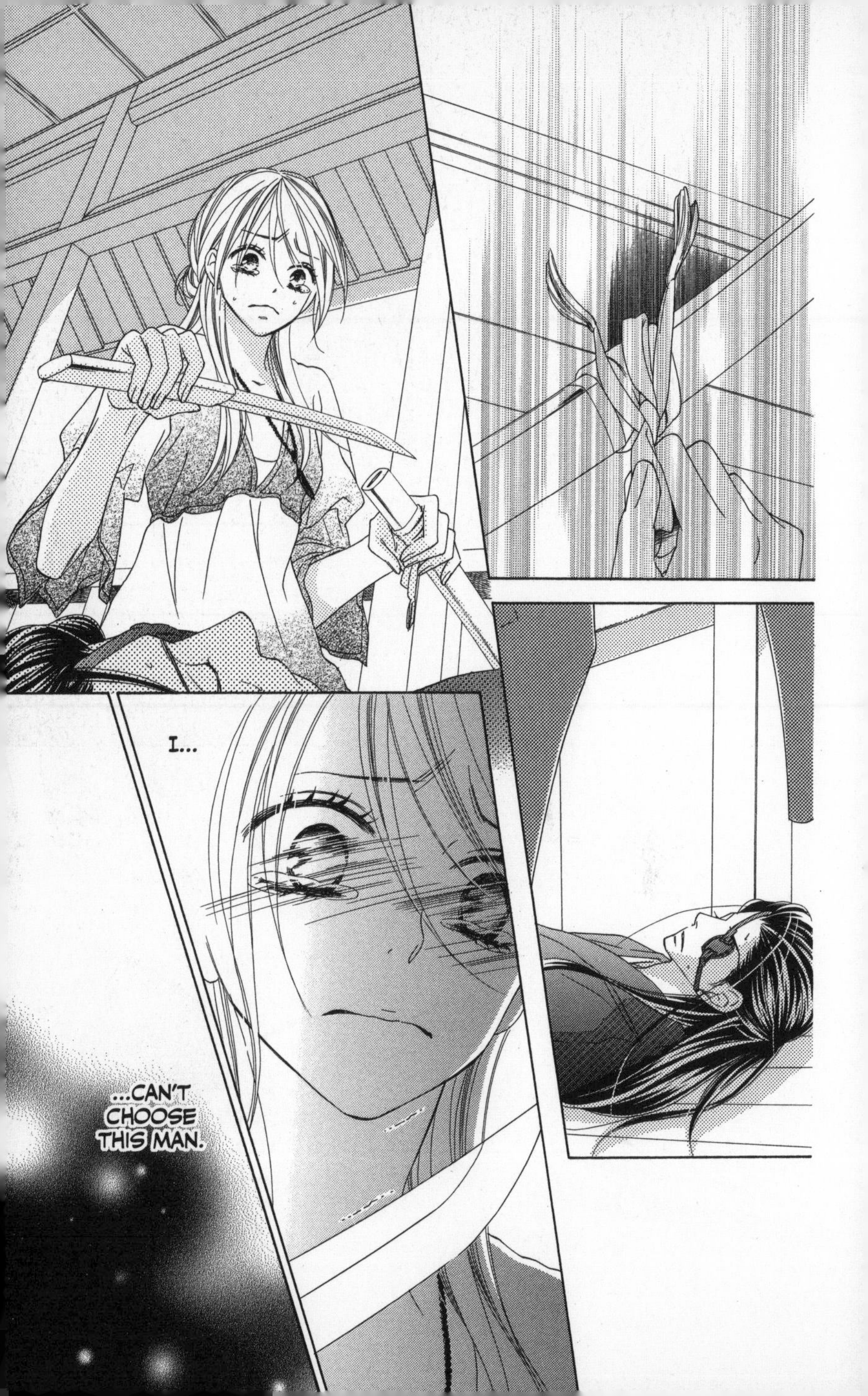
I...
...CAN'T CHOOSE THIS MAN.

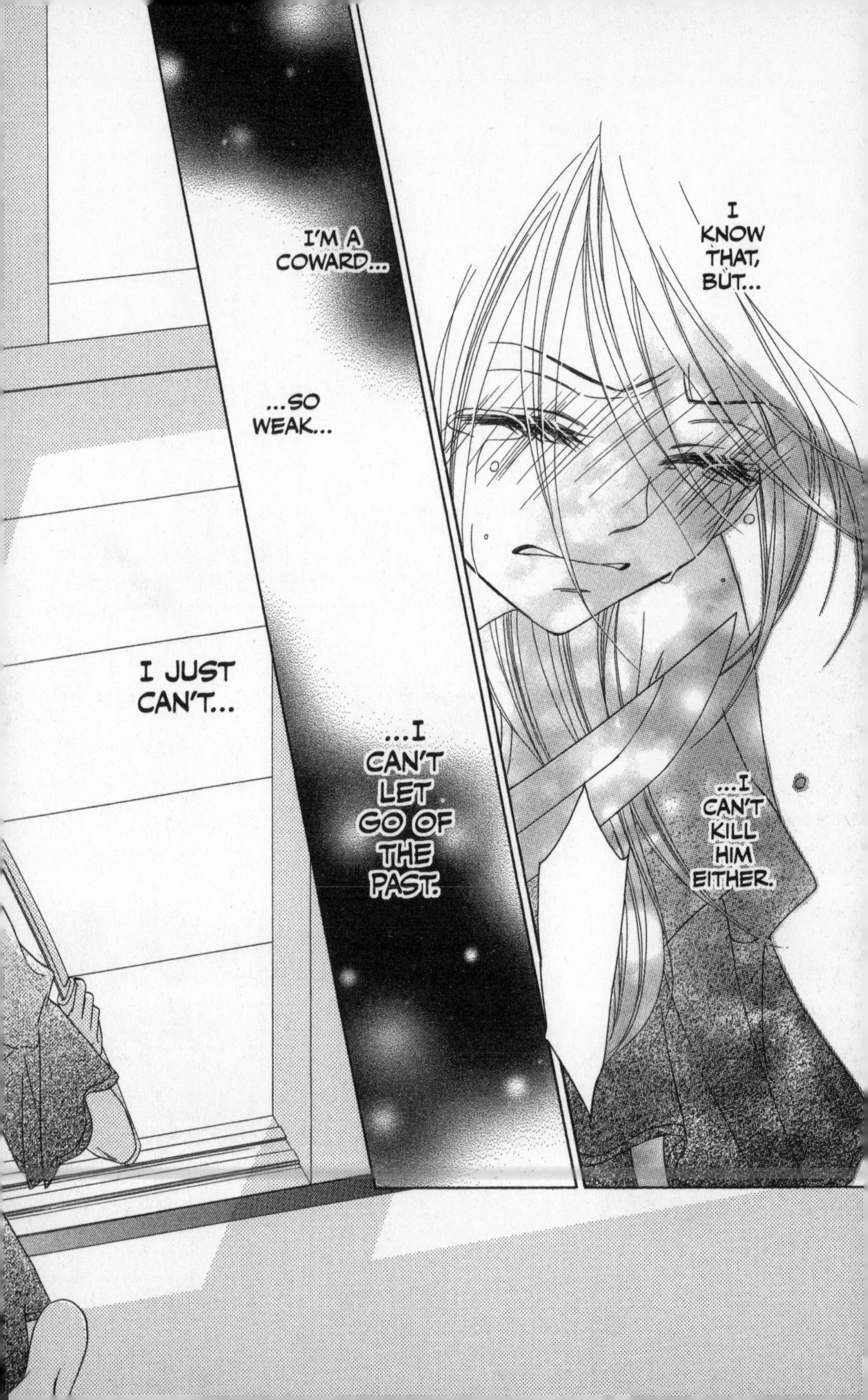
I KNOW THAT, BUT...
...I CAN'T KILL HIM EITHER.
I'M A COWARD...
...SO WEAK...
I JUST CAN'T...
...I CAN'T LET GO OF THE PAST.

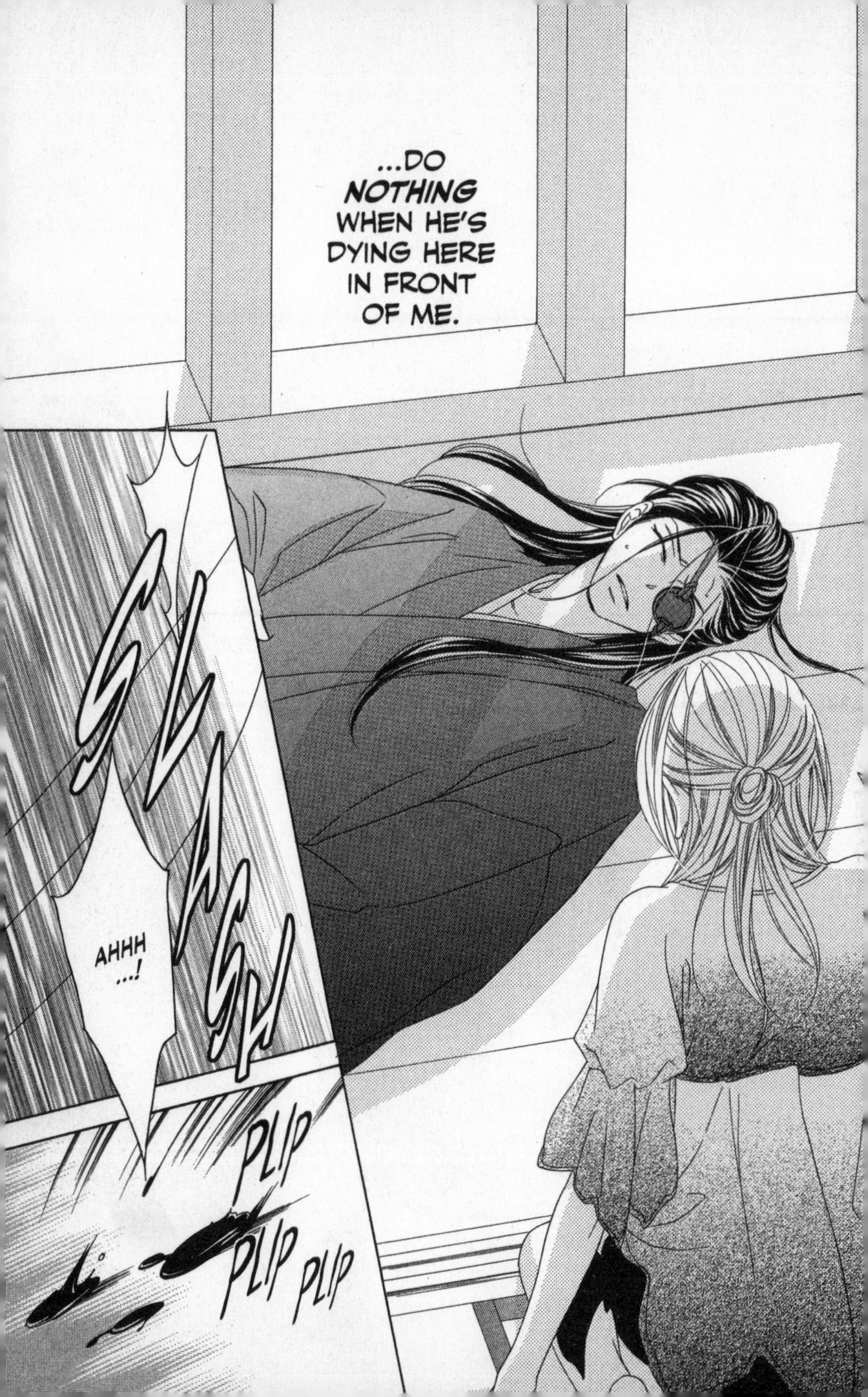
...DO *NOTHING* WHEN HE'S DYING HERE IN FRONT OF ME.
SWASH
AHHH ...!
PLIP
PLIP
PLIP

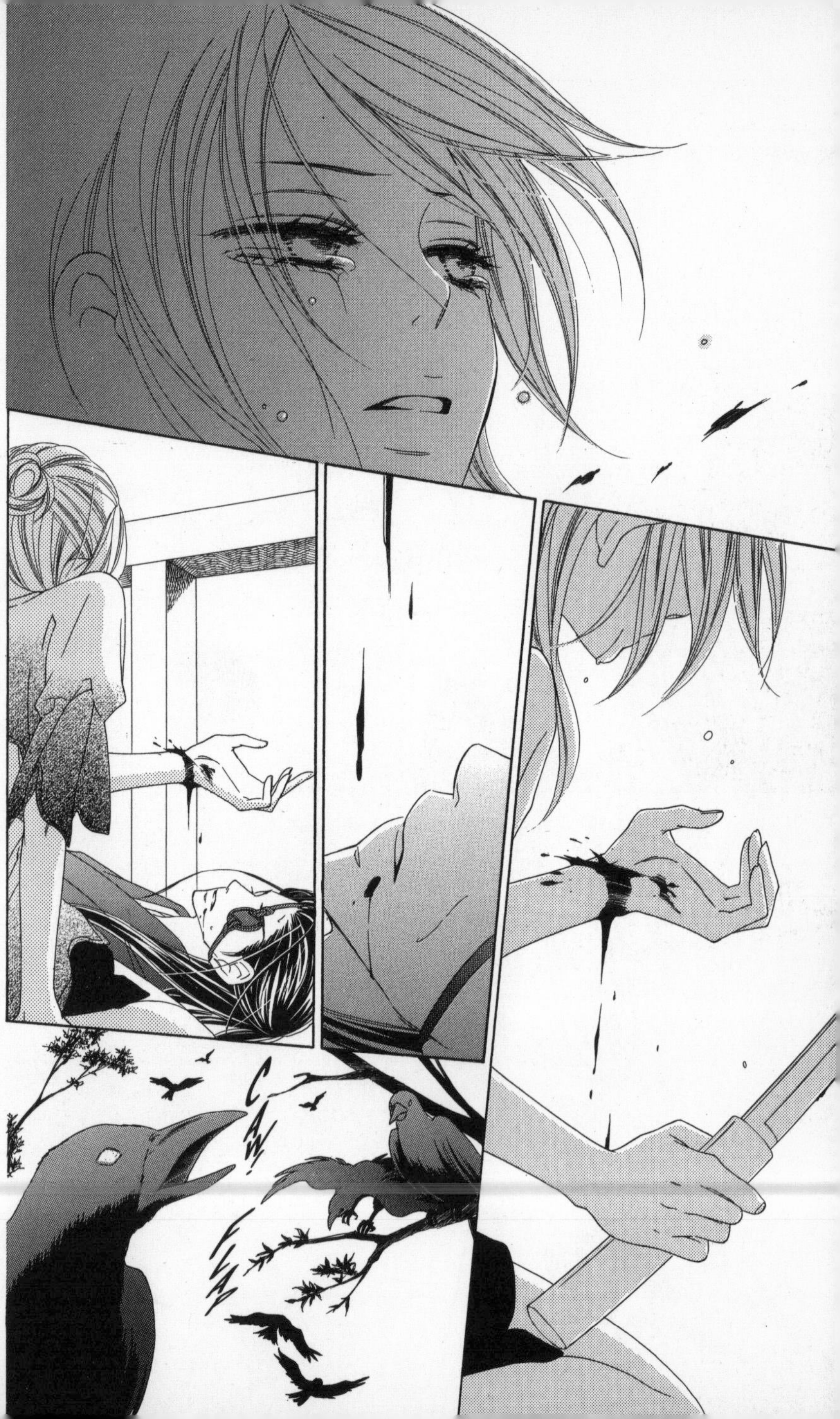
CAW!
FWM

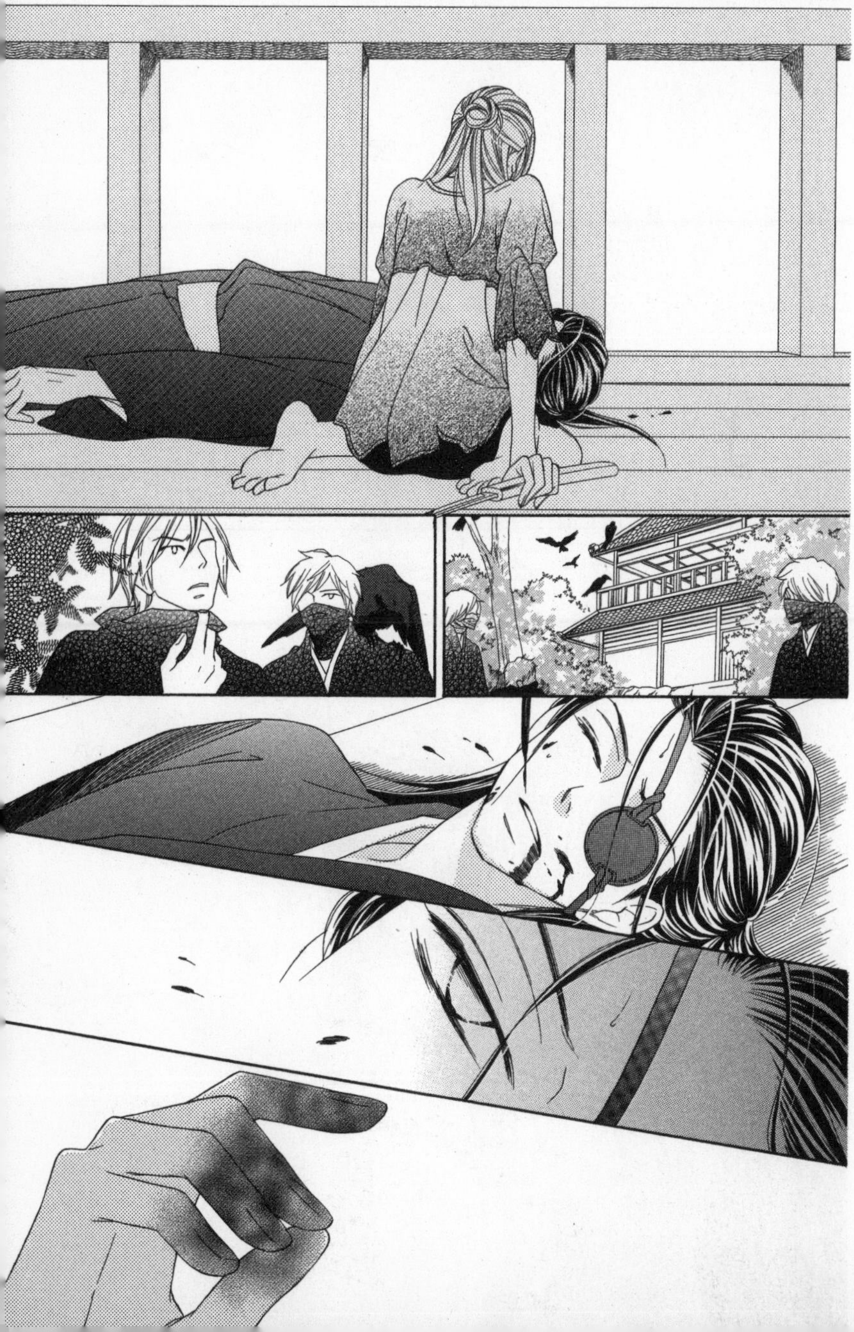

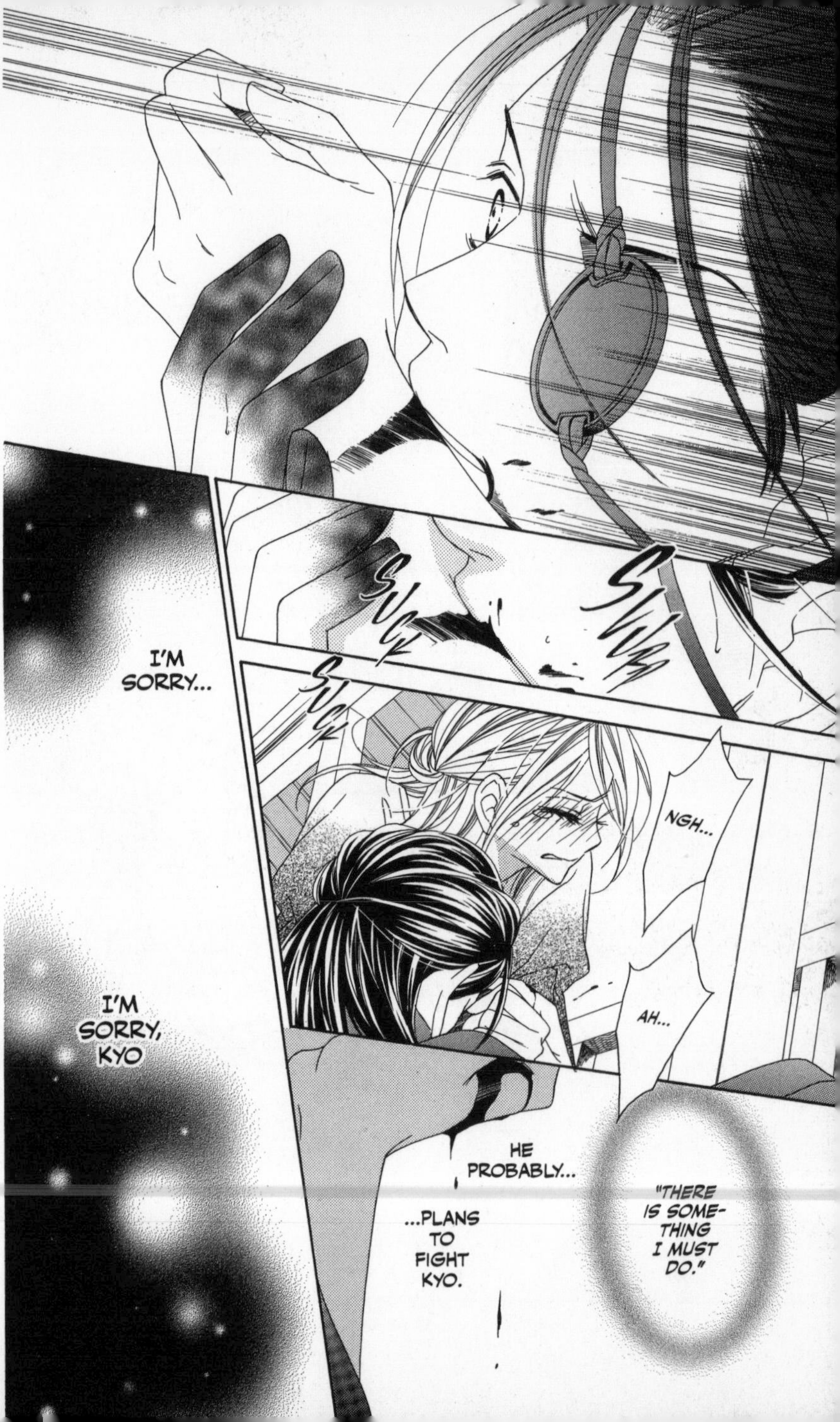

SLAM
SUCK
SUCK
NGH...
AH...
"THERE IS SOME-THING I MUST DO."
HE PROBABLY...
...PLANS TO FIGHT KYO.
I'M SORRY...
I'M SORRY, KYO

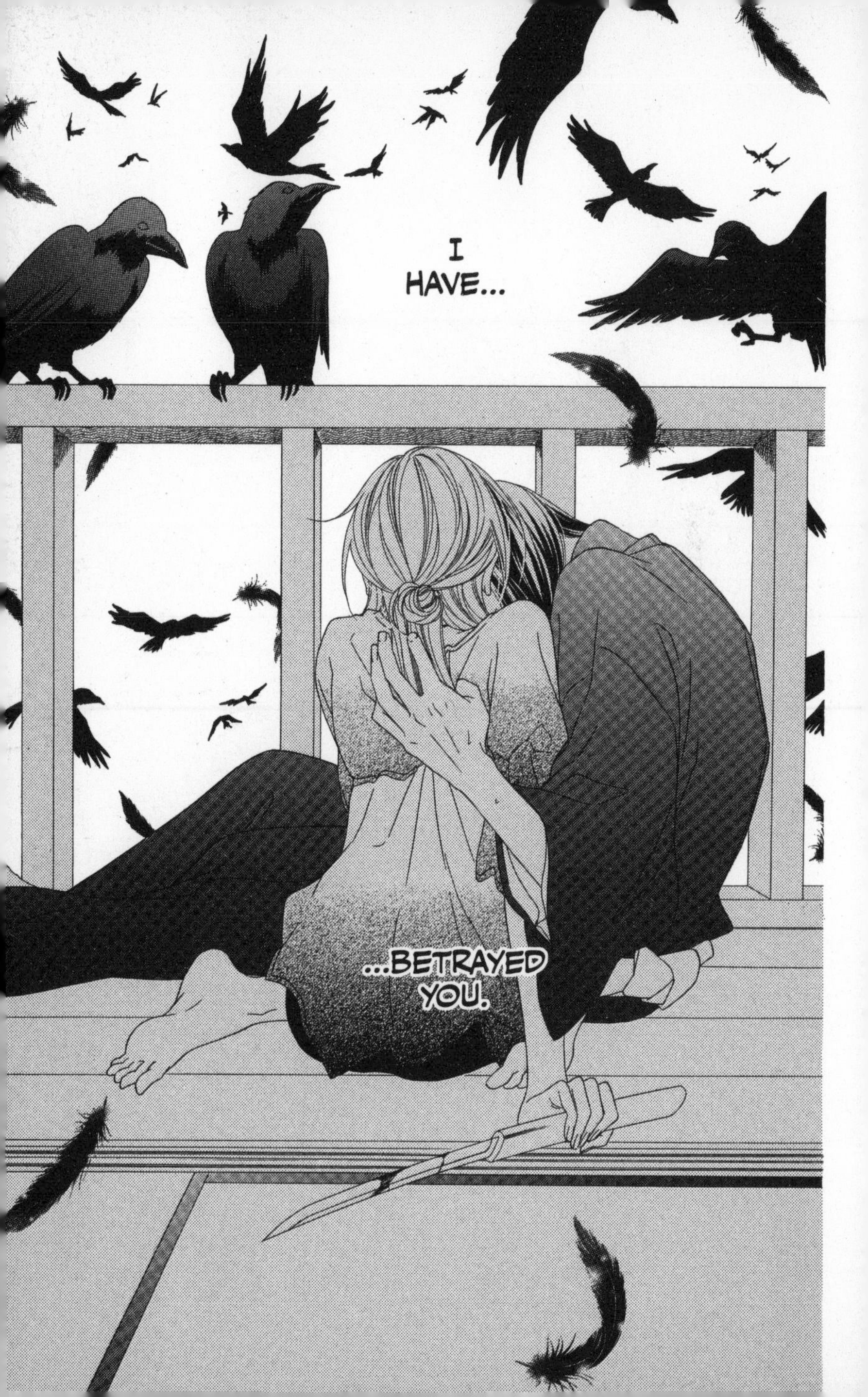
I HAVE...
...BETRAYED YOU.

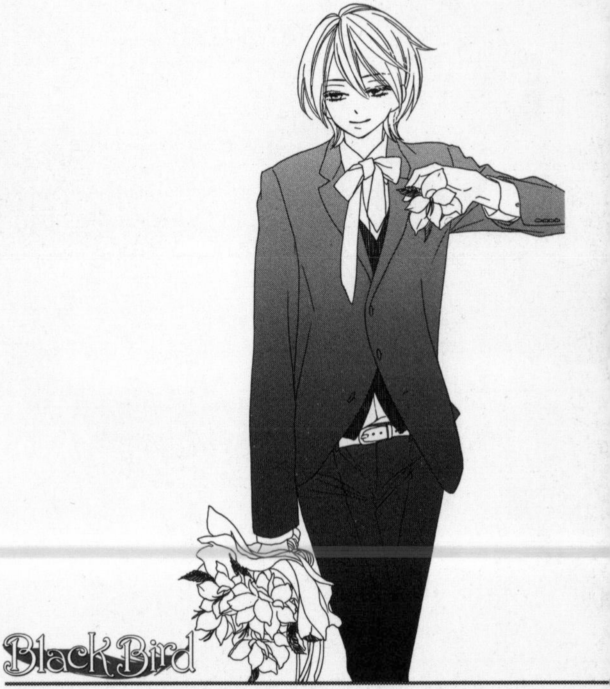
Black Bird

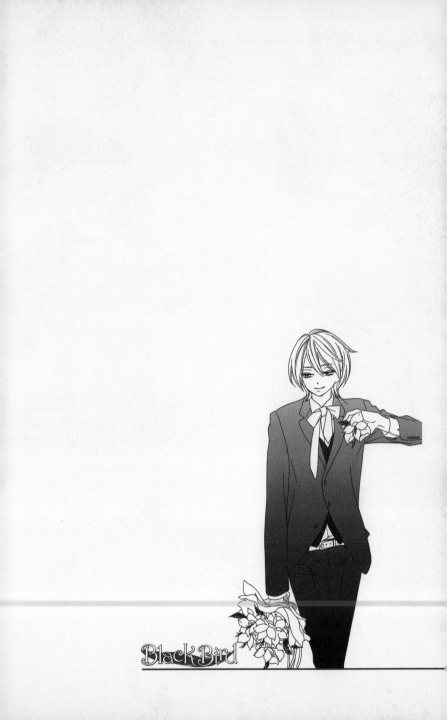

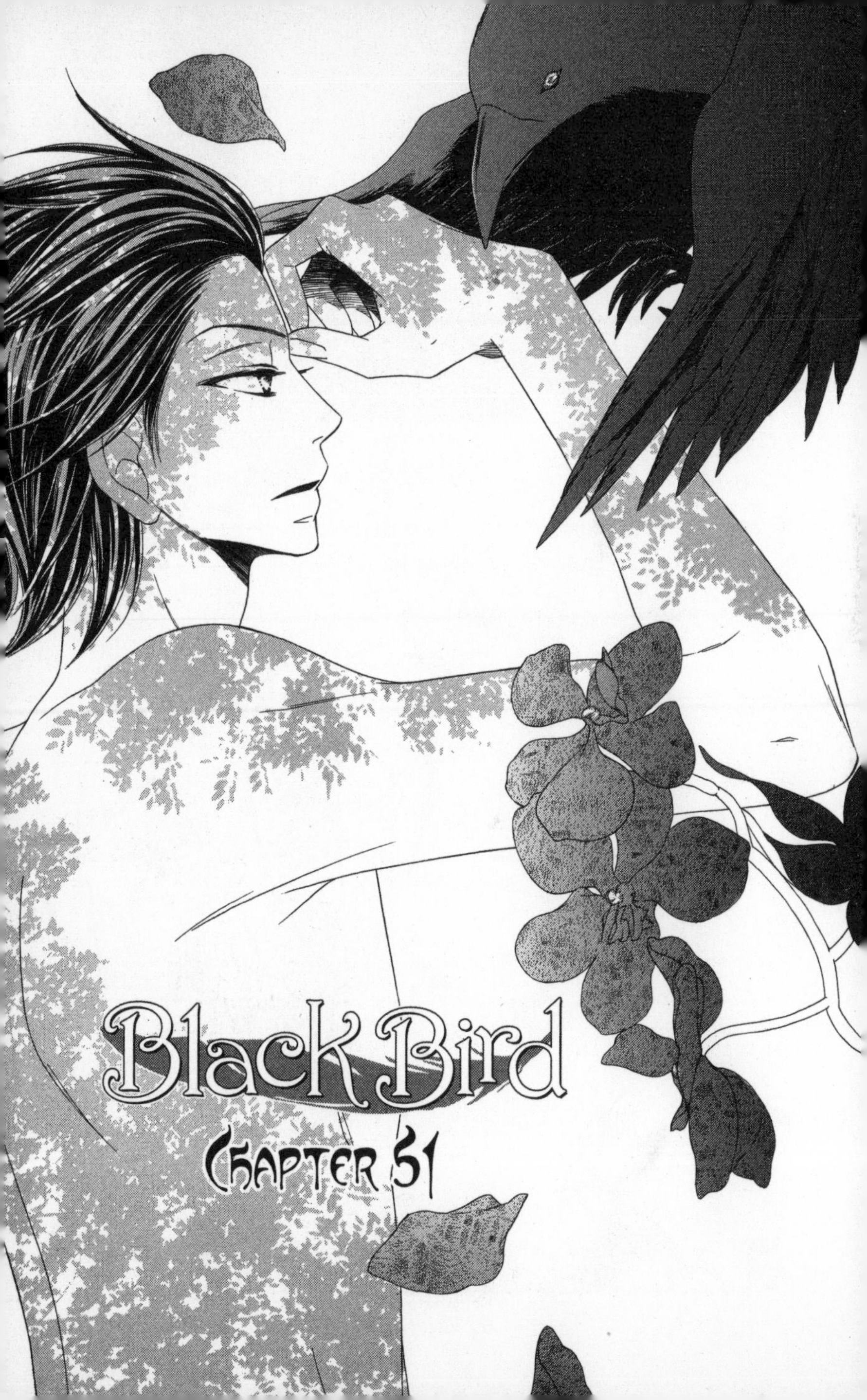
Black Bird
Chapter 51

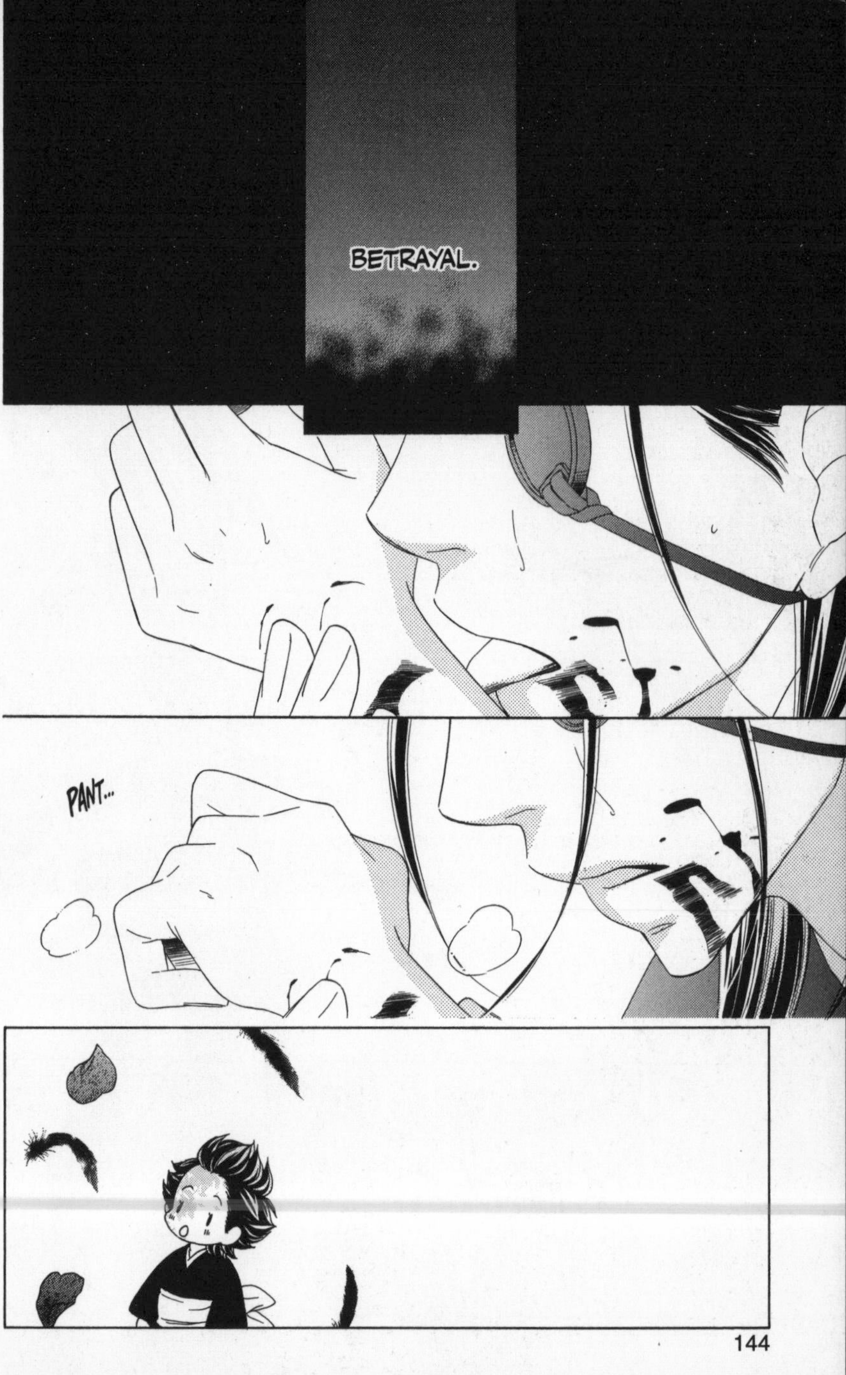
BETRAYAL.
PANT...

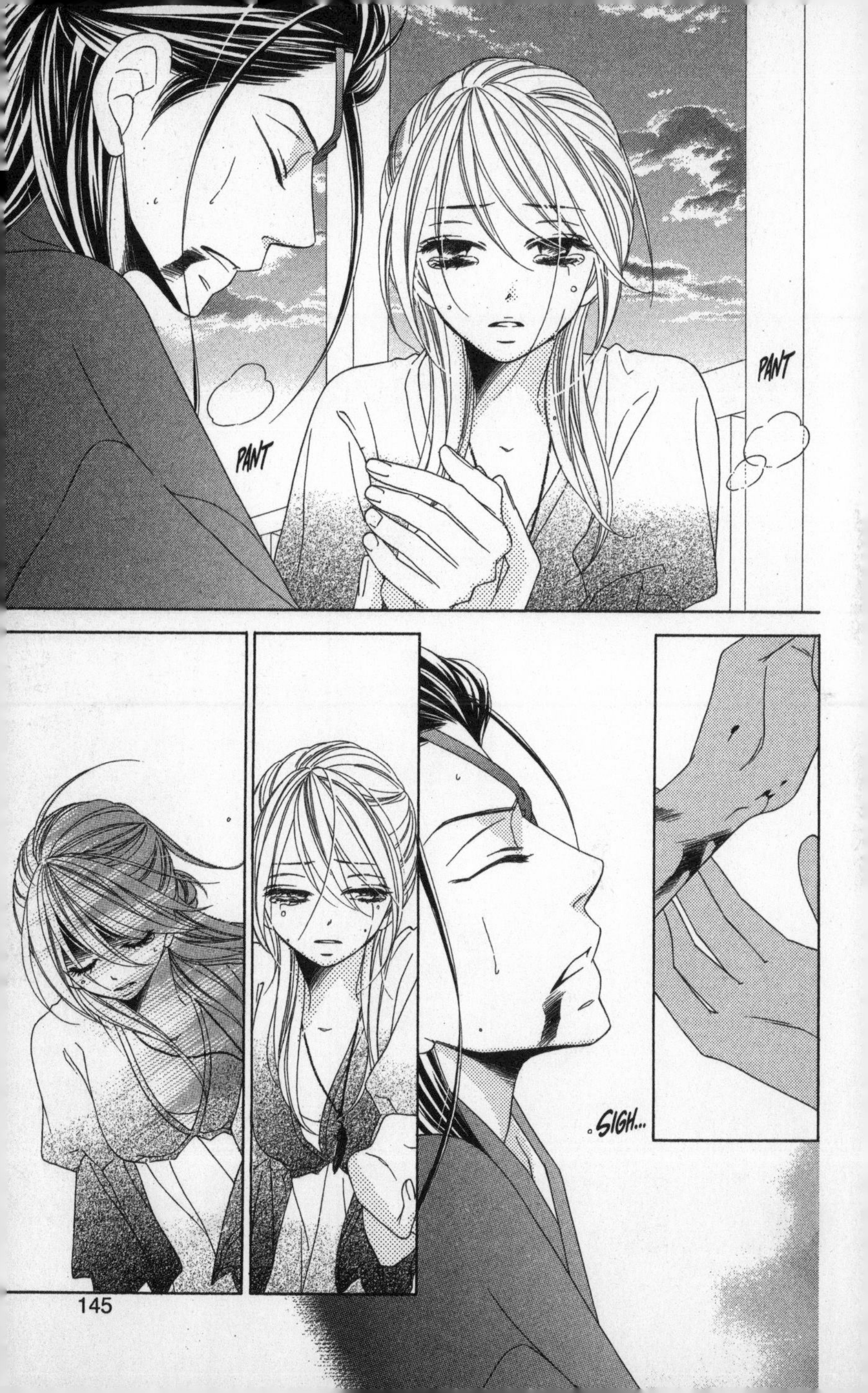
PANT
PANT
SIGH...

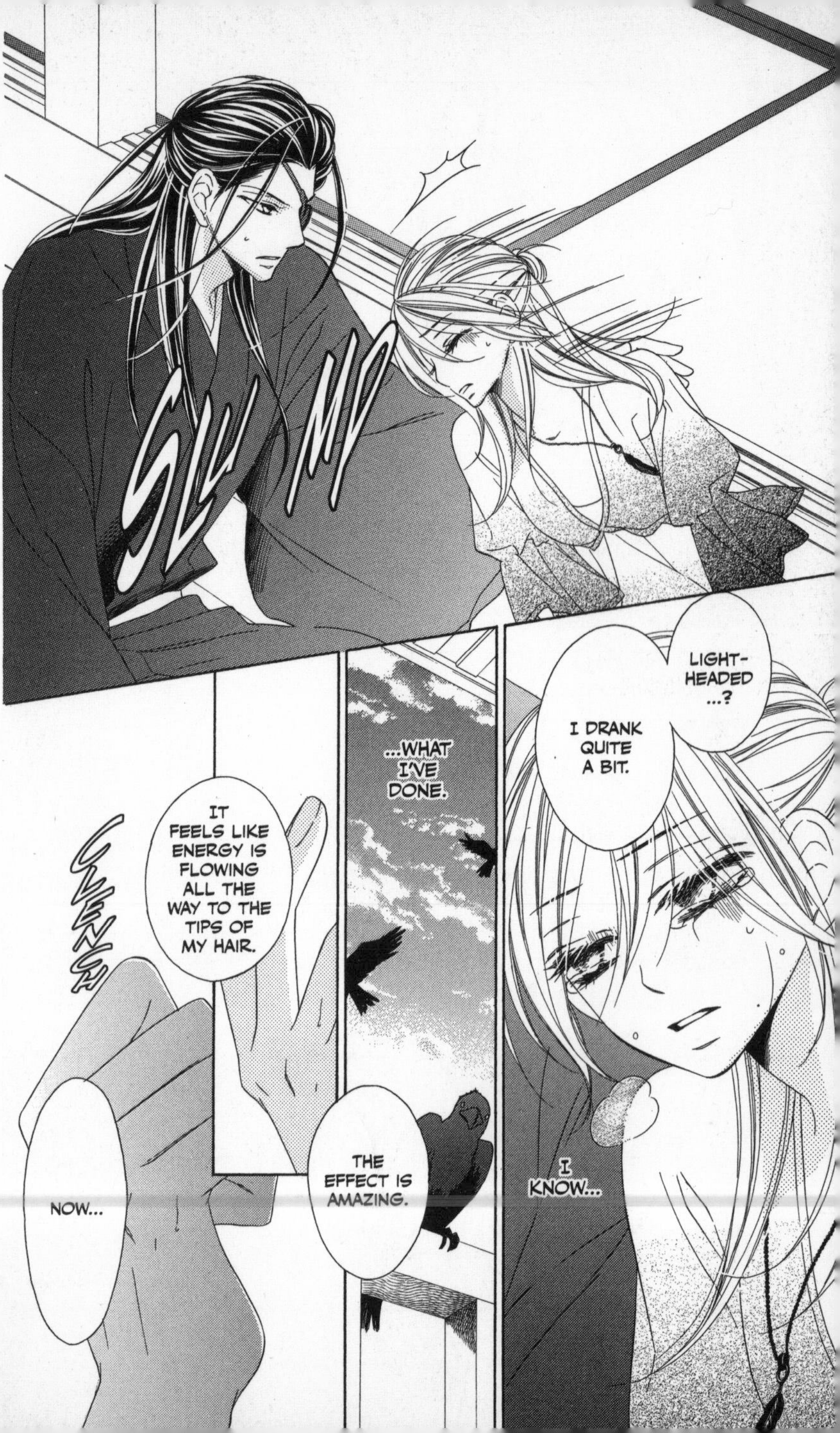
SLUMP
LIGHT-HEADED ...?
I DRANK QUITE A BIT.
I KNOW...
...WHAT I'VE DONE.
THE EFFECT IS AMAZING.
IT FEELS LIKE ENERGY IS FLOWING ALL THE WAY TO THE TIPS OF MY HAIR.
CLENCH
NOW...

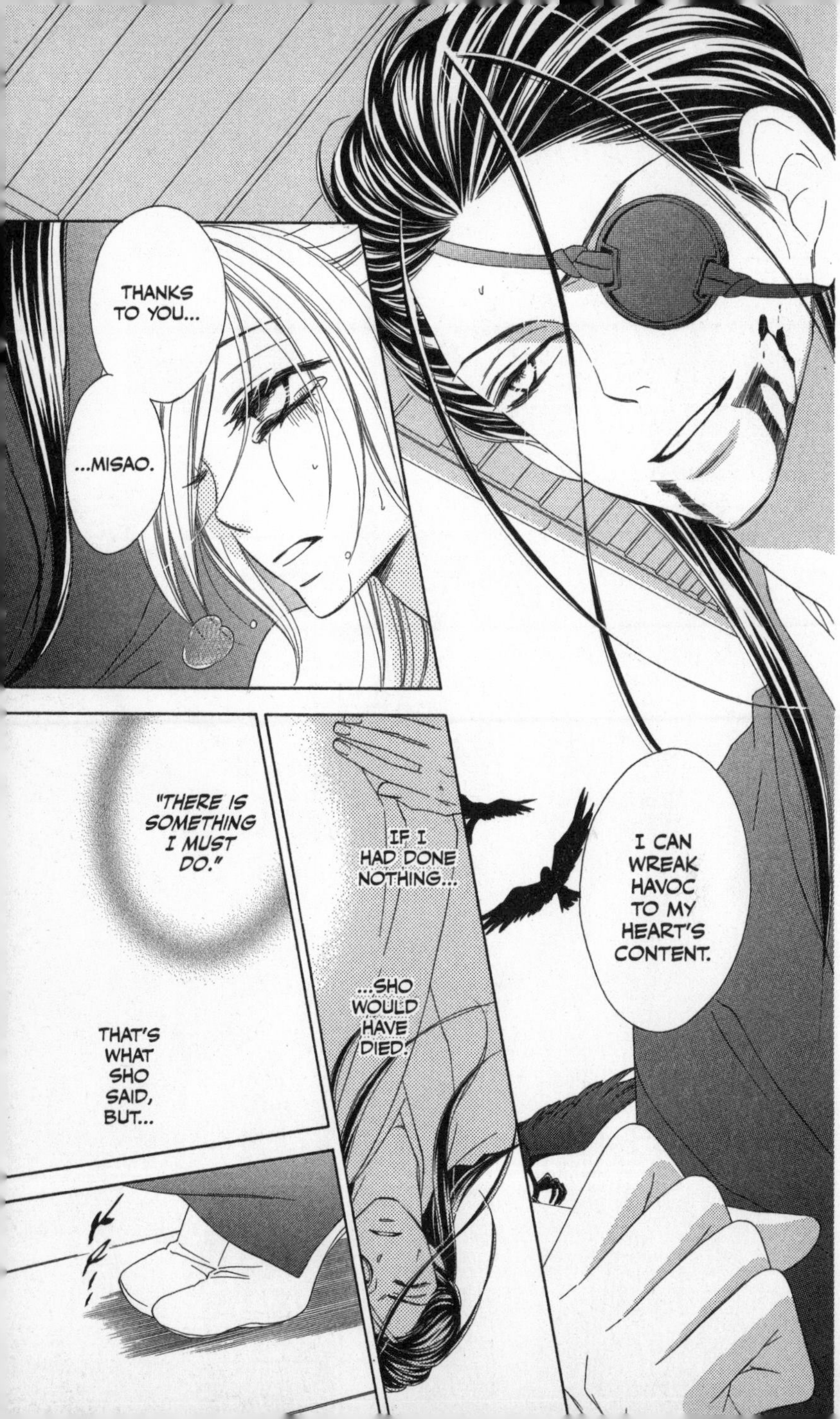
THANKS TO YOU...
...MISAO.
I CAN WREAK HAVOC TO MY HEART'S CONTENT.
IF I HAD DONE NOTHING...
...SHO WOULD HAVE DIED.
"THERE IS SOMETHING I MUST DO."
THAT'S WHAT SHO SAID, BUT...

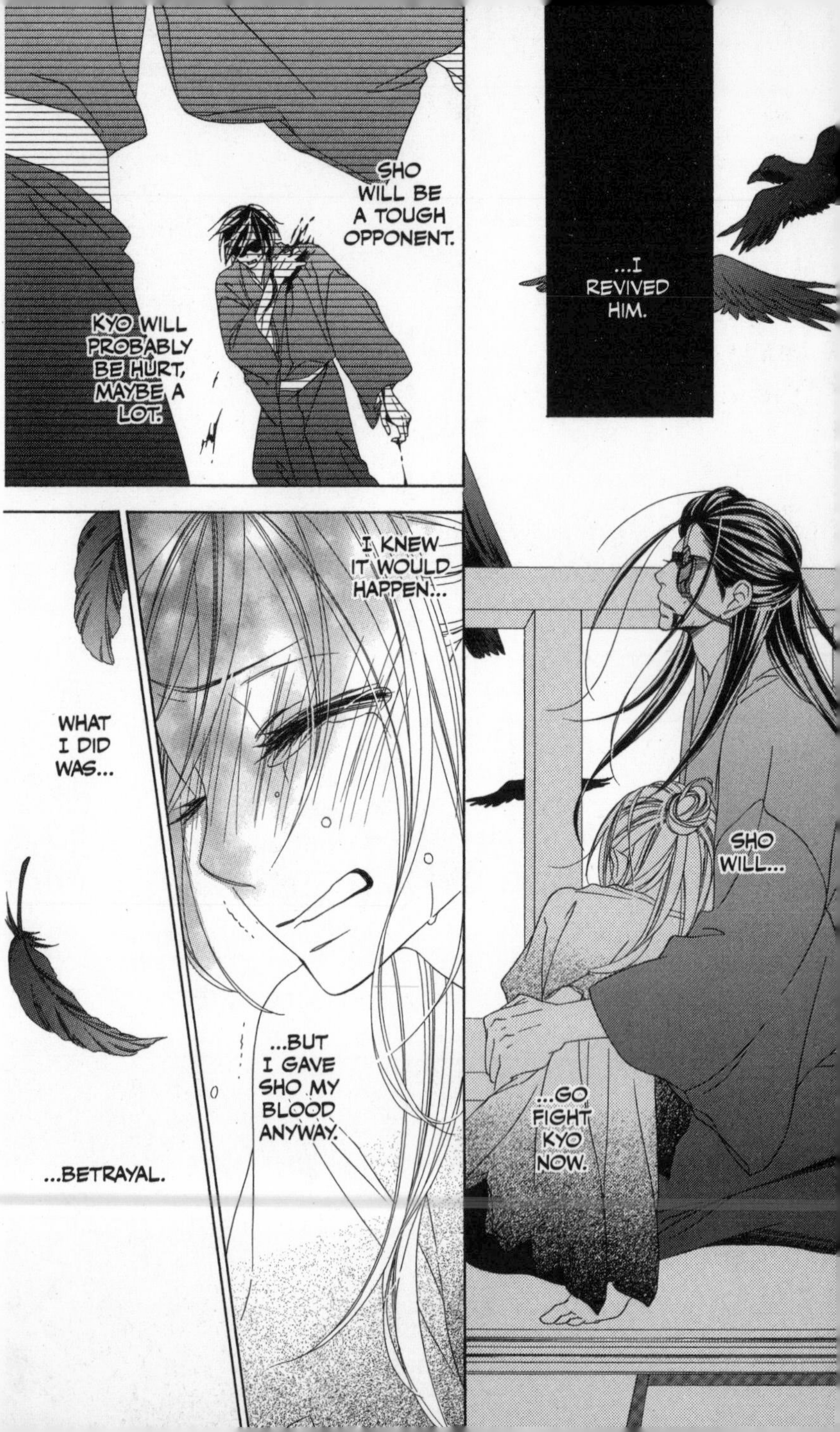
...I REVIVED HIM.
SHO WILL BE A TOUGH OPPONENT.
KYO WILL PROBABLY BE HURT, MAYBE A LOT.
SHO WILL...
...GO FIGHT KYO NOW.
I KNEW IT WOULD HAPPEN...
...BUT I GAVE SHO MY BLOOD ANYWAY.
WHAT I DID WAS...
...BETRAYAL.

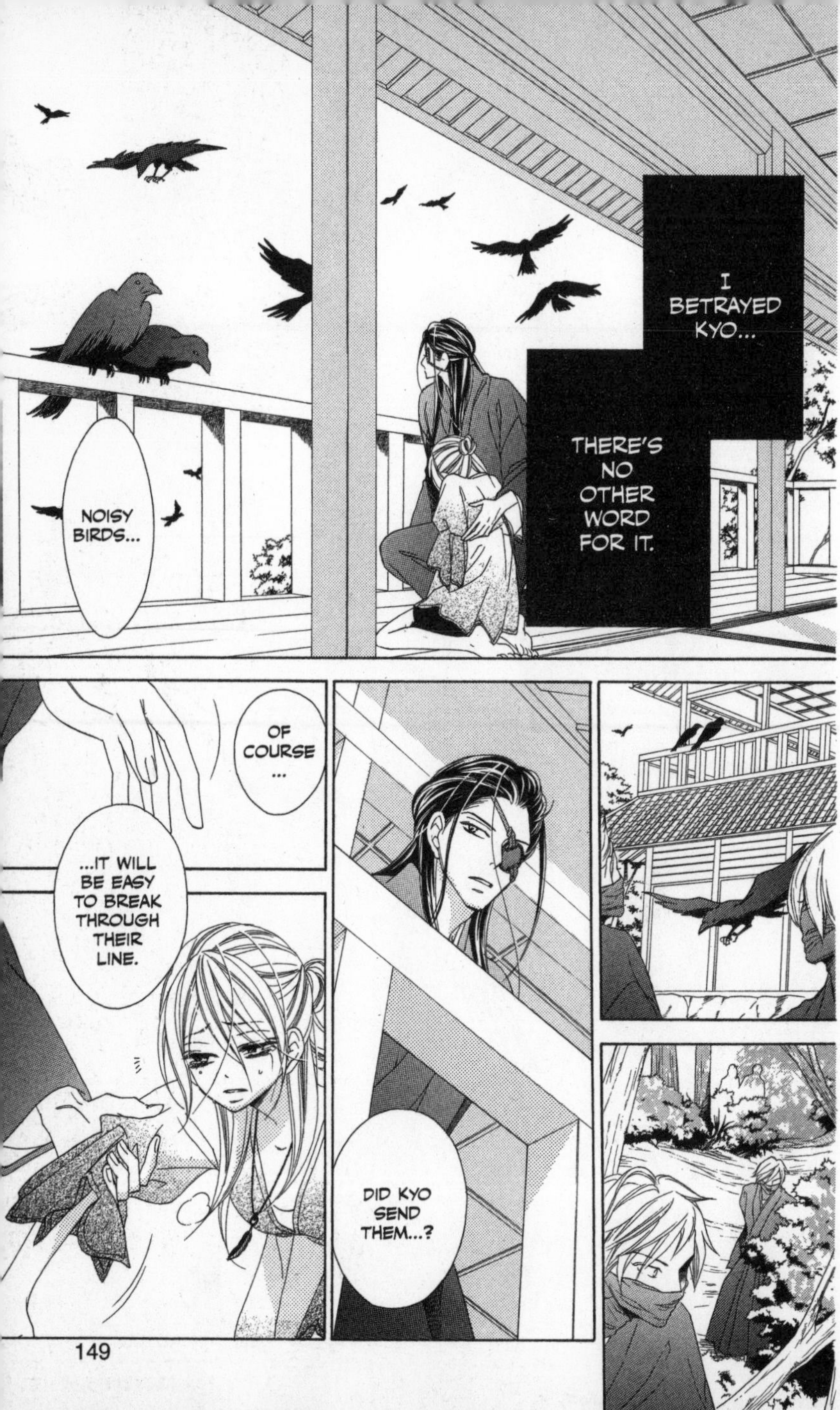
I BETRAYED KYO...
THERE'S NO OTHER WORD FOR IT.
NOISY BIRDS...
DID KYO SEND THEM...?
OF COURSE...
...IT WILL BE EASY TO BREAK THROUGH THEIR LINE.

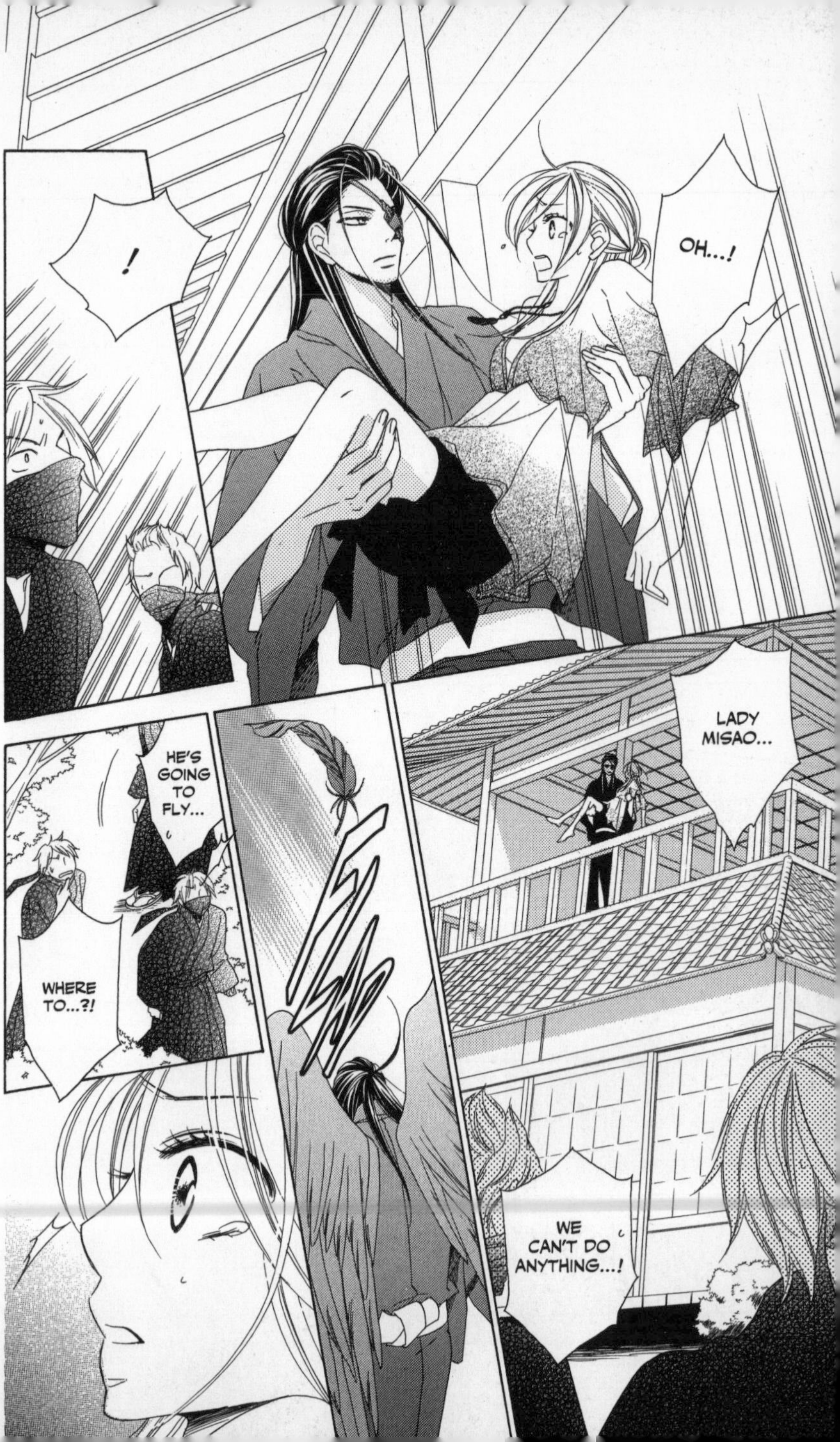
OH...!
!
LADY MISAO...
HE'S GOING TO FLY...
WHERE TO...?!
WE CAN'T DO ANYTHING...!

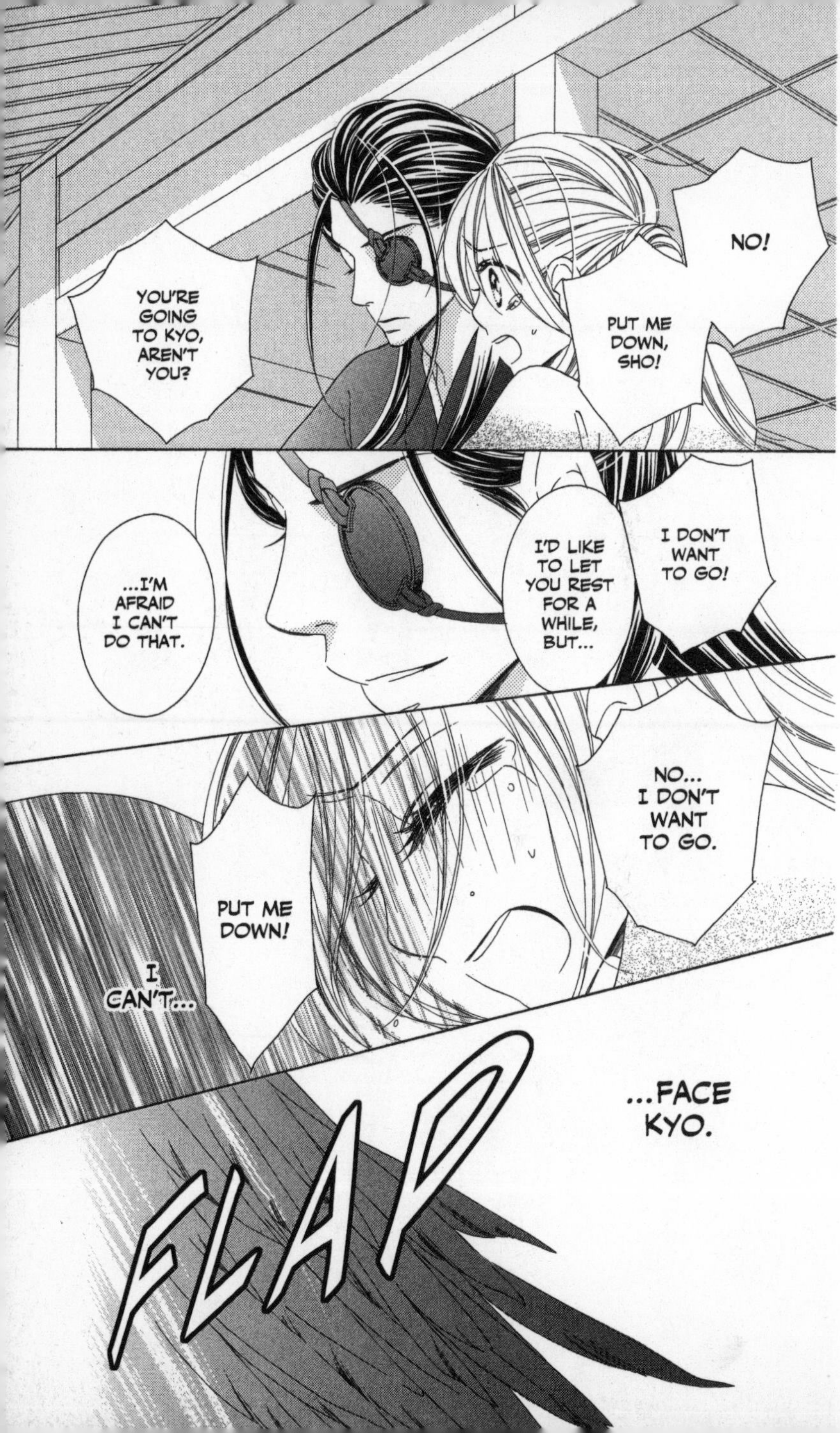
NO!
PUT ME DOWN, SHO!
YOU'RE GOING TO KYO, AREN'T YOU?
I DON'T WANT TO GO!
I'D LIKE TO LET YOU REST FOR A WHILE, BUT...
...I'M AFRAID I CAN'T DO THAT.
NO... I DON'T WANT TO GO.
PUT ME DOWN!
I CAN'T...
...FACE KYO.
FLAP

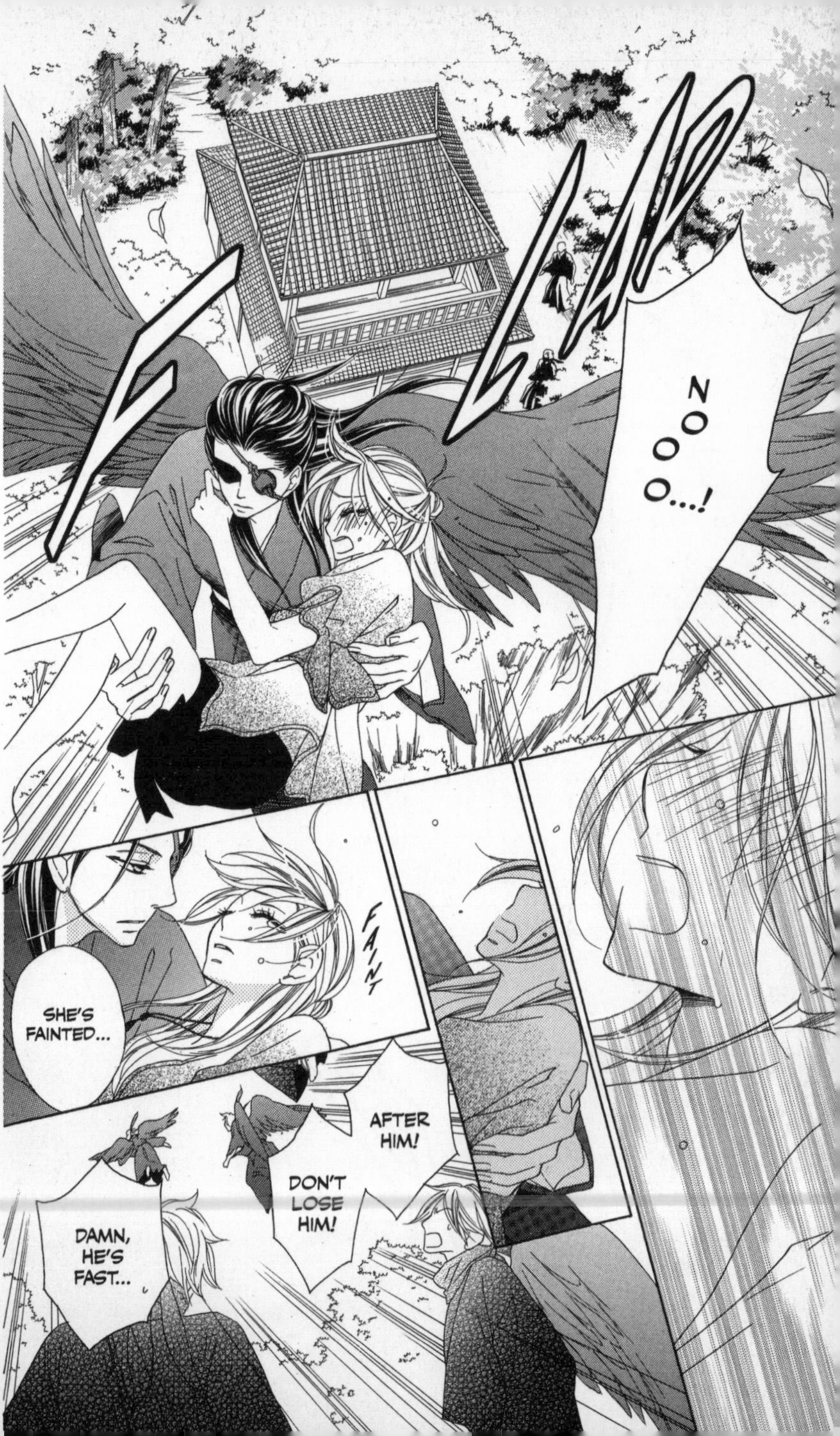
NOOOO...!
FAINT
SHE'S FAINTED...
AFTER HIM!
DON'T LOSE HIM!
DAMN, HE'S FAST...

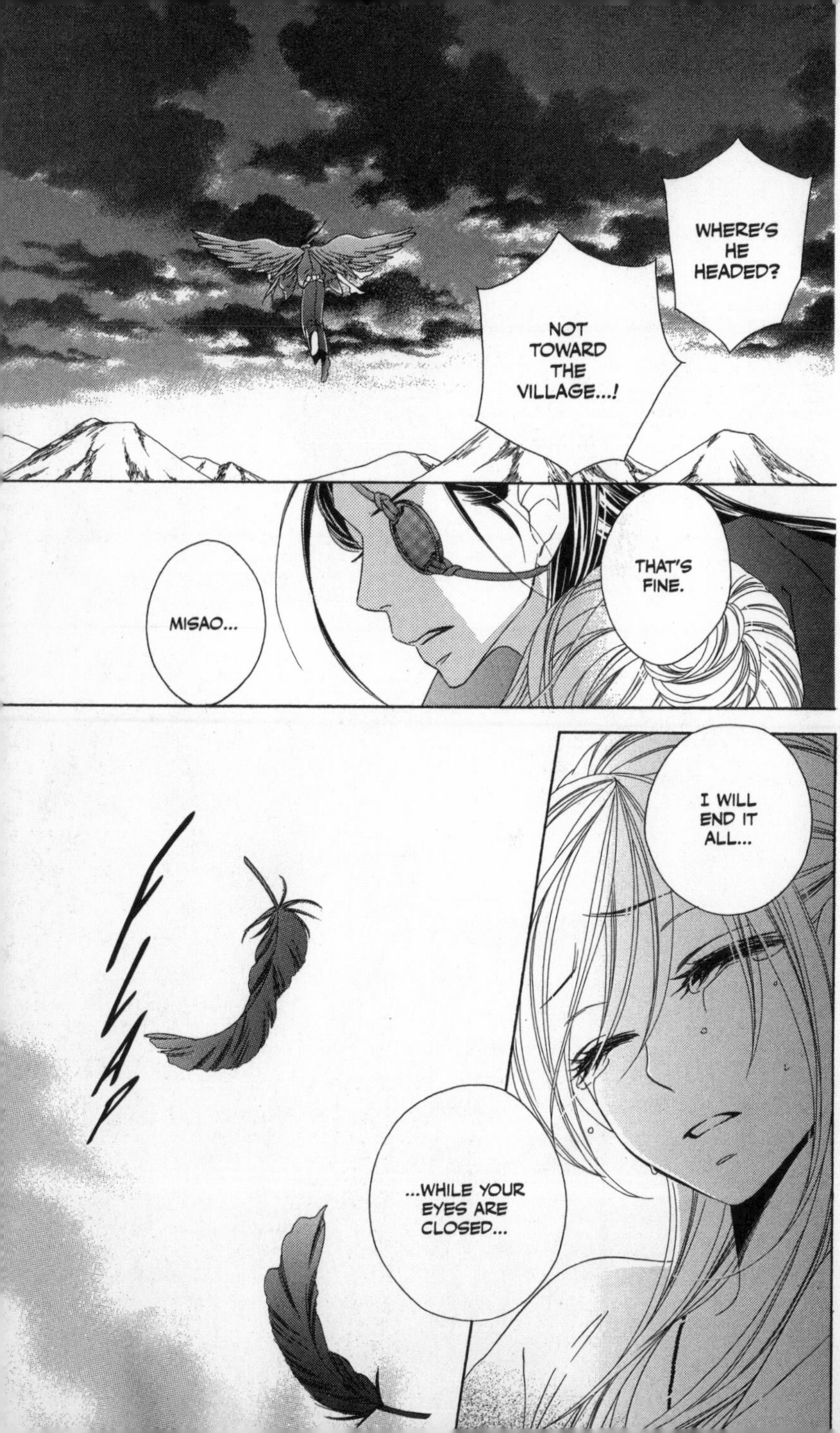
WHERE'S HE HEADED?
NOT TOWARD THE VILLAGE...!
THAT'S FINE.
MISAO...
I WILL END IT ALL...
...WHILE YOUR EYES ARE CLOSED...

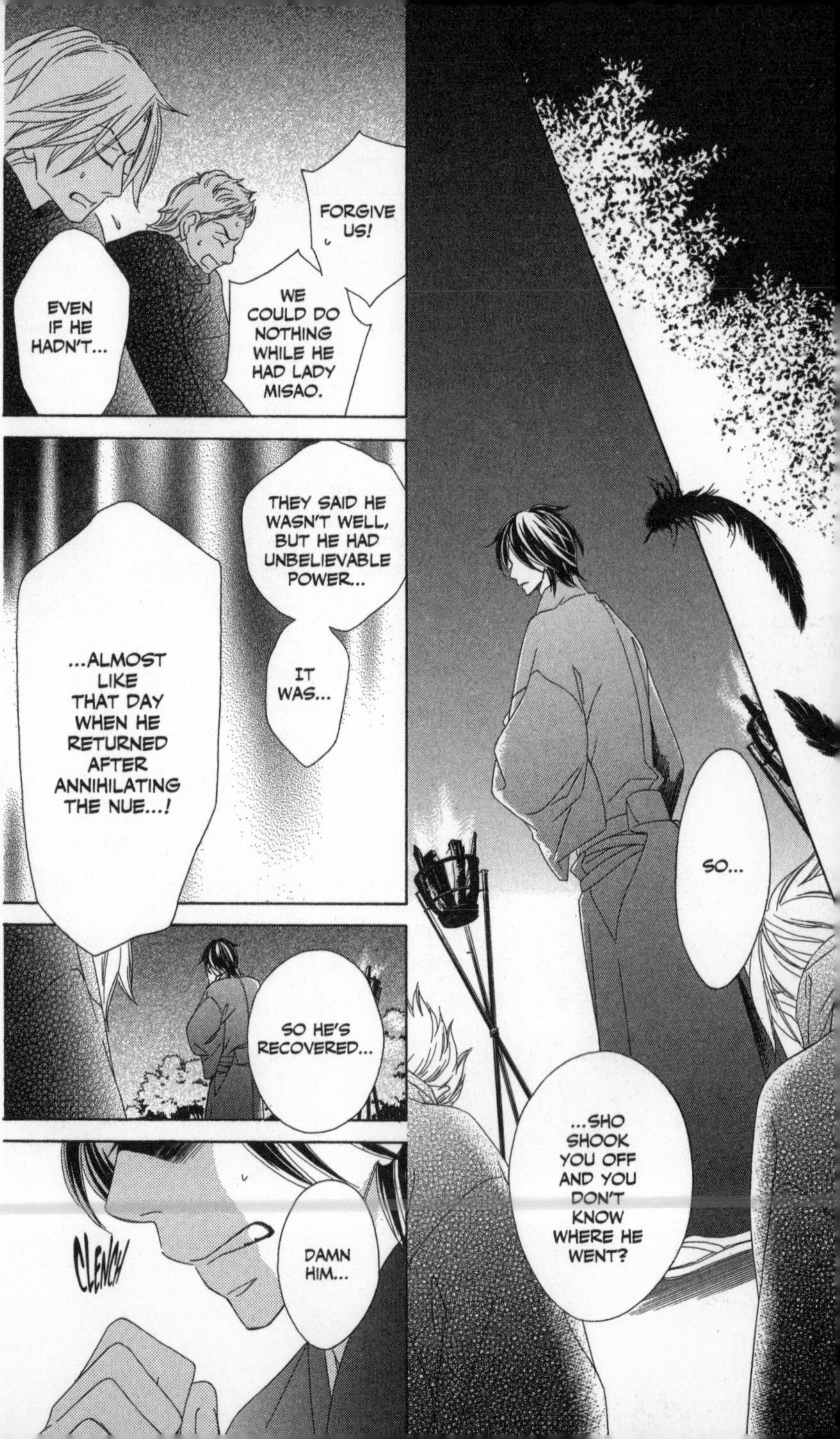
SO...
...SHO SHOOK YOU OFF AND YOU DON'T KNOW WHERE HE WENT?
FORGIVE US!
WE COULD DO NOTHING WHILE HE HAD LADY MISAO.
EVEN IF HE HADN'T...
THEY SAID HE WASN'T WELL, BUT HE HAD UNBELIEVABLE POWER...
IT WAS...
...ALMOST LIKE THAT DAY WHEN HE RETURNED AFTER ANNIHILATING THE NUE...!
SO HE'S RECOVERED...
CLENCH
DAMN HIM...

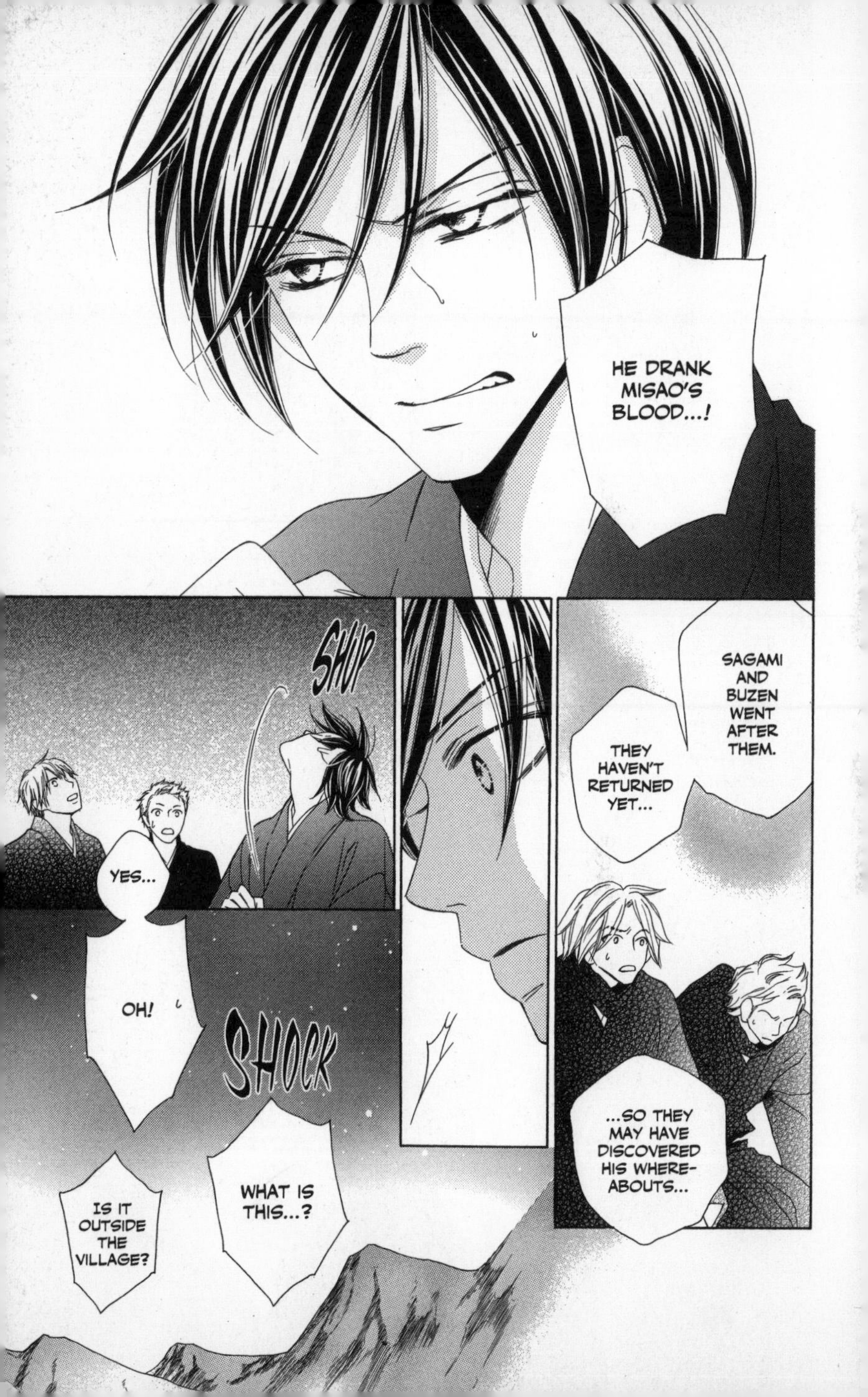
HE DRANK MISAO'S BLOOD...!
SAGAMI AND BUZEN WENT AFTER THEM.
THEY HAVEN'T RETURNED YET...
...SO THEY MAY HAVE DISCOVERED HIS WHERE-ABOUTS...
SHIP
YES...
SHOCK
OH!
WHAT IS THIS...?
IS IT OUTSIDE THE VILLAGE?

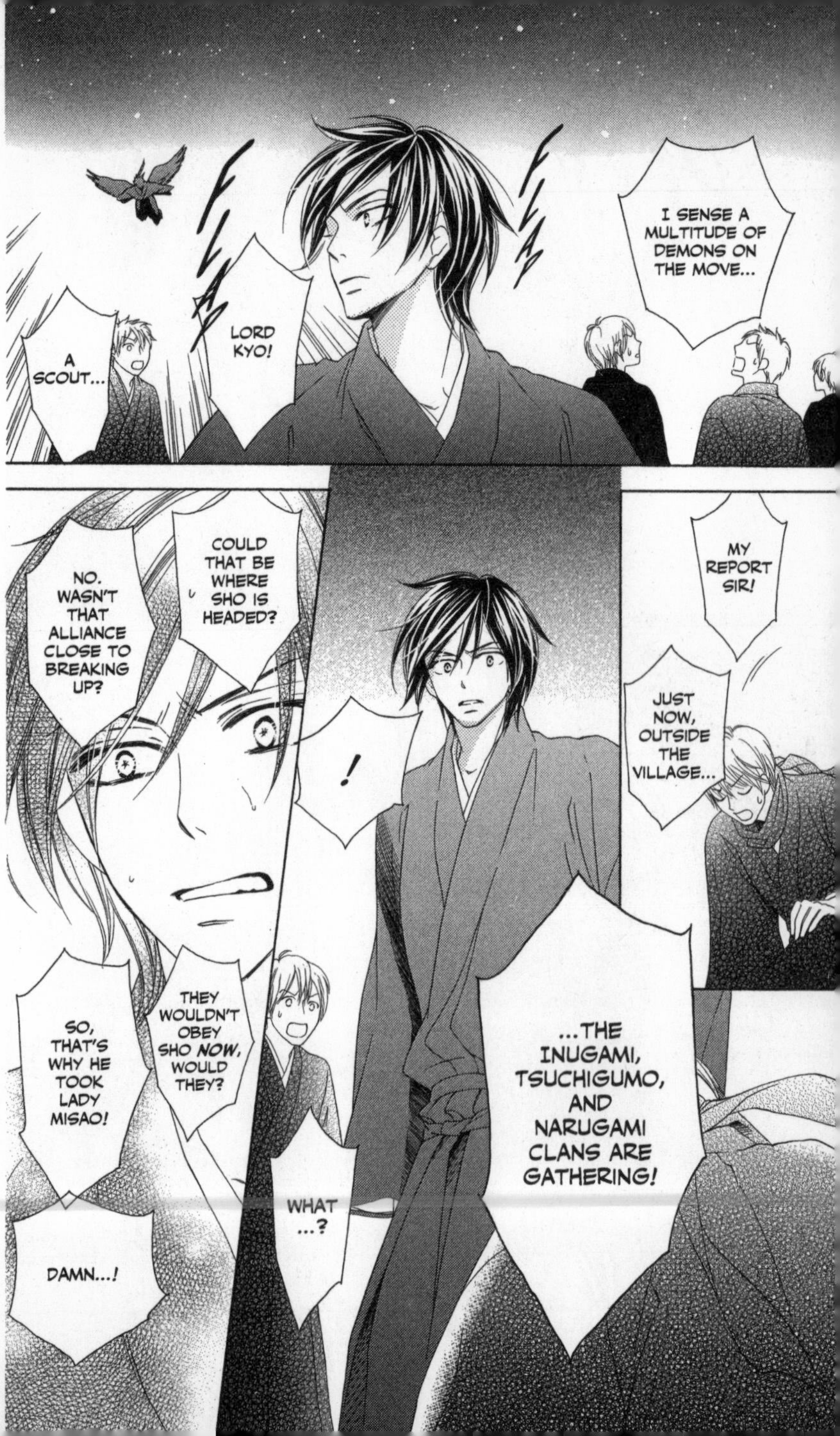
I SENSE A MULTITUDE OF DEMONS ON THE MOVE...
LORD KYO!
A SCOUT...
MY REPORT SIR!
JUST NOW, OUTSIDE THE VILLAGE...
!
...THE INUGAMI, TSUCHIGUMO, AND NARUGAMI CLANS ARE GATHERING!
WHAT ...?
COULD THAT BE WHERE SHO IS HEADED?
NO. WASN'T THAT ALLIANCE CLOSE TO BREAKING UP?
THEY WOULDN'T OBEY SHO *NOW*, WOULD THEY?
SO, THAT'S WHY HE TOOK LADY MISAO!
DAMN...!

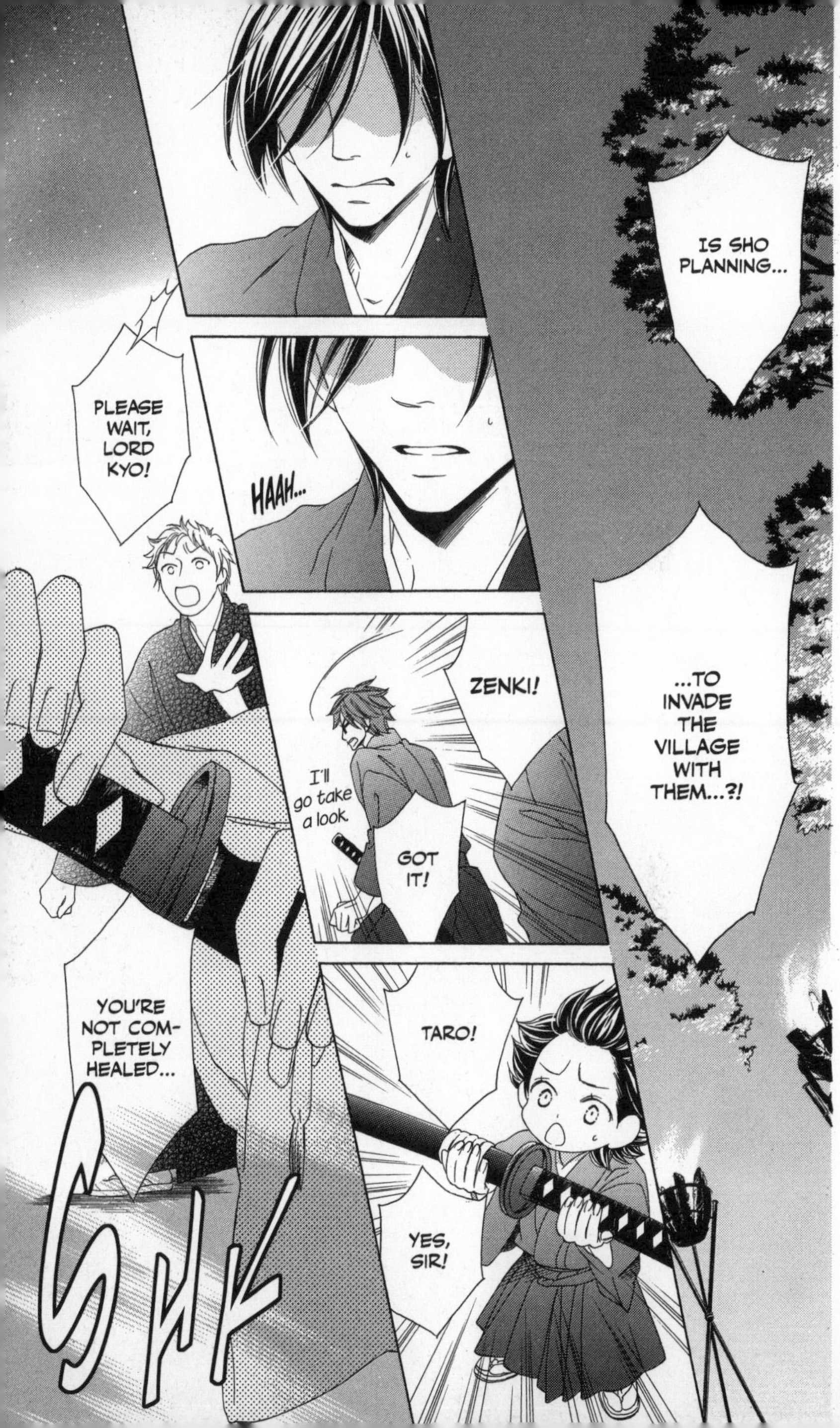
IS SHO PLANNING...
...TO INVADE THE VILLAGE WITH THEM...?!
HAAH...
PLEASE WAIT, LORD KYO!
ZENKI!
I'll go take a look.
GOT IT!
TARO!
YES, SIR!
YOU'RE NOT COM-PLETELY HEALED...
SHK

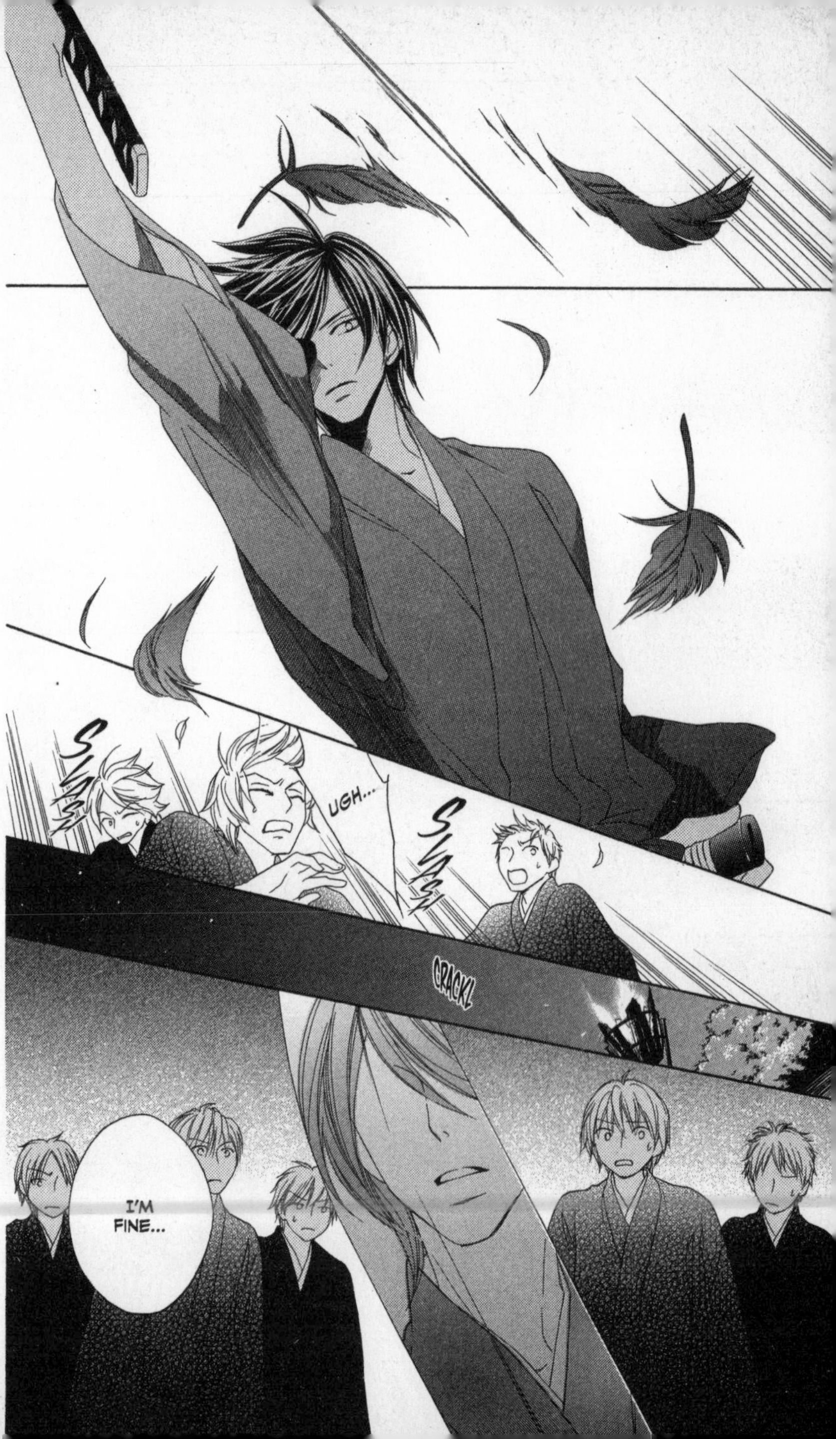
SLASH
UGH...
SLASH
CRACKL
I'M FINE...

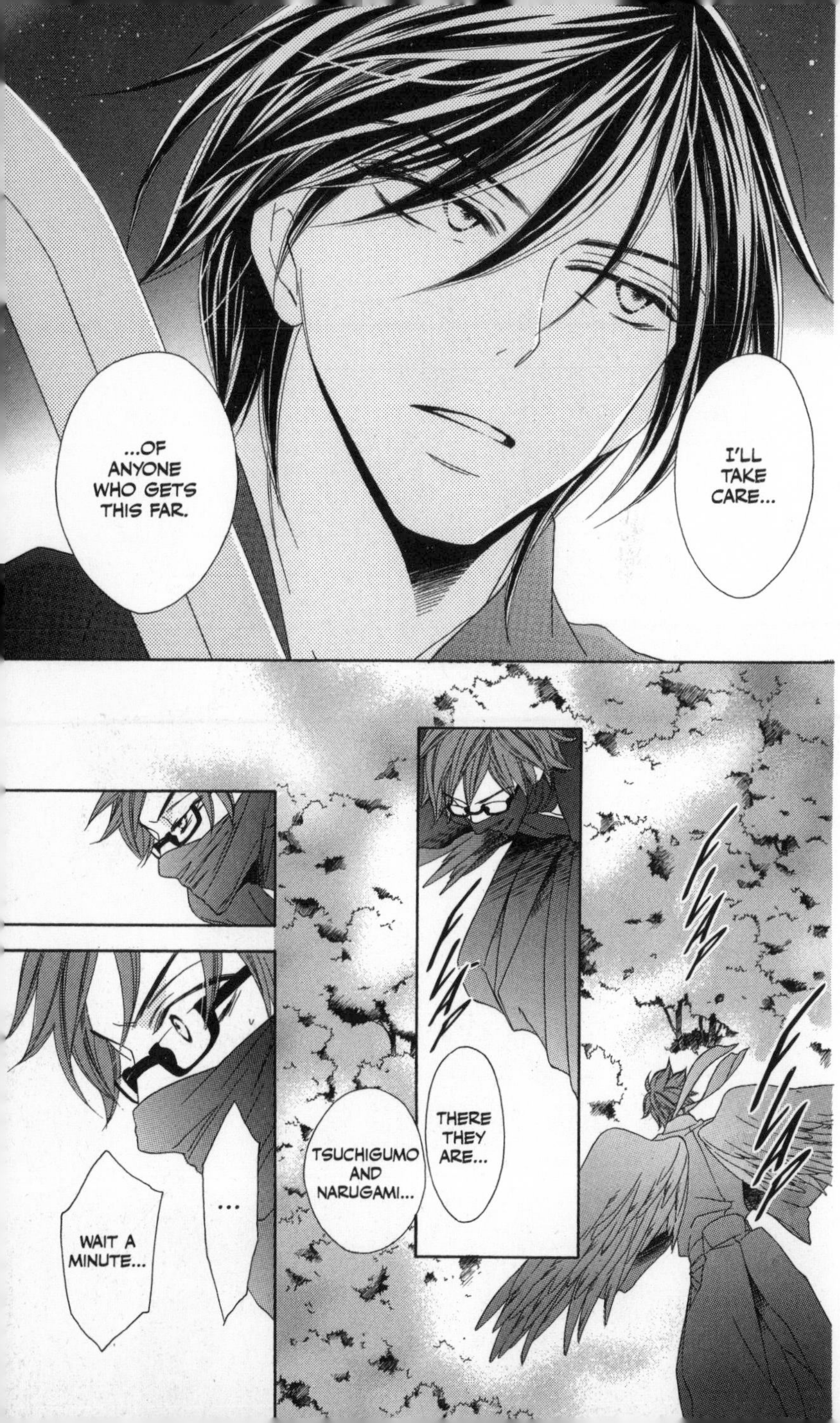
I'LL TAKE CARE...
...OF ANYONE WHO GETS THIS FAR.
THERE THEY ARE...
TSUCHIGUMO AND NARUGAMI...
...
WAIT A MINUTE...

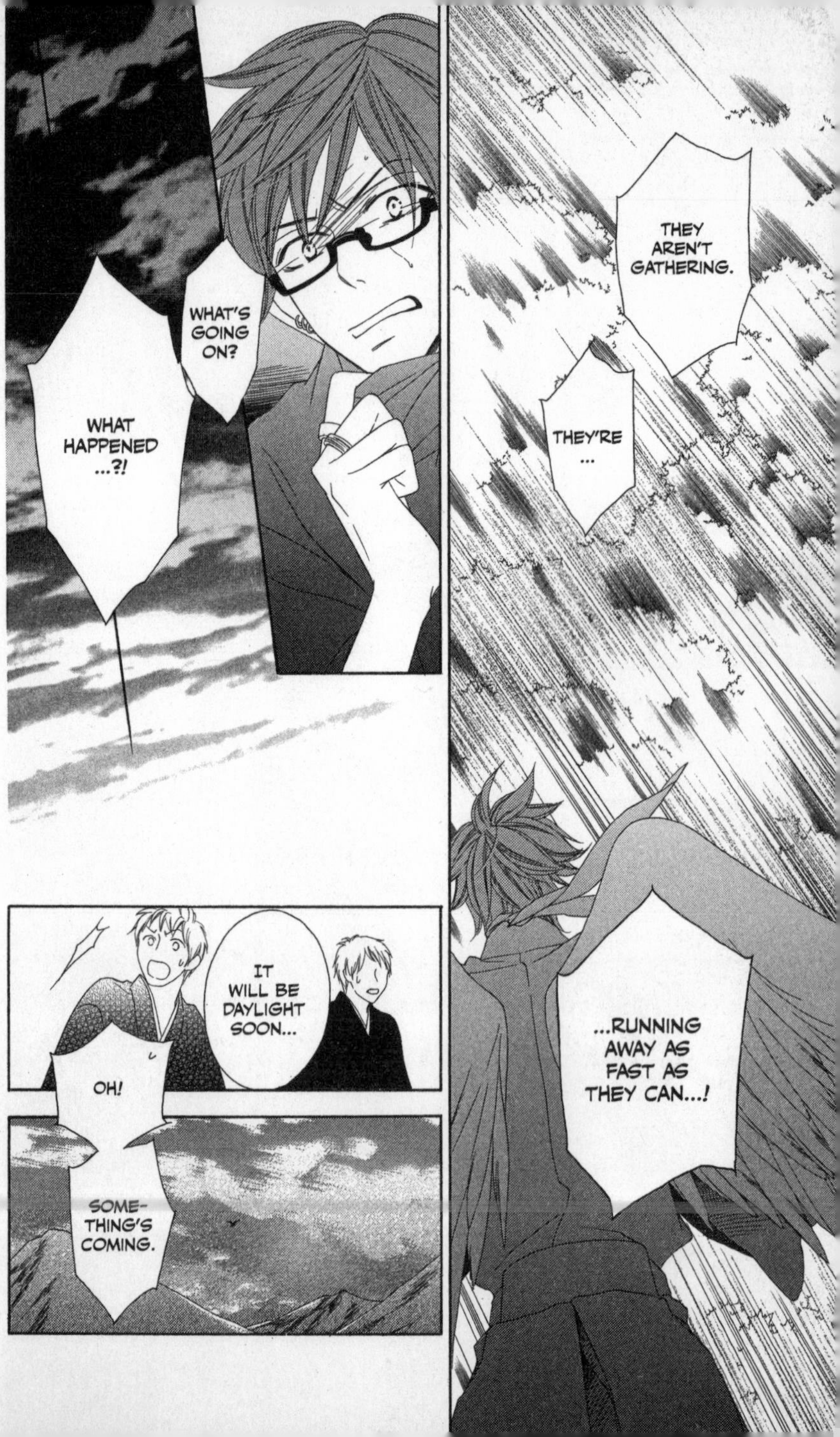
THEY AREN'T GATHERING.
THEY'RE ...
...RUNNING AWAY AS FAST AS THEY CAN...!
WHAT'S GOING ON?
WHAT HAPPENED ...?!
IT WILL BE DAYLIGHT SOON...
OH!
SOME-THING'S COMING.

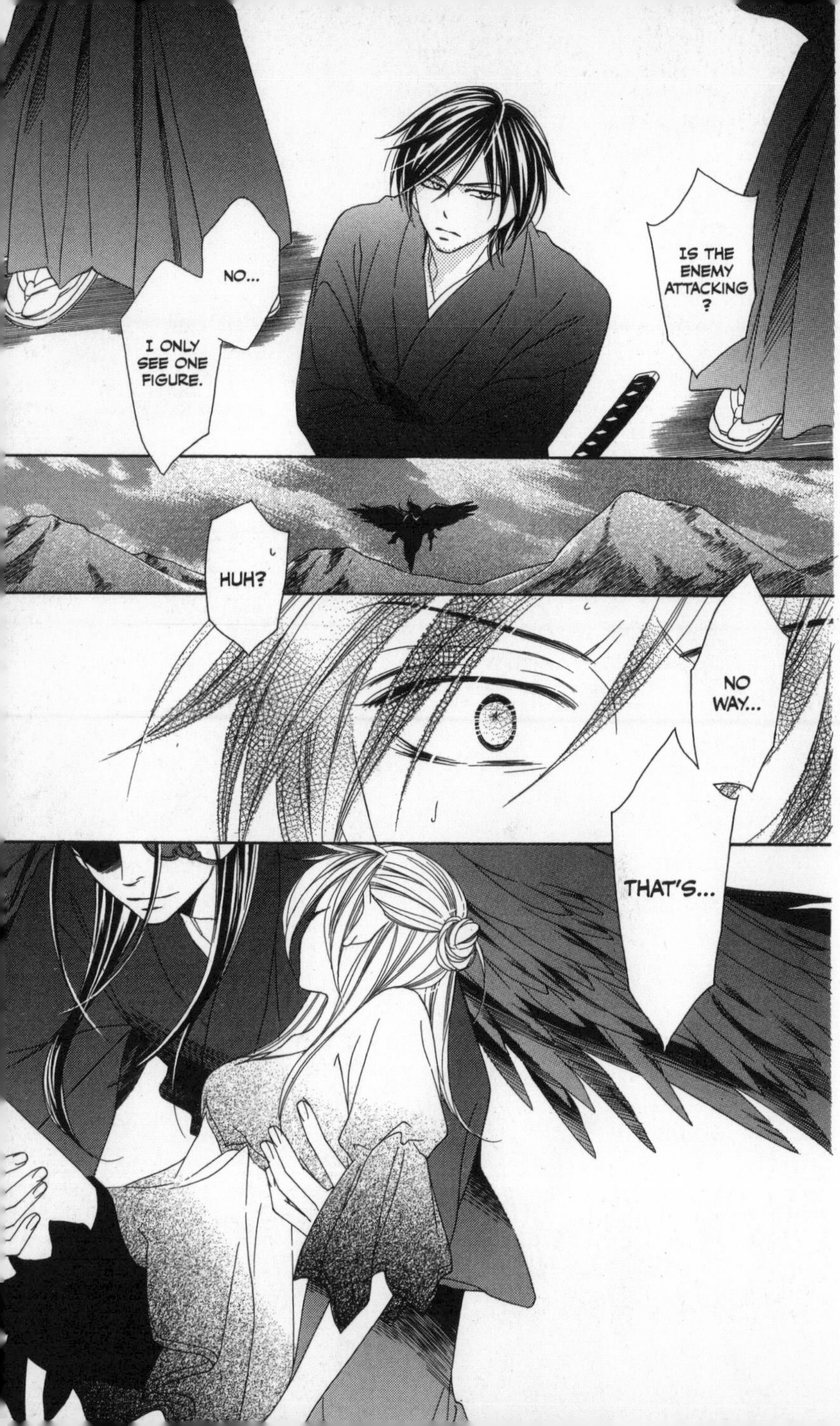
IS THE ENEMY ATTACKING?
NO...
I ONLY SEE ONE FIGURE.
HUH?
NO WAY...
THAT'S...

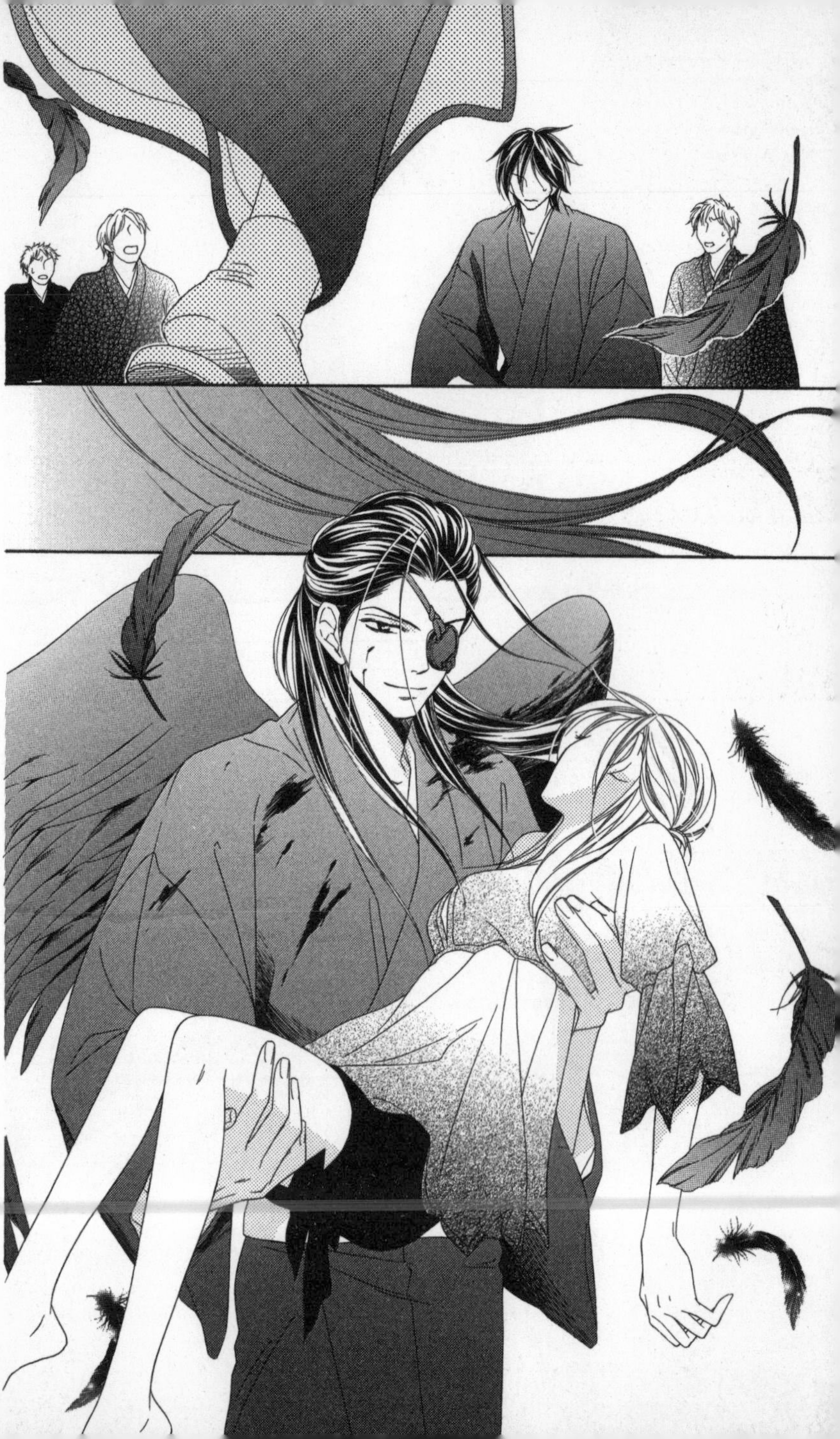

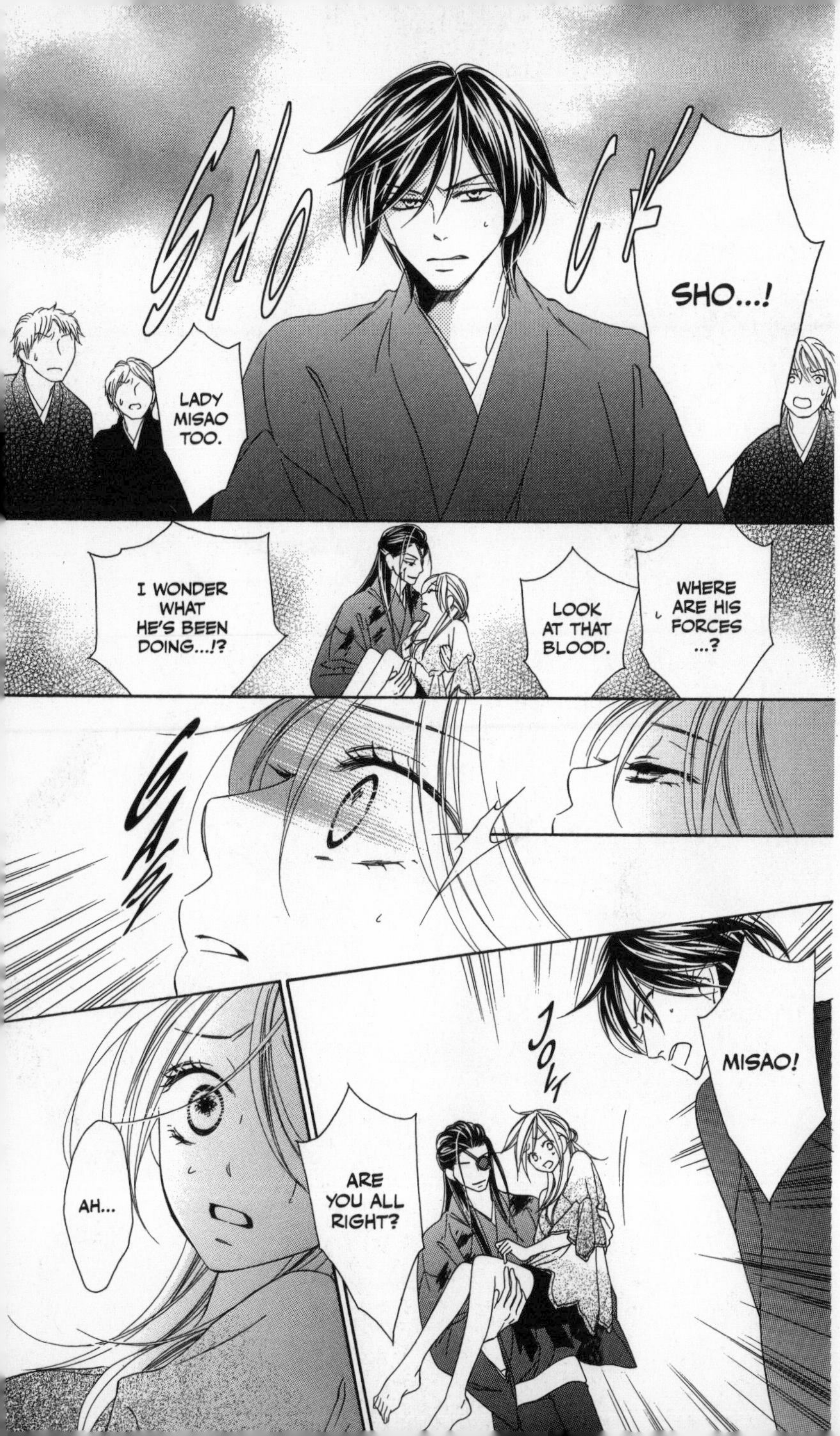
SHOCK
SHO...!
LADY MISAO TOO.
WHERE ARE HIS FORCES ...?
LOOK AT THAT BLOOD.
I WONDER WHAT HE'S BEEN DOING...!?
JOLT
MISAO!
ARE YOU ALL RIGHT?
AH...

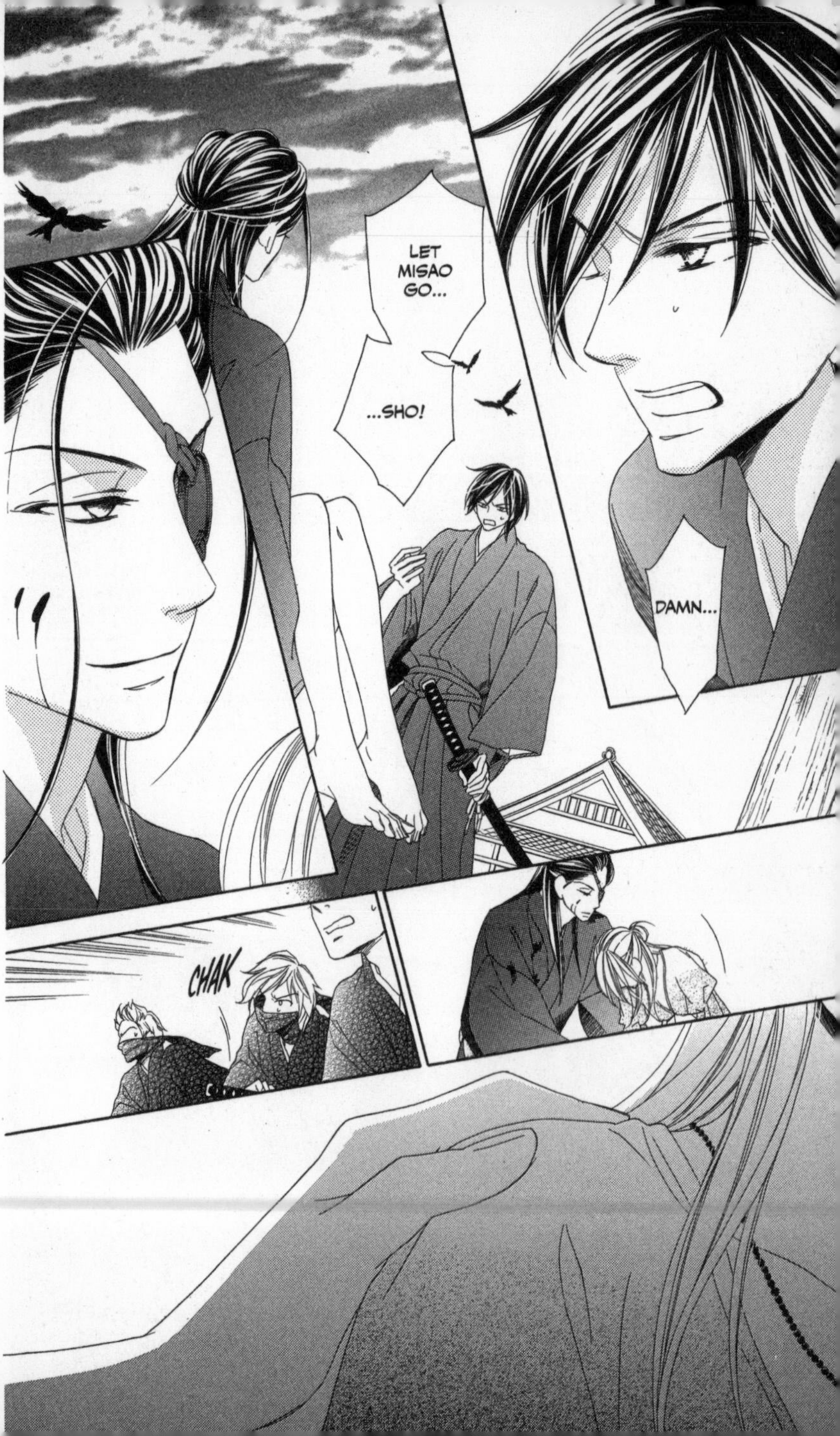
DAMN...
LET MISAO GO...
...SHO!
CHAK

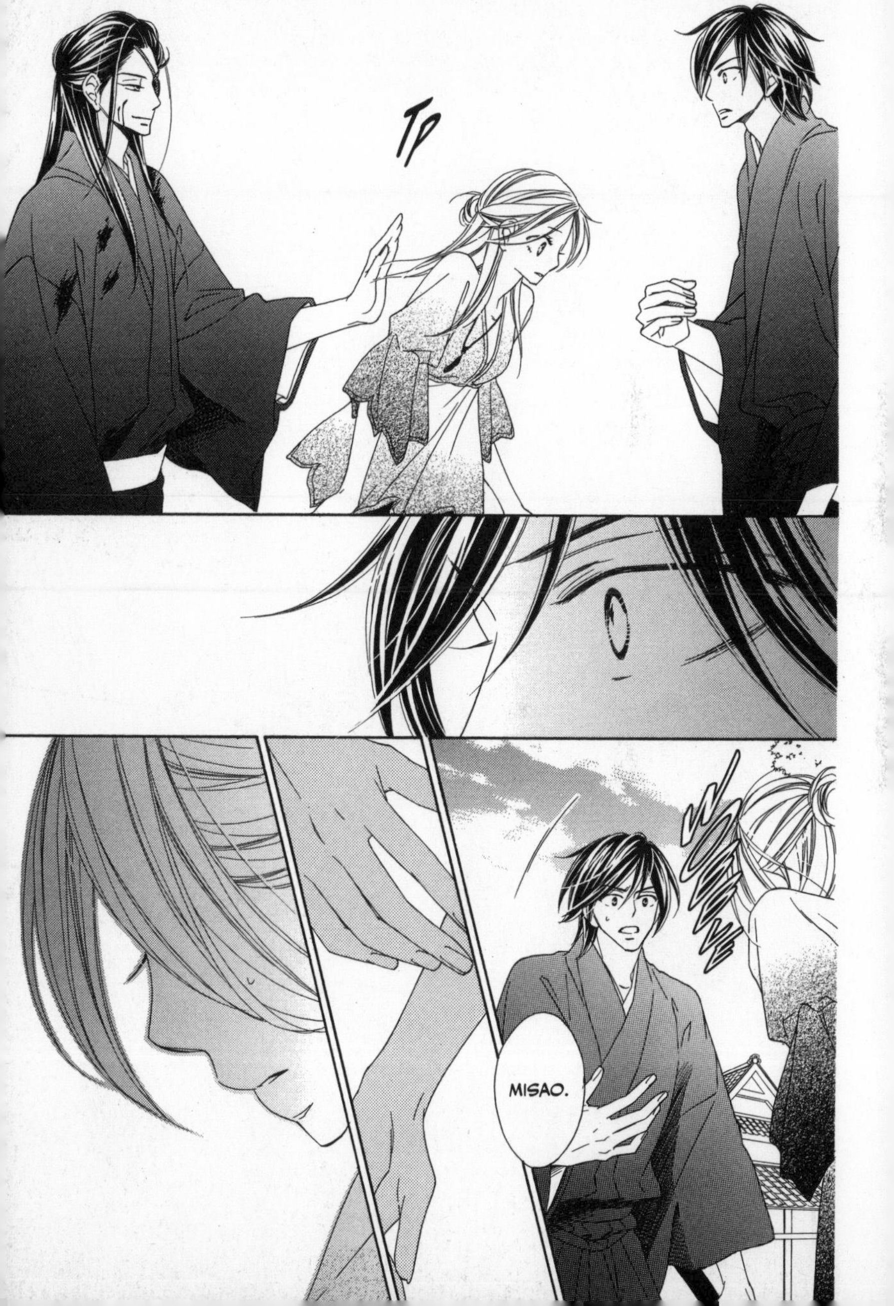
TP
MISAO.

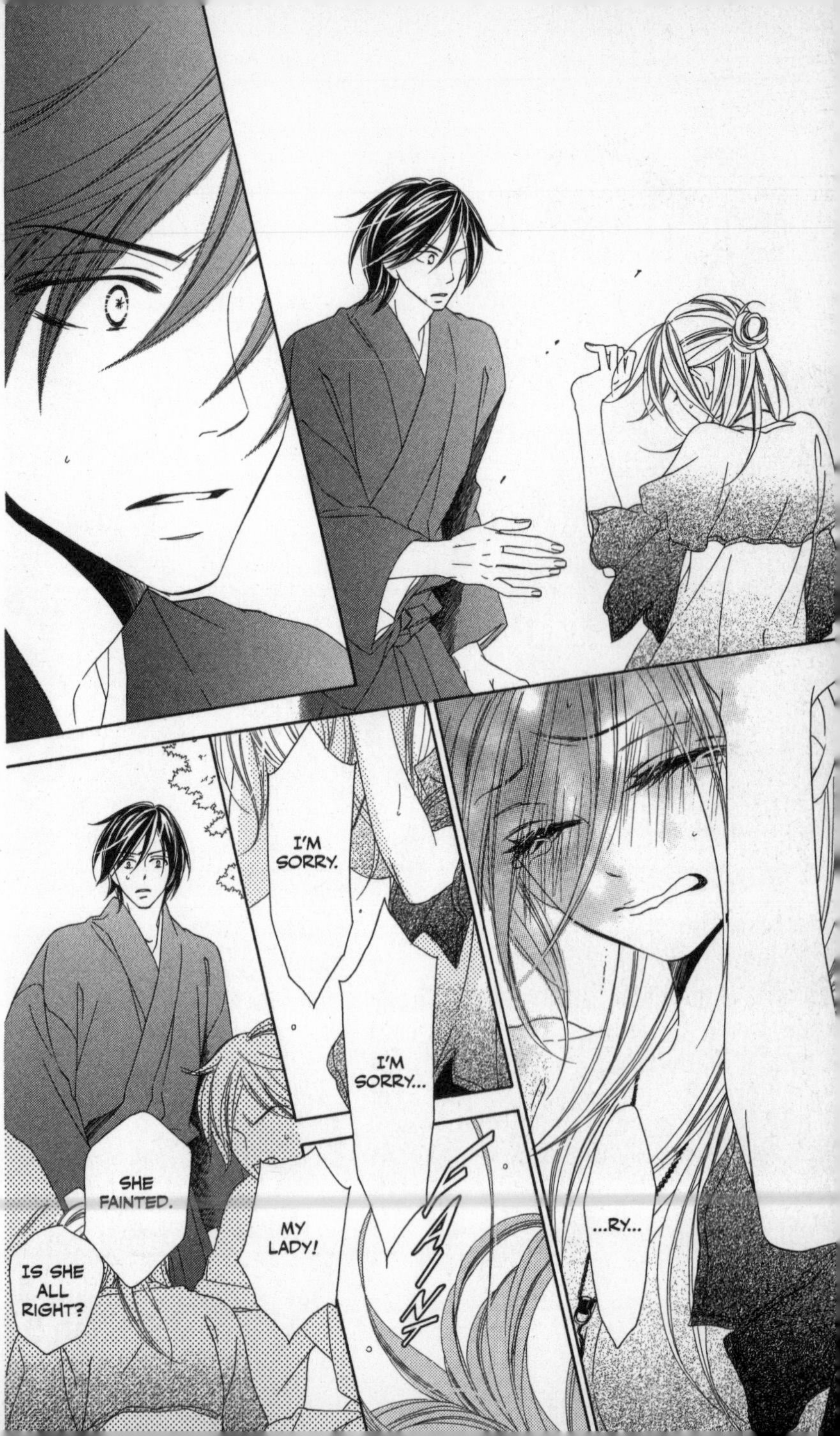
I'M SORRY.
I'M SORRY...
...RY...
MY LADY!
SHE FAINTED.
IS SHE ALL RIGHT?

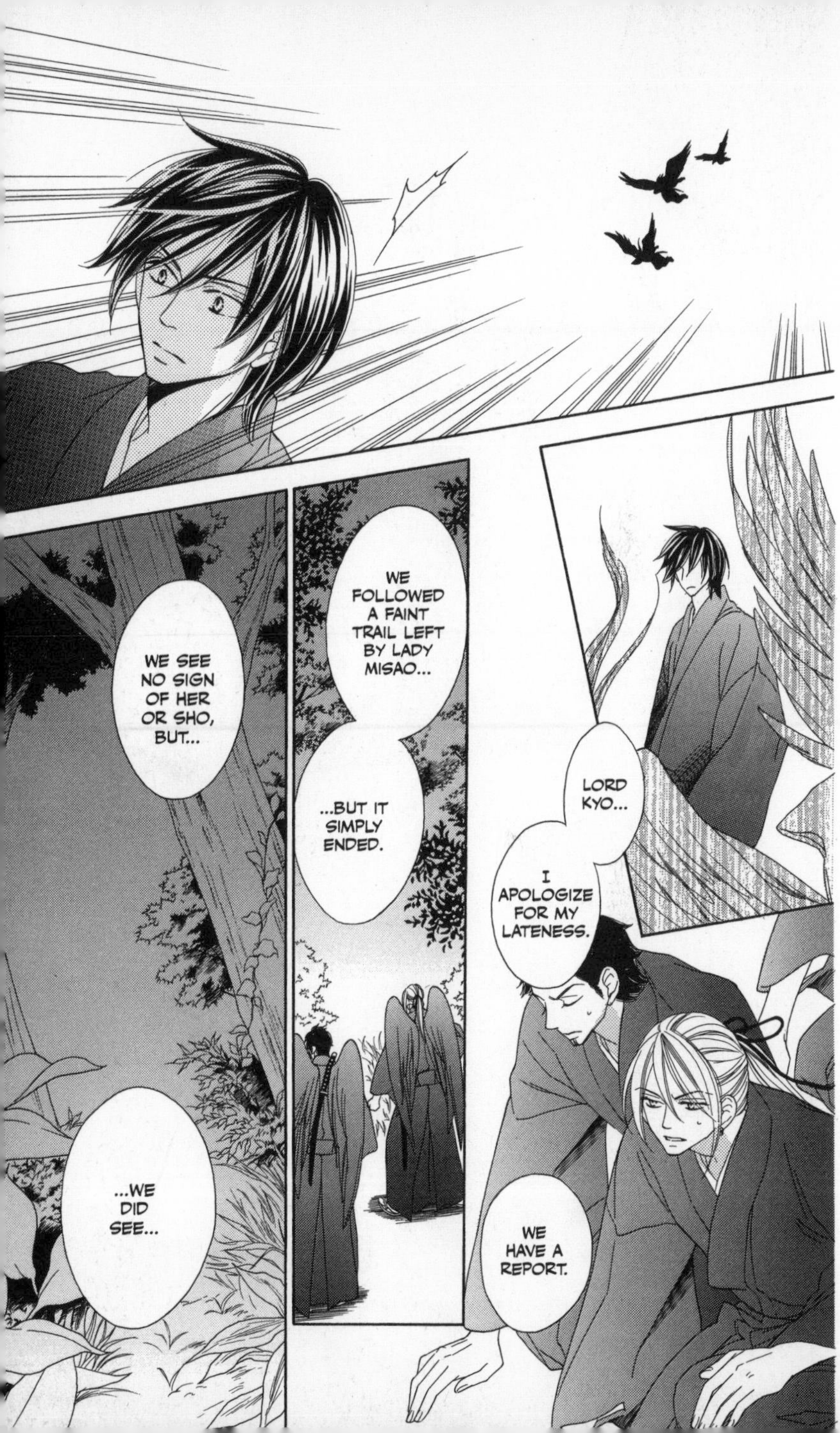
LORD KYO...
I APOLOGIZE FOR MY LATENESS.
WE HAVE A REPORT.
WE FOLLOWED A FAINT TRAIL LEFT BY LADY MISAO...
...BUT IT SIMPLY ENDED.
WE SEE NO SIGN OF HER OR SHO, BUT...
...WE DID SEE...

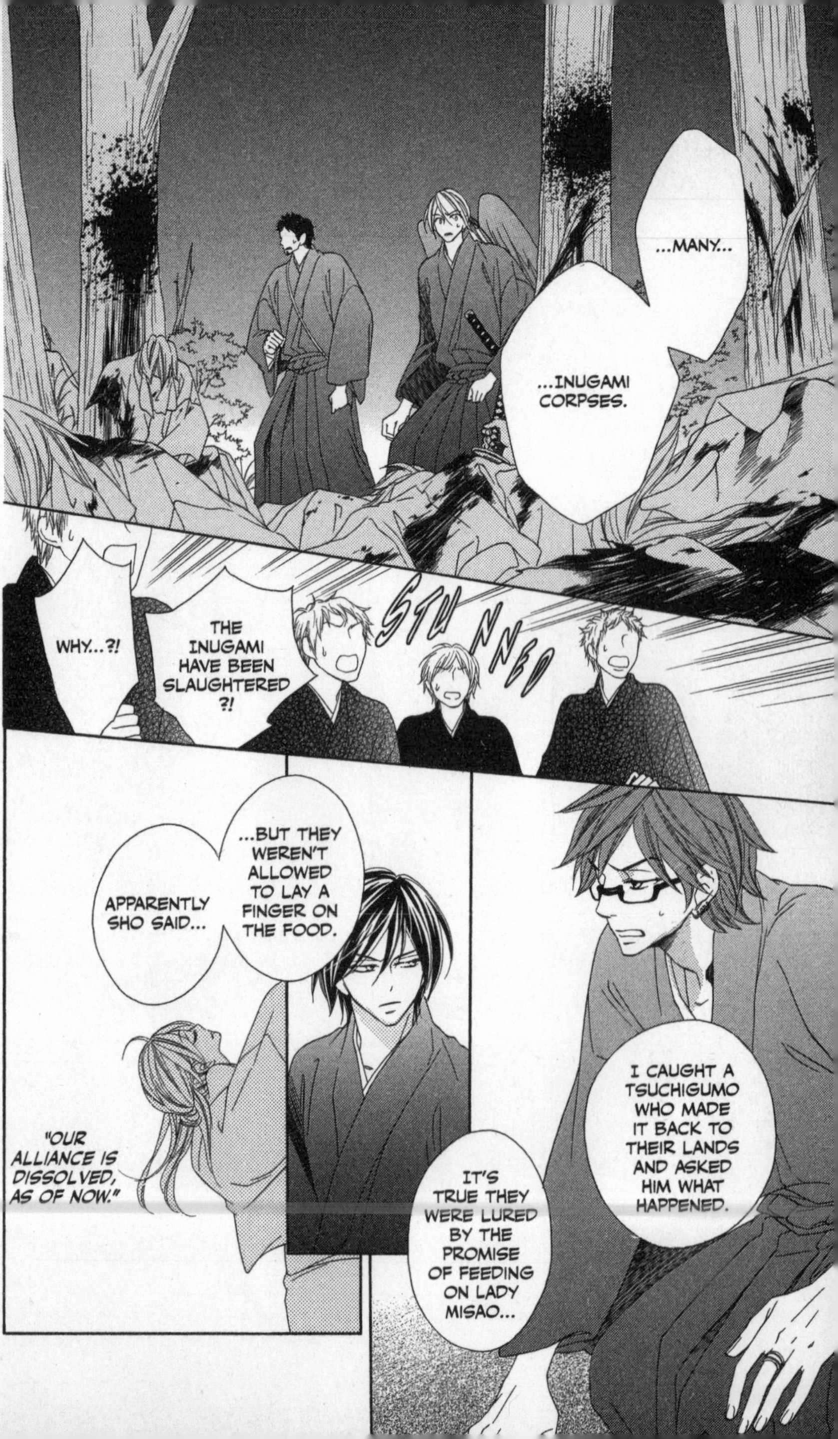
...MANY...
...INUGAMI CORPSES.
STUNNED
THE INUGAMI HAVE BEEN SLAUGHTERED ?!
WHY...?!
I CAUGHT A TSUCHIGUMO WHO MADE IT BACK TO THEIR LANDS AND ASKED HIM WHAT HAPPENED.
IT'S TRUE THEY WERE LURED BY THE PROMISE OF FEEDING ON LADY MISAO...
...BUT THEY WEREN'T ALLOWED TO LAY A FINGER ON THE FOOD.
APPARENTLY SHO SAID...
"OUR ALLIANCE IS DISSOLVED, AS OF NOW."

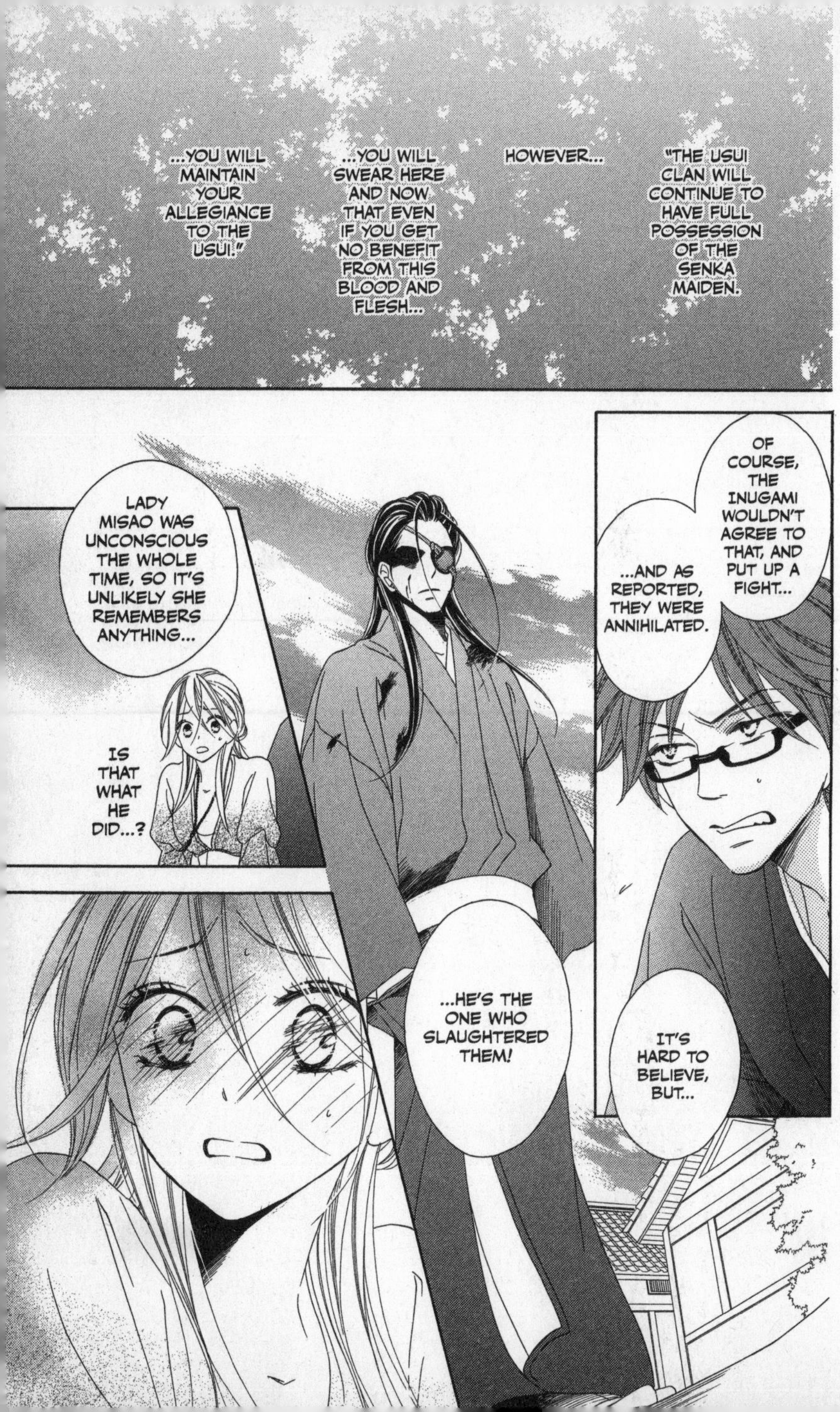
"THE USUI CLAN WILL CONTINUE TO HAVE FULL POSSESSION OF THE SENKA MAIDEN.
HOWEVER...
...YOU WILL SWEAR HERE AND NOW THAT EVEN IF YOU GET NO BENEFIT FROM THIS BLOOD AND FLESH...
...YOU WILL MAINTAIN YOUR ALLEGIANCE TO THE USUI."
OF COURSE, THE INUGAMI WOULDN'T AGREE TO THAT, AND PUT UP A FIGHT...
...AND AS REPORTED, THEY WERE ANNIHILATED.
IT'S HARD TO BELIEVE, BUT...
...HE'S THE ONE WHO SLAUGHTERED THEM!
LADY MISAO WAS UNCONSCIOUS THE WHOLE TIME, SO IT'S UNLIKELY SHE REMEMBERS ANYTHING...
IS THAT WHAT HE DID...?

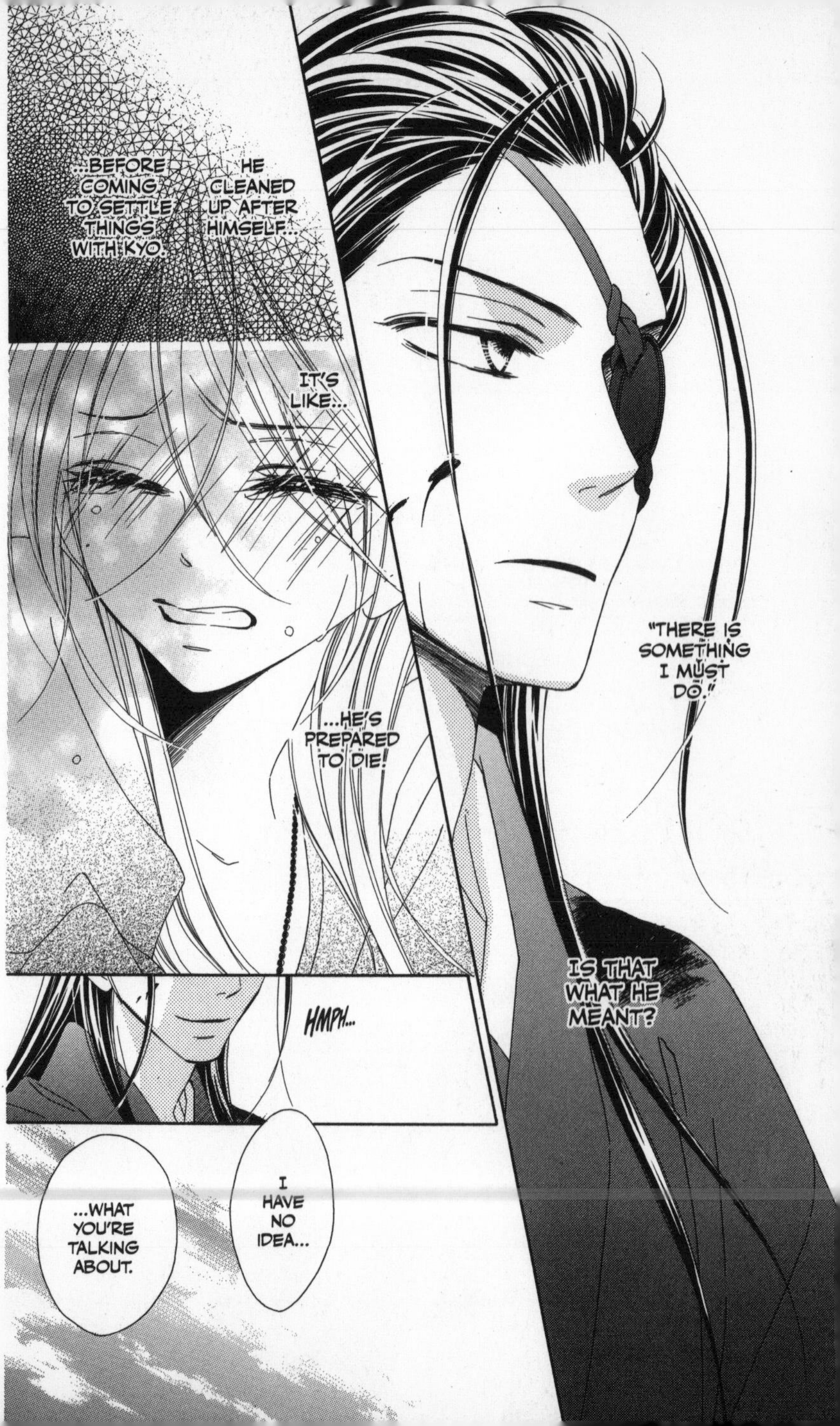
"THERE IS SOMETHING I MUST DO."
IS THAT WHAT HE MEANT?
HE CLEANED UP AFTER HIMSELF...
...BEFORE COMING TO SETTLE THINGS WITH KYO.
IT'S LIKE...
...HE'S PREPARED TO DIE!
HMPH...
I HAVE NO IDEA...
...WHAT YOU'RE TALKING ABOUT.

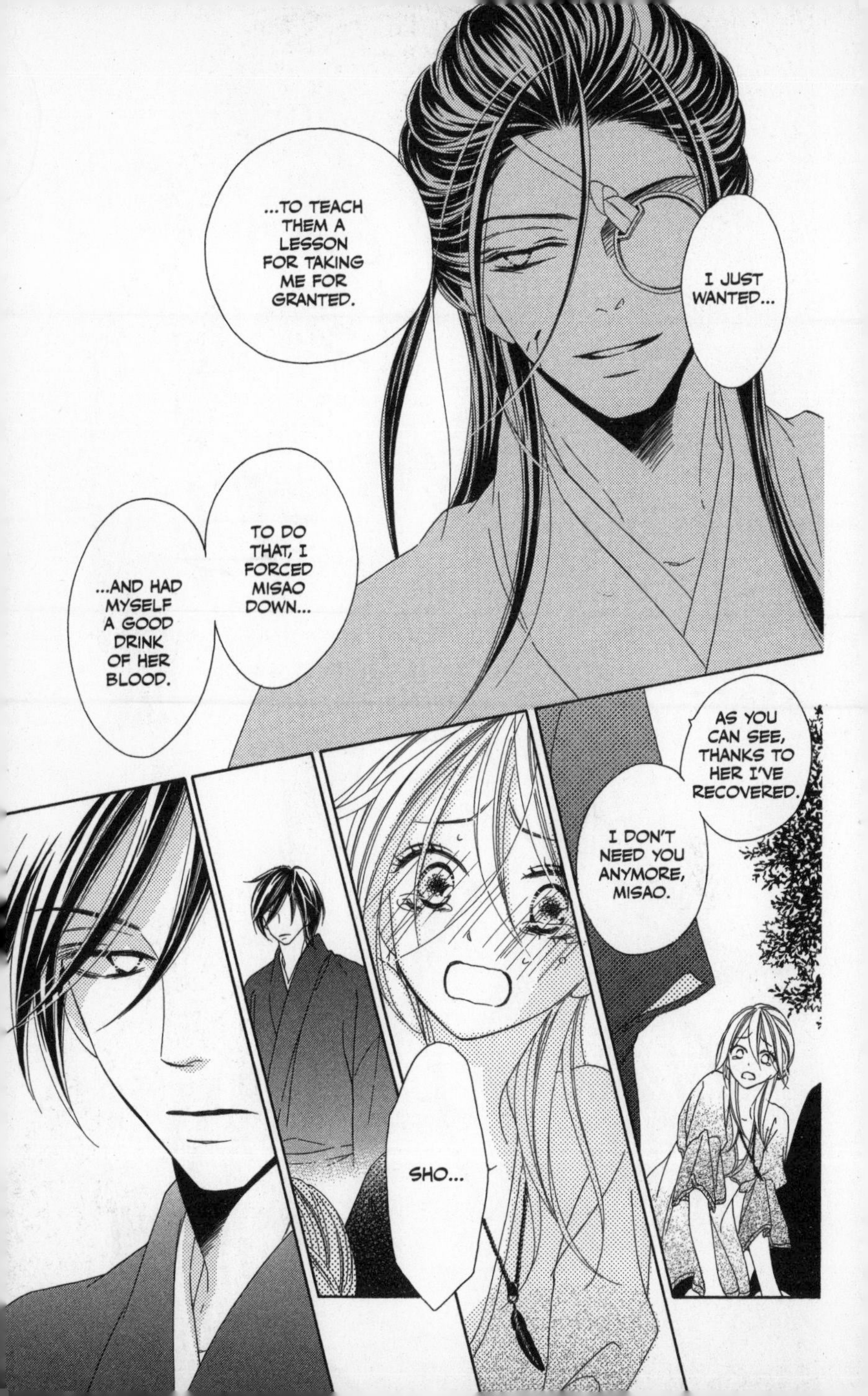
I JUST WANTED...
...TO TEACH THEM A LESSON FOR TAKING ME FOR GRANTED.
TO DO THAT, I FORCED MISAO DOWN...
...AND HAD MYSELF A GOOD DRINK OF HER BLOOD.
AS YOU CAN SEE, THANKS TO HER I'VE RECOVERED.
I DON'T NEED YOU ANYMORE, MISAO.
SHO...

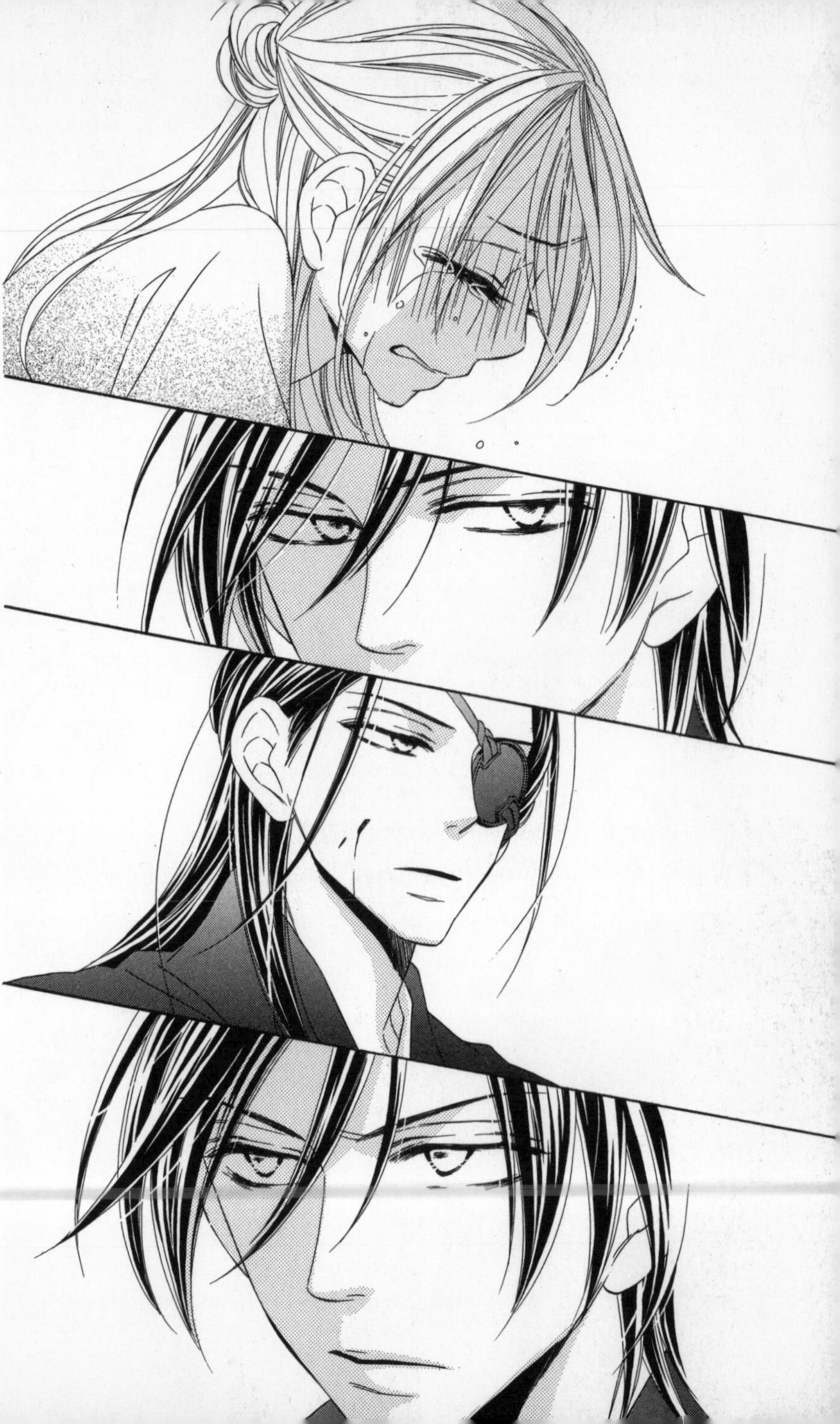

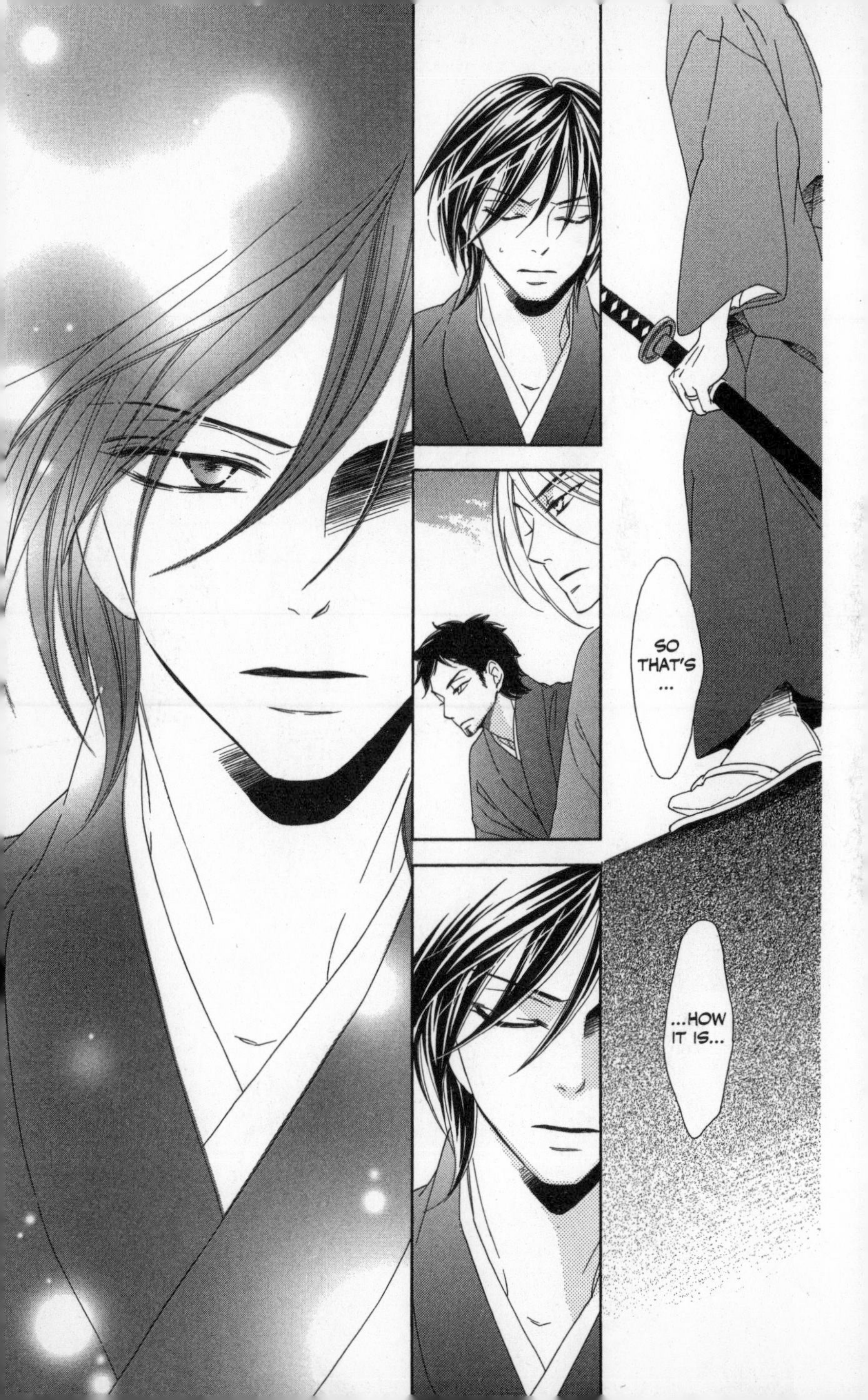
SO THAT'S ...
...HOW IT IS...

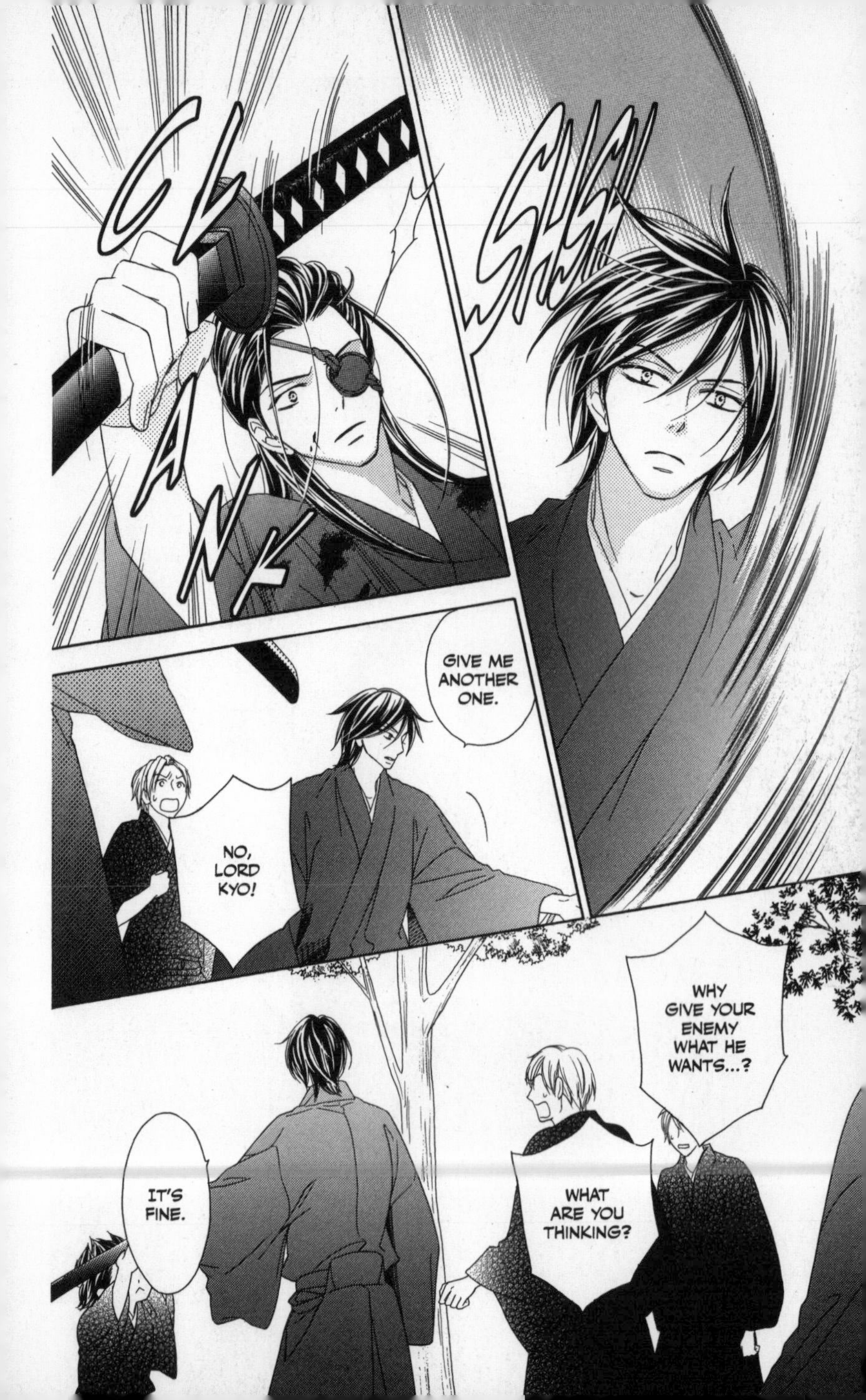
CLANK
GIVE ME ANOTHER ONE.
NO, LORD KYO!
WHY GIVE YOUR ENEMY WHAT HE WANTS...?
WHAT ARE YOU THINKING?
IT'S FINE.

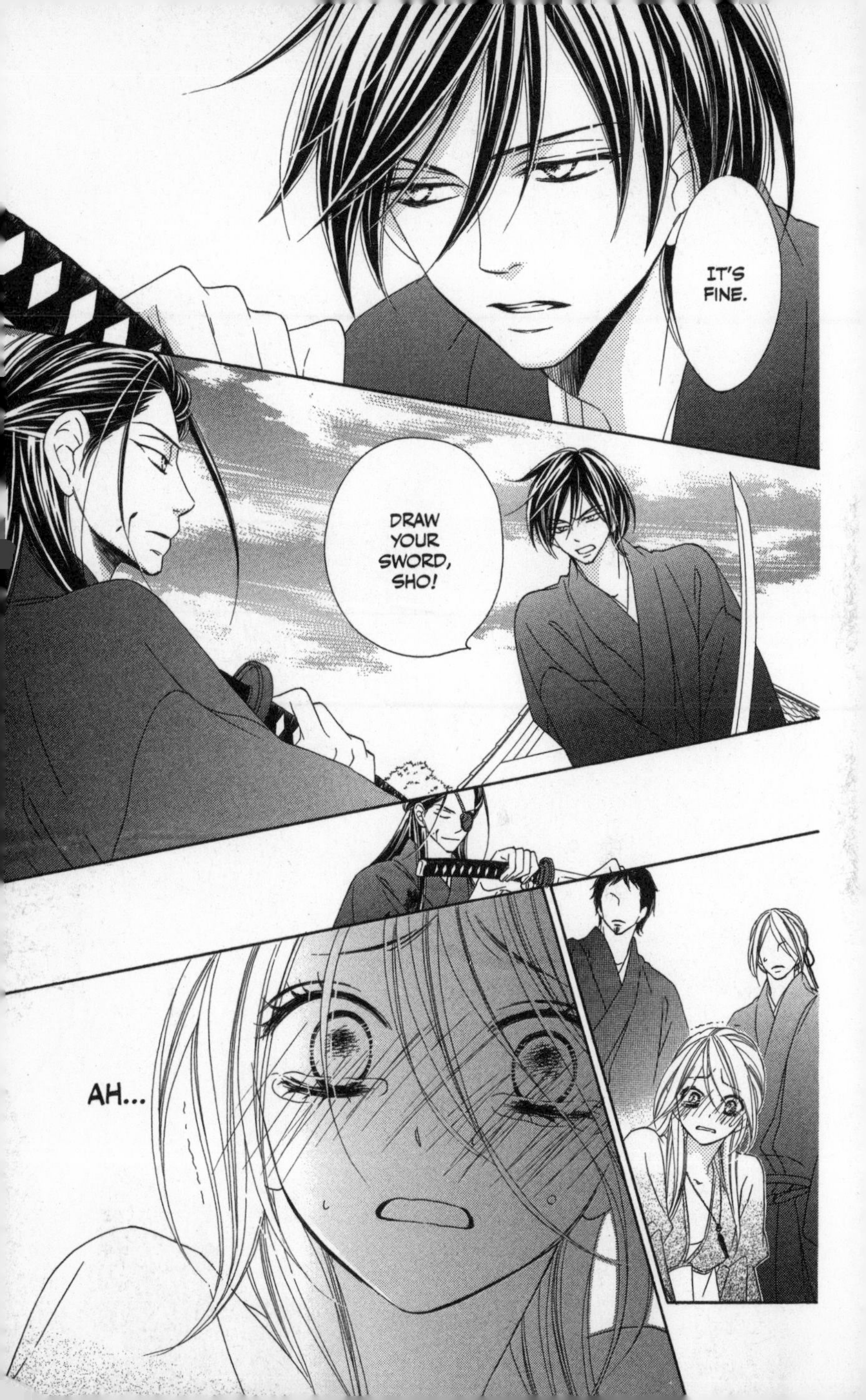
IT'S FINE.
DRAW YOUR SWORD, SHO!
AH...

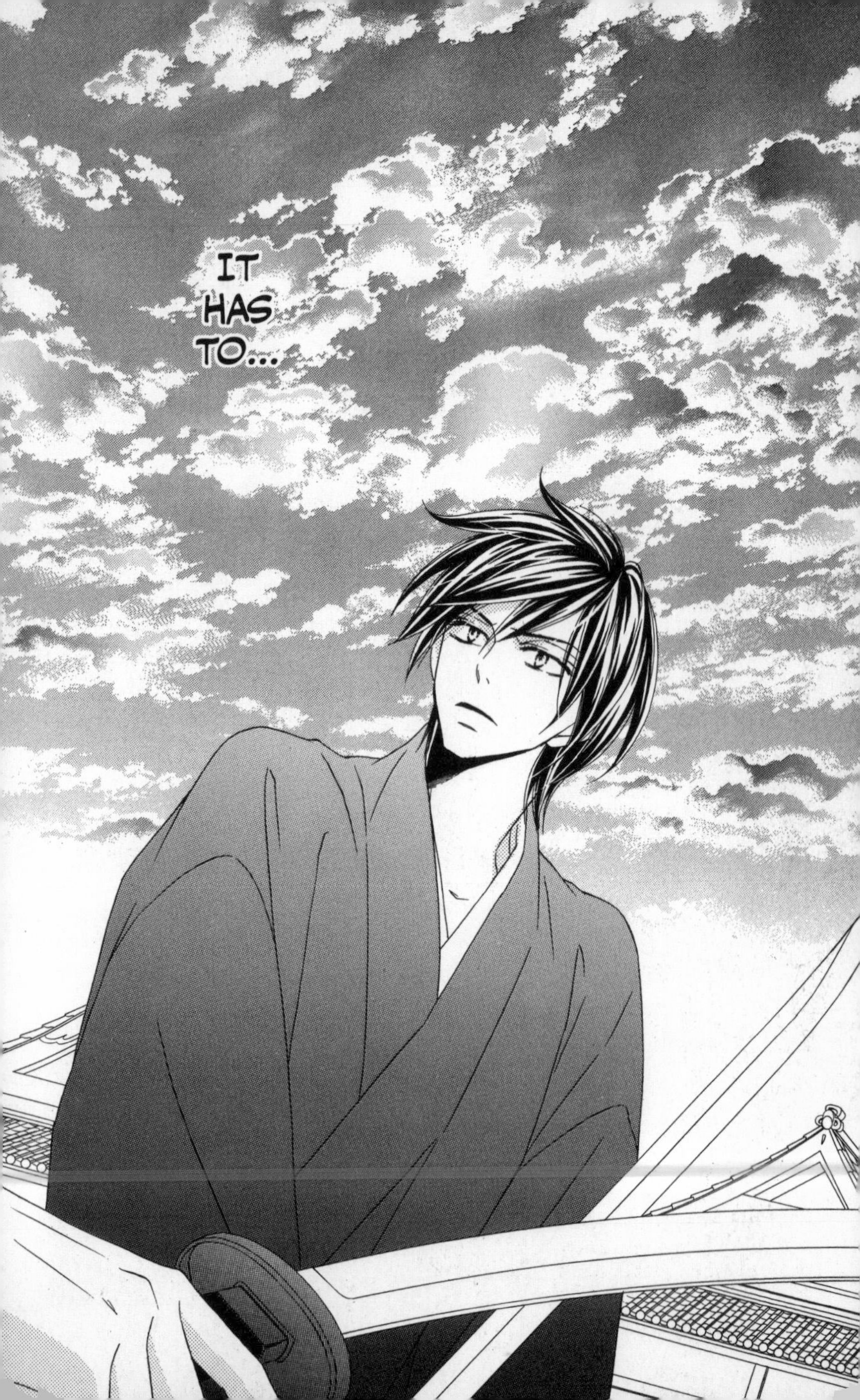
IT HAS TO...

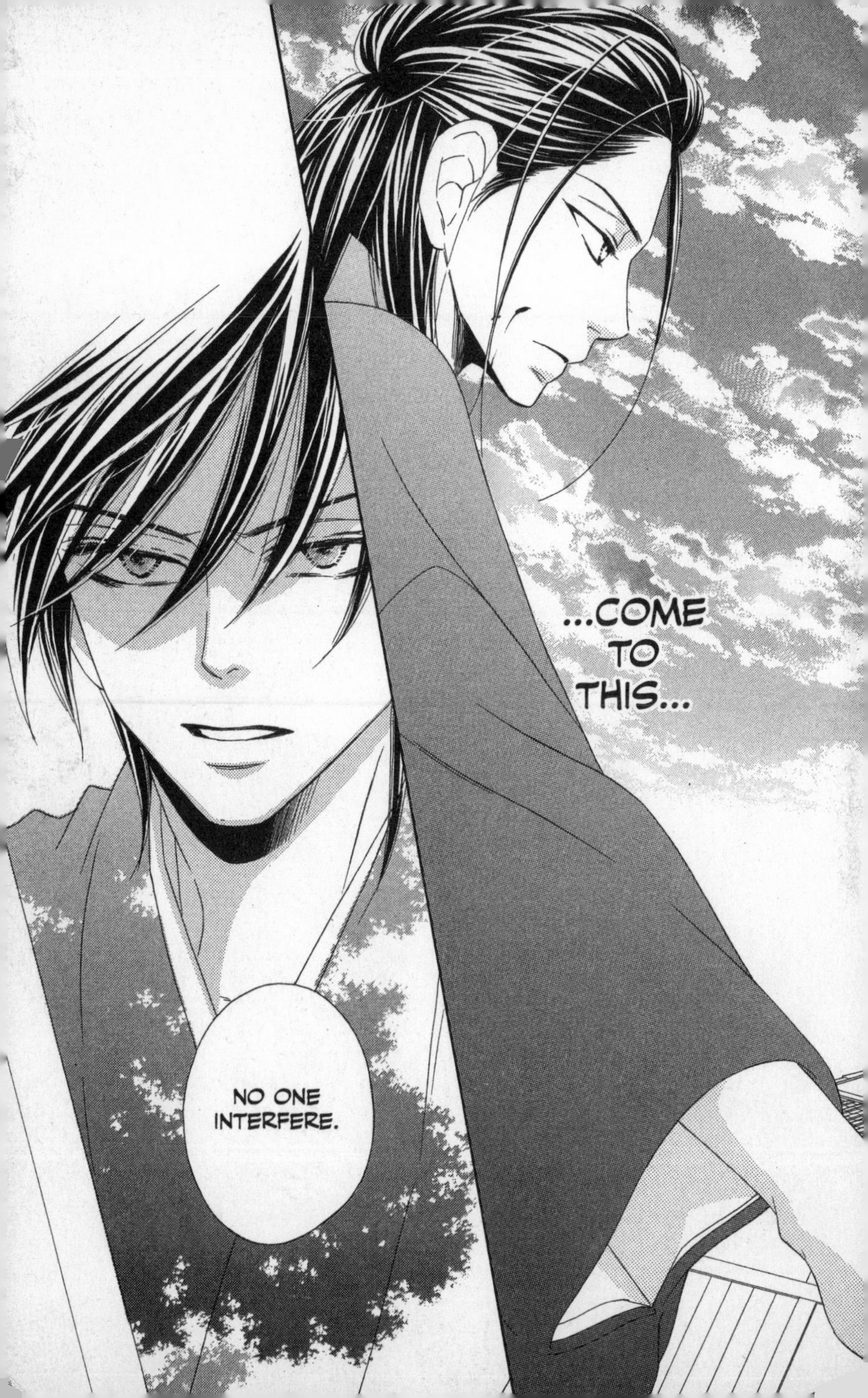
...COME TO THIS...
NO ONE INTERFERE.

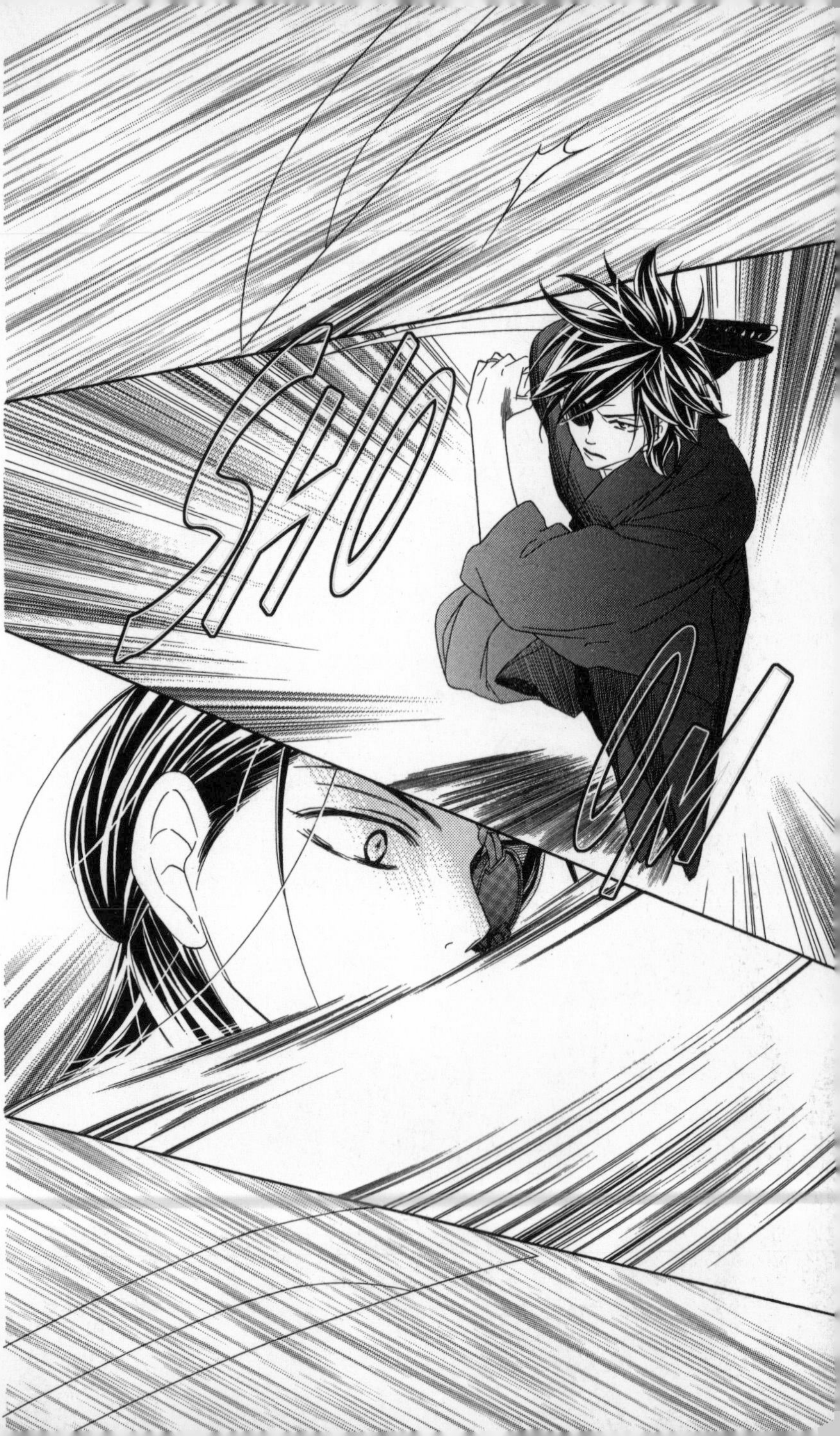
SHO
OM

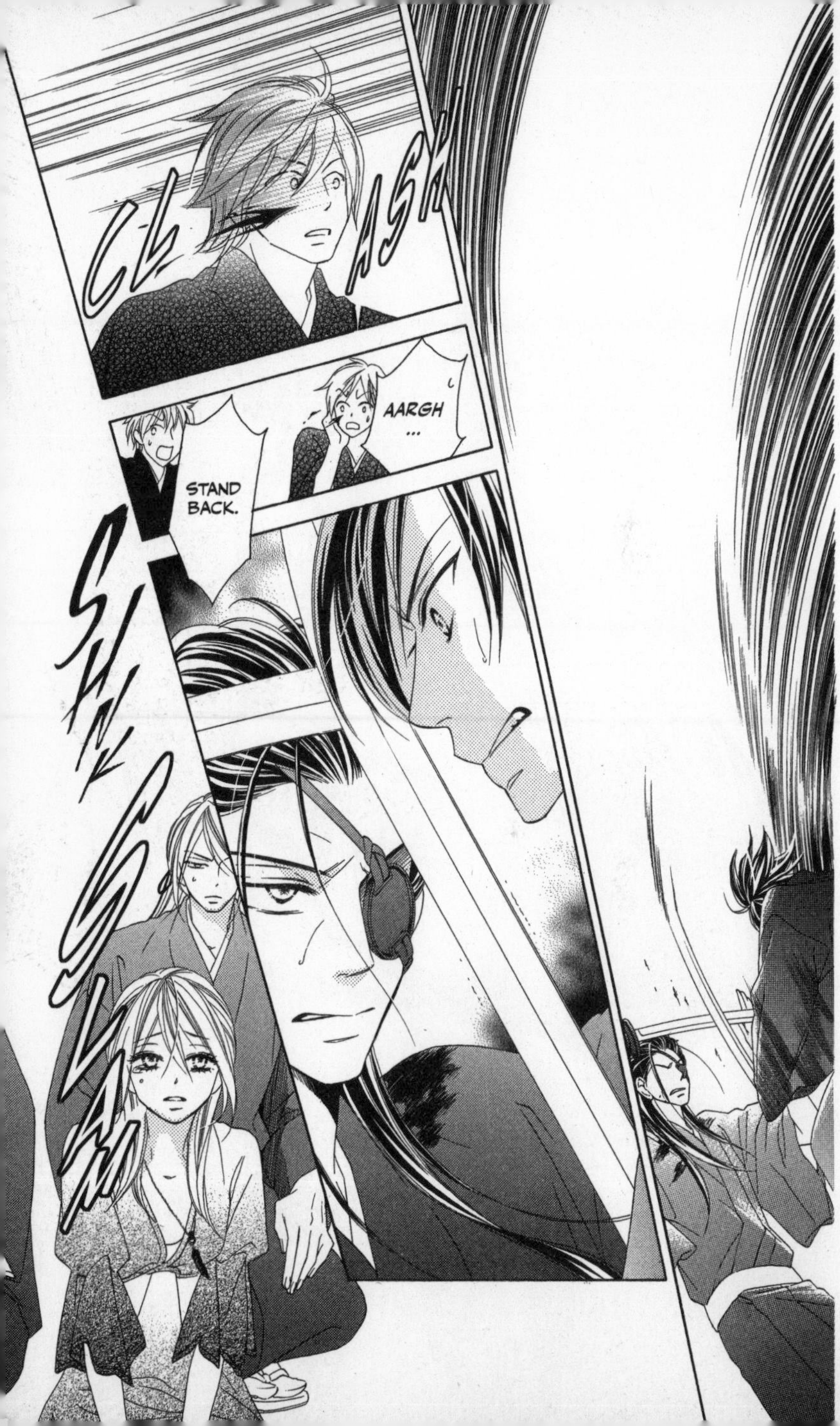
CL-ASH
AARGH ...
STAND BACK.

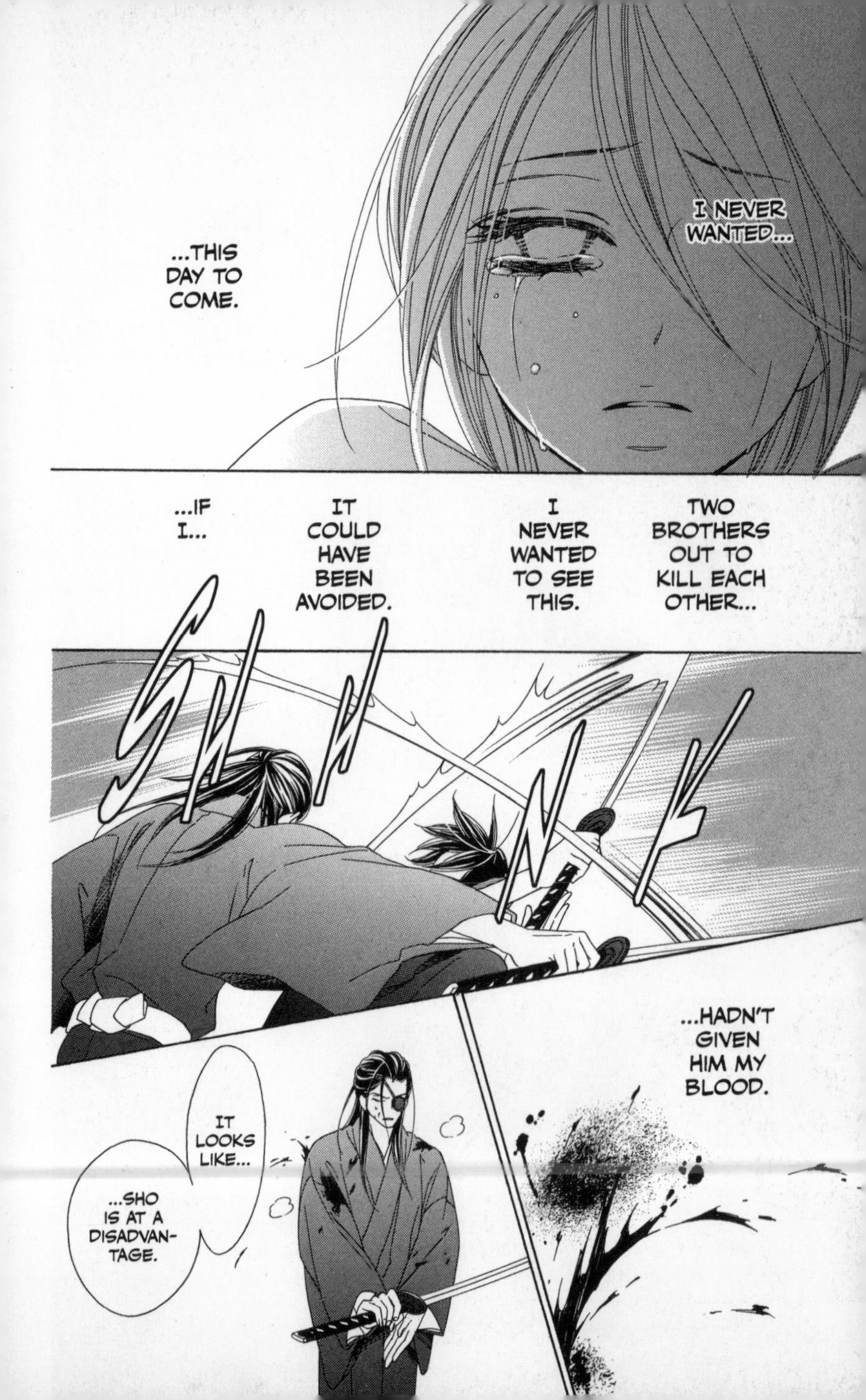
I NEVER WANTED...
...THIS DAY TO COME.
TWO BROTHERS OUT TO KILL EACH OTHER...
I NEVER WANTED TO SEE THIS.
IT COULD HAVE BEEN AVOIDED.
...IF I...
SHHNK
...HADN'T GIVEN HIM MY BLOOD.
IT LOOKS LIKE...
...SHO IS AT A DISADVAN-TAGE.

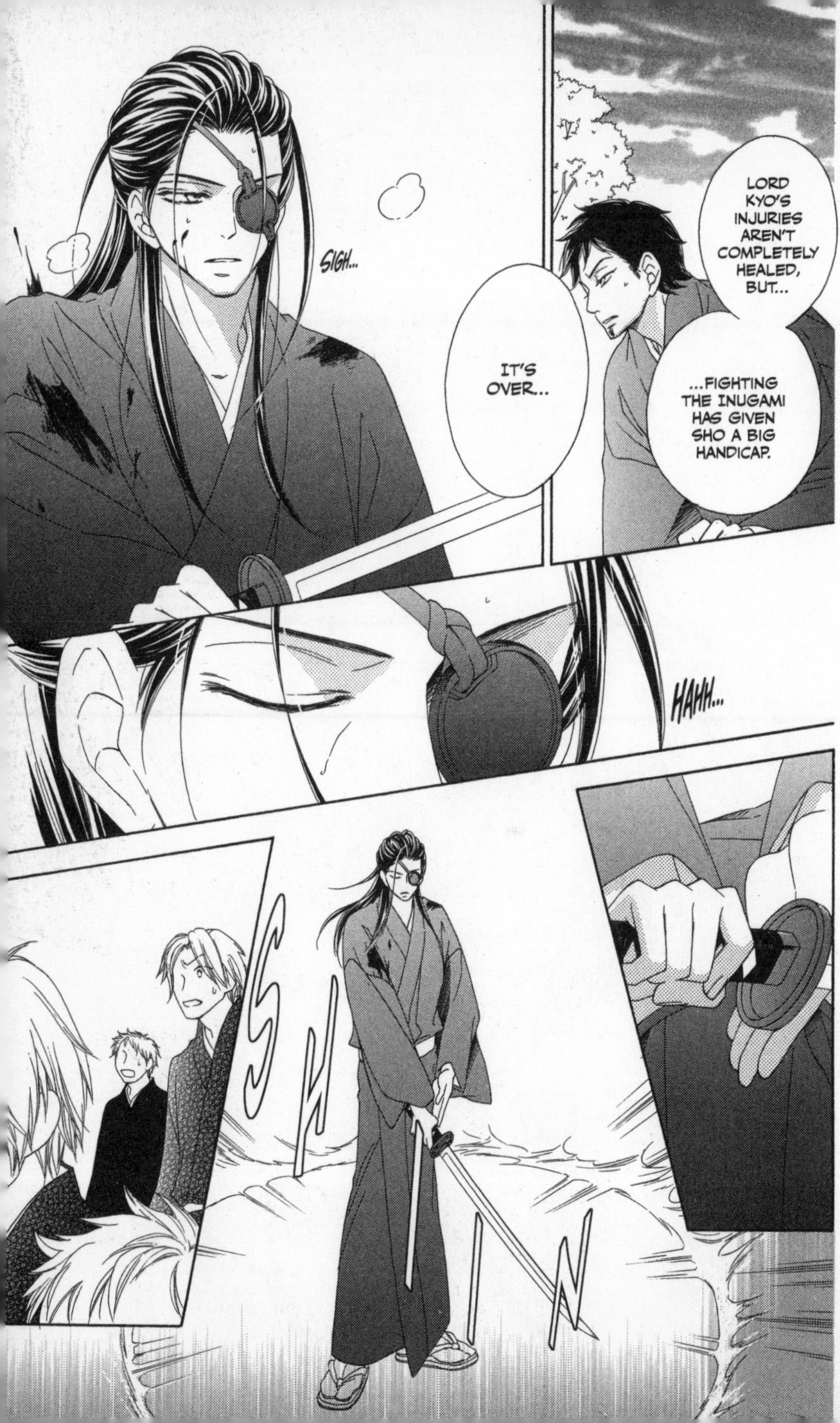
LORD KYO'S INJURIES AREN'T COMPLETELY HEALED, BUT...
...FIGHTING THE INUGAMI HAS GIVEN SHO A BIG HANDICAP.
IT'S OVER...
SIGH...
HAHH...
SHIN

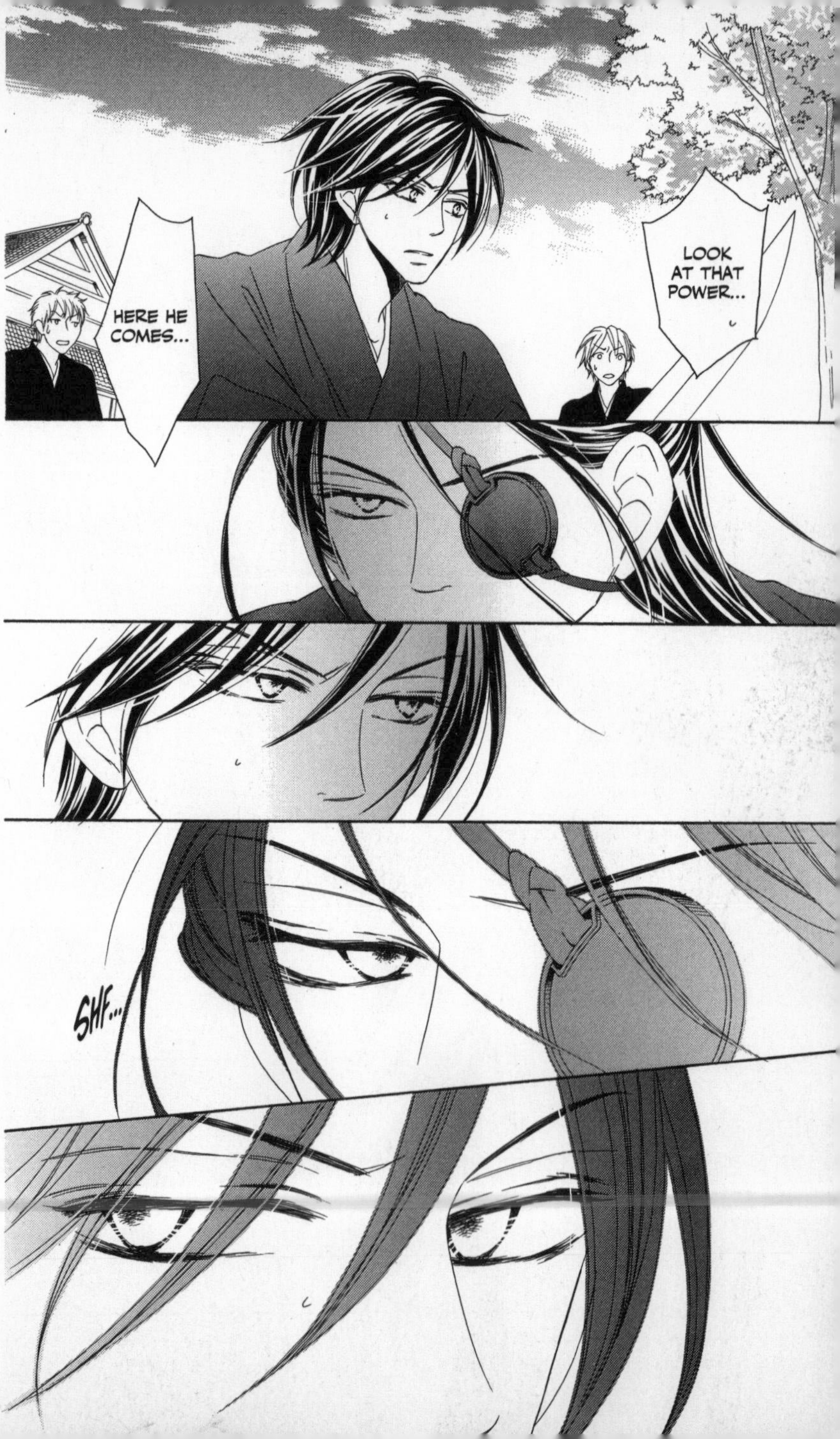
LOOK AT THAT POWER...
HERE HE COMES...
SHF...

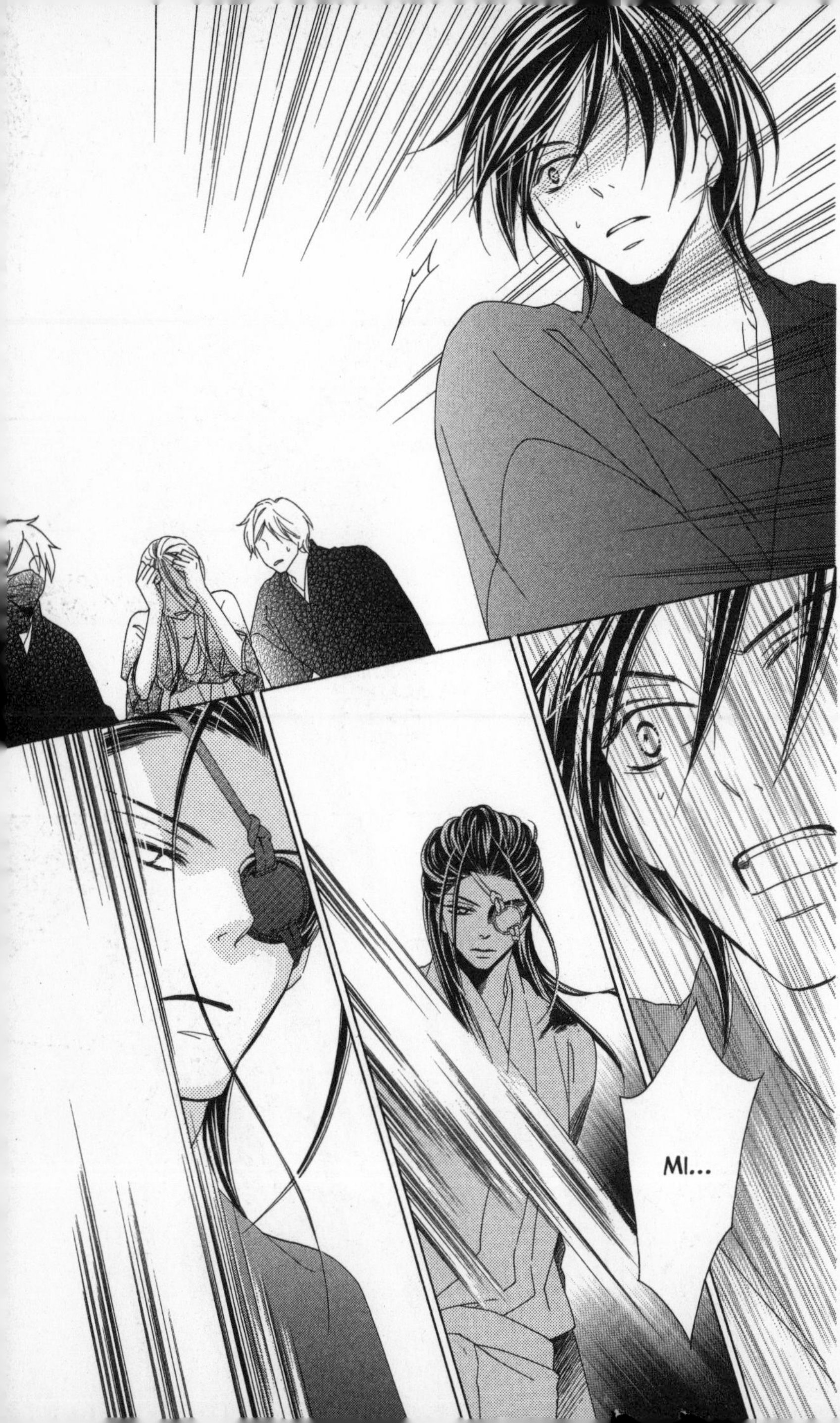
MI...

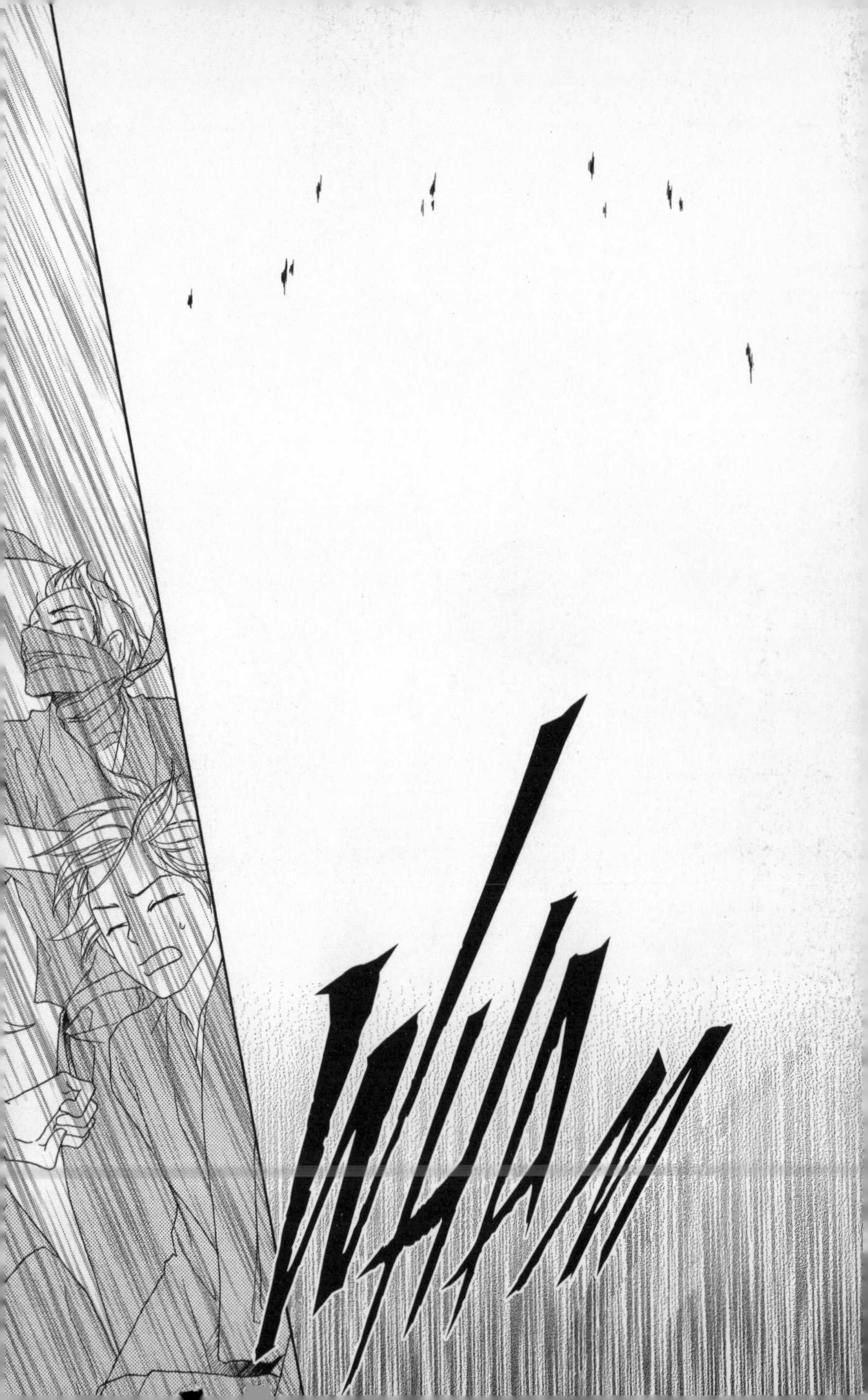

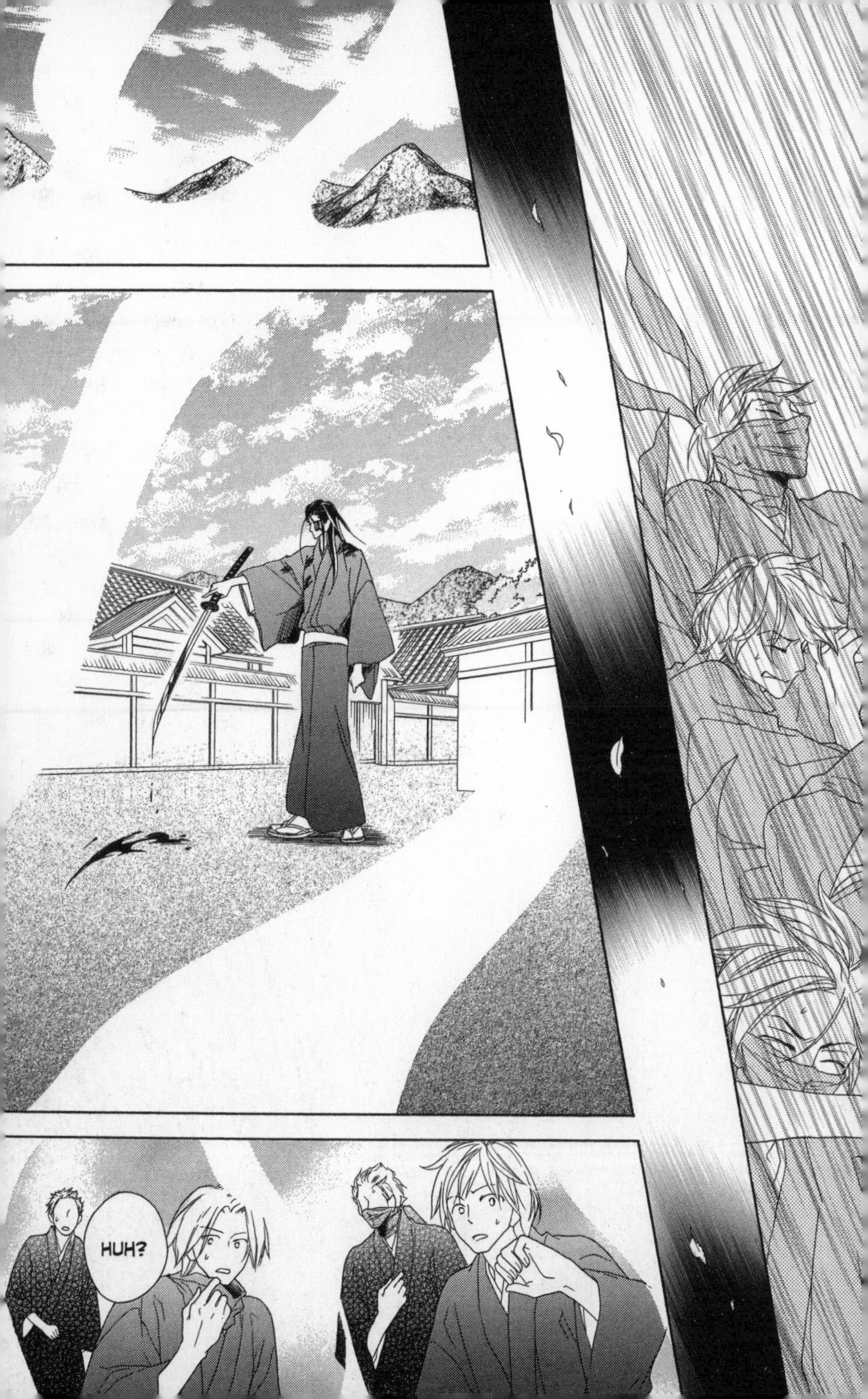
HUH?

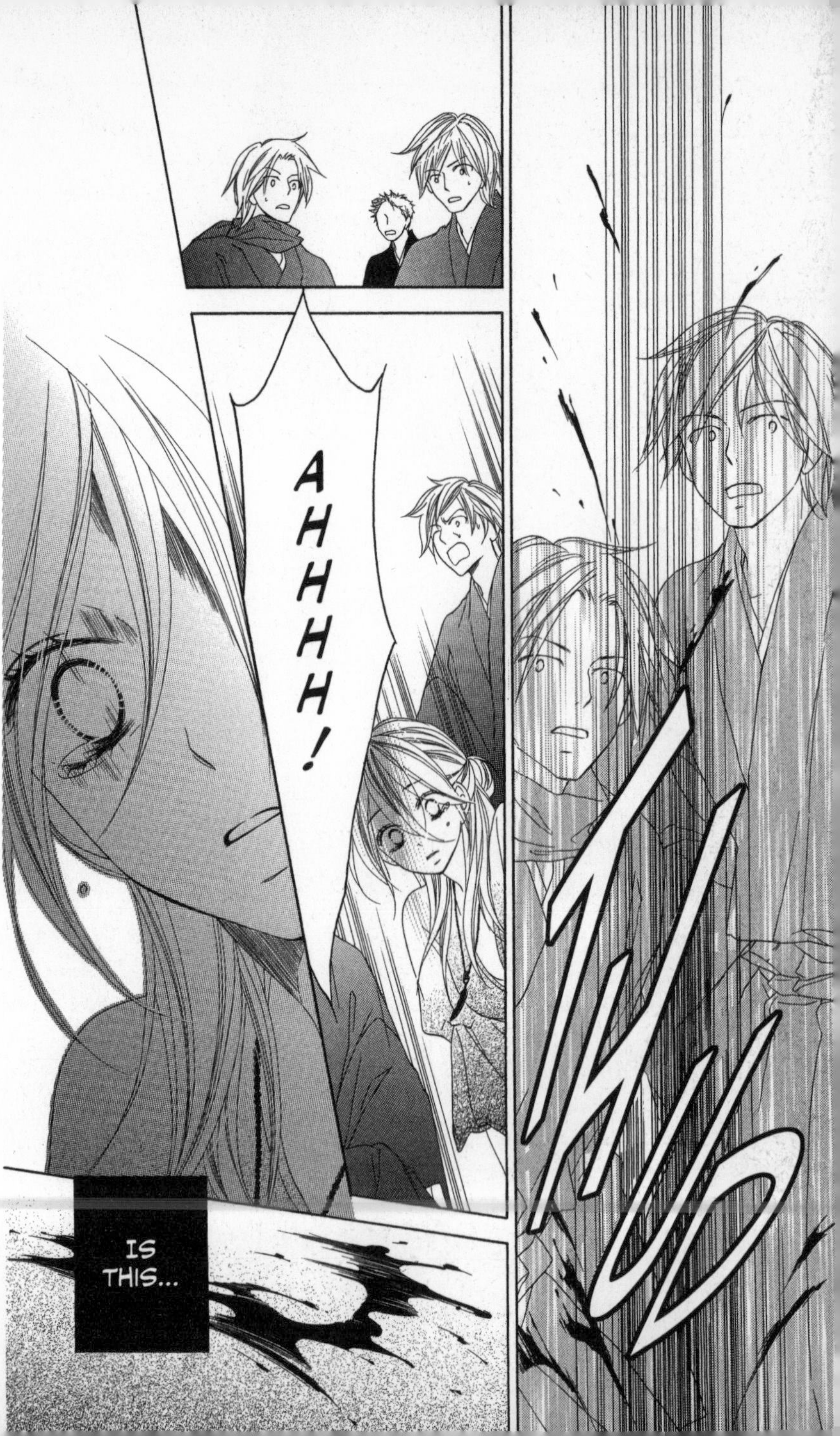
AHHHHH!
IS THIS...

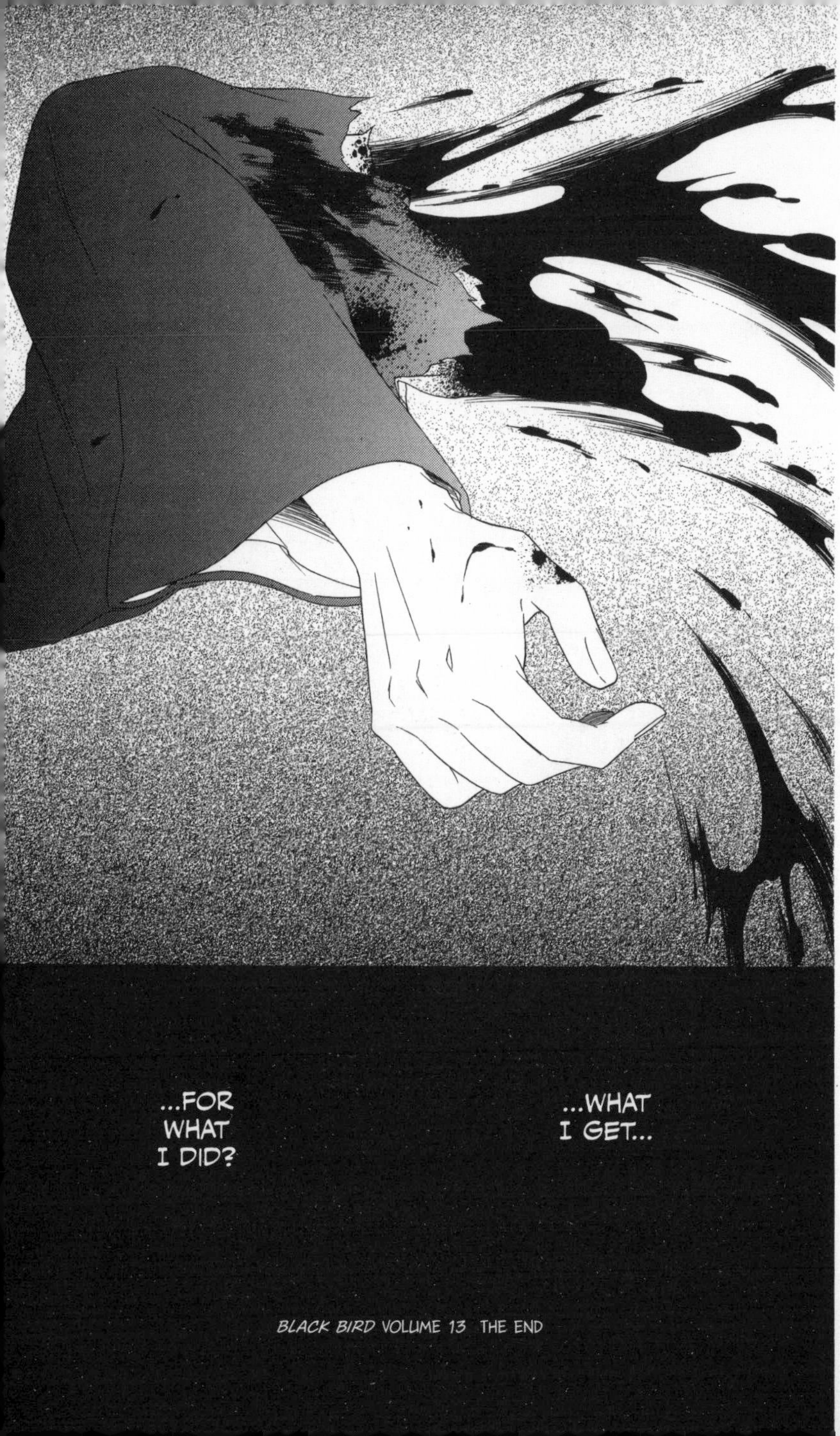
...WHAT I GET...
...FOR WHAT I DID?
BLACK BIRD VOLUME 13 THE END

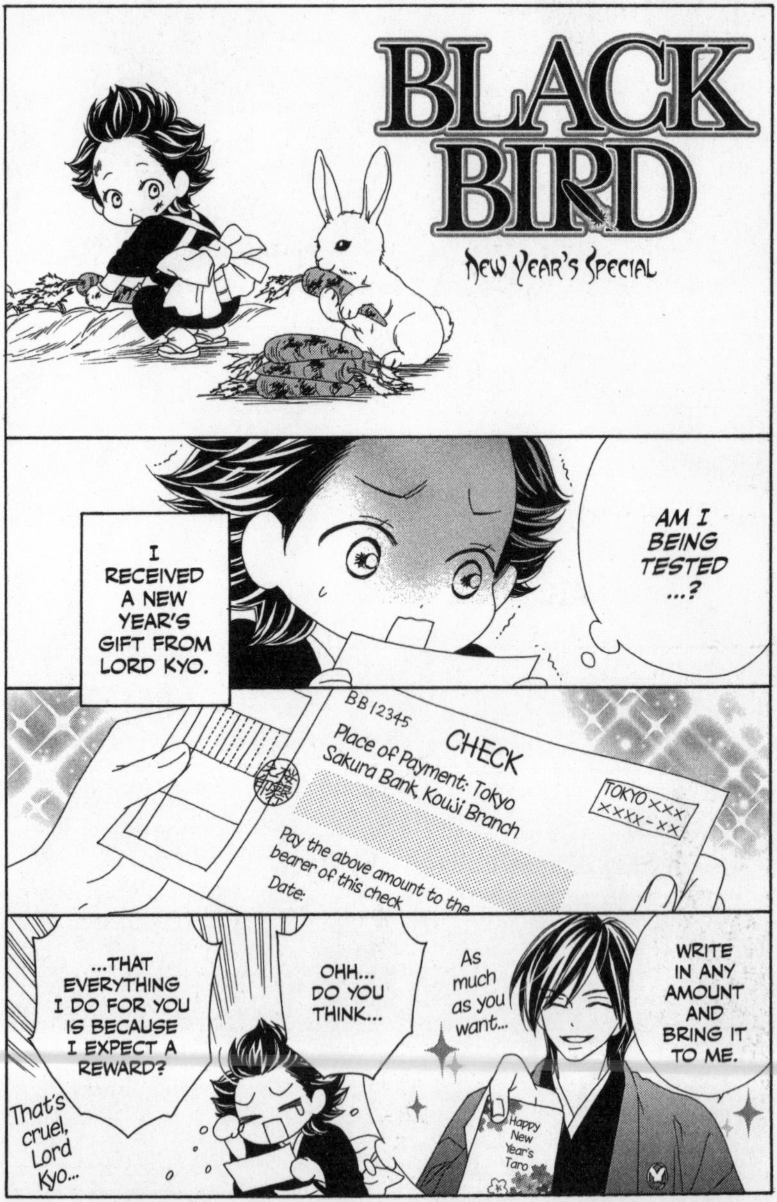

BLACK BIRD
New Year's Special
AM I BEING TESTED ...?
I RECEIVED A NEW YEAR'S GIFT FROM LORD KYO.
BB12345
CHECK
Place of Payment: Tokyo Sakura Bank, Kouji Branch
TOKYO XXX XXXX-XX
Pay the above amount to the bearer of this check
Date:
WRITE IN ANY AMOUNT AND BRING IT TO ME.
As much as you want...
Happy New Year's Taro
OHH... DO YOU THINK...
...THAT EVERYTHING I DO FOR YOU IS BECAUSE I EXPECT A REWARD?
That's cruel, Lord Kyo...

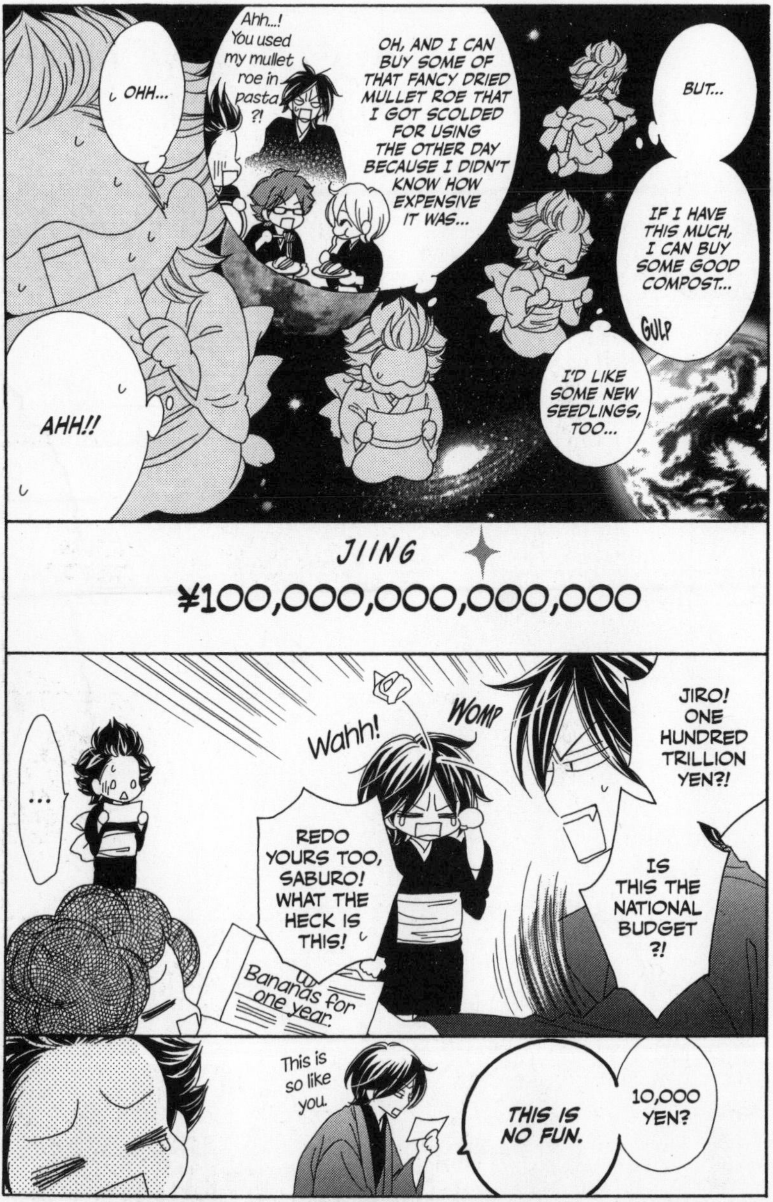
BUT...
IF I HAVE THIS MUCH, I CAN BUY SOME GOOD COMPOST...
GULP
I'D LIKE SOME NEW SEEDLINGS, TOO...
OH, AND I CAN BUY SOME OF THAT FANCY DRIED MULLET ROE THAT I GOT SCOLDED FOR USING THE OTHER DAY BECAUSE I DIDN'T KNOW HOW EXPENSIVE IT WAS...
Ahh...! You used my mullet roe in pasta?!
OHH...
AHH!!
JIING
¥100,000,000,000,000
JIRO! ONE HUNDRED TRILLION YEN?!
IS THIS THE NATIONAL BUDGET?!
WOMP
Wahh!
REDO YOURS TOO, SABURO! WHAT THE HECK IS THIS!
Bananas for one year.
...
10,000 YEN?
THIS IS NO FUN.
This is so like you.

BLACK BIRD NEW YEAR'S SPECIAL FEATURE / THE END
PRINTED IN THE SUPPLEMENT TO *BETSUCOMI* JANUARY 2011

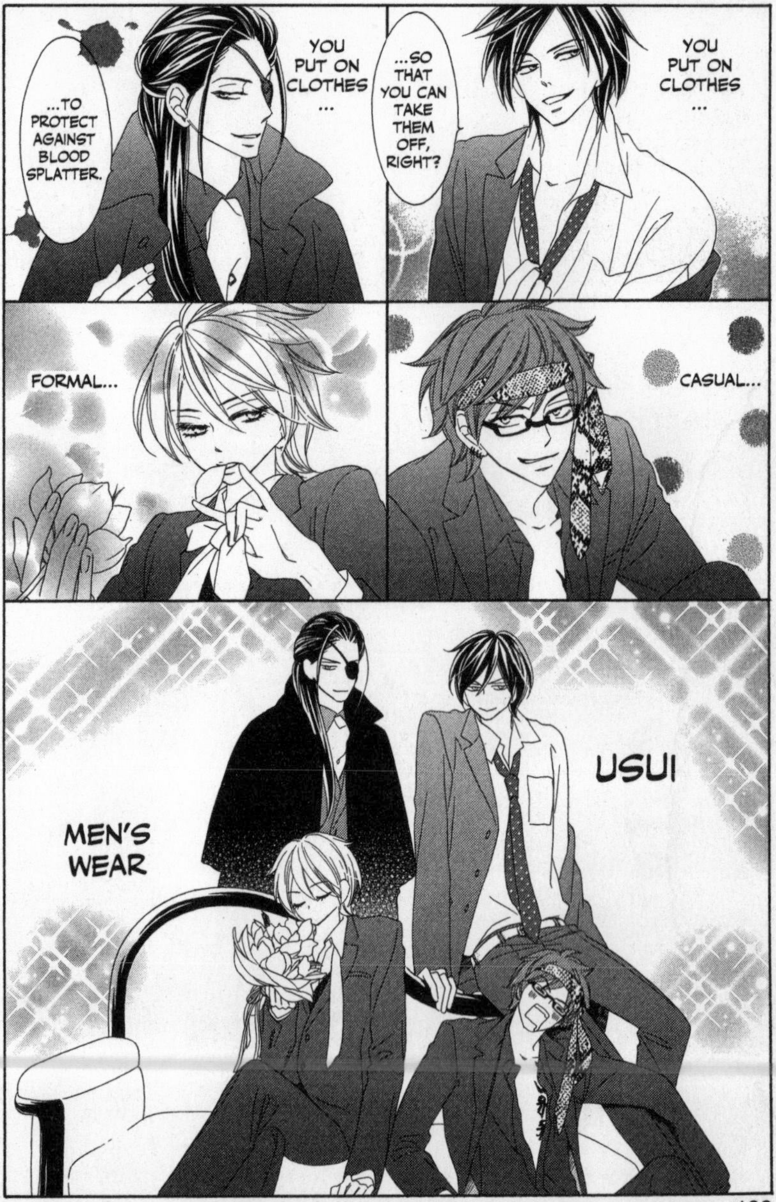
YOU PUT ON CLOTHES ...
...SO THAT YOU CAN TAKE THEM OFF, RIGHT?
YOU PUT ON CLOTHES ...
...TO PROTECT AGAINST BLOOD SPLATTER.
CASUAL...
FORMAL...
USUI
MEN'S WEAR

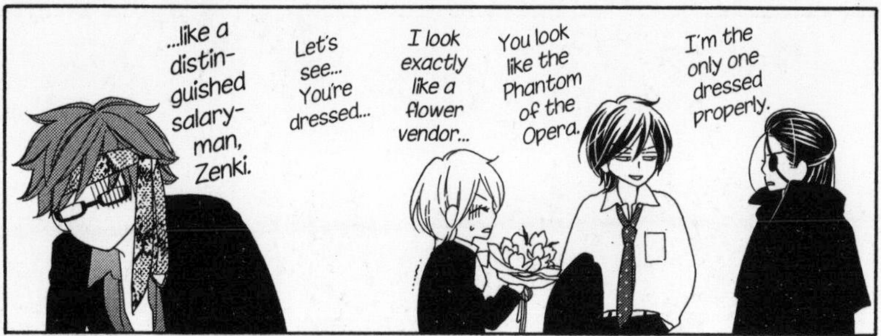
I'm the only one dressed properly.
You look like the Phantom of the Opera.
I look exactly like a flower vendor...
Let's see... You're dressed...
...like a distinguished salaryman, Zenki.

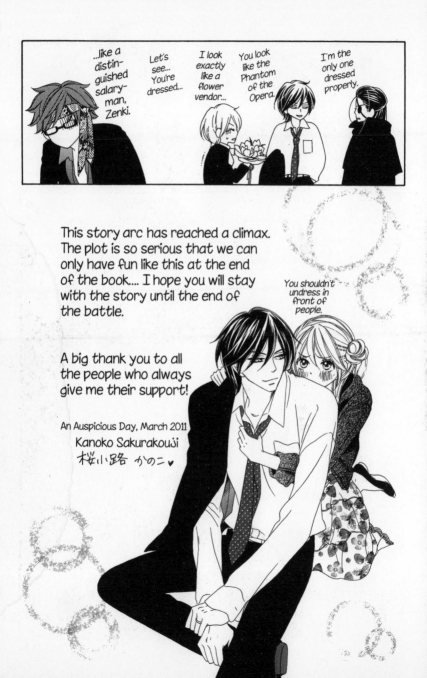

This story arc has reached a climax. The plot is so serious that we can only have fun like this at the end of the book.... I hope you will stay with the story until the end of the battle.

A big thank you to all the people who always give me their support!

An Auspicious Day, March 2011

Kanoko Sakurakouji

桜小路 かのこ♥

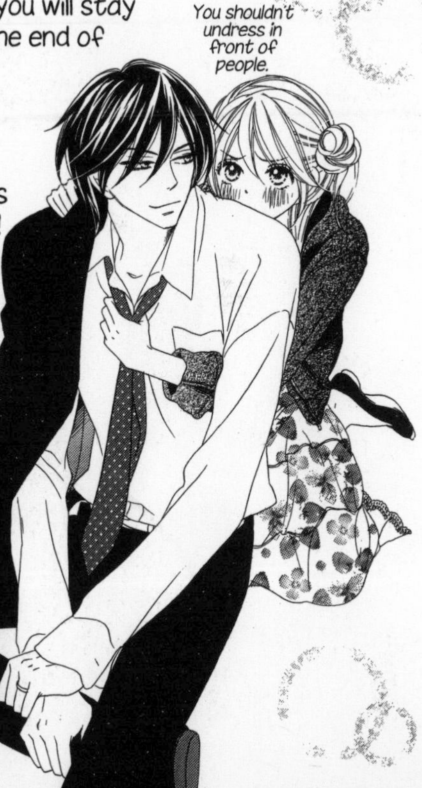
You shouldn't undress in front of people.

GLOSSARY

PAGE 188, PANEL 2: NEW YEAR'S GIFT
Money given to children on New Year's,
called *otoshidama* in Japanese.

Kanoko Sakurakouji was born in downtown Tokyo, and her hobbies include reading, watching plays, traveling and shopping. Her debut title, *Raibu ga Hanetara*, ran in *Bessatsu Shojo Comic* (currently called *Bestucomi*) in 2000, and her 2004 *Bestucomi* title *Backstage Prince* was serialized in VIZ Media's *Shojo Beat* magazine. She won the 54th Shogakukan Manga Award for *Black Bird*.

BLACK BIRD
VOL. 13
Shojo Beat Edition

Story and Art by KANOKO SAKURAKOUJI

© 2007 Kanoko SAKURAKOUJI/Shogakukan
All rights reserved.
Original Japanese edition "BLACK BIRD" published by SHOGAKUKAN Inc.

TRANSLATION JN Productions
TOUCH-UP ART & LETTERING Gia Cam Luc
DESIGN Amy Martin
EDITOR Pancha Diaz

BFT 9116 5.99

Printed in the U.S.A.

Published by VIZ Media, LLC
P.O. Box 77010
San Francisco, CA 94107

10 9 8 7 6 5 4 3 2 1
First printing, March 2012

www.shojobeat.com   www.viz.com

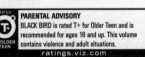

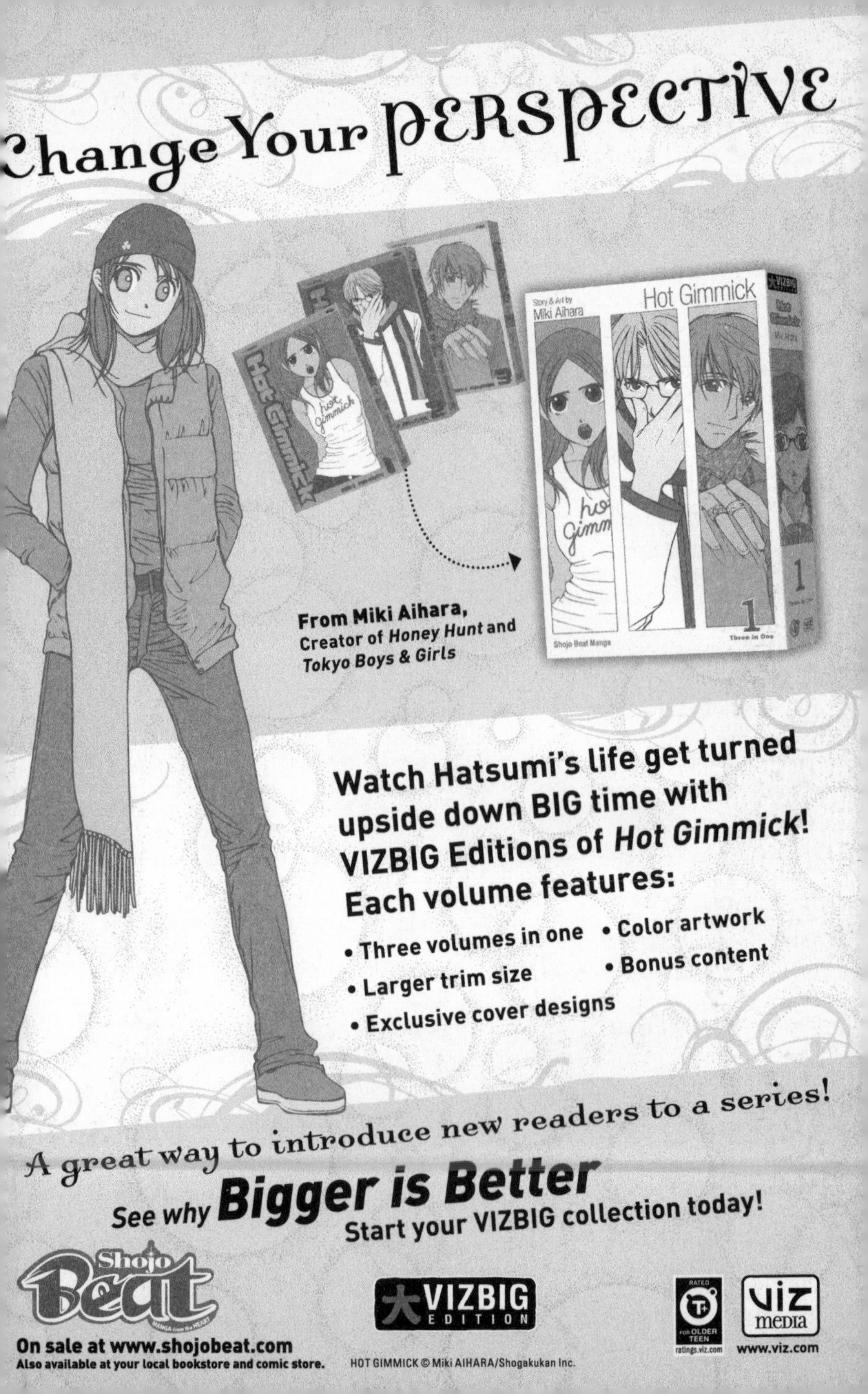
Change Your PERSPECTIVE
Hot Gimmick
Story & Art by
Miki Aihara
Shojo Beat Manga
1
Three in One
From Miki Aihara,
Creator of Honey Hunt and
Tokyo Boys & Girls
Watch Hatsumi's life get turned upside down BIG time with VIZBIG Editions of Hot Gimmick!
Each volume features:
• Three volumes in one
• Color artwork
• Larger trim size
• Bonus content
• Exclusive cover designs
A great way to introduce new readers to a series!
See why Bigger is Better
Start your VIZBIG collection today!
Shojo Beat
MANGA from the HEART
VIZBIG EDITION
RATED T+ FOR OLDER TEEN
ratings.viz.com
viz media
www.viz.com
On sale at www.shojobeat.com
Also available at your local bookstore and comic store.
HOT GIMMICK © Miki AIHARA/Shogakukan Inc.

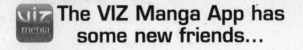